National Parks
The Family Guide

A complete family travel guide to all America's National: parks, monuments, memorials, battlefields, seashores, lakeshores, historical parks, historic sites, parkways, rivers & recreation areas.

by
Dave Robertson
and
Dr. June Francis

Sequoia & Kings Canyon National Parks COURTESY NPS

ACKNOWLEDGEMENTS

Thanks to our travel companions and research associates, our children, Tammy and David, our nephews, Jason and Meshach, and Mama, their grandmother who withstood our rigorous pace.

Special thanks to *On Site! 86* and *On Site! Expo* co-authors, Linda Cekal for early editorial assistance and Bob Heyman for his design contributions including the production of the maps. In addition, we would like to thank Jim Miller for his pictorial contributions and to paternal grandparents, Glenda and Robby Robertson, for their support.

It has been our privilege and pleasure to visit the national parks while conducting our research for our books. We'd like to thank all the National Park Service staff and volunteers who enhanced our understanding and enjoyment of their sites. For those park service people who sent us information, pictures and reviewed our material for inaccuracies, we'd like to give a special thanks.

Editor: Maggie M. Paquet; Proof Reader: Lynne Henderson; Cartographer: Robert Heyman; Cover design: V Group Design; Typesetting: The Typeworks; Photographs: The NPS and Jim Miller; Printer: Daily Journal of Commerce; Cover Photographs: NPS for Wildlife (Theodore Roosevelt NP), Kids (Grand Portage NM), Wonders (Mount Rushmore NMem), Theodore Roosevelt NP, Death Valley NM, Bighorn Canyon NRA, Ozark NSR, Frederick Douglass NHS, Bent's Old Fort NHS, Biscayne NP, Cedar Breaks NM, Voyageurs NP and Jefferson NEM.

ON SITE! Publications
Box 540
Pt. Roberts, WA 98281
604/733-5288

Canadian Cataloguing in Publication Data

Robertson, Dave, 1949-

National Parks - The Family Guide

Includes index.

ISBN 0-9692549-3-8

1. National parks and reserves--United States--Guide-books. 2. United States--Description and travel--1981- --Guide-books. 3. Family recreation--United States--Guide-books. I. Francis, June, 1955- II. Title.

E160.R62 1991 917.304'928 C91-091289-0

PRINTED IN THE USA

INTRODUCTION

National Parks - The Family Guide is a unique travel guide for families. The book focusses on the national parks' exceptional recreational and educational opportunities. Where else can a family see so many of the world's natural and man-made wonders? Where else can they learn so much about the events and the people that shaped this country? Where else can they enjoy such a variety of recreational opportunities? Where else can a family pay so little for admission or, better yet, get in for FREE to enjoy such an array of year-round educational entertainment?

The Authors

We have successfully co-authored and published *Whiz Trips with Kids The Best of the Rockies and the Southwest*; a Canadian bestseller: *On Site! 86* and an Australian bestseller: *On Site! EXPO*. We are professional educators and, more importantly, the parents of a girl and a boy. We wanted to stimulate our children's interest in travel, geology, history, cultural lifeways, archaeology and paleontology. As a family, we wanted to have fun together. As parents, we wanted to share America's national treasures with our kids. We set out across this vast land with four kids in tow, ours plus two nephews. We walked, hiked, drove, canoed, caved, climbed and swam. We rode horses, trams, canal boats, ferries, trains and merry-go-rounds. We saw audio-visuals, photographs, sculptures, paintings and artifacts. We visited museums, ruins, homes, cemeteries, deserts, beaches, swamps, battlefields, ranches, farms and forts. We evaluated everything we saw from the perspective of the oldest through the youngest; then we asked others for their opinions. At every point in our travels and our writings we considered each attraction from the perspective of a family. In *National Parks - The Family Guide*, a member of the Whiz Trips Guides series, we describe all the park sites according to their educational and recreational components.

How to use National Parks - The Family Guide

Because the national parks are spread throughout the country, we have provided a map detailing all the sites administered by the park service. Each state is listed in alphabetical order.Each site is alphabetically listed within the state it is located. Using the table of contents and the index, you can locate the site you are interested in. We have specified how long it should take a family to see the attraction properly (**Allow**) and whether there is an admission fee or not. In our review of each park we have detailed the **Highlights** that you should make a point of seeing. Under the heading **Whiz Tips**, we have identified what kind of interpretive programs are offered and what you will learn. **Kids' Stuff** tells you about the park's special features for kids like Jr. Ranger programs and which hikes are particularly good for families. At the end of our synopsis, we have provided the park's location (**Access**), the opening hours (**Days/Hours**), nearby public camping facilities (**Camping**), the park's annual special events (**Special Events**), whether the park has a teacher/leader's guide for large groups (**Teacher's Guide**) and who to contact for more information and to book reservations with for popular programs in peak times (**For info.**).

Tips for Families Visiting the National Parks

We strongly suggest that the first thing anyone does upon coming to a park, is to go to the visitor center for a synopsis of what is available to see and do at the park. This stop will greatly enhance your visit if you ask very specific and detailed questions. For example, ask about Jr. Ranger programs or living history presentations or upcoming events. We would like to say that in all our travels with our children, we found few places as welcoming as the national park sites.

For less than a one day admission fee for a family to a major amusement park, you and your family can buy an annual pass (*Golden Eagle Pass*) to all national park sites. "The pass admits the permit holder and any accompanying passengers in a single, private, noncommercial vehicle. Where entry is not by private vehicle, the pass admits the holder, spouse, children and parents. The *Golden Eagle* pass does not cover use fees, such as fees for camping, parking and cave tours." People 62 years or older qualify for a FREE *Golden Age Passport* which works like the *Golden Eagle Pass*. In addition, *Golden Age Passport* holders can qualify for a discount on camping fees. On Aug. 24th, the National Park's Birthday, entry fees to park sites are waived and many parks put on special presentations with an emphasis on families. All in all the national park annual pass is without doubt the BEST DEAL in America for a family vacation.

The National Park Service

Although the country's (and the world's) first national park (Yellowstone) was established on March 1, 1872, the park service recognizes August 24, 1916 as its birthday. It was then that the guidelines were set for the park service. "The service...shall promote and regulate the use...by such means and

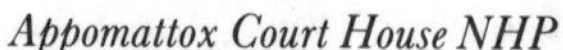

Appomattox Court House NHP COURTESY NPS

measures as to conform to the fundamental purpose of the said parks...to provide for the enjoyment...as will leave them unimpaired for the enjoyment of future generations." When one thinks of the national parks, one thinks of the big parks that have the term national park incorporated in their name like Yellowstone. These units of the park service are designated national park because they preserve an area of land and/or water which contains resources which are multi-varied and of national significance. National monuments differ in that they are more focussed protecting a natural reservation, prehistoric ruin, fossil site, a fortification or a monument. Places known for their commemorative value are proclaimed national memorials. Primarily military sites have been called national military park, national battlefield park, national battlefield site and national battlefield. However, a number of these places also fall into other categories such as national historical parks because of the complexity of the site. National historic sites individually focus on one subject but collectively cover a wide range of subject matter. Shoreline areas are clearly designated national seashores or national lakeshores while national rivers, wild and scenic riverways and national recreation areas generally indicate those units containing bodies of water. It should be noted that the Forest Service and the Department of Agriculture also oversee recreation areas. Thoroughfares that have been set aside as significant are called national parkways and national scenic trails. A recent designation has been national preserves which allow commercial use such as mining and hunting. We have also included a number of sites which while not directly administered by the park service are affiliated. While this is not an exhaustive list of the nomenclature used by the park service it does cover most of the names you will encounter within.

Death Valley NM COURTESY NPS

National Park Service Sites

Appalachian Trail
Saint Croix Island
MAINE
Acadia
VT.
N.H.
Saint-Gaudens
NEW YORK
Saratoga
Salem Maritime
Lowell
Saugus Iron Works
Cape Cod
MASS.
Fort Stanwix
Springfield Armory
Women's Rights
Martin Van Buren
Roger Williams
R.I.
CONN.
Vanderbilt Mansion
Home of Franklin D. Roosevelt
Upper Delaware
Eleanor Roosevelt
Delaware
Sagamore Hill
Steamtown
Fire Island
Delaware Water Gap
Morristown
Edison
St. Paul's Church
PA.
N.J.
Edgar Allan Poe
Independence
Thaddeus Kosciuszko
Cuyahoga Valley
Allegheny Portage Railroad
Hopewell Furnace
Valley Forge
Johnstown Flood
Eisenhower
Gettysburg
Hampton
Fort McHenry
Fort Necessity
Catoctin
Friendship Hill
Antietam
Harpers Ferry
DEL.
MD.
Manassas
Chesapeake & Ohio Canal
Prince William Forest
Shenandoah
Assateague Island
Fredricksburg & Spotsylvania
George Washington Birthplace
Gauley River
Richmond
Maggie L Walker
W. VA.
Petersburg
New River Gorge
Colonial
VA.
Bluestone
Appomattox Courthouse
Booker T. Washington
Wright Brothers
Blue Ridge Parkway
Fort Raleigh
Guildford Courthouse
Andrew Johnson
Cape Hatteras
Cape Lookout
N.C.
Great Smoky Mountains
Kings Mountain
Cowpens
Moores Creek
Chickamauga and Chattanooga
Ninety Six
S.C.
Congaree Swamp
Chattahoochee River
Charles Pinckney
Fort Sumter
Martin Luther King Jr.
GEORGIA
Fort Pulaski
Ocmulgee
Andersonville
Fort Frederica
Cumberland Island
Timucuan
Fort Caroline
Castillo de San Marcos
Fort Matanzas
Canaveral
De Soto
FLORIDA
Big Cypress
Biscayne
Everglades
Fort Jefferson
Grand Portage
Isle Royale
Apostle Islands
Pictured Rocks
St. Croix
Lower St. Croix
Sleeping Bear Dunes
WISCONSIN
MICHIGAN
Theodore Roosevelt Inaugural
Perry's Victory
Indiana Dunes
Herbert Hoover
IND.
OHIO
ILLINOIS
Mound City Group
William Howard Taft
Lincoln Home
George Rogers Clark
Jefferson National
Expansion Memorial
Lincoln Boyhood
KENTUCKY
Abraham Lincoln Birthplace
Mammoth Cave
Big South Fork
MISSOURI
Scott
Ozark
Cumberland Gap
Wilson's Creek
Obed
George Washington Carver
Fort Donelson
Stones River
Pea Ridge
TENNESSEE
Carl Sandburg Home
Buffalo
Shiloh
Russell Cave
ARK.
Fort Smith
Brices Cross Roads
Tupelo
Kennesaw Mountain
Hot Springs
Arkansas Post
Horseshoe Bend
Natchez Trace Parkway
Natchez Trace Trail
Tuskegee Institute
MISS.
ALABAMA
Vicksburg
LA.
Natchez
Gulf Islands
Big Thicket
Jean Lafitte
BOSTON AREA
Adams
Boston
Frederick Law Olmsted
John Fitzgerald Kennedy
Longfellow
Minute Man
NEW YORK AREA
Castle Clinton
Federal Hall
Gateway
General Grant
Hamilton Grange
Statue of Liberty
Theodore Roosevelt Birthplace
WASHINGTON AREA
Arlington House
Clara Barton
Constitution Gardens
Ford's Theatre
Fort Washington
Frederick Douglass
George Washington Parkway
Greenbelt
John F. Kennedy Center
Lincoln Memorial
Lyndon Baines Johnson
Monocacy
National Capital Parks
National Mall
Pennsylvania Avenue
Piscataway
Potomac Heritage Trail
Rock Creek
Theodore Roosevelt Island
Thomas Jefferson Memorial
Vietnam Veterans Memorial
Washington Monument
White House
Wolf Trap Farm

TABLE OF CONTENTS

ALABAMA

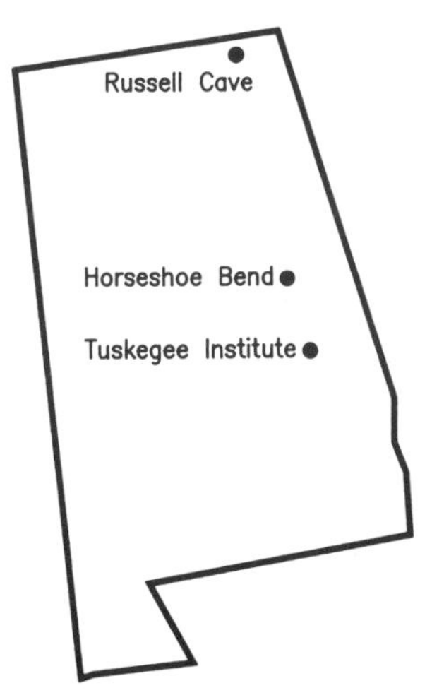

Horseshoe Bend National Military Park

Allow: 1-2 hrs. *Fee*

"When asked by an anthropologist what the Indians called America before the white men came, an Indian said simply, 'Ours'."
Vine Deloria, Jr.

On March 27, 1814, 1000 Upper Creek warriors prepared to defend themselves behind their wooden barricade at the horseshoe bend of the Tallapoosa River. By the day's end, 800 would lie dead. The man who directed this assault against them? It was Andrew Jackson, the future (7th) president of the United States, who was rated in a 1983 historian's poll interestingly enough as the 7th most effective president (out of 36). Jackson's success here, and later that year at the Battle of New Orleans, catapulted him to the nation's highest office.

Highlights

★ The interpretive walk takes you past noteworthy landmarks which help explain the fighting that took place. The Creek chose the horseshoe because they believed the surrounding water made it defensible. Unfortunately, out manned and out armed, their "sanctuary" became their prison.

Whiz Tips

💡 The visitor center has exhibits explaining the Creek culture and the events leading up to this battle. Also described is the battle's aftermath, including the expulsion of the tribe to the so-called Indian Territory in what is now Oklahoma (see Fort Smith NHS, AR). The rangers will, on occasion, demonstrate the loading and firing of flintlock rifles.

💡 During the War of 1812, the U.S. was in an expansionary stage, flexing its might and influence westward. The Creek nation was split over how much interference in its affairs it would accept. The Upper, or Red Stick, Creeks retaliated for an attack on one of their ammunition trains by killing 250 settlers at Fort Mims. Eight months later, Jackson and 3,000 well-armed men circled 1,000 poorly armed warriors and 350 women and children and executed their revenge, capturing essentially just the women and children.

Kids' Stuff

🟊 The 2.8-mi.-long nature trail leading through the fortification site past the river is a good family hike.

🟊 Kids like to fish the river for catfish, bass, sunfish and crappie.

Access: 12 mi. N of Dadeville or 18 mi. E of Alexander City on AL 49. **Days/Hours:** Daily 8-4:30. **Camping:** Wind Creek State Park on Hwy. 63 (669 sites, elec. & shwrs.). **For info.:** Superintendent, Horseshoe Bend National Military Park, Rte.1, Box 103, Daviston, AL 36256. 205/234-7111.

Russell Cave National Monument

Allow: 1-3 hr. *FREE*

In northeast Alabama is a cave that has witnessed human development for over 9,000 years. It isn't much to look at, but then again people did not to choose to live here because of its beauty. The park details the Native Americans who used the cave because of its shelter and running water.

Highlights

★ Once inside the cave entrance, you can quickly see why it served as a desirable home for prehistoric hunters. You are shielded from the elements, and the cave's natural warmth prevents the stream from freezing, thus offering a reliable source of water. With a fire, you could remain nice and cozy on even the coldest Alabama winter day.

Whiz Tips

Upon request, the rangers will demonstrate various pre-historic skills such as corn grinding, flint-flaking, leather cutting, heat-transfer cooking and use of the throwing stick (atlatl). Russell Cave provides us with impressions of man's progress through the ages. From 7000-500 B.C., we see little change in what were primarily hunter/gatherers. Toward the end of the period, the bow and arrow was utilized, and pottery and jewelry are in greater evidence. Over 1,100 years ago, a still more advanced culture appears, the Mississippian or mound-builders. Utilizing the rich river bottom lands, these people created a complex social culture which exacted large amounts of free (leisure) time to build ceremonial mounds and buildings. The Cherokee Indians were the native culture found in the area when the Europeans first arrived.

You can explore the park's 35,000-foot-long wild cave with the superintendent's permission and the proper equipment.

Kids' Stuff

★ Children enjoy seeing how early people coped with everyday life and often times are allowed to participate

Russell Cave National Monument COURTESY NPS

in the demonstrations. Very few places have such an open invitation for visitors.

Access: 8 mi. from Bridgeport on Cty. Rd. 75. **Days/Hours:** Daily 8-5 (clsd. Dec.25). **Camping:** State and county campgrounds within 10 miles of park. **Special Events:** 3rd April Sat., Indian Day. **Teacher's Package:** Available. **For info.:** Superintendent, Russell Cave National Monument, Rte. 1, Box 175, Bridgeport, AL 35740. 205/495-2672.

Tuskegee Institute National Historic Site

Allow: 2-3 hrs. *FREE*

"...not for the select few, but for the masses."
Booker T. Washington

It was a different time, a different place, and it called for different measures. African-Americans had moved from slavery to freedom, but sharecropping offered little more than the slave system it had replaced. In 1881, Booker T. Washington was recommended as the person to oversee the building of a black educational institute in Alabama. He had very definite ideas about what this school should teach and how. His goal was to teach the students life skills that would allow them to prosper within a country that limited their potential. Tuskegee Institute taught agriculture, building, basket-weaving, in short, practical skills. However, it attracted outstanding academics like George Washington Carver, who would have been a star at any post-secondary school. The site includes two historic buildings, Booker T. Washington's home, the Oaks and George Washington Carver Museum. The still functioning campus features historic buildings, many of which were built by the students as part of their curriculum.

Highlights

★ Tuskegee is a living example of how important education was for African-Americans. Both Booker T. Washington's and George Washington Carver's lives mirror those of their students. Born into slavery, both had little except overwhelming curiosity and ambition to bolster them. They had to work their way

Founder of Tuskegee Institute—Booker T. Washington

through school and felt their greatest lessons were learned from doing manual labor.

Whiz Tips

The park conducts tours (which they can tailor to families) of Booker T. Washington's home, The Oaks. You'll see how this man, who was a slave, rose to become a confidant of presidents (see Booker T. Washington NM, VA).

At George Washington Carver Museum you can see the many discoveries this noted scientist made for the uses of crops that could flourish in the South. Carver felt that black farmers should avoid the trap of banking their bets on cotton as a one-crop economy and grow crops like peanuts and soy beans, for which he had found a multitude of uses (see George Washington Carver NM, MO).

Kids' Stuff

★ We use visits to places like this to challenge our children's imaginations. We ask them to imagine themselves living in a backwoods log cabin and wanting to go to school so bad that they would have to leave us and travel far away just because they wanted to learn more. We ask them if they would be willing to sweep floors, cut wood, do odd jobs just so they could afford books. Then we tell them, if they did, maybe they could build something like this which has educated hundreds of thousands of people over 100 years.

Access: Just outside Tuskegee, off US 81 S on AL 126. **Days/Hours:** Daily 9-5 (clsd. Thanksgiving, Dec.25 & Jan.1). **Camping:** Tuskegee National Forest, primitive camping; Chewalca State Park (elec. & shwrs.). **For info.:** Superintendent, Tuskegee Institute National Historic Site, P.O.Drawer 10, Tuskegee Institute, AL 36088-0010. 205/727-3200.

ALASKA

Aniakchak National Monument & Preserve

Allow: 1 week *FREE*

Don't go looking for any roads, boats or even hiking trails leading to the monument. Pretty much the only way to see one of the largest (30 sq. mi.) craters in the world is to fly in. Discovered in the 20s, the volcanic caldera last erupted in 1933. Today it hosts a lake, a river and a unique profusion of wildlife which have made their home in this precarious setting.

Highlights

★ Visitors come for the wilderness experience and they must pay to fly in for the pleasure. They can take float trips and fish in truly pristine waters. They can see animals that will regard the sight of a human being as a "first."

Whiz Tips

Aniakchak is part of the North American portion of the Pacific Ring of Fire, which extends as far south as Lassen Volcano NP, CA. The fault movement between the Pacific plate and the continental plate is creating pressures beneath the earth's surface which relieve themselves through volcanic fissures like Aniakchak's.

Kids' Stuff

★ Parents and children visiting here must be very self-sufficient or travel with experienced guides.

Access: By plane. **Days/Hours:** Daily. **Camping:** Primitive. **For info.:** Superintendent, Aniakchak National Monument & Preserve, Box 7, King Salmon, AK 99613-0007. 907/246-3305.

Bering Land Bridge National Preserve

Allow: 1 week *FREE*

Whether our native populations came via the Bering Land Bridge or some other means may always be open to argument. However, the existence of this geologic formation is not. It appears as though the receding ice ages sufficiently raised the oceans' water levels covering the land linking Asia to the Americas. It is estimated the land bridge may even have been as wide as 1,000 miles. The remains of this land bridge just 50 miles from Siberia can still be seen. The region also holds particular interest for naturalists because of the summer amassing of birds from seven continents.

Highlights

★ The preserve has a profusion of wildlife. Polar bears and grizzlies share the land with wolves. Some of their quarry are the 112 species of birds who stop over.

Whiz Tips

❢ There are no visitor services, so you are left to your own devices as you seek to find out more about the area. The Inuits who live here continue to survive through subsistence hunting and by managing reindeer herds.

Family at Denali

COURTESY NPS

Kids' Stuff

★As with so many of Alaska's parks, families have to be able to fend for themselves or nature will prevail.

Access: By plane. **Days/Hours:** Daily. **Camping:** Primitive. **For info.:** Superintendent, Bering Land Bridge National Preserve, Box 220, Nome, AK 99762-0220. 907/443-2522.

Cape Krusenstern National Monument

Allow: 1 day *FREE*

For over 4,000 years Inuits have continued to hunt the seals and whales and fish for char and salmon along the sea coast. Over 114 distinct beach ridges have formed, recording human presence here. Each provides a historical treasure chest of Eskimo leavings which archaeologists study to determine their lifestyles. Visitors can enjoy the Arctic coastal experience.

Highlights

★ The Inuits still exact a living from the sea. Many of their practices which helped their culture survive the millennia are still used today.

Whiz Tips

This is a key site for scientists to study the people of the north. Its proximity to the Bering Land Bridge may provide clues of human migration. Some of the animals you might see are musk-ox, caribou, walrus, lynx, wolves, moose, seals, grizzlies, black bears and polar bears. In summer, waterfowl use the lagoons.

Kids' Stuff

★ Children can see how remote Inuit settlements maintain their culture. Angling families can catch Arctic char, grayling and whitefish.

Access: By plane. **Days/Hours:** Kotzebue H.Q., M-F, 8-5; Kotzebue Visitor Center, daily, summer only 9-7. **Camping:** Primitive. **For info.:** Superintendent, Cape Krusenstern National Monument, P.O.Box 1029, Kotzebue, AK 99752. 907/442-3760/3890.

Denali National Park & Preserve

Allow: 3-5 days *Fee*

Midway between Anchorage and Fairbanks is the home to the tallest mountain in North America, Mount McKinley or as the Athabaskans called it, Denali. Although named for the mountain, the park was initially set aside as a nature sanctuary and this is what it remains, with access beyond Mile 15 limited to the park's FREE tour buses. "Trip of a lifetime" visitors find the fact that McKinley seems perpetually shrouded disappointing but wallow in the wealth of wildlife they can view and photograph.

Highlights

★ The subarctic wilderness has huge areas of permafrost-ground which has remained frozen for thousands of years. Taiga and tundra expanses support animals who can withstand the rigors of the interminable deep cold. Caribou, moose, grizzly bears, Dall's sheep, wolves:

Denali National Park & Preserve COURTESY NPS

these are some of the large mammals who wander freely. Visitors may also sight fox, weasel, wolverine, snowshoe hare, lynx and beaver. Visitors who don't come prepared with binoculars and camera (at least 200mm telephoto lens) leave less satisfied.

Whiz Tips

❢ The park's auditorium in the Denali Park Hotel has a number of programs to orient you to the park. You should make sure to attend the short ranger talk about the park and try to catch the award-winning "Denali Wilderness" film that's shown twice daily. For early risers, there's the Morning Walk, a 1-2 hr. ranger-led stroll through the spruce forest. Others plan their day around the sled dog demonstration that's held three times each day. There are also hikes and evening programs which expose visitors to the many different aspects of the region. Visitors must get a coupon for the shuttle buses which will carry them 170 mi. in 10 hrs. through the near-pristine wilderness.

Kids' Stuff

★ The daily interpretive Discovery Hike although 3-4 hrs. in length, is a good one for families if the trail planned is gauged more toward "easy" than "strenuous."

★ The park's Jr. Ranger Program caters to the very young (6 & under) as well as the more typical age groupings (6-8 & 8-12). To qualify for a certificate, children must complete a set of activities which helps them learn about the park. For example, children ages 9 to 12 link predator to prey, recount the importance of ground squirrels to the park's ecosystem, match animals to their tracks and create a story about the animals to qualify.

Access: 240 mi. N from Anchorage or 120 mi. S from Fairbanks on AK 3. **Days/Hours:** Visitor Access Center, daily, summer 8-8; Eielson Visitor Center, daily summer 9-8:15. **Camping:** Park's drive-in sites are Riley Creek (102 sites), Savage River (34 sites) & Teklanika River (50 sites); bus-in sites are Sanctuary River (7 sites), Igloo Creek (7 sites) & Wonder Lake (28 sites). **For info.:** Superintendent, Denali National Park & Preserve, P.O.Box 9, Denali National Park, AK 99755-0009. 907/683-2294.

Denali National Park & Preserve COURTESY NPS

Gates of the Arctic National Park & Preserve

Allow: 3-5 days *FREE*

In the far reaches of Alaska sits the Brooks Range, the northernmost Rockies. This is a wild place, a place where people who visit don't come to see other human beings. The park, lying entirely inside the Arctic circle, was created to protect the integrity of the arctic environment; no visitor facilities are provided.

Highlights

★ For the true wilderness seeker, it doesn't get any better than this. Flying in is the norm. However, you can hike in from the Dalton Highway. The nearest settlement is an Eskimo village within the park. Winter temperatures vary from freezing to 70 below. Summer weather is also extremely variable but tends to be cool and rainy. Caribou, grizzlies, wolves, Dall's sheep and moose may be sighted but are widely dispersed because the land yields so little food.

Whiz Tips

❢ When you visit here, plan to survive on your own, although there are two ranger stations in case of an emergency.

❢ There are six wild rivers running through the park and the preserve encompassing 8.4 million acres. If you include its adjacent national park and preserve, Kobuk Valley NP and Noatak NPreserve, this is one of the largest park areas in the world.

Kids' Stuff

★ Fishing and arctic wildlife and landscapes will interest all, but both you and your children should be very knowledgeable about the wilderness. Rivers are gentle and easily navigated, but hiking is strenuous and not recommended for small children.

Access: Air. **Days/Hours:** Daily. **Camping:** Backcountry camping only on gravel beds, hardy moss or heath. **For info.:** Superintendent, Gates of the Arctic National Park & Preserve, P.O.Box 74680, Fairbanks, AK 99707-4680. 907/456-0281.

Glacier Bay National Park & Preserve

Allow: 3-5 days *FREE*

"At length the clouds lifted a little, and beneath their gray fringes I saw the berg-filled expanse of the bay, and the feet of the mountains that stand about it, and the imposing fronts of five huge glaciers, the nearest being immediately beneath me. This was my first general view of Glacier Bay, a solitude of ice and snow and newborn rocks, dim, dreary, mysterious..."

John Muir

Located in southeastern Alaska, the park can only be reached by boat or plane, usually from Juneau, which lies to its east. Most visitors fly into Gustavus, where a bus services Bartlett Cove. The major feature of the park is the 16 tidal glaciers, 12 of which calve icebergs into the ocean. Visitors who sail into the bay may see minke, humpback or orca whales gliding about or bald eagles, cormorants and gulls using the wandering icebergs to rest.

Highlights

★ This is a stunning coastline. The mountains rise straight out of the sea. Glaciers grind to the water's edge and offer their sacrificial portions. Icebergs bob along seemingly at peace with the world, belying the potential damage they can do to man's crafts.

Whiz Tips

❢ At Bartlett Cove, daily naturalist-led walks explain how quickly plants and animals fill the void left by the receding glaciers.

❢ What we are witnessing is the retreat of the last ice age, the Little Ice

Age. When Captain Vancouver sailed into this region in 1794, he found Icy Strait choked with ice. John Muir (see Muir Woods NM & John Muir NHS) came less than a century later and found the ice had receded 48 mi. In 1916, the ice was 65 mi. away from Vancouver's encounter. This is the most rapid glacial retreat ever recorded.

❢ Glaciers are created when snowfall exceeds snow melt. Landed snow changes into an icy granular shape that becomes compacted into solid ice. Gravity causes these masses of ice to flow down out of the mountains until the object reaches an equilibrium, i.e., the melting equals the snowfall. The glacier's end is called the "snout." At Glacier Bay, the 12 glaciers with their snouts at the water's edge are called tidal glaciers.

❢ The park suggests waterproof packs, clothes and matches, because the summers average about 50 degrees F. and are very wet.

Kids' Stuff

★ As you can imagine, the park is not overrun with children. Essentially, its programs are geared for adults, but most park service programs can be tailored to help kids understand.

★ There is fishing for cutthroat trout, Dolly Varden, salmon and halibut.

Access: Air or boat. **Days/Hours:** Mid-May to mid-Sept., daily 8-7. **Camping:** Park's Bartlett Bay Campground (FREE). **For info.:** Superintendent, Glacier Bay National Park & Preserve, Bartlett Cove, Gustavus, AK 99826-0140. 907/697-2230.

Iditarod National Historic Trail

In the late 1800s, gold-seekers from around the world flocked to Alaska to search for gold (see Klondike Gold Rush NHP, AK & WA). This 2,037 mi. trail, composed of a network of main and side routes, covered the area from Seward to Nome.

For info.: Iditarod National Historic Trail, Alaska Region, National Park Service, 2525 Gambell St., Anchorage, AK 99503.

Kenai Fjords National Park COURTESY NPS

Katmai National Park & Preserve

Allow: 3-5 days *FREE*

Encompassing 400 mi. of coast along the Alaskan peninsula, Katmai is another of the remote land masses preserved for the enjoyment of the determined nature lover. Initially set aside for its volcanic importance, the park has grown to include the pristine coast, the largest freshwater lake of any park (Lake Naknek) and a superb habitat for the Alaskan brown bear.

Highlights

★ Even the most resolute angler can't help but pay the bears some attention. The park contains the largest population of protected brown bears in the world and Brooks Camp is set up to facilitate both the bears and the tourists. Alaskan brown bears are coastal grizzlies. They grow to much larger sizes than the inland bears because of their higher protein diet (fish).

★ An estimated 50,000 well-to-do fishing fanatics fly in for world renowned fishing. At Brooks Camp, huge brown bears vie for the spawning salmon. Anglers cast their line for trophy rainbow trout, Dolly Varden, grayling and lake trout as well as salmon.

★ The most noted phenomena produced by the 1912 volcanic explosion of Novarupta was an eerie valley filled with steaming and hissing vents, known as the Valley of the Ten Thousand Smokes. Although the valley looks as though it's suffering from an anti-smokers campaign, it still warrants a visit. When the park was founded, it was felt Yellowstone's thermal output was lessening and this park would replace it. To paraphrase Mark Twain: the rumors of Yellowstone's death have been greatly exaggerated as have the predictions of this area's thermal longevity.

Whiz Tips

The 1912 volcanic eruption was one of the most explosive the world has ever witnessed. The effect was 10 times more powerful than Mount St. Helens. If it had happened in Manhattan, the Big Apple would be no more and Chicagoans would have heard the blast.

The park has over 50 major prehistoric/historic archaeological finds. This long period of inhabitancy has resulted in the largest collection of pit houses within any park.

Kids' Stuff

★ The park has been experiencing a large growth in family visitation. While the big draw is the bears, with the rich variety of open-air experiences available like hiking, there's certainly plenty to do here if your children enjoy the great outdoors.

Access: Air. **Days/Hours:** Visitor center, daily 8 a.m.-10 p.m. **Camping:** Brooks Camp on Naknek Lake (bring your own food). **For info.:** Superintendent, Katmai National Park & Preserve, P.O.Box 7, King Salmon, AK 99613. 206/442-7220.

Kenai Fjords National Park

Allow: 2 days *FREE*

"The Gulf of Alaska is a wilderness on the edge of a wilderness, remote by water, remote by land, rimmed with ice fields, glaciers, and the second highest coastal mountains in the world."

Boyd Gibbons
National Geographic

On Alaska's south central coast, Kenai Fjords NP encompasses one of largest non-polar ice fields in the country. Between 400-800 inches (33-66 ft.) of snow feed the ice field and its glaciers each year. These glaciers pour out of the mountains to the sea gouging softer rock and making deep valleys for the ocean to fill in as they recede. These deep water bays are called fjords. The fjords are getting even deeper as the Kenai Mountains are slowly slipping into the sea. The mountains' slow slide into the sea is a result of the shifting of the Pacific crustal plate. In just one day in 1964, the Alaskan Good Friday Earthquake caused the shore to sink about 6 ft. This earthquake caused a great tidal wave known as a "tsunami," which covered the shoreline trees in salt water, killing many of them.

Highlights

★ Exit Glacier allows visitors to get close to a moving glacier. Glaciers move because they accumulate more snow in winter than melts each summer. Gravity works to pull the compressed ice downhill. About 400 in. of snow is added to Exit Glacier each year causing the glacier to flow at a rate of almost 2 ft. per day or 600 ft. per year. Exit Glacier's snout or terminus reaches the ocean where it deposits (calves) blocks of ice made up of snow which fell on it about 50 years earlier.

★ Most visitors take a cruise to see the park. During their voyage they may see sea otters, seals, sea lions, bald eagles and 100 kinds of birds. If they're lucky, they may see whales. The all-day tours include the Chiswell Islands in the Alaska Maritime National Wildlife Refuge.

Whiz Tips

The park's rangers conduct interpretive programs at the visitor center in Seward and guided hikes at Exit Glacier. Evening programs at the visitor center include nature talks, water safety demonstrations or presentations on indigenous people. They also conduct daytime walks and talks.

Kids' Stuff

★ Children fortunate enough to travel here enjoy the many opportunities to see wildlife. All who visit are awed by the glaciers and the magnificent fjords.

Access: Exit Glacier, 12 mi. from Seward. **Days/Hours:** Daily, summer 8-7 & winter 8-5. **Camping:** Near Exit Glacier (10 primitive sites). **Special Events:** On Earth Day and the park' services day (Aug. 25), the park puts on special programs. **For info.:**

Kenai Fjords National Park COURTESY NPS

Kenai Fjords National Park, 1212 Fourth Ave., P.O.Box 1727, Seward, AK 99664. 907/224-3874.

Klondike Gold Rush National Historical Park

Allow: 2 hrs. *FREE*

"In the 1890s only Alaska remained as an adventurous escape, but to take off for Alaska for adventure alone was not sociably acceptable. To go in search of wealth, to find a fortune in gold, was acceptable."

David B. Wharton
The Alaska Gold Rush

Two national parks, one located in Skagway, AK and the other in Seattle's (see Klondike Gold Rush NHP, WA), commemorate the great Klondike Gold Rush of 1896-99. After gearing up in Seattle, gold seekers had to choose from a number of routes to the gold fields in Canada's Yukon Territory. Most couldn't afford the all-water route up the Yukon River from St. Michael. This left the long climb up the White Pass or the Chilkoot Trails as their path. Skagway competed with neighboring Dyea to see which would serve as the final jump-off place before the would-be miners hit the trail. And for what? Sure gold was lying along the banks of the Klondike River, but resident Yukon prospectors had quickly laid claim to every likely patch of land. At Skagway, you can still see the historic buildings constructed to feed the frenzy. The Klondike Hwy. traverses the White Pass and ardent hikers retrace the 33-mile overland path through the Chilkoot Pass to Lake Bennett.

Highlights

★ An amalgamation of private and public interests has preserved the look and feel of turn-of-the-century Skagway. Horse-drawn wagons and false-fronted buildings remind us of the days when folks in these parts just came for the good times and moved along.

Whiz Tips

The park rangers give walking tours of Skagway, talks about the gold rush and present a special interest program. 💡 The tales of the Klondike Gold

Klondike Gold Rush National Historical Park–Seattle, Wa COURTESY NPS

Rush are not of the riches plucked from the earth but of the immense determination thousands of men and women displayed to get at those riches. The Chilkoot Trail required individuals to lug a ton of supplies up to the summit before the Canadian Mounties would allow them to carry an ounce of it down the other side. Carrying loads of 30-70 lbs. on their backs, the stampeders had to hike up to the summit at least 20-30 times in order to get their load over. The White Pass was equally unattractive. Facing the same supply requirement, men so over-loaded their pack horses that the trail was littered with over 3,000 dead horses and mules. Getting over the pass wasn't the end of their struggles. Once in Canada, prospectors built all manner of boats to sail down the Yukon River to the Klondike fields over 500 mi. away. They left Lake Bennett when the ice melted.

Kids' Stuff

★ This is the scene of one of the most interesting quests in history. From all over the globe, dreamers flocked to the frozen north. They battled the elements and each other, and undertook immense hardship for a dream of finding their fortunes. Children are as enthralled by this story as anybody.

Access: In Skagway, via Alaska & Klondike Hwys, ferry or plane. **Days/Hours:** Summer, daily 8-8 & winter M-F 8-5. **Camping:** Primitive sites. **For info.:** Superintendent, Klondike Gold Rush National Historical Park, P.O.Box 517, Skagway, AK 99840. 907/983-2921.

Kobuk Valley National Park & Preserve

Allow: 1 week *FREE*

Kobuk Valley follows the Kobuk River to the Chukchi Sea, serving as an important migration route for caribou. The river begins near the Continental Divide in Gates of the Arctic National Park. The river valley has been populated for 12,500 years. People fished its waters and hunted the caribou and moose. An unusual phenomenon in the area is the Great Kobuk Sand Dunes, the world's largest dunes at this latitude.

Highlights

★ You can take float trips, hike, fish and sightsee. As you would expect, the caribou herds attract large carnivores. Grizzly and black bears compete for the fish and feed on the old and weak caribou, while wolves band together to claim their prizes.

Whiz Tips

! There are villages running the length of the river where natives exist at subsistence levels, taking what nature provides.

! The dunes are created by winds carrying the sand into the mountain-enclosed valley. The sand, produced by long-ago glacial action, reaches as high as 150 ft. and covers fossils of Ice Age mammals.

! Visitors often spot grizzlies, black bears, caribou, wolves, moose and lynx.

Kids' Stuff

★ The park provides no services, so your family must be able to cope on its own. The river hosts grayling, Arctic char, sheefish and salmon.

Access: By plane. **Days/Hours:** Kotzebue H.Q., M-F, 8-5; Kotzebue Visitor Center, daily, summer only 9-7. **Camping:** Primitive. **For info.:** Superintendent, Kobuk Valley National Park, Box 1029, Kotzebue, AK 99752. 907/442-3890.

Lake Clark National Park & Preserve

Allow: 3-5 days *FREE*

The park has three spectacular mountain ranges, the Alaskan, the Aleutian and the Chigmits, 50 mi. long Lake Clark and two active volcanoes, Redoubt and Iliamna. People typically visit this wild area by float plane.

Highlights

★ On the east flank of the mountains you can see the two volcanoes breathing. Cook Inlet offers fruitful ground for a host of winged creatures, seagoing whales and seals.

★ On the west side of the park is Lake Clark, trophy fishing and a wide array of land mammals, including grizzlies, moose, caribou and Dall sheep.

Whiz Tips

The land demands self-sufficiency. Summer brings rain. Winter is long. Mountain peaks shadow valleys from the sun's rays for months. The animals and the Dena'ina Indians adapted and survived. Today's interlopers must arm against the elements for their short sojourns. Respect for the vagaries of climate and bears is mandatory for survival. Summer tem- peratures are in the 50s and 60s and winter is no stranger to -40 degrees F.

Kids' Stuff

Families who visit here must be very experienced in the backcountry.

Access: Air. **Days/Hours:** Daily. **Camping:** Backcountry throughout the park. **For info.:** Superintendent, Lake Clark National Park & Preserve, 4230 University Dr., Ste. 311, Anchorage, AK 99508. 907/271-3751.

Noatak National Preserve

Allow: 1 week *FREE*

Designated an International Biosphere Reserve by UNESCO, the preserve contains the largest undeveloped river basin in the country. Although humans have used the region for 5,000 years, as proven by the 200 or so archaeological sites, only

Sitka National Historical Park COURTESY NPS

one village endures as testimony to man's existence.

Highlights

★ Float trips and fishing are the major recreation pursuits for those travelling to this remote wilderness. The river is quite gentle and slow-moving allowing canoeists, kayakers and floaters to set their own pace.

Whiz Tips

The Noatuk River begins in the Brooks Range inside Gates of the Arctic National Park, allowing visitors to see a range of landscape. At the Brooks Range, there is still thin coniferous forests which change to Arctic tundra as the river wends its way to the Chukchi Sea. River travelers may see caribou, wolves, grizzlies, black bears and lynx.

Kids' Stuff

Like most Alaskan parks, families have to be self-sufficient to venture here. Those that do can fish the Noatak for Arctic char, whitefish, grayling and salmon.

Access: By plane. **Days/Hours:** Kotzebue H.Q., M-F, 8-5; Kotzebue Visitor Center, daily, summer only 9-7. **Camping:** Primitive. **For info.:** Superintendent, Noatak National Preserve, Box 1029, Kotzebue, AK 99752. 907/442-3890.

Sitka National Historical Park

Allow: 1-2 hrs. *FREE*

"In 1867, U.S. Secretary of State William Seward bought the unknown region from the Russians in a widely derided move that led to Alaska's first nicknames, Seward's Folly and Seward's Icebox."

Mike Edlehart & James Tinen
America The Quotable

Sitka was established as the capital of the Russian colony and focal point of its rich fur trade. For almost forty years, Russia was able to monopolize trade for the seemingly unending bounty of luxurious sea otter and fur seal skins. Spiriting them to ready markets in China, the Russians were able to command fantastic prices. When news of this secret source of supply was revealed, Russia realized it had to establish permanent colonies to control the trade and Sitka,

Sitka National Historical Park COURTESY NPS

known to American sailors as the "Paris of the Pacific," became their key port. Unfortunately, it was already occupied by native people called Tlingits, who were accustomed to defending their turf from interlopers. This they were able to do, expelling the first Russian attempt at colonization. However, in 1804, the Tlingits were forced to abandon their fort and Sitka was established. The National Historical Park was established to acknowledge the 1804 Battle of Sitka. The park has since added a town site, including the Russian Bishop's House, which has been restored to show how the colony's Eastern Orthodox bishop fared in the mid-1800s.

Highlights

★ Sentinels of a living culture stand guard at the entrance to the visitor center. The Haida and Tlingit totem poles are not the only native art represented here. Utilizing ancient techniques, today's artisans display the same vigilance to their efforts that their forefathers did. For some, the religious aspect has diminished, but it is transplanted by the need to stem the tide of cultural extinction.

Whiz Tips

❢ Visitors are introduced to all aspects of totemic art on ranger-led walks. Many of the totem poles presented here are not indigenous to Sitka. They are reproductions of a collection of poles gathered from all over southeastern Alaska for the Louisiana Purchase Exhibit of 1904 and sent here at its completion.

❢ Guided walks explaining the Battle of Sitka or touring the Russian Blockhouse are less regular events.

Kids' Stuff

★ Kids like the large colorful totem poles and watching the local people craft their creations. During school periods, the park is more likely to put on specific children's programs.

Access: Sitka on Baranof Island, by Alaska State Ferry, cruise ship or by air. **Days/Hours:** Visitor center & Russian Bishop House, summer, daily 8-5. Visitor center, winter, 6 days/wk. 8-5. **Camping:** 6 mi. N on FR 11, Starrigan campground (30 sites). **For info.:** Superintendent, Sitka National Historical Park, P.O.Box 738, Sitka, AK 99835. 907/747-6281.

Wrangell-St. Elias National Park & Preserve

Allow: ".5 days or a lifetime" *FREE*

Bordered by Yukon Territory, British Columbia, Canada's Kluane National Park and the Gulf of Alaska, Wrangell-St. Elias, America's largest national park, encompasses three mountain ranges and 9 of the nation's 16 highest peaks. Although it's difficult to comprehend its scale, people familiar with Yellowstone could try to imagine six Yellowstones. Paved roads run past the western boundary and two gravel roads reach tenuously into the wilderness. These pathways of civilization are the exception. The park is a solitary experience and only the self-sufficient need apply.

Highlights

★ Together with Kluane, this is the premier mountain region on the continent. Mountaineering and kayaking are increasing in popularity among the park's visitors. Backcountry hikers can expect to see a rich variety of wildlife including bears, moose, Dall's sheep, buffalo, and caribou. Visitors who drive up the Nabesna Road into the Mount Sanford foothills or up the McCarthy Road into Mount Blackburn foothills will find incomparable scenery.

Whiz Tips

❢ These mountains are part of the Pacific Ring of Fire, the chain of volcanoes which encircle the Pacific Ocean. Volcanic action is still seen at Mount Wrangell in the form of steam vents, even though the last eruption was in 1930.

ô Temperatures have been known to reach the 70s in summer. Spring and early summer are prime mosquito-feeding periods. September may be the best time to visit, as there are fewer mosquitoes and the days are usually clear and crisp (emphasis on crisp).

Kids' Stuff

★ This is a wild place with few facilities for visitors, let alone children. Families travelling here must be well-versed in coping in the outdoors.

Access: Air or road from Chitina or from Slana. **Days/Hours:** Visitor stations, daily, summer-only 9-6. **Camping:** Backcountry camping; nearby State and the Bureau of Land Management, developed camping. **For info.:** Superintendent, Wrangell-St. Elias National Park & Preserve, P.O.Box 29, Glennallen, AK 99588. 907/823-2205/907/822-5238.

Yukon-Charley Rivers National Preserve

Allow: 1 week *FREE*

The preserve contains all 118 miles of the Charley River that drains out of Canada and the 130 miles of Yukon River it joins. The region is a critical nesting ground for the endangered peregrine falcon. The rivers first came into prominence at the end of the last century when gold was found on their banks (see Klondike Gold Rush NHS, AK & WA). Today, they are more noted, particularly the Charley, as prime float waters.

Highlights

★ The Charley is regarded among the best white water streams in Alaska, a world-class waterway. Surprisingly, the park's summer temperatures compare favorably with Grand Teton's. June and July visitors can enjoy the experience of continuous daylight or twilight while December visitors can only hope for 6 or 7 hours of daylight and 50 below or worse temperatures.

Whiz Tips

The Yukon River remains an important resource for the Athabaskan native peoples. Its waters have provided salmon and sustenance for centuries. With the coming of gold prospectors, these people sought security by banding together and small villages continue to border the Yukon's banks.

There are over 150 species of birds which have been spotted in the region. Some of the more common birds even the novice bird-watcher can recognize are: the Arctic loon, bald and golden eagles, peregrine falcon and sandhill crane.

Kids' Stuff

★ Families with older children can make use of the floating possibilities that exist within the reserve. The stretch of the Yukon River between Eagle and Circle is an especially appealing trip for families as it is free of rapids with a current of about 4-6 mi./hr.

★ The fishing opportunities include grayling, northern pike, burbot, sheefish, whitefish and salmon.

Access: Taylor Hwy. from the Alaska Hwy. to Eagle or Steese Hwy. from Fairbanks to Circle. **Days/Hours:** Daily. **Camping:** Both Eagle and Circle have campgrounds. **For info.:** Superintendent, Yukon-Charley Rivers National Preserve, P.O.Box 167, Eagle, AK 99738. 907/547-2233.

AMERICAN SAMOA

The National Park of American Samoa

Allow: 1 week *FREE*

This recent (Oct., 1988) addition to the park service contains 2 rain forest preserves, a magnificent white sand beach and one of the best preserved coral reefs in the Pacific. The parkland is planned to include portions of 3 different islands; Tutuila, the largest, Ta'u, the easternmost and Ofu. Like many people who live close to the land, the native Polynesians show their respect by calling their islands "Samoa," or "sacred earth." The U.S. portion of these islands consists of 5 islands and 2 atolls. Within the designated wild areas are the enedangered flying fox, a fruit bat with an enormous wing span (as big as an eagle's), Pacific boa, tortoises and a colorful array of birds and fish.

For info.: c/o Pacific Area Office, P.O.Box 50165, Honolulu, HI 96850 or American Samoa Office of Tourism, P.O. Box 1147, Pago Pago, American Samoa, 96799. 684/699-9280.

ARIZONA

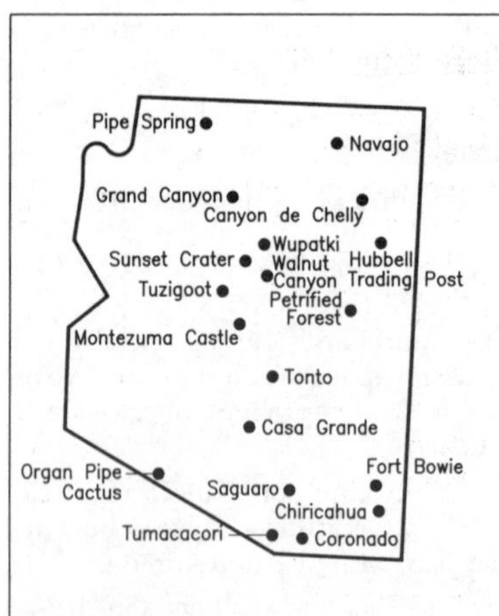

Canyon de Chelly National Monument

Allow: 1-2 days *FREE*

Deep in Navajo land is the last-ditch fortress of the Navajo Nation, Canyon de Chelly. Still regarded as a sacred place by the Navajo, Canyon de Chelly National Monument restricts visitor access. As a result, without either the assistance of a Navajo guide or park ranger, use of the canyon is limited to the overlooks and White House Trail. Still, that is more than enough. The tiny Navajo ranches nestled peacefully under the watch of the ancient Anasazi ruins, the meandering river playing tag with the dirt lane and the sheep scattered here and there as though placed by some giant child, are symbols of simpler times and simpler ways.

Highlights

★ Take the trail to White House Ruins, a challenging but easier excursion than it appears. Along the way you go through a small tunnel carved in the rock and have to ford the shallow Rio de Chelly.

★ Some canyon walls have been caught standing alone and encircled by the river to form vertical islands. One such island, 800 foot tall Spider

Rock in Monument Canyon, is a favorite for photographers.

Whiz Tips

The somewhat strenuous ranger-led canyon treks and the special hikes to visit the archaeologists at work at the Mummy Cave offer unparalleled scenery and a wealth of information about the region. For traditional Navajo, Hopi, and many other Indians, some Anasazi dwellings are holy places. Few would enter a ruins unless they were going for a special religious ceremony. As a result, Anasazi ruins were left intact until the arrival of the Europeans.

In 1863, Kit Carson was sent to subdue the Navajo. His first attempt met with disaster as the Navajo dug in at Canyon de Chelly and repelled him. However, Carson burnt their crops and slaughtered their sheep causing massive starvation. Weakened and bowed, the Navajo were forced to undergo the "Long March," across New Mexico to Fort Sumner. As fate would have it, famine struck and for four years the Navajo continued to suffer. Finally, the U.S. government relented and offered them three options: they could go to the rich farmlands in Oklahoma's Indian Territory, stay put, or return to their desert homelands. It was no contest. The Navajo have a special relationship with this barren land and believe it is a living thing. They returned to flourish, becoming the continent's largest Native American nation.

Kids' Stuff

★ What better way to teach your children about the history of their country than to visit a place so steeped in western history. The trail to the White House is a great one for kids with the tunnel and a river crossing.

Access: 3 mi. E of Chinle. **Days/Hours:** Visitors center, daily 8-5. **Camping:** Park's Cottonwood Campground (75 sites & shwrs.). **For info.:** Superintendent, Canyon De Chelly National Monument, P.O.Box 588, Chinle, AZ 86503. 602/674-5436.

Casa Grande Ruins National Monument

Allow: 1-2 hrs. *Fee*

East off I-10 midway between Tucson and Phoenix is a unique Hohokam archaeological ruins. The Casa Grande, the Big House for which the monument is named, is notable because archaeologists believe one of its uses may have been as a pre-historic observatory. The Casa Grande and the smaller ruins in the vicinity were built by the Hohokam in the early 1300s out of caliche, a desert soil similar to concrete.

Highlights

★ The Casa Grande is the tallest and most massive Hohokam structure in evidence today. It is quite impressive when viewed from a distance or close up.

Whiz Tips

Sometime during the 1400s, the Hohokam culture declined and the site was abandoned. While no one knows for sure what became of these master irrigationists, the O'odham (Pima & Papago Indians) in this region may be their descendants.

The rangers give interpretive talks at various times during the year explaining the significance of the monument. In addition, there is a self-guiding trail.

Kids' Stuff

★ There's a Kid's Guide to the ruins which provides information and questions, fun for the whole family.

Access: Halfway btwn., Phoenix & Tucson E of I-10. **Days/Hours:** Daily 7-6. **Camping:** 26 mi. W Picacho Peak State Park (38 sites, elec. & showers). **For info.:** Superintendent, Casa Grande Ruins National Monument, 1100 Ruins Dr., Coolidge, AZ 85228. 602/723-3172.

Chiricahua National Monument

Allow: .5 days *Fee*

In the southeast corner of Arizona are the former stomping grounds of the formidable Chiricahua Apaches. This mountain retreat was wrested from them, turned into a Dude Ranch and finally a national monument. The monument is distinctive because of its extraordinary geology. The enormous boulders balancing upon huge pedestals were formed from ashes of a cataclysmic volcano. The rocks were melded together by time and pressure, finally to be whittled by wind and rain. The Chiricahua named the land the "Land of the Standing-up Rocks."

Highlights

★ The eight-mile drive up to these formidable formations is chock-full of pull-overs for camera buffs. The rocks take on special life of their own as the light and shadows create their own masterpiece.

Whiz Tips

❢ Tours of the Faraway Ranch house are given year round. It's worth timing your trip to coincide with these programs so you can find out more about these remarkable pioneers.

❢ Few names commanded so much respect and fear among the pioneers, stagecoach drivers and soldiers as those of Cochise and Geronimo, the famous Chiricahua Apache war chiefs. You can learn a little about their lives and their battles at the park and nearby Fort Bowie NM.

Kids' Stuff

★ The ranch hike from the campgrounds is a good size for children.

Access: S. of Willcox (I-10) on AZ 186. **Days/Hours:** Visitor center daily 8-5 (clsd. Dec.25). **Camping:** Park campground (25 sites). **For info.:** Superintendent, Chiricahua National Monument, Dos Cabezas Rte., Box 6500, Willcox, AZ 85643. 602/824-3560.

Casa Grande Ruins National Monument COURTESY NPS

Coronado National Memorial

Allow: 1-2 hrs. *FREE*

Abutting the Mexican border where the Huachuca Mountains peter out, Coronado Memorial overlooks the valley where the first major European expedition entered what is now the American Southwest. The memorial was established in 1952 to commemorate Francisco Vasquez de Coronado's expedition of 1540-42 and the Spanish influence on the history of the Southwest.

Highlights

★ The view from Coronado Peak reveals an overview of the topography of the land Coronado and his cohorts trudged across. A line of cottonwood trees marks the San Pedro River which the expedition followed. It's hard to picture why a large troop of armored Spaniards would take on such a journey. What a sight they must have been to the natives who lived and dressed so close to the land!

★ The memorial maintains the environs much the way they would have been when the Coronado Entrada journeyed here. Oak and pine trees, agave and yucca plants provide food and shelter for the many animals the Spaniards would probably be encountering for the first time.

Whiz Tips

At the rear of the visitor center is a 14 ft. glassed wall overlooking a small wildlife sanctuary. On-lookers have spotted over 160 species of birds here as well as javelina (a wild pig-like animal found only in the Americas), coatimundi (a recent immigrant to the Southwest, nicknamed "hog-nosed coon"), cous white-tail deer and gray fox. The added bonus for interested photographers is the ability to take exceptional close-ups without disturbing the wildlife.

Kids' Stuff

★ There is a short hike to a cave which you can explore. It is a dry cave and you should have the proper equipment (caving books recommend a minimum of three flashlights) before exploring the cave. The hike leaves very near the visitors

Coronado National Memorial COURTESY NPS

center then up a steep trail. Although the cave has been badly vandalized, there are still stalagmites, stalactites and flowstone to be seen. You should be aware that even so much as touching a cave formation damages it as the oils on your skin leave a residue.

Access: 22 mi. S of Sierra Vista or 35 mi. W of Bisbee on AZ 92. **Days/Hours:** Daily 8-5. **Camping:** Coronado National Forest to the N & W; state's Parker Lake Canyon (18 mi. E.) and Carr Canyon (10 mi. N). **For info.:** Superintendent, Coronado National Memorial, RR 2, Box 126, Hereford, AZ 85615. 602/366-5515.

Fort Bowie National Monument

Allow: 3 hrs. *FREE*

Just inside southern Arizona from the New Mexican border is a dirt road turn-off leading to a gravel pull-over. Remote scrub-brush hills give no hint why the shaded picnic tables and accompanying bulletin board should be there. This is your jump-off point for your visit to Fort Bowie. Trekking over the harsh desert hills, you wonder why anybody would build anything here. Down gullies, over dry washes, through scrub brush, you're constantly on the alert for rattlers. You begin to realize how soldiers, cowboys and miners must have felt in these hills as they worried about Apache attacks. The stunted desert trees provide perfect camouflage for marauders. Any sign of "civilization" would be welcome. Unfortunately, the first structure you come upon is the remnants of the Butterfield Stagecoach Station. Not a good sign. Oh, oh!...a grave yard. Next you are confronted by an Apache wickiup, proof you are not alone. Finally, Old Glory tops the hill marking where the fort stands... er...stood.

Highlights

★ The view from atop the hills on your return trip looks down on the fort and the wild country it sought to control. Thinking of the spring below, you reflect on how the presence of water forced the use of the trail even though it took travelers through some pretty tough country. Given the danger of dying of thirst or by

Fort Bowie National Historic Site

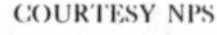
COURTESY NPS

Apache attack, it's clear the Apache were no match.

Whiz Tips

❢ You ponder the over zealousness of Lieutenant George Bascom, who so enraged Cochise, the Chiricahua Apache chief, that the area's history for the next eleven years would be written in blood. Bascom erroneously accused Cochise of stealing some cows and a rancher's 12 yr. old child. To add insult to injury, he arrested Cochise, his wife and some male relatives. Cochise made a daring escape by cutting his way out of a tent. His wife and relatives didn't make it. Unfortunately, Bascom compounded the problem when he hanged some of Cochise's innocent relatives in retribution when Cochise took hostages to trade.

Kids' Stuff

★ There's some "hands-on" exhibits at the ranger station near the fort. Children can examine a replica cavalry saber, bugle, military hats, Springfield rifle and mountain howitzer. The hike is fun for kids as long as you make it an adventure and not a duty. If they don't feel up to it, don't force them. Take plenty of water!

Access: Trailhead S of Bowie off I-10 12 mi. on graded road. **Days/Hours:** Daily from 8-5 (clsd. Dec.25). **Camping:** Nearby (28 mi.S) Chiricahua National Monument (25 sites). **Special Events:** First wknd. after Labor Day, Fort Bowie Days Festival. **For info.:** Superintendent, Fort Bowie National Historic Site, P.O.Box 158, Bowie, AZ 85605. 602/847-2500.

Grand Canyon National Park

Allow: 2-7 days *Fee*

"On either side of us were hills from 1,000 or 1,500 feet high, wooded from crest to heel. As far as the eye could range forward were columns of steam in the air, misshapen lumps of lime, mist-like preadamite monsters, still pools of turquoise-blue stretches of blue cornflowers, a river that coiled on itself 23 times, pointed boulders of strange colors, and ridges of glaring, staring white."

Rudyard Kipling
American Notes

No matter who you ask for recommendations for places to visit in the

Grand Canyon National Park

West, everybody's list includes the Grand Canyon, one of America's 19 World Heritage Sites. Over 200 miles long and 12 miles wide, this northern Arizona canyon offers a myriad of vistas that you can gulp down or sip slowly. The artist who sculpted this phenomenon is the Colorado River, the nation's second longest river. When our noisy crew first stopped to see what all the fuss was about, the four kids and Grandma tumbled out of the van, headed pell-mell to the viewpoint and fell into a church-like hush. For the next few minutes you could have heard a pin drop. Then Grandma, having spent most of her life in Jamaica and knowing little if anything about the Grand Canyon, said in an authoritative but awed whisper, "This is it...this is the greatest of them all."

There are two different regions to the park: the most popular and populated South Rim and the North Rim. Because of the five hour drive between the two, each has their own newspaper detailing the programs its offered.

Highlights

★ The Canyon at any time of the day, at any angle, provides dazzling scenery. Colors change, shadows grow and lessen, a slight turn of your head and you encounter a totally different perspective. Miles of fluted canyon wall fill your field of vision. Use a telescope and the magnified vision before you is no less detailed, no less compelling. It's no wonder visitors return again and again as the landscape is far too vast to take in no matter how long or how closely you look at it.

★ The Tusayan Ruin and Museum utilizes the small prehistoric pueblo ruins as the central focus in showing the life of the ancient Anasazis in the canyon.

Whiz Tips

Our experience with the park's interpretive programs is you can't go wrong. They provide background information on the history of the Canyon and the park, as well as relevant geological and natural history.

It doesn't really matter if we give you this tip because everybody feels (s)he must visit the South Rim BUT if you want fewer crowds and the same rewards, visit the North Rim.

Most people recommend you take the overnight mule trip down to the Canyon bottom. Although seemingly perched precariously close to disaster, these beasts of burden are extremely sure-footed and also dread the possibility of descending too quickly. Please be advised: after riding these critters, you will wonder if your knees will ever have close communion again. Cowboys didn't walk funny just because it was macho.

Kids' Stuff

★ The children's interpretive programs featured a puppet show about the canyon and games about the wildlife. Kids receive their own newspaper entitled *The Young Adventurer* which details the requirements for the Jr. Ranger program. Our kids' participation in the Junior Ranger Program culminated in a Town Crier-like announcement complete with "Hear Yea, Hear Yea" and bell-ringing proclaiming their completion. They were thrilled by all the attention.

Access: South Rim 60 mi. N of Williams or 57 mi. W of Cameron on AZ 64. North Rim 45 mi. S of Jacob Lake on Hwy. 67. **Days/Hours:** South Rim year-round; North Rim from mid-May to late-Oct. Visitor centers daily, summer 8-8. South Rim visitor center, daily, winter 8-5. **Camping:** Park's 4 campgrounds (3 resrvtns.); Mather (showers), North Rim (Ticketron), Trailer Village (elec.-602/638-2401). **Teacher's Package:** Available. **For info.:** Superintendent, Grand Canyon National Park, P.O.Box 129, Grand Canyon, AZ 86023. 602/638-7888.

Hubbell Trading Post National Historic Site

Allow: .5 days *FREE*

Just 10 years after the Navajos returned to their northeastern Arizona homeland from their enforced exile to eastern New Mexico, John Lorenzo Hubbell set up his trading post near their reservation. Today, at the reservation's oldest continually active trading post, you can still buy provisions or Navajo blankets.

Highlights

★ The post reeks of authenticity right down to the musty smell and wooden counters darkened with stains. Trade goods still hang from walls and rafters. Make no mistake this is the real thing; an Indian trading post.

★ The self-guided tour of the homestead demonstrates the delicate balancing act the Hubbells had to perform as they succeeded in bridging the white and red worlds. The ranger-led house tour is not to be missed if only to see the beautifully designed Navajo rugs and fine basket work which cover the ceilings.

Whiz Tips

In the visitor center there's usually a Navajo artisan, weaving or silversmithing.

Hubbell's success is a lesson to us even today. Research into intercultural exchange demonstrates the immense value placed on trust. Hubbell recognized in order for people to trust him he had to be himself. He did not try to become "Indian" but rather retained his cultural roots and acted in good faith. His continued success was due to his scrupulous honesty.

Kids' Stuff

By providing a little background information for your kids before your visit you can greatly enhance their interest and learning. Tell them a little about reservations, trading posts and the goods that both worlds desired from each other.

Access: 1 mi. W of Ganado and 55 mi. NW of Gallup on AZ 264 or 40 mi. N of Chambers on US 191. **Days/Hours:** Daily 8-5, summer 8-6 (clsd. Thanksgiving, Dec.25 & Jan.1). **Camping:** Nearby Canyon De

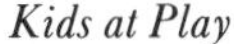

Kids at Play

Chelly (75 sites). **For info.:** Superintendent, Hubbell Trading Post National Historic Site, P.O.Box 150, Ganado, AZ 86505. 602/755-3475/7.

Montezuma Castle National Monument

Allow: .5 days *Fee*

The park consists of two sites, Montezuma Castle and Well which are about a 30 minute drive apart. Both are serviced by the Yavapai-Apache Visitor center, mid-point between them. Although early European explorers named these fantastic structures after the famed Aztec leader, Montezuma, there is no evidence the Mexico City empire held any sway over this part of the New World. In all probability, the connection was made more out of the hope the Europeans would unearth riches similar to those found by the Spaniards in Mexico City.

Highlights

★ The visitor center, a cooperative national monument facility and Yavapai-Apache center, has three audio-visual viewing areas with a variety of presentations you can see. In addition, it has a large exhibit hall and a Native American craft shop.

★ Because climbing will increase erosion, you can only gaze up at Montezuma Castle, a dazzling feat of architecture and perseverance. There is, however, a nature walk through the Indian ruins at the base of the cliffs (the dwellings of those who suffered acrophobia, dread of high places?).

★ Montezuma Well would be an attraction even without the presence of Sinagua ruins. A huge natural cistern, you walk up its sides to gaze down on the oasis below. The Sinagua built cliff-dwellings in the wall face and on the floor of the basin. They channeled the water escaping the well through an underground stream into the fields to grow crops.

Whiz Tips

Although we are not sure why the Sinagua built Montezuma Castle, we at least learn how they managed to complete such a difficult feat.

The Yavapai-Apache Center is a good place to learn about the unusual association between the Yavapai and Apache Indians. Differing in cultural and linguistic roots, the two tribes formed a friendship that grew as the Europeans flooded their lands. Both tribes suffered a major joint defeat when their warriors were cornered at Skull Cave and were decimated by bullets ricocheting off the cave's walls. Today, they still share reservations.

Kids' Stuff

Both sites offer fun walks for the youngsters. Neither of the trails are arduous and both have ruins. Of the two, children like the Well better because they could go down into it and they could see the underground stream emerge.

Access: Visitor center 2.5 mi. off I-17 S of Flagstaff. **Days/Hours:** Daily, summer 8-7 & winter 8-5. **Camping:** National Forest's Clear Creek at Camp Verde (18 sites). **For info.:** Superintendent, Montezuma Castle National Monument, P.O.Box 219, Camp Verde, AZ 86322. 602/567-3322.

Navajo National Monument

Allow: .5 days *FREE*

In northeastern Arizona, deep in Navajo territory, is Navajo National Monument, the home of the Kayenta Anasazi. Responsible for the preservation of three ruins, the park provides access to two. Keet Seel, Navajo for "broken pieces of pottery," is open to visitors who reserve a place and invest a day or two to complete the rugged 16 mi. round trip. Betatakin, Navajo for "ledge house," has regular tours from May-Sept.

Highlights

★ Even as you view Betatakin from the Sandal Trail overlook near the visitors center, you recognize the architectural mastery of the ancient Anasazi. There is a mysterious feeling that is hard to explain when you visit these cliff-dwellings. Spiritual "Doubting Thomases" find it hard to account for the sense of intimacy we all share with the lost Anasazi.

Whiz Tips

As you tour the ruins with the rangers, you learn more about the Kayenta branch of the Anasazi. The other two major branches, Mesa Verde and Chaco, are best represented at Mesa Verde National Park and Chaco Canyon. The three branches have been primarily identified through their differences in pottery styles, architecture and religious practices. It is generally accepted that the Kayenta people were not as architecturally advanced as their cousins but their pottery is comparable. Located as far west as the Grand Canyon and as far north as southern Utah, the Kayenta had their most advanced pueblos located here. The current theory for the demise of their culture about 1300 AD is a century-long drought compounded by severe erosion of their canyon bottom farmland. Many feel the Anasazi are the ancestors of the Hopi and Pueblo peoples.

The national parks on the reservation joins the Navajo in their observance of Daylight Savings Time. Arizona and the Hopi Reservation don't change their clocks. The result? In summer, the reservation time is one hour later than the rest of Arizona but the same as Colorado, Utah and New Mexico.

Kids' Stuff

★ The park offers a Jr. Ranger program which asks the children specific questions about how they would live in this area. When they've completed the work sheet, they receive a certificate.

★ The Betatakin hike is a 5 mi. round trip and 5-6 hours long, not an excursion every family wants to take. To compound the challenge, the sites

Navajo National Monument COURTESY JIM MILLER

are located about 7300 ft. above sea level and the thin air poses problems for unfit hikers. The park recommends two quarts of water and sturdy shoes for each person. If your children are up to it, this could be the highlight of their vacation.

Access: 50 N of Tuba City or 22 mi. SW of Kayenta on US 160 turn onto Rte. 164. **Days/Hours:** Daily, spring & summer 8-5 & winter 8-4:30 (clsd. Thanksgiving, Dec.25 & Jan.1). **Camping:** Park's campground (30 sites); primitive camping at Keet Seel. **For info.:** Superintendent, Navajo National Monument, HC 71 Box 3, Tonalea, AZ 86044-9704. 602/672-2366/7.

Organ Pipe Cactus National Monument

Allow: 2-3 days *Fee*

516 square miles of Sonoran Desert nestled along the Mexican border safeguard over 225 species of birds and 28 types of cactus. The monument, one of the country's 19 World Heritage Sites, was created to preserve the only place in the U.S. you'll find organ pipe cacti living in the wild. The organ pipe cactus is shaped like a large "bush" with a number of branches rising from the ground, rather than from a "trunk." May and early June are excellent times to see these cacti bloom, turning the desert ablaze with color.

Highlights

★ Hiking through the desert scenery offers rare rewards not duplicated elsewhere. One is sometimes startled by the profusion of wildlife. Creatures you might see include roadrunners, javelinas, tortoises, hawks, coyotes, gila woodpeckers, gila monsters and rattlesnakes.

★ Two scenic drives on dirt roads begin near the visitor center. The Puerto Blanco drive takes you around its namesake mountains past Golden Bell Mine, Bonita Well, Quitobaquito Oasis and along the Mexican border, leading you to Senita Basin picnic grounds. The Ajo Mountain Drive takes you through the Diablo Mountains to the base of the Ajo Mountains.

Whiz Tips

Summer temperatures include about 50 days when the red line rises above 100 degrees F. As recent as 1990, the record high was 118 degrees F; get out the skillet, let's fry some eggs.

Of particular interest to desert aficionados is when the plants bloom. Your best bet for blooming cacti are May-June; annuals and perennials peak in March. You may see flowering of some plants virtually any time of the year because of "second" flowering. Plants you will find include Saguaro, Ocotillo, Brittlebrush, Prickly Pear, Cholla, Creosotebush, Mesquite and Elephant Tree.

Kids' Stuff

★ There are several hiking trails in the park. The children-sized trails include the Desert View Nature Trail and the Paloverde Trail. Children can suffer long-term effects if they become dehydrated and the park stresses summer hikers should carry at least a gallon of water.

Access: 142 mi. S of Phoenix on AZ 85 or 140 mi. W of Tucson on AZ 86 & 85. **Days/ Hours:** Daily 8-5. **Camping:** Park's Headquarters Campground (208 sites). **For info.:** Superintendent, Organ Pipe Cactus National Monument, Rte. 1, Box 100, Ajo, AZ 85321. 602/387-6849.

Petrified Forest National Park

Allow: 2 hrs. *Fee*

Encompassing a part of the Painted Desert, this 28 mile drive off of I-40 in northeastern Arizona has pockets of stark beauty amid mostly desert country. Scattered in the south part of the park is Nature's rubble heap, the petrified wood for which the park is noted. Recent scientific finds have renewed the importance of the park. Some unusual finds still being analyzed and not yet available for public display indicate truly unique discoveries.

Highlights

★ At the park's eastern portal, you drive through a portion of the Painted Desert. Weird shades of blue and purple mix in with hues of red and pink. About half-way through the park, take the turn-off for Blue Mesa for a closer inspection of these tinted geologic formations.

★ There are a number of petrified attractions in the park. Agate Bridge is an 111-foot long petrified tree trunk spanning a small arroyo. Agate House is evidence of use of the best available materials (petrified wood) to build a domicile. The Rainbow Forest is a collection of fallen trees turned into rock and battered and broken by the earth's convulsions.

Whiz Tips

Although the park personnel are concerned with the preservation of the petrified wood (thieves take an enormous quantity each year), you can still learn about the theories of petrification. It is currently believed petrification (fossilization) takes place when organic matter is replaced by mineral matter or the cells are filled by mineral matter.

Kids' Stuff

The park's Jr. Ranger Program includes activities for 6 and under (a group often excluded), 7-9 and 10 and up. Each participant has to complete three projects to qualify for a badge and certificate.

Watch your kids carefully. Even after warning our children to look and not touch, our three year-old forgot and started to add to his rock collection. Fortunately, we saw him in time and left his small collection in the Rainbow Forest.

Access: 26 mi. E of Holbrook on I-40. **Days /Hours:** Daily daylight hours (clsd. Dec.25 & Jan.1). **For info.:** Superintendent, Petrified Forest National Park, AZ 86028. 602/524-6228.

Petrified Forest National Park

Pipe Spring National Monument

Allow: 2-3 hrs. *Fee*

On the Kaibab Indian Reservation in northwestern Arizona, is a preserved Mormon fort standing guard over the Pipe Spring and its precious commodity, water. Brigham Young sent groups of Mormons out to build new communities to claim ownership over vast tracts of land and to grow enough foods to survive. However, by spreading out, they left themselves open to attack and had to build fortifications like Pipe Spring's Winsor Castle to defend themselves.

Highlights

★ The tours given by costumed rangers elaborate on the daily lives of the intrepid travelers. By limiting access to the Spring, the Mormons incurred the wrath of the native peoples. After crossing the prairies as so many of the faithful did, it must have been disheartening to find their peace still unsettled in the new land.

Whiz Tips

The Navajos didn't take kindly to interlopers. The first Pipe Valley settlers, cattlemen Dr. Whitmore and Robert McIntyre were slaughtered by the locals. In 1868, the Mormon Militia established the spring as its southern-most outpost. After Maj. John Wesley Powell, of Grand Canyon fame, negotiated a peace with the natives, Brigham Young made plans to construct a more permanent presence.

Although the cowboys who worked this stretch of country didn't drive their cattle to market like their Great Plains counter-parts did, they utilized many of the same tools and technology. The park presents a cross-section of exhibits demonstrating how these symbols of Western America went about earning their beans and biscuits.

Why is it called Pipe Spring? Back before there was a fort, a famed sharp-shooter William Hamblin was challenged to shoot a hole through a bandanna. Well, William "missed" the shot as the bullet merely pushed the hanging soft cloth aside. Not too pleased at this trick, Hamblin "borrowed" one of his taunters' pipes and proved his skill by shooting the bottom of the pipe's bowl out without scratching its sides. Needless to say, this made quite an impression on the jokers and the name for the Spring has stuck.

Kids' Stuff

★ The fort, the memorabilia and the costumed hosts all provide a colorful and eventful stop for children.

Access: 14 mi. W of Fredonia on US 89A via AZ 389. **Days/Hours:** Open daily, summer 8-6, winter 8-4:30 (clsd. Thanksgiving, Dec.25 & Jan.1). **Camping:** 13 mi. N of Kanab, UT, Coral Pink Sand Dunes State Park (22 sites). **For info.:** Superintendent, Pipe Spring National Monument, Moccasin, AZ 86022. 602/643-7105.

Saguaro National Monument

Allow: 1 day *Fee-Rincon Mtn. (Tucson Mtn.-FREE)*

The symbol of the Great American Deserts, the saguaro cactus (also known for good reason as the "Giant Cactus") is only found in the Sonoran Desert, in Arizona. Fictionally, it is shown as a lonely sentinel with a solitary buzzard perched atop one of its three arms and a cow skull at its feet. In reality, it is generally found in a forest of saguaros, has many arms and plays host to an abundance of wildlife. The Sonoran Desert is one of the hottest and driest zones in North America and, yet, it has the lushest variety of flora and fauna of any neighboring desert. While saguaros are found throughout the desert, Saguaro National Monument oversees two areas of saguaro cacti deemed noteworthy by the national parks. Bordering east (Rincon Mtn. District) and west (Tucson Mtn.District) of Tucson, both locations lie on the flanks of the city and its adjoining mountain ranges.

Highlights

★ By taking the nature walks or a longer hike, you quickly see and hear the profusion of birds and animals who make this harsh desert their home. Prepared or not, the wealth of wild life encountered on such a foray is astonishing. Drives through either of the monument's two sections take you past this regal plant for which the West is so well known. Like armies of captured outlaws, these desert giants reach for the sky.

Whiz Tips

Every day there is a nature walk explaining the saguaro and other life forms in the desert. The saguaro is a remarkably well adapted desert survivor. Living up to 150 hundred years or more and reaching over 35 ft. high, the saguaro may weigh several tons supported by a 70 ft. root system. Saguaros with no or few arms are mere babes about 75 years old. With corrugated trunk and branches it can expand like a bellows during a wet period, storing the water for up to four years. The tiny spines studding the plant act like toy sun umbrellas shading the plant and protect it from hungry or thirsty animals. The plant is fed by its enormous root system which flares out in all directions staying just below the surface so it can soak in whatever moisture is available before it evaporates. Its flowers bloom in May and early June nights and last until noon allowing for night-time pollination by bats. Their fruit which ripens right after the blossoms, is edible. The local Native Americans, the only people permitted to harvest the saguaro fruit, turn it into many delicacies, the most common of which is jam.

Kids' Stuff

★ This is a strange new world for most visitors and no less so for kids. The desert park offers a good opportunity to demonstrate to your children how plants and animals have come to survive here. Most of us assume the climate is so harsh, very

Saguaros at Tonto National Monument COURTESY NPS

few creatures can exist. Dawn or dusk walks quickly demonstrate the fallacy of that assumption. Your main task will be to make sure your kids are sufficiently well-watered as they explore the desert.

Access: Both are short drives from Tucson. **Days/Hours:** Daily, summer 7-7 & winter 8-5. Visitor center 8-5. (clsd. Dec.25) **Camping:** E Coronado National Forest's 5 campgrounds on the Catalina Hwy; W Gilbert Ray Campground (elec.) in the Tucson Mtn. County Park; Catalina State Park (shwrs.) 10 mi. N. of the city on Hwy. 89. **For info.:** Superintendent, Saguaro National Monument, 3693 S. Old Spanish Trail, Tucson, AZ 85730-5699. 602/296-8576.

Tonto National Monument

Allow: 3-4 hrs. *Fee*

No, this is not a monument to the Lone Ranger's erstwhile buddy, Tonto. Rather these cliff-dwelling ruins were named after the Tonto Basin where the Salado Indians grew their crops. The basin is now home to Roosevelt Lake, supplying water and electricity to the Phoenix area about 2 hours to the west. The Salado like the Anasazi, the Mogollon and the Sinagua practiced the art of erecting stone buildings and cliff-dwellings. There is cause to believe the Salado people built their cliff-dwellings because over-population forced them to optimize their fertile soil. One current theory is that the Tonto Basin was host to one of the largest communities in North America, at the time.

Highlights

★ The Upper Ruins is noted for having many intact buildings. As a result, visitors receive a more comprehensive picture of the living conditions the Salado people experienced. Because of the relative isolation of the monument, they do recommend you call for reservations for this winter-only tour. Don't despair if you don't get on that tour; there is a self-guiding tour to the Lower Ruins which is well worth the trip.

★ The famed Apache Trail (Hwy. 88) is a long dirt road which winds around deep chasms in a never-end-

Tonto National Monument COURTESY NPS

ing series of switchbacks. It ranks with the most scenic drives in the west but it is not for the faint-at-heart nor for those of you who prize a flawless paint job. The Trail takes you past the supposed home to the Lost Dutchman Gold Mine, the Superstition Mountains and historic Tortilla Flat.

Whiz Tips

❢ You learn about the lives of the Salado from their remaining artifacts. It's clear these people had leisure time to develop their artistry in many areas. The Salado were expert weavers, jewelers, tool-makers and potters. It's not clear where they came from as they seem to have blended their ways from their neighboring Hohokam, Mogollon and Anasazi. In the visitor center you can see the evidence of this expertise. Their culture outlasted these other cultures until just before the arrival of the Apaches. However, like their earlier contemporaries, they also mysteriously disappeared.

Kids' Stuff

★ Your children will not complain about their visit as there's a spectacular view of valley and lake. They will find the ruins to be an exciting and intriguing place to explore. On our climb to the ruins we encountered foraging deer, an unexpected bonus.

Access: 28 mi. from Globe/Miami & US 60 on AZ 88. **Days/Hours:** Open daily 8-5, trail closes at 4 (closed Dec.25). **Camping:** Nearby Roosevelt Lake (primitive). **Teacher's Package:** Available. **For info.:** Superintendent, Tonto National Monument, P.O.Box 707, Roosevelt, AZ 85545. 602/467-2241.

Tumacacori National Historical Park

Allow: 1 hr. *Fee*

A pleasant stop between Tucson and Nogales are two mission ruins, Guerari and Calabazas. These missions, lonely outposts in a foreign and sometimes threatening world, survived for longer than there has been an Anglo-Saxon influence in this same region.

Highlights

★ The missions are concrete evidence of the Catholic Church's inroads in spreading the faith. However, rumors of buried riches brought the greedy who ravaged the mission, leaving only ruins.

Whiz Tips

❢ For two hundred years, missionaries and Indians tried to reach a balance of Judeo-Christian and Native American beliefs. Unlike elsewhere, the Pimas actually requested more priests than Europe could supply. The Jesuits were the first to establish a mission here but political problems with King Carlos resulted in their replacement by Franciscans. Apparently Carlos felt he could better control the Franciscans who take an oath of poverty than the Jesuits who saw their role as scholars and educators.

Kids' Stuff

★ The relationships forged between the Europeans and the Native Americans is interestingly told. Children don't often see the Native American's perspective and how even the missionaries coming to "save," placed additional burdens upon them.

Access: 45 mi. S of Tucson or 18 mi. N of Nogales on I-19. **Days/Hours:** Daily 8-5 (clsd. Thanksgiving & Dec.25) **Camping:** Pena Blanca Lake and Patagonia Lake State Park (82 sites, elec. & shwrs.). **Spe-**

cial Events: Every first Sunday in Dec., FREE Tumacacori Fiesta featuring crafts, food and fun. **For info.:** Superintendent, Tumacacori National Historical Park, P.O. Box 67, Tumacacori, AZ 85640. 602/398-2341.

Tuzigoot National Monument

Allow: 1 hr. *Fee*

Close to Jerome, you'll accomplish a feat early looters and archaeologists didn't...discover ancient Sinagua Indian ruins. Unlike so many areas where ruins of ancient Indian communities are found, Tuzigoot was discovered virtually intact. Today, it still looks as though people could farm the land and prosper. The valley is still watered by the Verde River and has rich deposits of topsoil from the river silt and flooding. Indeed, if the Spanish had viewed this setting at their first encounter with the ruins of the Sinagua culture, the name Sinagua (without water) would never have been applied. The remains give evidence of a community numbering 50 or so which doubled and redoubled as it appears northern Sinaguas fled here before a drought. We can only speculate why all abandoned this seemingly rich agricultural area.

Highlights

★ Over time, the Sinagua added one hundred and ten rooms forming a 500 by 100 foot pueblo. Climbing to the roof of the two story building atop the hill gives you a marvelous view of the valley and Jerome in the distance. The hill, a limestone ridge, rises 120 feet above the valley floor, making an imposing sight.

Whiz Tips

The ruins shows you the masonry talents which were shared across the Southwest amongst several cultures, all of whom abandoned their "cities" and their architecture around the same time.

Kids' Stuff

★ Who can resist climbing up to a roof. No youngster we've ever encountered can. The Southwest has so many Indian ruins that even the most ardent of us can become "non-plussed." However, we found our children were always "up" for visiting one of these architectural marvels.

Access: 2 mi. E of Clarkdale. **Days/Hours:** Open every day 8-5. **Camping:** Nearby Dead Horse Ranch State Park (45 sites, elec. & shwrs.); National Forest campgrounds N towards Flagstaff. **For info.:** Superintendent, Tuzigoot National Monument, P.O.Box 219, Camp Verde, AZ 86322. 602/634-5564.

Walnut Canyon National Monument

Allow: 2 hrs. *Fee*

Although it is a national monument preserving the cliff-dwelling ruins of a long-ago peoples, it's not hard for today's visitor to imagine living in this semi-suburb of Flagstaff. We could easily envision water piped in, electrical hook-ups, paved roads winding through the canyon valley leading to secluded bungalows. Of course, few of us could survive by living off the land as the Sinagua did. They grew dryland crops, mostly on the mesa top. As with all cliff-dwellers, we wonder why they would create logistically difficult homes. Everyday they had to clamber down or up canyon walls for water, to farm, to hunt, to visit, to get wood, etc. Why? What caused them to add these burdens to a life of manual labor?

Highlights

★ Trekking down the steep trail

into the canyon to the ruins takes you to 25 ruins, providing you close-up views of many more. Unfortunately, the ruins were discovered early in European settlement of the area and pot hunters destroyed many of the structures in their search for Indian artifacts.

★ This is a beautiful little canyon offering relatively pleasant summer temperatures and stunning fall colors.

Whiz Tips

! During the summer, the rangers give daily talks and walks explaining the people and how they survived.

! There is a white strata of limestone in the canyon walls which was left when the area was covered by sea water. In the Kaibab limestone are some 80 species of sea fossils. Today, they rest at 6500 feet above sea level.

Kids' Stuff

★ The kids love climbing around and through the ruins. Plus the canyon becomes a great "I saw it first" place as you are constantly on the lookout for the 300-plus ruins which dot the landscape. Save the relatively flat rim trail for last and use it as an enticement for your kids on the way back up. You'll get a panoramic view of the wealth of ruins located in the canyon.

★ In the exhibit area, your kids can try their hand at grinding corn into flour using the Sinagua's grinding stones. This simple exhibit shows how labor-intensive even relatively simple looking tasks were. The park asks kids to collect garbage for which they will reward them with a badge.

Access: 10.5 mi. E of Flagstaff off I-40. **Days/Hours:** Daily 8-5 (clsd. Thanksgiving & Dec.25). **Camping:** Coconino National Forest has 8 campgrounds within 35 mi. of Flagstaff. **For info.:** Superintendent, Walnut Canyon National Monument, Walnut Canyon Rd., Flagstaff, AZ 86004. 602/526-3367.

Kids in the Southwest

Wupatki & Sunset Crater Volcano National Monuments

Allow: 3-4 hrs. *FREE*

Wupatki and Sunset Crater Volcano are adjacent, forming one large attraction just to the north of Flagstaff. Sunset Crater preserves the evidence of volcanic activity and Wupatki, the proof of Indian settlement (est. 2,000 Indians) immediately following the eruption. The 2600-plus ruins at Wupatki are of special significance because the Sinagua Indians appear to have had trade connections to the Indians of Mexico and Central America. Today, the strongest evidence we see of this relationship is a ball court at Wupatki Ruins which has withstood 700 years.

Highlights

★ The Wupatki Ruins, one pueblo within the monument, has a number of interesting features. Like some of the other ruins in the park, it has portions of its buildings built in and around existing rock outcrops. Whether this was done to add stability or to save on the number of rocks used in construction, we don't know. Beside the ball court, there is a round amphitheater which is unique to these ruins. Make sure you check out the "Blow Hole" at Wupatki. It is a fissure in the ground which will expel or "inhale" air depending on the surface atmospheric pressure. When it's "exhaling" it feels like a natural air conditioning unit in summer or a heater in winter.

Whiz Tips

The Sinagua, Anasazis and others came to settle and take advantage of the slightly richer soils. You learn how the Sinagua cultivated the soil and what crops they depended on. Some people believe the Sinagua became the Hopi.

At Sunset Crater Volcano National Monument, you can hike through the lava beds and around the outside base of this 1,000 foot high crater. The nature trail through these beds takes you past a small lava cave.

Kids' Stuff

★ Kids enjoy Wupatki Pueblo more because of the unusual structures, the ball court, the amphitheater and the blow hole. The blow hole doesn't always work because there has to be a variance between the surface pressure and the hole's.

Access: 15 mi. N of Flagstaff on US 89. **Days/Hours:** Visitor center, daily, summer 7-7 & winter 8-5 (clsd. Dec.25 & Jan.1). **Camping:** National Forest Bonito Campground just W of Sunset Crater Volcano. **For info.:** Superintendent, Wupatki/Sunset Crater Volcano/Walnut Canyon National Monument, 2717 N. Steves Blvd., Ste. #3, Flagstaff, AZ 86001. 602/527-7040.

Family at Hot Springs

COURTESY NPS

ARKANSAS

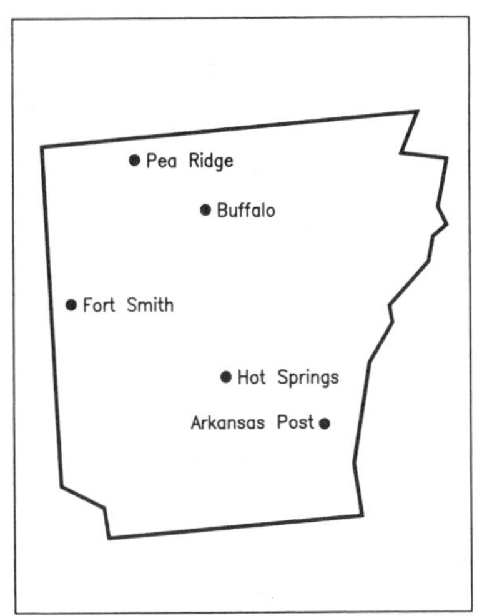

Arkansas Post National Memorial

Allow: 2-3 hrs. *FREE*

"It is a flat alluvial country, full of oxbow lakes or bayous, where the river used to live, and full of swamps and cypress knees and water moccasins and buzzards and sharecroppers."

Clyde Davis
The Arkansas

Such is the country where the Arkansas River moseys down to meet the Mississippi. As early as 1683, Europeans sought to control the trade with the natives to the west and the local Quapaw, Osages and Chickasaw. Although the French, then the Spanish and then the French again hoped for jewels and gold, they were content to settle for furs. The post saw encounters in the American Revolution and in the Civil War and was the short-lived capital of the territory. Today, little remains of any of the 10 or more forts which were built here as the river has been continually changing its mind and now meanders over their foundations.

Highlights

★ The post has had a colorful, if not notable history, which the park re-

Arkansas Post National Memorial COURTESY NPS

lates through its movie, exhibits, interpretive programs and self-guided walks.

Whiz Tips

From 1683 to 1765, the French used the waters west of the Mississippi as their personal storehouse, trading with the native peoples. Arkansas Post was an ideal link for supplies going in and out of the wilderness. After the French and Indian War, France ceded the lands in this region to Spain. Although the Spaniards were less adventurous than the French, they still maintained a presence at the post for trade. In 1800, because of events in Europe, Spain returned Louisiana and the post to France, which did little else than sell it off for $17,000,000 to the Americans. Although Arkansas Post was declared the territorial capital in 1819, within two years, folks had concluded this region was too swampy and moved their capital upstream to Little Rock.

Kids' Stuff

★ The park has a Jr. Ranger program and offers special programs for kids on weekends, including puppet shows and costumed interpreters. There's a film festival on weekends at 2 and 4.

★ The trails in the park are fun for kids to explore as long as they are protected from biting insects. Birding and fishing are other pleasures your family can take in. The park suggests carrying binoculars to aid you in your nature walks.

Access: 7 mi. S of Gillett or 20 mi. NE of Dumas off US 165 on AR 169. **Days/ Hours:** Daily, summer 8-6 & winter 8-5 (clsd. Dec.25). **Camping:** 4 US Army Corps of Engineers campgrounds nearby; closest Moore's Bayou Park, 2 mi. **Special Events:** Black History Month and Columbus Day celebrations, as well as Civil War encampments and early fur trader days. **For info.:** Superintendent, Arkansas Post National Memorial, Rte.1, Box 16, Gillett, AR 72055. 501/548-2432.

Buffalo National River

Allow: 2-3 days *FREE*

Although the Ozarks rise less than 2,500 ft. above sea level, they stand in stark contrast to their surroundings. They join Arkansas, Missouri and Oklahoma in a recreation heaven of picturesque wooded valleys, sheer cliffs and tumbling rivers. Buffalo River is one of the few wild rivers in the country to be preserved in its natural state throughout its length.

Highlights

★ The river is famed for its float trips. In spring, folks make good use of the headwaters of the river, as this is usually the only time you can travel it. The middle river, also good water at this time, lasts through to late summer. The lower portion of the course, the most remote section, is floatable later in the year than the other two, but there is a 24 mi. stretch with no land access.

★ Although the summer heat can dampen some visitors' walking spir-

Buffalo National River

COURTESY NPS

its, the newly constructed 25 mi. Buffalo River Hiking Trail has plenty of rewarding overlooks. The park has several more established trails leading to caves, waterfalls, pioneer homes, farm steads, mines and Indian rock shelters.

Whiz Tips

❢ Like most natural parks, the average visitor to Buffalo River comes to recreate. However, the rangers have several guided programs so you can learn about the region as well. Among the more interesting offerings are a cave tour, a canoe float trip, a ghost mining town trip, a mystery canyon journey and a Native American walk. Like Texas' Big Thicket National Preserve, the Ozarks were just to the south of the region's last Ice Age. The result is an unusual mixture of about a thousand northern, desert and southern plant species.

❢ Why is it called Buffalo River? While nobody knows for sure, the story we favor is that the first European travelers to the area saw buffalo here and named the river after their find. Although the buffalo have long since disappeared from the region, there are deer, raccoons, opossum, bobcats, mink, beaver and even bears. In addition, elk have just recently been introduced.

Kids' Stuff

★ With fishing, hiking, boating, swimming, exploring and the great outdoors, there's plenty to keep any family entertained. Kids really enjoy exploring the trails leading to caves and pioneer homesteads.

Access: Buffalo Point 17 mi. S of Yellville off AR 14. **Days/Hours:** Daily. **Camping:** 13 FREE campgrounds & 2 fee campgrounds Buffalo Point (shwrs. & elec.) & Tyler Bend (shwrs.). **For info.:** Superintendent, Buffalo National River, P.O.Box 1173, Harrison, AR 72602-1173. 501/741-5443/449-4311.

Fort Smith National Historic Site

Allow: 1 hr. *Fee*

"There's no Sunday west of St. Louis, and no God west of Fort Smith."

Glen Shirley
Law West of Fort Smith

On the border of Arkansas and Oklahoma, Fort Smith was originally founded to keep the peace between the indigenous Osage and the Cherokees who were being pressured to move westward by white encroachment. The fort's second edition was built to protect white settlers from the large numbers of eastern Native Americans who were being exiled westward into the so-called Indian Territory. When no real problems occurred between these people, the fort was again abandoned and taken over by Judge Isaac C. Parker, who ruled the western "no-man's land" with an exact view of justice. Today's visitors can see many of the second fort's original structures, the ruins of the first fort and exhibits on justice in the Indian Territory.

Highlights

★ This is where the wild west met civilization. Although the soldiers at the fort saw little action, Judge Parker's deputies were in daily life and death struggles. No less than 100 officers of the court would lose their lives in the execution of their duties. The reconstructed gallows is proof that the court, too, demanded its due, as 79 of the 160 sentenced to meet their maker stretched the hemp.

Whiz Tips

❢ Fort Smith was the final border crossing for the Cherokee, Creek, Choctaw, Chickasaw and Seminole Nations, the so-called "five civilized tribes" who were stripped of their eastern lands. Andrew Jackson's presidency saw the beginning of what could easily be termed these tribes' "Holocaust." The administration termed the mass removal of the Indians westward, the "Great Experiment," but history would come to refer to it as the people most affected (one in four died during the march) called it, "The Trail of Tears."

Kids' Stuff

★ Children delight in seeing the way people lived in the last century. At the fort, they can see the history of soldiers, Indians, outlaws and lawmen. Stories of the exploits of the people in this time have kept Americans enthralled for decades. Here's where fiction meets its equal in fact.

Access: Downtown Fort Smith. **Days/Hours:** Daily 9-5. **Camping:** Lake Fort Smith State Park off US 71 (12 sites, elec. & shwrs.) **For info.:** Superintendent, Fort Smith National Historic Site, P.O.Box 1406, Fort Smith, AR 72902. 501/783-3961.

Hot Springs National Park

Allow: .5 days *FREE*

"Any city frequented by troubled joints has a tendency to start its day slowly."

Philip Hamburger
An American Notebook

Once called "The National Spa," this still popular mecca drew throngs of visitors seeking cures for a host of maladies. As early as 10,000 years ago, man was drawn to the hot waters. Their existence was so well-known by the infant American nation that one of the first acts President Jefferson took after concluding the Louisiana Purchase was to commission a study of the hot springs. In 1832, at the same time as Andrew Jackson's government was creating a separate Indian Territory just to the west, four sections of the area were proclaimed the nation's first natural reserve. Today, visitors can still utilize the waters from 47 hot springs, even though their medicinal value is questionable. The country's smallest national park has adaptively restored the Fordyce Bathhouse as a visitor center and

Fort Smith National Historic Site COURTESY NPS

regulates the condition of the other bathhouses.

Highlights

★ Whether or not the springs are curative, they are most certainly pleasurable: 4,000 years old, hot (143 degrees F), naturally sterile water bubbles out of the earth to soak into muscles and bones you didn't even remember you had.

★ A good way to see what contraptions the bath houses used to channel the waters for particular "remedies" is to take a self-guided tour of the Fordyce Bathhouse's 24 refurbished rooms and 3 exhibit halls.

Whiz Tips

❢ Rangers and park volunteers conduct a number of summer interpretive programs. Past subjects have been a thermal features walking tour, Historic Bathhouse Row, the Indian Quarry Hike (2 hrs.) and evening campfire programs.

❢ The hot springs' daily production is 850,000 gallons of water so sterile that NASA used it to preserve moon rocks. We automatically assume hot springs are the result of volcanic activity. Not here. Rainwater seeps into deep environs of the earth where the increased pressure heats it. The deeper into the earth it goes, the higher the temperature gets. When it hits the cracks and faults in the Hot Springs Sandstone, the pressure propels it to the surface where it arrives roughly a year later (not exactly WARP speed).

Kids' Stuff

★ Because small children generally lack the fat to insulate their still-growing organs from the water's heat, their exposure time to the heated water should be limited.

★ Some of the over 30 mi. of trails in the vicinity are: Grand Promenade, a .5 mi. walkway past the covered springs, Peak Trail, another .5 mi. jaunt up to Hot Springs Mountain, 1.4 mi. Dead Chief Trail, linking up with Short Cut Trail and the Gulpha

Hot Springs National Park COURTESY NPS

Gorge Trail. Active children can handle most of these short hikes with ease.

Access: Downtown Hot Springs. **Days/ Hours:** Daily 9-5 (clsd. Dec.25 & Jan.1). **Camping:** Park's Gulpha Gorge Campground. **Special Events:** In Oct., Octoberfest's Volksmarsch (people's walk). **For info.:** Superintendent, Hot Springs National Park, P.O.Box 1860, Hot Springs, AR 71902. 501/623-1433.

Pea Ridge National Military Park

Allow: 1-2 hrs. *Fee*

In the Ozarks of northwestern Arkansas, Pea Ridge is considered one of the most significant battles in the "Trans-Mississippi" campaign. Missouri, a Confederate border state, played an early role in the Civil War. The only major battle, Wilson's Creek (see Wilson's Creek NB, MO) had been won by the South but had resulted in losses which caused them to regroup south. At Pea Ridge, the Confederates gave a concerted effort to re-enter Missouri to capture St. Louis and northern access to the Mississippi. The park details the two days of fighting and preserves the rebuilt Elkhorn Tavern, a site of much of the action.

Highlights

★ You can drive (7 mi.), hike (10 mi.) or ride a horse (11 mi.) around the battlefield to get an excellent view of what transpired. The first day, the South tried a two-pronged onslaught. The eastern thrust at Elkhorn was very successful. However, the western one at Round Top resulted in the gutting of the entire Southern command, as Generals McCulloch and McIntosh were killed and their ranking colonel was captured. On the second day, with both the Confederates and the Federals focussing at Elkhorn, the fighting was pretty even until the Confederates ran out of ammunition. Fortunately for the South, the Union army chased the wrong band of fleeing soldiers, allowing the main body to escape, leaving Missouri firmly in the hands of the North. The Elkhorn Tavern, an excellent example of the period's architecture, was rebuilt after being destroyed during the war.

Pea Ridge National Military Park

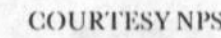
COURTESY NPS

Whiz Tips

During summer, the park offers daily interpretive programs starting at the visitor center. The introductory AV and exhibits at the center provide a good overview of the Trans-Mississippi encounters, a less-well known segment of the Civil War. Both armies made the control of the Mississippi a priority because of its transportation capability. When the Federals succeeded in accomplishing this goal (see Vicksburg NMP, MS), they had cut the Southern forces in half and effectively determined the war's outcome.

1,000 Oklahoma Territory Cherokee Indians joined the Confederates, becoming the only Native Americans involved in a major battle. They captured a Union gun emplacement early in the fighting, but were thrashed by Union cannons and withdrew to assist as scouts for the remainder of the action.

Kids' Stuff

★ Many families enjoy hiking the park. The best way to do this is to do some prior research so you can more fully appreciate the significance of the geography in determining the outcome. Plaques and monuments mark the key battle points.

Access: 10 mi. N of Rogers off US 62. **Days /Hours:** Daily 8-5 (clsd. Thanksgiving, Dec.25 & Jan.1). **Camping:** Nearby Beaver Lake, the Army Corps of Engineers' Lost Bridge Campground (10 mi.). **Special Events:** On March 7 & 8, battle anniversary; Labor Day Weekend, the Encampment of Civil War Living History Soldiers. **For info.:** Superintendent, Pea Ridge National Military Park, Pea Ridge, AR 72751. 501/451-8122.

CALIFORNIA

Cabrillo National Monument

Allow: 1-3 hrs. *Fee*

In 1542, Juan Rodriguez Cabrillo left a small Mexican port on the Pacific Coast in search of new lands and new fortunes. Midway through his journeys, he landed at San Diego's Point Loma. To honor Cabrillo, who lost his life in search of his dreams, the park has exhibits telling his tale. In addition, it preserves Old Point Lighthouse and maintains a whale overlook from which visitors can see the great migrating mammals.

Highlights

★ Touring the historic 1855 lighthouse gives you a sampling of how people coped living in these isolated outposts. For low pay ($1,000/yr.)

and housing, the keeper had to tend to the lamp, clean the lens, maintain the working parts and keep vigil from dusk to dawn with the aid of a (lower-paid) assistant.

★ December through early March, the Whale Overlook is one focal point where visitors search the waters for the mighty gray whales. The whales actually pass quite close to the park on their way south toward the lagoons in Baja California. In late spring, they return to their summer feeding grounds in the northern seas of Alaska.

Whiz Tips

❢ There are ranger-led talks and walks throughout the year explaining Cabrillo, the gray whales, the tidepools and the lighthouse.

❢ Cabrillo was actually replacing Pedro de Alvarado as captain of the enterprise. Alvarado had been killed in an Indian uprising. Cabrillo made it well up the California coast before he broke a limb while rushing to the defence of his men who were scuffling with some natives. In all probability, gangrene set in, because he died within six weeks of the injury. His men, under their third leader Bartolome Ferrer, made it as far as southern Oregon before turning back.

Kids' Stuff

★ Kids love exploring the intertidal area found within the park. Although the creatures dwelling there are protected by the park, you and your family can touch, just don't take or harm them. Sea anemone, crabs, limpets and occasionally octopus, are seen during low tides. A good outing is the 2 mi. roundtrip Bayside Nature Trail.

★ The lighthouse is an intriguing place for children. Restored to the 1880s time period, children can imagine a life very different from theirs.

Access: Southern end of Point Loma in San Diego. **Days/Hours:** Daily 9-5:15 (summer, sunset). **Camping:** Silver Strand State Park, beach camping 15 mi. from monument; 50 mi. E, Cuyamaca Rancho State Park & Laguna Mountain Recreation Area. **Special Events:** Last Sept. wknd., Cabrillo festival (ethnic food, dancing and landing reenactment); Oct. 13th, Cabrillo NM birthday; Nov. 15th, Lighthouse birthday; sometime in Jan., gray whale watching week. **Teacher's Package:** Available. **For info.:** Superintendent, Cabrillo National Monument, P.O.Box 6670, San Diego, CA 92166. 619/557-5450.

Channel Islands National Park

Allow: 2-3 days *FREE (ferry fee)*

"California is a queer place in a way, it has turned its back on the world, and looks into the void of the Pacific."

D.H. Lawrence

Eight smallish islands lay splattered off the coast of Los Angeles. Five of them have been designated Channel Islands National Park. Although the islands appear ever-so-close, the nearest, Anacapa Island (actually three islets), is 11 miles from the mainland. At the Ventura mainland visitor center you can see an introductory AV, photos, Chumash Indian artifacts, a simulated caliche ghost forest, tidepool and, on weekends, special presentations.

Highlights

★ The five islands are: Anacapa, an important pelican rookery and whale-watching locale; Santa Cruz, the largest; Santa Rosa, the second largest and a vital harbor seal breeding ground; San Miguel, the westernmost with a caliche forest; and Santa Barbara, the southernmost. The islands offer excellent underwater exploration, challenging wildlife hikes and beautiful beaches.

Whiz Tips

❢ A less obvious part of the park is the mile of water around each of the park's islands. Beneath the surface is a wealth of plant and sea life which serves to nourish the world's largest creature, the blue whale. Other mammals that frequent these waters are the gray whale, the Pacific white-sided dolphin, Steller's sea lion, the northern elephant seal, the California sea lion, the northern fur seal and the Guadalupe fur seal.

Sheep raising probably had the biggest impact on the island's native plants and animals. Introduced hogs, cats and rabbits have also played significant roles in changing the landscape. On Santa Barbara, a South American iceplant has been waging (and winning) a battle to claim land from the island's indigenous plants.

Kids' Stuff

★ As Mom used to say, "Half the fun is getting there." The boat ride over to the islands is filled with anticipation. On weekends, the park's staff conducts tidepool feedings for children. It also holds nature walks so everybody can learn more about these special places.

Access: At Ventura, southbound on US 101 take Seaward exit or northbound on US 101 take Victoria exit. **Days/Hours:** Visitor center daily, summer 8-5:30 & winter 8-5. **Camping:** Permit-only primitive camping; Anacapa (must be able to carry camping gear up a steel rung ladder and 154 steps, then .5 mi. to the campsite); Santa Barbara 9 sites, less strenuous to reach; San Miguel limited access; near Ventura, mainland state campgrounds. **Special Events:** In the spring, Land by the Sea Fair. **For info.:** Superintendent, Channel Islands National Park, 1901 Spinnaker Dr., Ventura, CA 93001. 805/644-8262.

Death Valley National Monument

Allow: 2-3 days *Fee*

"Its physical credentials are formidable the hottest and driest spot in the United States and the lowest point in the Western Hemisphere. From one end to the other, it appears as an unyielding slice of desert that penalizes the unlucky and the unprepared..."

Donald Dale Jackson
Sagebrush Country

Straddling the Nevada/southern California border, Death Valley National Monument offers surprisingly diverse attractions. The park in-

Channel Islands National Park COURTESY NPS

cludes most of the Amargosa and the Panamint Ranges, two mountain ranges which bracket the valley. The resulting 2 mi. difference in elevation accounts for a tremendous variety of wildlife. Native American presence in the region dates back to when it had a lake, as hard as that may be to imagine. Tales of mineral wealth attracted more recent inhabitants. The monument's abandoned domiciles attest to the desert's perseverance for solitude.

Highlights

★ Who can resist Scotty's Castle? An extravagant mansion complete with a tower and a "gianormous" swimming pool built "behind God's back." Formally called the Death Valley Ranch, it was built as a vacation home. The owners' good friend, Death Valley Scotty, was given full run of the place. Scotty was rumored to have a gold mine up in the hills, which he secretly visited when his funds got low. Because of the mansion's popularity, many visitors use their waiting time to run up to Ubehebe Crater (16 mi. return) where they can inspect a Maar volcanic crater .5 mi. wide and 750 ft. deep.

★ At the Furnace Creek Visitor Center, you can learn all about the monument and its Borax connection. Those familiar with the park service know that Stephen Mather, its first director, was a driving force in shaping the parks we enjoy today. Before his public career, he was a "Borax-man" who came up with the brand name "20-Mule-Team" based on the method by which borax was transported out of Death Valley.

★ Other sights to see are the Sand Dunes, Salt Creek, the Devil's Golf Course (salt pinnacles), Artists Drive, Eureka Mine and the Charcoal Kilns. Stunning viewpoints include: Zabriskie Point, Red Cathedral, Dantes View and Badwater (279 ft. below sea level).

Death Valley National Monument COURTESY NPS

Whiz Tips

❢ Most park interpretive programs take place in the vicinity of the visitor center. Topics range from nature to the borax mining. Scotty's Castle tours have a new twist as the rangers have taken to donning '30s togs to re-create the era.

❢ Death Valley was formed when the earth shifted along several faults, leaving the mountains towering while the valley tipped below sea level. Essentially, the valley and the western Panamint Mountains are actually rotating toward the east. The western mountain ranges create a rainshadow causing the valley's aridity (avg. precipitation 1.91 in./yr.) and some startling statistics. In 1974, there were 134 days when the mercury went over 100 degrees F. On July 15, 1972, the thermometer recorded 201 degrees F. The lowest recorded temperature was 15 degrees F. in 1913.

Kids' Stuff

★ While children have always enjoyed Scotty's, the recently introduced living-history program will make this a highlight for them. You'll also have trouble pulling your kids away from the Charcoal Kilns, 10 beehive-shaped stone kilns, which are great echo chambers. Families can explore the relatively safe Eureka Mine with a flashlight, while the sand dunes always make for fun play when the temperature complies. On holiday weekends, the park usually has special programs just for children.

Access: E from US 395 on CA 190 & CA 136; W from US 95 on NV 267, 374 & 373; NW from I-15 on CA 127. **Days/Hours:** Visitor center, daily, summer 8-5 & winter 8-8. Scotty's Castle tours, daily 9-5. **Camping:** Park has 9 campgrounds (over 1500 campsites); Furnace Valley-Ticketron reservation. **Special Events:** Death Valley '49er Encampment on the 2nd weekend of Nov. **Teacher's Package:** Available. **For info.:** Superintendent, Death Valley National Monument, Death Valley, CA 92328. 619/786-2331.

Devils Postpile National Monument

Allow: 2 hrs. *FREE*

"...a massive faulting of the earth's crust forced the edge of Nevada down below California and thrust up the Sierra Nevada, sheerest of mountain ranges. Gabriel might have raised it there, barricade before paradise."

Richard Rhodes
"Harper's", 1970

Epitomizing this barricade is Devils Postpile, a formation of columnar basalt that spilled from the Earth's depths and cooled at such a rate that it cracked vertically. The volcanic rock column has weathered the effects of time to tower above the surrounding landscape. Also within the monument is well-named Rainbow Falls, a 101 ft. high waterfall and Soda Springs, a cold, carbonated spring that stains the river gravel a reddish brown.

Highlights

★ At Devils Postpile, you can see the enormity of this phenomenon as evidenced by the size of the pieces of broken columns at the structure's base. The cracks that formed during the cooling period have been polished by ice and scoured by glaciers. World renowned Giant's Causeway in Ireland is another example of columnar basalt.

★ Rainbow Falls is bracketed by andesite and rhyodacite cliffs. At its base, refreshing waters bring life and sustenance to wildflowers.

Whiz Tips

❢ You can attend guided walks or evening talks to learn more about the geological make-up of the park.

❢ During summer, visitors use the monument's shuttle bus.

Kids' Stuff

★ The walks around the park's major features are excellent ones for families. At Rainbow Falls, there is a stairway leading to the base. Devils Postpile can be easily circumnavigated. There's also trout fishing in the park's streams.

Access: 17 mi. W from US 395 on SR 203. **Days/Hours:** Daily. **Camping:** Park has summer campground (21 sites). **For info.:** Superintendent, Devils Postpile National Monument, P.O.Box 501, Mammoth Lakes, CA 93546. summer-619/934-2289 & winter-209/565-3341.

Eugene O'Neill National Historic Site

Allow: 2-3 hrs. *FREE*

"The past is the present, isn't it? It's the future, too."

Eugene O'Neill

The 1920s belonged to Eugene O'Neill. Accredited with invigorating American playwriting, O'Neill won three of his four Pulitzer prizes for his plays (*Beyond the Horizon*-'20, *Anna Christie*-'21 and *Strange Interlude*-'27) during the decade. To top off his feats he was the first American and only American playwright awarded the Nobel prize for literature (1936). It was with the prize money from the Nobel Prize that O'Neill was able to build his Danville, California residence, "Tao House." You must make reservations to join the twice daily park service tours.

Highlights

★ It was at "Tao House" that O'Neill's best-known plays *The Iceman Cometh* and *Long Day's Journey Into Night* were written. The great American novelist Sinclair Lewis, said he "... has done nothing much in the American drama save to transform it utterly...from a false world of neat and competent trickery to a world of splendor, fear and greatness." His plays rarely, if ever, were without controversy. Brendan Gill said "...[*The Iceman Cometh*] is the most boring play ever written. But

Death Valley National Monument COURTESY NPS

immediately after *The Iceman Cometh*, O'Neill sat down and wrote *Longest Day's Journey into Night*. It is easily the greatest play written in English in my lifetime." It also won him his fourth Pulitzer.

Whiz Tips

O'Neill was steeped in theatrical experience. He spent his childhood travelling the country watching his father playing the role of the Count of Monte Cristo over 1,000 times. His mother became addicted to morphine during her recovery from Eugene's birth. He grew to be an unsettled young man, attempting suicide and living in squalor. A stay at a sanitarium with a bout of TB, gave him a new start which took him to Harvard to study drama. Although his triumphs would seem enough to make anyone satisfied, until his death O'Neill seemed to personify "melancholy."

Kids' Stuff

★ O'Neill's topics and handling of the material are usually beyond most pre-high school students. The park's programs are geared for an adult audience.

Access: By park van. **Days/Hours:** Tour twice daily. **Camping:** Anthony Chabot Regional Park (reservations e838-0249f, 73 sites & shwrs.) and Del Valle Regional Park (150 sites & shwrs.). **For info.:** Superintendent, Eugene O'Neill Historic Site, C/O John Muir National Historic Site, 4202 Alhambra Ave., Martinez, CA 94553. 415/838-0249.

Golden Gate National Recreation Area

COURTESY JIM MILLER

Golden Gate National Recreation Area

Allow: 2-3 days *FREE*

"East is East, and West is San Francisco, according to Californians."

O.Henry
"A Municipal Report"

Golden Gate National Recreation Area, the most visited park in America (20,000,000/yr.), serves as an umbrella administration for a number of sites within the Bay area. It flows from Aquatic Park toward the Golden Gate Bridge, where it forks back south around the point and down the coast and north over the bridge to take in the Marin Headlands. Mostly, it provides beach access and greenways for all to enjoy within reach of public transport. Noteworthy sites are the famed Alcatraz Island, Fort Point National Historic Site, Fort Mason, Baker, China & Ocean Beaches, the Cliff House, Fort Funston, Sweeney Ridge and Tennessee Valley.

Highlights

★ Probably the most popular site for out-of-towners is Alcatraz (fee ferry access). We all come with vivid images of this inescapable island prison surrounded by voracious man-eating sharks. The rangers recount the island's history starting before its prison days.

★ One of the best places to take in the coast is from Cliff House Visitor

Center. Nature lovers bring binoculars to watch the antics of California sea lions and marine birds on the Seal Rocks.

★ After the War of 1812, the U.S. government embarked on a major program of fortifying its coastal waters. While most forts were built on the more populated east coast, San Francisco's Fort Point was constructed during this era. Like the eastern forts, its masonry construction was rendered useless when rifled cannons were introduced in the Civil War (see Fort Pulaski NM, GA).

Whiz Tips

❢ Several units offer interpretive programs where rangers explain the area's unique features. The National Maritime Museum has one of the most extensive maritime collections in the country. San Francisco Maritime National Historical Park also includes 6 historic vessels lining the Hyde St. Pier, allowing close-up views. Two of these, the *C.A. Thayer*, a schooner, and the *Eureka*, a commuter ferry, let you clamber around on board. The *Balclutha*, a square-rigged Cape Horn sailing ship, has a re-carved masthead.

Kids' Stuff

★ The great thing about these areas is their proximity to the city. Children don't have to contend with long drives to reach places where they can learn about nature. Beaches, hikes, bike trails and historic sites complement each other, providing parents with a myriad of alternatives.

★At both the Marin Headlands and Muir Woods visitor centers, kids can check out "Discovery Packs" which enable them to explore nature using bug boxes, binoculars, pocket microscopes and dip nets.

★Fort Point has daily Civil War artillery drills and weekend rifle drills. Also once a month they have Civil War sing-a-longs.

★Other great family outings include the Marine Mammal Center, a mammal research, conservation and rehabilitation facility; the Bay Area Discovery Museum, a "hands-on" center and Slide Ranch, a demonstration farm and environmental education center.

Access: Just E of Fisherman's Wharf in downtown San Francisco. **Days/Hours:** Daily 10-5. **Camping:** E Anthony Chabot Regional Park in the Oakland area (73 sites) & N Spring Lake County Park near Santa Rosa. **For info.:** Superintendent, Golden Gate National Recreation Area, Fort Mason, San Francisco, CA 94123. 415/556-0560.

John Muir National Historic Site

Allow: 2-3 hrs. *Fee*

"The mountains are calling and I must go."
John Muir

And so it was for the adventurous John Muir, even after he married, had a successful fruit farm and two children here in Martinez, just east of San Francisco. Visitors can see his home, the Martinez Adobe House (his eldest daughter's home) and some of the orchards he tended. As for the mountains, few can claim to have done as much as Muir to preserve America's natural treasures.

Highlights

★ As you watch the introductory AV and tour Muir's home, you can't help but wonder about what drove this man. He set off on mind-boggling walks with little but a change of clothes. He spent months alone in the wilderness. His passion for these lonely outposts drove him to become a one-man lobby for preserving wild places. Like a modern-day Johnny Appleseed, Muir wandered the land. He planted seeds of doubt about the pillage of the wild and beautiful places. His ideas bore the fruit of five of the nation's greatest national parks, Teddy Roosevelt's initiation of a significant national park system and a groundswell of popular support for conservation. It's almost strange to visit this splendid ranch to learn about him. Somehow an isolated rocky overhang where silence sits in a golden haze would seem a better place. But Muir didn't go into the deep woods and hide like some hermit. He understood that ideas have to be accessible. And so, this site surrounded by a huge and growing populace serves to convey his message.

Whiz Tips

The Martinez adobe home is an excellent example of mid-19th century California architecture. The Martinez family has a long and distinguished role in the area. The Grand Patron was San Francisco's third mayor. His son built the house on lands his father had secured. Muir's father-in-law acquired the property and Muir's eldest daughter, Wanda, lived here.

Kids' Stuff

★ With the revitalization of conservation and environmental awareness, most children are familiar with the concepts Muir taught. The park's intent is to make people aware of what he stood for and how he achieved his goals, worthwhile lessons for even older pre-schoolers.

Access: Just off Alhambra Exit of Rte. 4, 10 mi. E of I-80 or 5 mi. W of Rte. 680. **Days/Hours:** 10-4:30 (clsd. Mon. & Tues.). **Camping:** Anthony Chabot Regional Park (73 sites & shwrs.) and Del Valle Regional Park (150 sites & shwrs.). **Special Events:** Last Apr. Sat., John Muir Birthday Celebration. **Teacher's Package:** Available. **For info.:** Superintendent, John Muir National Historic Site, 4202 Alhambra Ave., Martinez, CA 94553. 415/228-8860.

Joshua Tree National Monument

Allow: 2-3 days *Fee*

"[On crossing the Mojave Desert] It's as though nature tested a man for endurance and constancy to prove whether he was good enough to get to California."

John Steinbeck
Travels with Charley

On the road from Phoenix to L.A., you drive from the lower, drier Colo-

Joshua Trees COURTESY JIM MILLER

rado Desert to the Mojave Desert, which is the home of the plant for which the monument is named. The Colorado Desert is distinguished by its growths of creosotebush. Scattered among the vastness of these desert lands are five fan-palm oases that attract wildlife like a magnet does iron.

Highlights

★ It feels strange to be out in the desert. Part of you says you can't survive here. Yet, you know air-conditioning has made existence not just tenable but to some, inviting. The parched land has hues only the desert light can reveal.

Whiz Tips

The Joshua tree is an overgrown member of the yucca family. Its arms, jutting out in all directions, sprout foot-long, white blossoms from their tips. Although the monument receives just a couple more inches of precipitation per year than Death Valley, it is far more vegetated. Some of the animals that enjoy this moisture are mountain sheep, coyotes, desert foxes and bobcats.

Kids' Stuff

★ Children enjoy visiting the desert because it is so different from what they are accustomed to. Like all of us, they are usually surprised at the variety of plants and animals that call the arid country home.

Access: 140 mi. E of L.A. on I-10 & Hwy. 60 to N entrances or 25 mi. E of Indio on I-10 to S entrance. **Days/Hours:** Daily 8-5 (clsd. Dec.25). **Camping:** Park has 9 campgrounds (over 300 sites). **For info.:** Superintendent, Joshua Tree National Monument, 74485 National Monument Dr., Twentynine Palms, CA 92277. 619/367-7511.

Lassen Volcanic National Park

Allow: 1 day *Fee*

Until Mount St. Helens buried the other Harry Truman in a sea of ash and mud, Lassen Volcano was the most recent volcanic action the lower 48 had witnessed. You can drive around three sides of this dramatic peak, possibly the world's largest plug dome volcano. On your way

Joshua Tree National Monument COURTESY ROBERT HEYMAN

there, you'll pass an almost complete array of thermal activity: sulfur vents, hot springs, fumaroles and mudpots. The northern California park preserves evidence of volcanic forces such as cinder cones, lava plateaus and lava pinnacles.

Highlights

★ The current thermal activity holds an almost unnatural fascination. We visit to see the power that lies beneath the surface, yet its very presence can lull us into believing it harmless (witness the death toll at Mount St. Helens). Lassen and/or Mount Shasta are predicted to join St. Helens in her fuming.

★ The park has a variety of outdoor recreational activities from winter skiing to summer boating and fishing. There is no shortage of hiking trails along which you can see the most diverse collection of plant life in the region. The park boasts 715 species compared to a "measly" 485 at nearby Mount Shasta.

Whiz Tips

Geologic occurrences dominate the park's many interpretive programs. However, the region's recent history is also covered. Like the rest of the Cascades, the newest North American mountains, Lassen were probably formed because of the expanding oceanic crust thrusting beneath the continental plates. The immense pressure caused by this grating melts the rock, which then seeks an outlet. Another interesting change we are witnessing is the regrowth of vegetation and repopulation of animals and birds in places which volcanic mud and ash rendered lifeless. Scientists are studying this area as a predictor of probable occurrences at Mount St. Helens.

Kids' Stuff

There's a Jr. Ranger program, 7-12 that meets most mornings each summer week for two hours of enjoyable discovery culminating in the awarding of a special patch.

Another patch can be earned by families or children over 12 when they complete their official task of exploring the volcanic phenomena. They then become members of the Cascade Volcano Club.

For younger children there's a unique program for 4-6 yr. olds which attempts to have the youngsters utilize all their senses. Regular interpretive offerings like Skin & Bones, Ooze & Ahs also allow youngsters to vent their tactile needs.

Good hikes for children include Lily Pond Nature Trail, Manzanita Lake and Bumpass Hell.

Access: From N or S on CA 89 & from E & W on Rte. 36 & 44; Redding 48 mi. W. **Days/Hours:** Daily 8-5. **Camping:** Park has 7 developed campgrounds; Manzanita Lake (shwrs.). **For info.:** Superintendent, Lassen Volcanic National Park, P.O.Box 100, Mineral, CA 96063-0100. 916/595-4444.

Lava Beds National Monument

Allow: 1-2 days *Fee*

Just shy of the Oregon border is the product of Medicine Lake volcano's utterances. As one park ranger put it, "The monument has text-book examples of classic volcanic formations." The most popular of these are the nearly 200 lava tube caves. Other formations include two kinds of lava: "aa," a jagged sharp type of lava best seen at Devils Homestead Flow and "pahoehoe," a relatively smooth, ropy flow. Cinder and spatter cones can also be seen.

Highlights

★ The best place to start is at the visitor center. Not only do they have a connecting lava cave to show you some of what you can explore, but they have an excellent AV introducing you to the monument as a whole. The Modoc War exhibit recounts not just this California Indian tribe's attempt to assert itself here but the bloodied pages of Native American struggles throughout the continent.

★ After you visit lighted Mudpot Cave, we'd suggest you try a dark one. Hard hats and three light sources are strongly recommended (the visitors center has hats you can buy and FREE lights).

Whiz Tips

There is a full slate of interpretive tours and programs offered during the summer.

Medicine Lake volcano is an unusual formation in the Cascades because it is a shield volcano very similar to the Hawaiian volcanoes (see Haleakala NP & Hawaii Volcanoes NP, HI). The largest volcano in the Cascades, its slopes are gentle as very fluid molten rock flowed out and down the flanks. This high fluidity accounts for the proliferation of lava tubes (caves) which form when the external surface of the lava cools, hardening into a well-insulated tube.

The area first came to international prominence in the winter of 1872/73, when the local Modoc Indians "tilting at windmills" tried to establish individual rights for themselves. For close to five months, 52 warriors held off a force twenty times their size. Their leaders were hanged for their audacity and the rest of the those involved in the war were banished to Oklahoma territory and oblivion. Those Modocs who did not participate remained in the area where their descendants are still found.

Kids' Stuff

Before undertaking exploration of a cave with smaller children, check with the rangers who can advise you which caves are more suitable. Special caves within the monument are ice caves which have ice even when the external temperature reaches 100 degrees F.

The site has a Jr. Ranger program which requires family involvement. They feel this way the whole family unit can learn and enjoy together.

Access: 30 mi. from Tulelake, CA or 58 mi. from Klamath Falls, OR, off Rte. 139. **Days /Hours:** Visitor center, daily, summer 9-6

Lava Beds National Monument

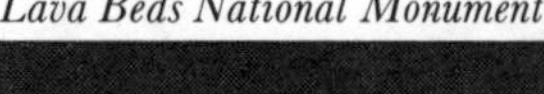

& winter 8-5 (clsd. Thanksgiving & Dec.25). **Camping:** Monument's Indian Well Campground (40 sites); National Forest campgrounds within 30 mi.**For info.:** Superintendent, Lava Beds National Monument, Box 867, Tulelake, CA 96134. 916/667-2282.

Muir Woods National Monument

Allow: 1-3 hrs. *Fee*

"This is the best tree lover's monument in all the forests in all the world."

John Muir

Ironically, this tribute to John Muir, the great conservationist (see John Muir NHS), exists today because of its once remoteness. Today, it receives thousands of visitors because of its close proximity (12 mi.) to San Francisco. The tall redwood trees still command homage as they stand quietly watching the curious and the concerned. Like court attendants, smaller trees and ferns spread their leaves to absorb the sounds that might disturb the royal redwoods.

Highlights

★ Strolling among the great California redwoods is at once a humbling and energizing experience. Their great heights and age make us realize how little right we have to endanger their continuance. Their very existence brings us a renewed wonder and faith in the tremendous possibilities of life.

★ This park can be appreciated during any season and has an added bonus in winter watching salmon spawn.

Whiz Tips

💡 While the tallest tree in the world (367.8 ft.), a California redwood, resides to the north in Redwood National Park, these smaller siblings (253 ft.) are potential successors. Redwoods are amazingly resilient to the vagaries of life. Their bark is highly fire and disease resistant. Many trees in this forest are over 1,000 years old. Almost any part of the tree can sprout new growth and you'll often find fallen redwoods, called "nurse logs," with new trees growing from them. The biggest threat to these giants, besides you

Big Tree at Redwood National Park

know who, is wind. Like their lumbering cousins the sequoias, redwoods have very shallow root systems and can be easily toppled. Although redwoods once ranged across the continent, the great mountain-building episodes that created the Rockies, the Sierra Nevadas and the coastal range created climates not conducive to redwoods. Now, they cling tenuously near the coast for its more moderate climate. The visitor center has a scale model of the redwood forest which makes their tremendous height a little clearer to discern.

Kids' Stuff

★ There are FREE Jr. Ranger Discovery Packs which you and your family can use to help you explore the forest.

★ We were quite surprised how awed our children were of these natural wonders. Our five-year-old still talks of these great trees and reacts enthusiastically to any nature trail which includes large trees.

Access: 17 mi. N of San Francisco on US 101 & CA 1. **Days/Hours:** Daily, 8-sunset. **Camping:** Nearby Mt. Tamalpais State Park. **Teacher's Package:** Available. **For info.:** Superintendent, Muir Woods National Monument, Mill Valley, CA 94941. 415/388-2595.

Pinnacles National Monument

Allow: 1 day *FREE*

South of the Bay area, mid-way between I-5 and the coast is remarkable Pinnacles National Monument. Pinnacles is mute testimony to the immense latent power of the San Andreas Fault. The rock spires that stand amongst the smoothed and rolling hills are part of a volcano that lies 125 mi. to the south. The shifting of the Pacific and North American plates has resulted in the sheering off of the Pinnacles portion of the Neenach Formation and its displacement up near San Francisco. Visitors can hike and go caving from either of the two unconnected roads leading into the park.

Highlights

★ There is a myriad of hiking trails through the striking and unusual outcrops. In addition, there are two main caving areas to explore, Bear Gulch Caves and Balconies Caves.

★ Spring is one of the best times to visit the park and see the blooming of the hill foliage.

Whiz Tips

❢ The San Andreas Rift consists of a number of faults which were formed when the Pacific Plate met North America. The collision resulted in a portion of the continent being ripped off to sit on the Pacific Plate. The tenuous strip of land includes all of Southern California that runs north from Baja to Point Reyes National Seashore, just north of San Francisco. The shifting of these plates caused the volcanic action creating Pinnacles and the region's famous earthquakes.

Kids' Stuff

★ There are weekend interpretive programs (east side only) which include some things of interest to families. Ranger-led walks and talks explain the geology of this atypical landscape. In addition, you can learn about the chaparral that grows so abundantly. The Bear Gulch Visitor Center has "hands-on" exhibits.

★ Children love exploring the "talus" caves in the park. Proper back-up lighting is a must when visiting these dark and mysterious places. At the visitor center, the rangers provide information about the caves which can make your explorations that much more rewarding. Ask about the "Adventure Packs."

Access: W from Hollister on CA 25 &

Hwy. 146, E from Soledad on CA 146. **Days /Hours:** Bear Gulch Visitor Center, daily, 9-5. **Camping:** W park allows camping at Chaparral Picnic Area (not during F-Su. from Feb-May) & Los Padres National Forest's Arroyo Seco Campground (45 mi. W); E Hollister Hills State Vehicle Recreation Area (35 mi. N) & Fremont Peak State Park (52 mi. N); **For info.:** Superintendent, Pinnacles National Monument, Paicines, CA 95043. 408/389-4485.

Point Reyes National Seashore

Allow: 1-2 days *FREE*

Point Reyes, where the San Andreas Fault meets the ocean, is an apt reflection of the California psyche. Its natural beauty is the work of a pounding ocean and moving landscapes. As you walk the point's trails or drive its scenic roadways, you are captured by its raw pleasures, until you are reminded of the great and threatening fault which created it. The recreational opportunities are boundless. Beach areas offer beachcombing, sea lion sightings, bird watching, spectacular scenes and whale watching. In the hills, you can hike, bike or drive to see tule elk, ocean overlooks, Morgan horses, the fault and Kule Loklo, a replicated Coast Miwok Indian village.

Highlights

★ California is blessed with miles upon miles of awe-inspiring coastline. The Point Reyes portion of the Pacific Ocean plays second fiddle to no other. The land challenges and the sea answers. The result is dramatic cliffs, sand-ridden coves and a frothy ebb and flow of sea water.

★ The park has recreated a Native American settlement with programs designed to introduce a way of life that existed for centuries before Sir Francis Drake happened upon this coast in 1579. The people "populating" the village demonstrate their handiwork for summer visitors.

★ Three other noteworthy sights you should take in, are the reintroduced tule elk herd on Tomales Point, the Point Reyes Lighthouse and the Morgan horses.

Whiz Tips

The naturalist programs include ranger-led walks and tours of the historic lighthouse. Some of the walk topics are: the migrating whales, the sea lions, the Morgan horses, the Miwok Indians, the San Andreas Fault, the birds and the tidal pools.

Point Reyes is the west coast's only national seashore. Unlike, the east coast seashores, which are mostly sand-swept barrier islands, Point Reyes is rocky, hilly and verdant.

In Jan. and Feb., you need to arrive early and hope for clear skies if you want to see the migrating gray whales just off Point Reyes Lighthouse. It's not that the whales only travel at dawn's early light (they travel 24 hrs./day) but that Californians bring their curious pastime of sitting in rush-hour traffic with them on their nature outings. The visitation is so great at this time of the year that the park shuttles visitors to the lighthouse.

Kids' Stuff

★ When you arrive at the park, pick up a Jr. Ranger pamphlet so your kids can earn a badge by attending several naturalist activities.

★ There are some excellent hikes for families here. For example, the Earthquake Trail and Woodpecker Nature Trail are both under a mile long.

★ Children love seeing the Morgan horses and how they're trained to be used for service throughout the national park system. Other highlights are the Native American weekend demonstrations of basket-weaving and other crafts at the Indian village.

★ While the Pacific-side of the point should be avoided by swimmers because of treacherous currents, Tomales Bay State Park offers families warmer water and a chance to break out the swimming togs and take a dip.

Access: 40 mi. N of San Francisco on US 101 & US 1. **Days/Hours:** Daily 9-5. **Camping:** Permit backcountry camping. **For info.:** Superintendent, Point Reyes National Seashore, Point Reyes, CA 94956. 415/663-1092.

Redwood National Park

Allow: 2-3 days *FREE*

"From them come silence and awe. It's not only their unbelievable stature, nor the color which seems to shift and vary under your eyes, no, they are not like any trees we know, they are ambassadors from another time."

John Steinbeck
Travels with Charley

The world's tallest trees are preserved within this northern California sanctuary, which runs 40 miles along the Pacific coast. At the end of a 3 mile round trip hike, visitors can enjoy the rare privilege of seeing not just the world's tallest tree, at 367.8 ft., but the world's third and sixth tallest in the same grove. The park maintains a wild coastline and a large number of Roosevelt elk, as well.

Highlights

★ For many, the redwoods are the ultimate forest experience. To walk among these towering trees is truly to commune with nature. You know they're alive. You feel their presence. Their height, while hard to determine, commands attention.

★ The Roosevelt elk (named for Theodore Roosevelt) are easily seen and photographed from the roadway. They are the largest of the North American elk species.

★ If you're fortunate, you may be able to see migrating gray whales from Crescent Beach Overlook and other coastal overlooks.

Whiz Tips

❢ Redwood National Park has a number of interpretive programs which range from talks to walks and kayak trips. The rangers focus primarily on three significant natural

Redwood National Park COURTESY NPS

phenomena: the trees, the wildlife and the tidepool and seashore life.

❢ The redwood cannot withstand droughts, so they live close to the coast just out of reach of the salt spray. Redwoods were widespread across the country but, as mountain ranges grew and the climate changed, its range was reduced to California's coast. They are extremely resistant to fire and disease, which accounts for their longevity. As you stroll through these woods, you'll see fallen trees with a new trees growing from them. There's a nearby museum made from redwood which has to be continually trimmed to cut off the new growth. Early pioneers used fire-ravaged, yet still flourishing redwoods to house their fowl. They called these hollowed out trees, "goose pens."

❢ At the tide pool walks visitors explore the rocky pools searching for anemones and sea stars. Overhead you may spot a bald eagle, peregine falcons, brown pelican or an Aleutian Canada goose.

Kids' Stuff

★ We were somewhat amazed to see how fascinated our children were by the redwoods. It's difficult to grasp their true size from the ground but even today our youngest child still compares all tall things to the redwoods. While the hike to the world's tallest tree (367.8 ft.) is a 3 mi. roundtrip with a somewhat steep trail, most families cope.

★ The mixture of coastal and forest explorations provides an excellent variety of experiences for children. They can recognize the differences between each environment and how one effects the other.

Access: On US 101 S from Oregon Coast or N from Eureka. **Days/Hours:** Daily. **Camping:** Park's 4 backcountry campgrounds (25 sites); 3 state parks 4 (350 sites, reservations-MISTIX e1-800/444-7275f, elec. & shwrs.); national forest has 6 campgrounds. **For info.:** Superintendent, Redwood National Park, 1111 2nd St., Crescent City, CA 95531. 707/464-6101.

Santa Monica Mountains National Recreation Area

Allow: 2 days *FREE*

Some 150,000 acres of canyons, ridges and southern California shoreline attract 35,000,000 visitors each year. The park service, state parks, county parks, community organizations and private interests have a stake and a say in the administration of the recreation area.

Highlights

★ This area epitomizes west coast living: rugged hills and coast, meeting under fair skies, colors that could only be bleached by the sun and the salt air. And people that O. Henry characterized as follows: "Californians are a race of people; they are not merely inhabitants of a state." The park preserves both the natural and cultural aspects of the area. The Santa Monica Mountains are home to hundreds of species of plants and animals that make this ecosystem unique. Of particular interest are the oak savannah areas of Cheeseboro Canyon, the coastal chaparral of Zuma and Trancas Canyons, the rugged peaks and cliffs of Circle X Ranch and the ravines of Pt. Mugu and Malibu Creek. At Ranch Sierra Vista/Satwiwa Site, you can learn about the Chumash people who lived in these hills and see a working horse ranch. Paramount Ranch, a still active movie location (only in L.A.), recreates a western ranch.

Whiz Tips

❢ Many visitors enjoy the green winter season the most of all. Hiking in the secluded oak groves offers respite from the summer sun and city life, a rare pleasure.

❢ The Santa Monica Mountains are one of the few North American mountain ranges running east to west. They're a young and ever-growing fault range with sharp angles and stark relief.

Kids' Stuff

★ Because of the number of interpretive programs put on in the park's environs, by the 30 different organizations, families have a veritable feast of alternatives to choose from. Make sure you visit the national park's visitor center to get a program of what's on.

★ Children really enjoy the Paramount Ranch tour with its old west facade and the weekend tours of the Rancho Sierra Vista ranch. Don't forget the over 25 miles of beaches where your kids can frolic in the surf and build sandcastles.

Access: Just N of Beverly Hills. **Days/ Hours:** M-Sa 8-5. **Camping:** Permit walk-in camping at Circle X Ranch; Point Mugu State Park (159 sites), Malibu Creek State Park & Leo Carrillo State Beach (136 sites & shwrs.) (reservations). **Special Events:** Year-round events including horse shows and outdoor concerts. **Teacher's Package:** Available. **For info.:** Superintendent, Santa Monica Mountains National Recreation Area, 30401 Agoura Rd., Ste.100, Agoura Hills, CA 91301. 818/597-9192.

Sequoia and Kings Canyon National Parks

Allow: 2-3 days *Fee*

"When a tree takes a notion to grow in California nothing in heaven or on earth can stop it.

Lilian Leland
Travelling Alone, A Woman's Journey Round the World

What the Grand Canyon is to geology, what Mesa Verde is to prehistoric architecture, what Yellowstone is to wildlife, that is what Sequoia and Kings Canyon are to plantlife. Nothing has so thoroughly instilled awe in us as the sequoias, the earth's largest living things. It's impossible to describe the tremendous respect one feels in their presence. Both Sequoia, the nation's second oldest national park, and Kings Canyon

Sequoia & Kings Canyon National Parks COURTESY NPS

are sanctuaries for these wood giants which are found nowhere else on earth.

Highlights

★ For some, visiting the largest tree, General Sherman, is the epitome. For others, the Nation's Christmas Tree-General Grant- is their highlight. For still others, it's the opportunity to be dwarfed by these monsters when driving through the Tunnel Log.

Whiz Tips

There are year-round interpretive programs. On winter weekends and holidays, you can don snowshoes and plod around with rangers who explain the forest's yule-tide mood. Summer brings a full slate of enlightening daily programs about the park's ecology, geology, sequoias, botany, animal life and stream life.

While there are taller trees (the redwoods on the coast), older trees (the bristlecone pine in the interior), even wider trees (the Montezuma cypress in Mexico), the sequoia is not just the biggest but it has height, width and great age. It is estimated that the General Sherman stands 275 ft., weighs 1385 T., is over 100 ft. in circumference and is about 2500 years old. Like the redwoods, the sequoias are amazingly resistant to fire and disease. Ironically, fire creates optimum conditions for their seeds to germinate. Unfortunately also like the redwoods, they have a very shallow root network and are subject to destruction from strong winds. Sequoia wood is extremely brittle, a fact which has saved them from being heavily logged and preserved them for the ages. Sequoias are only found on the western slopes of the Sierras and 90% of them are in state or federal parks.

Kids' Stuff

★ During the summer, the nature center is a hands-on natural science museum. Other summer programs include special children's walks and

Sequoia & Kings Canyon National Parks

COURTESY NPS

a kid's campfire before the nightly presentation.

★ Grant Grove and Giant Forest each have an abundance of hiking trails families can explore. At Cedar Grove, you can follow the river trail to Roaring River Falls and Zumwalt Meadow.

★ Kids relish exploring Sequoia's Crystal Cave, a marble cave (see Oregon Caves NM, OR) which can be toured during the summer (fee).

★ In winter, families visit the Giant Forest and Grant Grove to sled or tube down hills. Both have cross-country ski trails. On weekends and holidays, ranger-led snowshoe walks may be scheduled.

Access: Sequoia, E on CA 198 from US 99; Kings Canyon, E on CA 180 from US 99. **Days/Hours:** Visitor centers, daily, Ash Mountain, summer 8-5 & winter 8-4:30; Lodgepole 9-5; Grant Grove 8-5. **Camping:** Park has several campgrounds; Lodgepole (Ticketron reservation) and Grant Grove are near sequoia groves. **For info.:** Superintendent, Sequoia and Kings Canyon National Parks, Three Rivers, CA 93271. 209/565-3456.

Whiskeytown-Shasta Trinity National Recreation Area

Allow: 2-3 days *Fee*

Three park regions are joined under two agencies to form this national recreation area. The Shasta and Trinity sections are administered by the national forests while Whiskeytown in handled by the park service. All three reservoirs were created to channel water down to the Sacramento and Bay areas. The net effect for today's visitor is a freshwater playground and surrounding back-to-nature experiences.

Highlights

★ Visitors put a heavy emphasis on the "recreation" part of the park's name. Whiskeytown Lake enjoys more consistent water levels throughout the summer than its sister lakes. Water sport enthusiasts can water-ski, sail, canoe, power boat, swim, or even scuba dive. Fishing fanatics can cast for two species of trout (rainbow

Whiskeytown-Shasta-Trinity National Recreation Area COURTESY NPS

and brown), three species of bass (smallmouth, bigmouth and spotted) and a landlocked salmon called kokanee. Landlubbers can hike, pan for gold (permit needed) or take to two wheels on some of the best mountain bike trails in the state.

Whiz Tips

The recreation area offers a surprisingly diverse selection of ranger-led activities. How many places show you how to strike it rich by goldpanning, lend you the equipment and let you tap their treasures (by permit with small fee)? To learn more about the "Days of '49," you can join a ranger on a walk through the Tower House Historic District, see the remains of the El Dorado Gold Mine and Stamp Mill or visit the 1852 Camden House. The rangers don't ignore the lake as they conduct canoe and patio boat tours.

Kids' Stuff

★ There's a 1 hr. long, summer-only, Jr. Ranger program focussing on environmental activities and games. For example, your kids could study pond life, learn about birdwatching or about trees.

★ Children can attend their own programs called "Just for Kids." Here 6 to 12 yr. olds learn about the natural environment of the park. Fishing clinics are sometimes offered by the park rangers. If fishing is where your kids are at, then the lake's colder western waters are where you should head. However, swimmers prefer the warmer eastern end.

Access: Intersection of CA 299 & Kennedy Memorial Dr. **Days/Hours:** Visitor information center, summer, daily; fall & spring, W-Su; winter, S&S 9-5. **Camping:** Park has 2 campgrounds (87 sites). **For info.:** Superintendent, Whiskeytown-Shasta-Trinity National Recreation Area, P.O.Box 188, Whiskeytown, CA 96095-0188. 916/246-1225.

Yosemite National Park

Allow: 2-3 days *Fee*

"That first gaze up the opposite height! Can I ever forget it? The valley is here scarcely half a mile wide, while its northern wall of mainly naked, perpendicular granite is at least four thousand feet high probably more. But the modicum of moonlight that fell into this awful gorge gave to that precipice a vagueness of

Yosemite National Park

outline, an indefinite vastness, a ghostly or weird spirituality."

Horace Greeley
An Overland Journey from New York to San Francisco

There are few places in the country so familiar. Painters, photographers, writers and poets have sought to capture its essence. The images of Half Dome and El Capitan are national symbols, true Americana. Does it deliver? You bet it does. This is an "Incomparable Valley!" Its natural beauty caused President Abraham Lincoln to set it aside for posterity in 1864 as the nation's first state park.

Highlights

★ Take to the hills. The park offers little solitude if you remain with the hordes of visitors who drive the loop road, snap their mandatory shots and hit the villages. The famed valley is less than 1% of the park's area. There are 200 miles of roads and 800 miles in trails running through the mountains and valleys. For example, you could drive up 3,000 ft. to Glacier Point for a panorama of the valley and Half Dome. A short hike from there takes you to 8,000 ft. Sentinel Dome. Photographers take special care to time their visit to Glacier Point at sunset or during a full moon. Mariposa Grove and Tuolumne Grove are two outings that will reward you with close-up views of the spectacular giant sequoias. Mariposa has a museum explaining sequoias and contains probably the worlds oldest sequoia, Grizzly Giant, at 2,700 years old. At 8,600 ft., the Tuolumne region, a favorite with high country hikers, is awash with wildflowers in spring and early summer.

Whiz Tips

❢ There are a full range of interpretive programs focussing on the natural pleasures to be found here. During summer, you can attend ranger-led walks and talks at Camp Curry, Glacier Point, Crane Flats, Lower River, Lower Pine, Tuolumne Meadows, Bridalveil Creek, Wawona and White Wolf areas. Yosemite Lodge and the Valley Visitor Center feature year-round activities. A special treat are the programs found in the Wawona region relating its pioneer days.

❢ The valley is the product of glacial action. Alpine glaciers flowed down through the Merced River canyon carving the u-shaped valley. The entrance to the park on CA 140 shows the v-shaped scenery you would see if these glaciers hadn't scored Yosemite Valley. The best time to see the valley's many waterfalls is in spring or early summer.

Kids' Stuff

★ The park offers Jr. Ranger programs which allow children from 8-12 to participate in nature walks and classes while older children can go on special hikes.

Access: E from Merced on CA 140 & 120; N from Fresno on CA 41 or W from Lee Vining (summer only) on CA 120. **Days/ Hours:** Daily. **Camping:** Park has 5 campgrounds (reservations/Ticketron). **For info.:** Superintendent, Yosemite National Park, P.O.Box 577, Yosemite National Park, CA 95389. 209/372-0200.

COLORADO

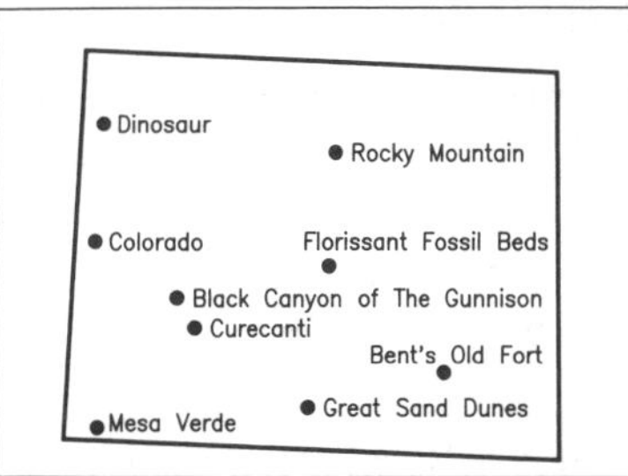

Bent's Old Fort National Historic Site

Allow: 2 hrs. *Fee*

In southeastern Colorado near La Junta, you'll discover a fort that looks just like you imagine. True it's a reconstruction and the fort was never attacked, but after seeing so many ruins, it's exciting to see what was. Standing on the parapet and looking out over the fort walls, you can almost see the mountain men and Indians camped in the field next to the river.

Highlights

★ Be sure to see the introductory film before you tour the premises. By putting the fort and its times in perspective, it allows you to make the most of your encounters with the fort's costumed "residents" as they go about their "1840's" daily routines.

Whiz Tips

The fort has summer tours explaining the people, places, and significant events in the life of the fort. Special demonstrations include frontier medicine, blacksmithing, adobe making, the hunter's role, and 1840's military skills.

William and Charles Bent entered into the fur trading business with Ceran St. Vrain in the 1820's. In 1832, they started work on a fort along the Arkansas River, a central

Bent's Old Fort NHS COURTESY BENT'S OLD FORT NHS

location for both the fur trade with the Indians and trade with the Santa Fe Mexicans. William, the principal manager of the fort, was regarded as a fair man by the Indians and mountain men. His reputation helped make Bent's Fort a success. In 1847, after the United States wrested control of New Mexico from Mexico, Charles became the first American governor of the new territory. Unfortunately, the Pueblo Indians and Mexicans were not thrilled at this change in the status quo and registered their concern by rebelling, assassinating Charles as an exclamation mark to their statement. The European markets for furs were already in a drastic decline and St. Vrain went his own way. William finally abandoned the fort in 1849 after a breakout of cholera brought by the '49ers headed for California's gold fields.

Kids' Stuff

★ Hey, this is a real adobe fort, built from soil and clay. Kids love to explore the buildings and to get up on the parameter of the walls and check out the countryside.

★ In mid-August, there's a day of activities for kids called Kid's Quarters. They get to play pioneer games and do frontier chores (amazing what a little make-believe can do to get your children to do something constructive).

Access: 8 Mi. E from La Junta or 15 mi. W from Las Animas on CO 194. **Days/Hours:** Daily, summer 8-6, winter 8-4:30 (clsd. Thanksgiving, Dec.25 & Jan.1). **Camping:** E to Hasty, Lake Hasty Recreation Area (65 sites). **Special Events:** Winter Quarters (late Mar.), June encampment, the Fourth of July festivities, early Aug. encampment, The Labor Day weekend Fur Trade Encampment, the "Diez Y Seis de Septiembre" Hispanic celebration (Sept.16), and Christmas' 1846 replication. **Teacher's Package:** Available. **For info.:** Superintendent, Bent's Old Fort National Historic Site, 35110 Hwy. 194 E., La Junta, CO 81050. 303/384-2596.

Black Canyon of the Gunnison National Monument

Allow: .5 days *Fee*

In western Colorado, between Gunnison and Montrose, is the Black Canyon of the Gunnison National Monument, a twelve-mile stretch of the deepest and darkest section of the Gunnison River. As you enter the park, suddenly the earth appears to open, allowing elfish mists to escape from the depths of a blackened wound. Reaching depths of 2700 feet, the river has cut and scraped a narrowing channel through hard rock, creating more a fissure than a canyon. Although the narrowness of the earth's incision limits light, it's the canyon's dark rock that accounts for its name. The park's more developed South Rim is about a three hour drive from its North Rim.

Black Canyon of the Gunnison NM

COURTESY NPS

Highlights

★ Tomichi Point view is the stuff of nightmares. If you were in California, you'd think you were witnessing the aftermath of an earthquake.

★ A number of the overlooks put you out on canyon precipices that offer panoramic views. The real wonder occurs when you look back at your previous viewpoint and see how little solid ground supported you.

Whiz Tips

The South Rim, has a visitor center, two nature trails and twelve overlooks. The North Rim with a visitor contact station, one nature trail, six overlooks and a campground is accessed via a gravel road which is closed in winter.

The amazing story of how this relatively small river has carved its way deep beneath the surface is one that impresses upon us the power of water and time to create change. Also overcoming many obstacles, the Montrose community introduced the Canyon to the park service and persistently petitioned them for its inclusion as a national treasure.

Kids' Stuff

★ The nature walks are all child-size although you will be walking along canyon walls. Using the park's booklets and signs, you can teach your children about the formation of the canyon and its wildlife.

★ During summer, children's programs are offered two or three times per week.

Access: South Rim 15 mi. E on US 50 & CO 347 from Montrose. North Rim 50 mi. W on CO 92 & gravel road (14 mi.) from Delta. **Days/Hours:** Visitor centers daily, summer. **Camping:** South and North Rims campgrounds, Corecanti National Recreation Area, Ridgeway Lake State Recreation Area and Crawford Lake State Recreation Area. **For info.:** Superintendent, Black Canyon of the Gunnison National Monument, 2233 East Main, Montrose, CO 81401. 303/249-7036.

Colorado National Monument

Allow: 1 day *Fee*

In Colorado, just across the Utah border from Arches and Canyonlands National Parks, is another spectacular area known as Colorado National Monument. With a Monument Mesa, an Independence Monument and a Monument Canyon, this is a "monumental" national park. We are tempted to say the park is "another example of the effects of water, wind, and time" and yet what a variety of rock formations these commonplace erosive tools have carved.

Highlights

★ There is a sense of adventure as you descend to get a closer look at these stones carved by a seemingly invisible hand. Whether you hike down to these haunting rock formations or peer at them from the many pull-overs, you'll be amazed at their beauty. If you're running out of film or travelling on a limited budget, save your shots for the best overlooks: Monument Canyon, Coke Ovens and Artists' Point Overlooks.

Whiz Tips

The park does a good job of introducing you to the semi-desert land and its wide diversity of wildlife through its interpretive programs. Squirrels, chipmunks, lizards and desert cottontails compete with the birds for food. Mule deer, desert bighorn sheep, fox and bobcats can be found. Even mountain lions, bears and elk have been spotted, but don't count on any close-up pictures. As part of the greater Colorado Plateau it shares the same geological strata as do Arches, Bryce, Zion, and the Grand Canyon. Wind, water, and frost have worn away at the softer rock leaving a collection of spires, domes, arches, windows, balanced rocks, and steep canyon walls.

Kids' Stuff

★ With child-size trails you can explore quite a bit of the landscape. The trails which most kids can handle are Window Rock, Canyon Rim, Coke Ovens, Alcove, John Otto's Trail (named after the chap who worked tirelessly to get this place included in the national park system, John Otto) and Devil's Kitchen.

Access: 4 mi. W of Grand Junction or 2 mi. S from Fruita off I-70. **Days/Hours:** Visitor center daily, summer 8-8 & winter 8-4:30. **Camping:** Park's Saddlehorn Campground (80 sites); Other federal and state campgrounds (within 1 hr.). **For info.:** Superintendent, Colorado National Monument, Fruita, CO 81521. 303/858-3617.

Curecanti National Recreation Area

Allow: 2 days *FREE*

The Gunnison River cuts deep through this hilly country. Over thousands of years it has carved a trough that collects the waters from the surrounding mountains. Today, a series of dams slows its progress, creating calm lake waters where bubbly froth once churned. Fisherfolk, windsurfers and boaters take to the three man-made lakes - Blue Mesa, Crystal and Morrow Point.

Highlights

★ This is a raw, rough country. Visitors are attracted by the craggy rocks and cold waters. Most like nothing better than to test their skill at hooking a tail-dancing trout. Some stalk the more numerous rainbow while others want the wily brown. Easterners enjoy the nostalgia when they catch a brookie, while trophy hunters hope to reel in a lumbering Mackinaw (up to 30 lbs.) from the deep holes.

Whiz Tips

❢ Rangers guide visitors on the Morrow Point Lake boat tour (fee). Some regions of the park are only accessible by boat or arduous hiking trails. You learn about the narrow-gauge railroad, the Scenic Line of the World, which ran through the area.

Curecanti National Recreation Area COURTESY NPS

There are also daily interpretive talks during the summer and on weekends.

Kids' Stuff

★ Most of the interpretive programs offered here can be adapted to include children. For example, at Elk Creek, your kids can help rangers feed fish at the fish pond. A Jr. Ranger program was in developmental stages and should be in place when you visit. Two relatively easy hikes with children are Neversink and Mesa Creek.

Access: Elk Creek Visitor Center 16 mi. W of Gunnison or Cimarron Information Center 20 mi. E from Montrose on US 50. **Days /Hours:** Elk Creek Visitor Center, summer, daily & winter, intermittently, 8-4:30. **Camping:** Park has 4 campgrounds; Elk Creek 179 sites & shwrs.), Lake Fork (87 sites & shwrs.), Stevens Creek (54 sites) & Cimarron (22 sites). **Teacher's Package:** Available. **For info.:** Superintendent, Curecanti National Recreation Area, 102 Elk Creek, Gunnison, CO 81230. 303/641-2337/0406.

Dinosaur National Monument

Allow: 2-3 days *Fee*

A glance at the map shows two main unconnected roads leading into Dinosaur National Monument. The entrance from Jensen, Utah takes you into the actual dinosaur digs and to a very distinctive display hall. The entrance from Dinosaur, Colorado takes you to the park headquarters and a scenic drive to some of the most spectacular canyon scenery in Colorado.

Highlights

★ In order to provide you with a memorable picture of a paleontologist's (that's what they call the dinosaur miners) chores, the park has enclosed a large cross-section of a dinosaur quarry. Each layer of rock exposes different fossils. The cross-sectional view is three stories high running almost a football field in length. The exposed surface is littered with different-sized bones, some bigger than a man. The top layer has the most recent remains and the bottom the oldest.

★ The scenic drive through the Colorado component of the park offers dramatic scenery, nature trails, wayside exhibits and Echo Park.

Whiz Tips

The recent excitement over dinosaurs echos the excitement of the major discoveries a century ago. It was only in the 1800s that scientists could prove the age of the items they had uncovered. Conventional wisdom at that time was a strict biblical interpretation; i.e., God took a literal seven days to create the earth; therefore, it was only 6,000 years old. With more accurate dating methods, scientists began to question where these huge bones came from. Backed by competing museums, a bevy of paleontologists scoured the West looking for the richest finds. This region's climate and geography collaborated to make it a prime location for preserving the prehistoric remains. When possible, tours of the grounds are given to help visitors visualize the field work the paleontologists conducted to unearth their finds.

There are fine examples of Fremont Indian petroglyphs along the drive from the quarry to Cub Creek. The Fremont exhibited hunting traits similar to those of the Great Basin Indians. It is thought that after their disappearance in the 1300s, they became the Shoshone or Ute peoples.

Kids' Stuff

★ There is a Young Naturalist program for the kids. Plus, there are a number of relatively short self-guided nature trails including Gates of Lodore, Red Rock, Harpers Corner, Plug Hat and Sounds of Silence.

Access: Quarry 20 mi. E on US 40 & N on UT 149 from Vernal, UT; H.Q. 39 mi. E on US 40 from Vernal or 2 mi. E on US 40 from Dinosaur, CO. **Days/Hours:** Visitor center daily, summer 8-7, winter 8-4:30 (clsd. Thanksgiving, Dec.25 & Jan.1). **Camping:** Park's two developed campgrounds (135 sites) are near the Quarry; Colorado access (3 primitive campgrounds). **Teacher's Package:** For purchase. **For info.:** Superintendent, Dinosaur National Monument, Dinosaur, CO 81610. 303/374-2216.

Florissant Fossil Beds National Monument

Allow: 2-3 hrs. *Fee*

To the west of Colorado Springs is a rather innocuous stretch of property which has since proven to be a fountain of information about the earth's natural history. Almost 35 million years ago, the park was a large lake bordered by giant sequoias. Enormous volcanic explosions expelled millions of tons of ash and buried the entire region. The plant and insect life were smothered alive and the ash turned to shale enclosing the skeletal remains of all these organisms. Over 60,000 fossils have been exhumed for examination. The park's visitor center and trails help explain the finds.

Highlights

★ The main attraction visitors see is a semi-petrified forest (the sequoias are partially petrified). Turn-of-the-century Coloradans were "stumped" when they tried to cut one of the trees to show at the World's Exposition in Chicago. The pieces of the defeated saw blades are still lodged in the fossilized stumps.

Whiz Tips

Probably the most interesting facet of the fossilization that occurred here, is the length of time it took. Over 500,000 years volcanic dust, ash and pumice settled in the area burying things alive. Some of these smothered objects settled at the bottom of what was then Lake Florissant. Embedded in very fine ash, they became fossilized, forming shale.

During the summer months, the rangers give regularly scheduled natural history talks, guided tours and wild flower walks. There are also two self-guiding (brochures) nature trails

Florissant Fossil Beds National Monument COURTESY NPS

and 15 mi. of hiking trails. In winter, cross-country skiing, snowshoeing and sledding are popular pastimes.

Kids' Stuff

★ There are several nature trails and the Hornbek Homestead house is inhabited on occasion by rangers who explain how the pioneers who lived here coped with the elements. In addition, the kids can examine the hands-on exhibits at the visitor center.

Access: 37 mi. W on US 24 & Cty. Rd. #1 from Colorado Springs. **Days/Hours:** Daily summer 8-7:30 & winter 8-4:30 (clsd. Thanksgiving, Dec.25 & Jan.1). **Camping:** Nearby U.S. Forest Service's 11 Mile Canyon Campground & 11 Mile Reservoir camping (state-reservations). **For info.:** Superintendent, Florissant Fossil Beds National Monument, P.O. Box 185, Florissant, CO 80816. 303/748-3253.

Great Sand Dunes National Monument

Allow: 1 day *Fee*

As the last Ice Age came to a close and the glaciers retreated, the South-Central Colorado mountain rocks they had dislodged began to crumble. The snow melt rivers battered the residue further breaking it up into smaller pieces leaving a fine silt along their banks. The rivers changed course, abandoning vast tracks of fine sand which dried off becoming a toy for the wind. The prevailing southwesterly breezes snatched this shifting sand and threw it against an unmoving barrier' the west side of the Rocky Mountains. Here, it has collected over the centuries forming 700 feet sand dunes, the tallest in North America.

Highlights

★ For a remarkable sight, go out on the dunes at dusk and see the animals emerging for their night of foraging. Deer walk by you like so many New Yorkers, ignoring your presence, bent on a night time of pleasure. Take a flashlight so you can stay after dark and catch whole communities of creatures performing their nightly chores. With the cool evening air, the respite from the harsh sun and the cover of darkness, troops of small desert animals make their way out onto the sand's surface.

Whiz Tips

💡 The park provides exhibits, an AV and interpretive programs explaining the dunes and the life they sustain. During summer, there are night programs and porch talks.

💡 Daytime heats the sand to 120 degrees F.; nighttime makes distances difficult to judge. NEVER go out on the dunes in an electric storm. You are the highest point on the horizon and in short work, you'll be toast.

Kids' Stuff

★ During summer, kids can earn a Jr. Ranger patch by completing the work booklets. On Saturday mornings a special program is offered for children ages 6-12.

★ This is a world-class sand box. It isn't unusual to see adults well into their prime frolicking on the dunes.

Access: 37 mi. E on Hwy. 150 from Alamosa. **Days/Hours:** Visitor center daily 8-5 (closed Thanksgiving, Dec.25 & Jan.1). **Camping:** Park's Pinyon Flats Campground (88 sites); plus primitive camping on the main dune mass other side of first ridge. **Special Events:** Summer Sundays, local concert artists; last Aug. wknd., 10K run. **Teacher's Package:** Available. **For info.:** Superintendent, Great Sand Dunes National Monument, Mosca, CO 81146. 303/378-2312

Hovenweep National Monument

Allow: .5 days *FREE*

Spanning the border between Utah and Colorado are six clusters of prehistoric Pueblo ruins. Hovenweep (Ute for "Deserted Valley") looks like a miniature Rhine Valley, with small castles (pueblos) and towers overlooking shallow canyons. Several of these structures are aligned to show the equinoxes and solstices. The Pueblo Indians grew corn, beans and squash on the mesa tops and canyon bottoms. After a long drought, they abandoned the area and moved south.

Highlights

★ The truly amazing towers have a storybook quality about them. They cause people to wonder why they were ever built. It is likely the towers served a number of functions including storage facilities, solar observation points and signalling posts.

★ The McElmo Canyon gravel road connecting just south of Cortez to the monument has some of the most beautiful scenery you'll find anywhere. Handsome redrock canyons, a meandering river and remote ranches are revealed around each turn.

Whiz Tips

Both the Pueblo and earlier Anasazi peoples adapted to this unforgiving environment for over 1300 years by utilizing hunting and gathering and farming lifeways. Yet they still had time to practice fine masonry, basketry and rock art.

Kids' Stuff

★ Using the park Jr. Ranger Program handout, children learn more about the monument. When they have successfully completed the tasks, they receive a badge.

★ All three self-guiding trails are fairly short and fun for kids as they "discover" the ruins.

Access: 45 mi. E from Blanding, UT or 43 mi. W of Cortez, CO on paved, gravel and dirt roads. **Days/Hours:** Ranger contact station, daily 8-5. **Camping:** Monument's campground (31 sites). **For info.:** Superintendent, Hovenweep National Monument, McElmo Rte., Cortez, CO 81321. 303/562-4248.

Mesa Verde National Park

Allow: 2-3 days *Fee*

Between Cortez and Durango in southwestern Colorado is truly a national treasure, Mesa Verde Na-

Mesa Verde National Park

tional Park. There are other Anasazi ruins and other Anasazi tours but this park has them all beat. If just on the basis of the wealth of cliff-dwellings alone, Mesa Verde would be a "MUST SEE." The park guides make the tours fun, interesting and exciting. Ask away, they'll answer, speculate and they'll speculate with you. This is truly a world class show...the WHIZZIEST of them all.

Highlights

★ Where do we start...Balcony House where you climb tall ladders and crawl through tunnels then pull yourself up the cliff side steps by chain. Sound dangerous? Our three-year-old did it and loved it!

★ How about Cliff Palace, the largest cliff-dwelling to be found in North America? Over 200 people lived their daily lives routinely climbing cliffs to mind their farms at the mesa top. Infants learned to walk along steep cliff faces and then, perhaps, to decode the climb to the top. You must start with the correct foot or you will end up in a precarious position. Interestingly, of the 400 Anasazi remains found at the park, there doesn't appear to be evidence of an unusual number of broken bones, attesting to their ease at scaling these heights.

★ Or Spruce Tree, by far the most genteel of the Mesa Verde cliff-dwellings with a spring so near at hand and gentler slopes around. Here you can go into a roofed kiva (they used this as a community center).

★ Or better yet...the Wetherill Mesa loop which is visited via tram (a reprieve for Grandma). This loop allows you to see the progression of homes the Anasazi built. They started off in pit houses then moved into above-ground pueblos and finally to cliff-dwellings before they "disappeared."

Whiz Tips

💡 The Anasazi Indians left no written history. Their name is taken from the Navajo who arrived in the area just before the Europeans and means "Ancient Ones." Who were they... what happened to them ... what can we learn from them? Mesa Verde comes the closest to answering these questions.

Mesa Verde National Park

Kids' Stuff

★ You'd think after a long arduous hike with rangers droning on about some long ago people, the last thing kids would want to do is see more...think again. Our crew reveled in this park. They loved the ladders, the tunnels, the long climbs up and down and the idea of those long ago Indians.

★ The park has a Jr. Ranger program in which the questionnaire the kids complete becomes their certificate of achievement.

Access: 10 mi. E from Cortez or 8 mi. W from Mancos on US 160. **Days/Hours:** The Park, the Chapin Mesa Museum and Spruce Tree House Ruins daily, winter 8-5. Rest of park daily, summer; Far View Visitor center 8-5 & museum 8-6:30. **Camping:** Park's campground (477 sites, May-Oct.). **For info.:** Superintendent, Mesa Verde National Park, CO 81330. 303/529-4465.

Rocky Mountain National Park

Allow: 2 days *Fee*

In northern Colorado, only two hours from Denver, is one of the most visited parks in U.S., outdrawing even Yellowstone. The park itself is an oasis of pristine nature even if its eastern portal isn't. The southeastern section offers an abundance of short- to medium-length trails over well-graded terrain. The interior goes from the high mountain valleys to the Rocky's precipices bridging the Continental Divide (the place where water falling to the west goes to the Pacific Ocean and water falling to the east goes to the Atlantic Ocean). In the early summer, the high meadows are ablaze with alpine flowers, while fall brings gold to the aspen and elk down from the heights.

Highlights

★ The wildlife in the fall is truly outstanding. It is not uncommon to take a short nature stroll and happen upon deer or elk. During a fall hike we had several sightings of both including a remarkable scene of a small herd of elk standing in the shallow bay of one of the lakes, feeding on the underwater growth.

★ The drive through the park offers outstanding views of the high country. This road is the highest (12,183 ft.) thoroughfare in the country, with 11 miles of highway running above the tree line. It allows everybody to get into the mountains, not just the ardent hikers.

Whiz Tips

❢ With 2,500,000 visitors a year, the park puts on a full slate of interpretive programs. You can go on photo walks, take in fishing lessons, birdwatch, learn how and what to video in the mountains, practice orienteering, sketch nature and explore after dark.

❢ The popular southeastern section of the park along the Bear Lake Road is very congested in the summer and the park warns that parking is nonexistent between 10 a.m. and 3 p.m.. There is a free shuttle bus service to this area to relieve the congestion. The schedule is posted in the park newspaper.

❢ The Old Fall River Road offers the enticement of a civilized back country trip to the mountain pass, but fails to deliver the scenery seen from Trail Ridge Road. Save yourself the thrills of this set of gravel switchbacks.

❢ The principal place to see exhibits pertaining to the geologic and natural make-up of the Rockies, is the Moraine Park Museum.

Kids' Stuff

★ With all that is offered, it is nice to see there is an emphasis on the smaller of our species. Junior Rangers are encouraged with several interpretive programs directed their way. Wildlife walks, puppet shows, coping with being lost in the woods and environmental games are but a few of the offerings.

Access: Just W of Estes Park on US 34/36 or NE of Grand Lake on US 34. **Days/ Hours:** Main visitor centers open daily from 8-5. (clsd Dec.25). Museum & Alpine Visitor center open summer only. **Camping:** Park's 5 campgrounds (over 575 sites), two (Ticketron 1/900/370-5566). **For info.:** Superintendent, Rocky Mountain National Park, Estes Park, CO 80517. 303/586-2371.

DISTRICT OF COLUMBIA

Constitution Gardens

Allow: 1 hr. *FREE*

Forty acres of landscaped park land sit between the Washington Monument and the Lincoln Memorial. The gardens have a 7.5 acre lake, a memorial to the Signers of the Declaration of Independence and an 1883 Lock House.

Constitution Gardens

COURTESY JIM MILLER

Highlights

★ Without this urban greenway, the other monuments and memorials would be cluttered among marbled government buildings. There is seldom a time during summer when somebody isn't setting up a small picnic or tossing a ball or frisbee.

Whiz Tips

The park consists of reclaimed land that at one time rested beneath the waters of the Potomac River. You can learn more about the Declaration of Independence by visiting the park's memorial.

Kids' Stuff

★ Strange as it may seem to out-of-towners, you and your kids can carry your fishing rods to downtown Washington, DC and bring back supper from the park's lake.

Access: Between the Reflecting Pool & Constitution Ave. **Days/Hours:** Daily. **Camping:** Greenbelt Park (175 sites) & Prince William Forest Park (80 sites). **For info.:** Superintendent, Constitution Gardens, National Capital Parks-Central, 900 Ohio Dr., SW, Washington, DC 20242. 202/426-6841.

Ford's Theatre National Historic Site

Allow: 1-2 hrs. *FREE*

"Next to the destruction of the Confederacy,

the death of Abraham Lincoln was the darkest day the South has ever known."

Jefferson Davis, Ex-Confederate President

In downtown Washington, stands Ford's Theater, where President Lincoln was the first U.S. President to be assassinated. Across the road stands the house where he died. The war was in its last throes. Lee had surrendered to Grant at Appomattox less than a week before. The unwary Lincoln, an inveterate theater-goer, attended a comedy called "Our American Cousin." Near the end of the play, a famous actor entered the presidential box and shot Lincoln in the back of the head. John Wilkes Booth, who dreamed of valor, would go down in infamy as the assassin.

Highlights

★ The theater looks as it did that sad eve. The president's box is festooned with the nation's flag. The lights are dim, the mood the same. How many wonder what would have been had the act failed?

★ In the theater's basement, the details of the prelude, the act and the aftermath are creatively displayed. Rangers give talks in the theater and tours of the house where Lincoln died. The world was harsh with the conspirators. Judgment and execution were quick. The nation struggled with his successor, Andrew Johnson. It fluctuated between healing the wounds between North and South and opening new ones. Eventually, the nation abandoned the will, if not the letter, of Lincoln's greatest feat, the *Emancipation Proclamation.*

Whiz Tips

❢ John Wilkes Booth joined the Richmond Grays (a Virginia Militia unit) when they went to guard the captured abolitionist, John Brown (see Harpers Ferry NHP, WV). Booth witnessed Brown's hanging. When the South seceded, he continued to follow his acting career and consoled himself that he served the South as a spy and conspirator. His first plan to kidnap Lincoln on a country outing failed when the president canceled his trip. A stop by Ford's Theater to pick up his mail provided Booth with Lincoln's plans. Booth's well-laid plan with co-con-

Ford's Theater National Historic Site

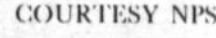
COURTESY NPS

spirators resulted in the death of the president, the wounding of the already infirm Secretary of State Seward and the alcohol-induced depression of fellow-conspirator, George Atzerodt, when he failed to attack Vice-President Johnson.

Pennsylvania Avenue National Historic Site is part of Pennsylvania Avenue that runs between the White House and the Capitol and includes Ford's Theatre.

Kids' Stuff

★ Children who have studied Lincoln or have a sense of him will benefit from a visit here. The ranger's talk on the tragedy was extremely thorough and presented the information in such a manner that even children could understand.

★ The kids took great pleasure in measuring themselves against Lincoln's image on a wall. We saw more than a few adults indulging in this activity.

Access: 511 Tenth St. NW in downtown Washington. **Days/Hours:** Daily 9-5 (clsd. Dec.25: theater clsd. Thurs., Sat., & Sun. matinees & rehearsals). **Camping:** Greenbelt Park (175 sites) & Prince William Forest Park (80 sites). **For info.:** Ford's Theatre National Historic Site, National Capital Parks-Central, 900 Ohio Dr., SW, Washington, DC 20242. 202/426-6924, TTD: 202/426-1749.

Frederick Douglass National Historic Site

COURTESY NPS

Frederick Douglass National Historic Site

Allow: 1-2 hrs. *FREE*

"Agitate! Agitate! Agitate!"

Frederick Douglass

As you drive through the bustling streets of this Washington, DC neighborhood, you wonder what kind of home Frederick Douglass owned. Atop the hill is a fine big house, a suitable dwelling for any successful person. If you had visited this 19th century ceaseless advocate for equality, you would have been greeted by a butler with an implement to hold your hat so human oils wouldn't soil it. If you came to dine, you would have had to dress appropriately in a formal suit or dress. Douglass may have advocated major changes in the social structure but he also advocated the social niceties. He saw himself as an equal with the leaders of the day and behaved accordingly.

Highlights

★ The guided tour of Douglass' home provides visitors with a little-known view of the man who "stold his body from slavery." After escaping to the North, Douglass displayed such eloquence that abolitionists had him tour the country to tell his tale and to seek support for equality. His home and governmental positions were scant reward for his efforts.

Whiz Tips

Douglass sought a larger audience by writing about his travails. He named names, becoming a target for slave hunters. Fleeing to England, he continued to drum-up abolitionist support in Europe. Ironically, English friends assisted him in buying his own freedom. Douglass eventually returned to America to promote his cause and to lend his name and support to women's rights (see Women's Rights NHP, NY). Aware of John Brown's plot to overthrow the slave owners by attacking Harper's Ferry (see Harpers Ferry NHP, WV), Douglass refused to join what he correctly believed to be a suicide mission. Douglass harried Lincoln throughout the Civil War until at last the *Emancipation Act* was signed and African American soldiers were paid comparable to their white counterparts. After the war, he supported Grant's bids for the presidency and began government service. At no time did he give up his fight for equality.

Kids' Stuff

★ Frederick Douglass was not anti-white. Rather, he was anti-slavery; he was anti-inequality; he was anti-hatred. He devoted his life to causes which provided all men and women the right to strive, to seek and to reap the rewards of a free society. This is an admirable lesson for any child.

Access: South of Anacostia River on hill at 14th & W St. **Days/Hours:** Daily summer 9-5 & winter 9-4. **Camping:** Greenbelt Park (175 sites) & Prince William Forest Park (80 sites). **For info.:** Superintendent, Frederick Douglass National Historic Site, 1411 W. St. S.E., Washington, DC 20020. 202/426-5960.

Hains Point

Just southeast of the Jefferson Memorial is this city park administered by the park service. Its centerpiece is an unusual statue, "The Awakening", which resembles a giant man rising out of the ground. The park has a playground and concession-operated attractions.

Access: In East Potomac Park. **Days/Hours:** Daily, dawn to dusk. **Camping:** Greenbelt Park (175 sites) & Prince William Forest Park (80 sites). **For info.:** Superintendent, Hains Point, National Capital Parks-Central, 900 Ohio Dr., SW, Washington, DC 20242. 202/426-6841.

John F. Kennedy Center for the Performing Arts

Allow: 2-3 hrs. *FREE*

"I am certain that after the dust of centuries has passed over our cities, we, too, will be remembered not for our victories or defeats in battle or politics, but for our contribution to the human spirit."

John F. Kennedy

Not far from the Lincoln Memorial, overlooking the Potomac and Theodore Roosevelt Island, is a wondrous complex devoted to the performing arts. The enormous building houses four major theaters, a movie theater and a theater lab. Close to 7,000 people can watch five different events on any given evening. The park service has a limited interpretive role at this site as the Friends of the Kennedy Center provides tours and information services. It also fund raise and administer a Specially Priced Tickets program for specific categories of deserving people.

Highlights

★ Although J.F.K. has received the most accolades for the completion of this "national" facility, the bill authorizing money for its construction was signed by President Eisenhower. Congress decided to name the center for President Kennedy after his assassination. They wanted it to be a "living" memorial representing the degree of importance the Kennedy administration placed on the arts. Work was finally begun in 1966, and, in 1971, the center opened its doors.

Whiz Tips

The tour of the facility focuses on the special features incorporated into the facility. Not the least of these are the many generous gifts from foreign nations. It's clear that the sentiments expressed above by President Kennedy are shared by the over 40 countries who have so enriched this memorial.

❢ To give you some idea how big this building is, the Washington Monument could easily be laid down inside its grand foyer.

Kids' Stuff

★ There are specially priced tickets for children. In addition, there are performances given for the younger age set. While the tour may prove a little too old for many children, kids need to be dragged away from the Swiss art piece called Appolla X by Willie Weber where they can see distorted views of themselves.

Access: At New Hampshire Ave. & F St. NW overlooking the Potomac River. **Days/Hours:** Tours run daily 10-1; Bldg. 10-midnight. **Camping:** Greenbelt Park (175 sites) & Prince William Forest Park (80 sites). **For info.:** General Manager, John F. Kennedy Center for the Performing Arts, Washington, DC 20566. 202/416-7910.

Lincoln Memorial

Allow: .5 hr. *FREE*

"The greatness of Napoleon, Caesar or Washington is moonlight by the sun of Lincoln. His example is universal and will last thousands of years."

Leo Tolstoy, 19th century Russian novelist and historian

Abraham Lincoln seated in calm repose ranks as one of the most familiar statues in the world. The alabaster image conveys to even the most unfamiliar visitor the esteem with which Lincoln is held. Some great men of their day don't withstand the test of time; others grow in magnitude. Lincoln has definitely proved to be a pre-eminent member of the latter group. It's rare to find a historian who doesn't name Lincoln among the best presidents the country ever had. And most of those would call him the best. In fact, a 1983 poll of 900 prominent historians ranked him the nation's greatest president.

Highlights

★ Make sure you ask the rangers

John F. Kennedy Center for the Performing Arts

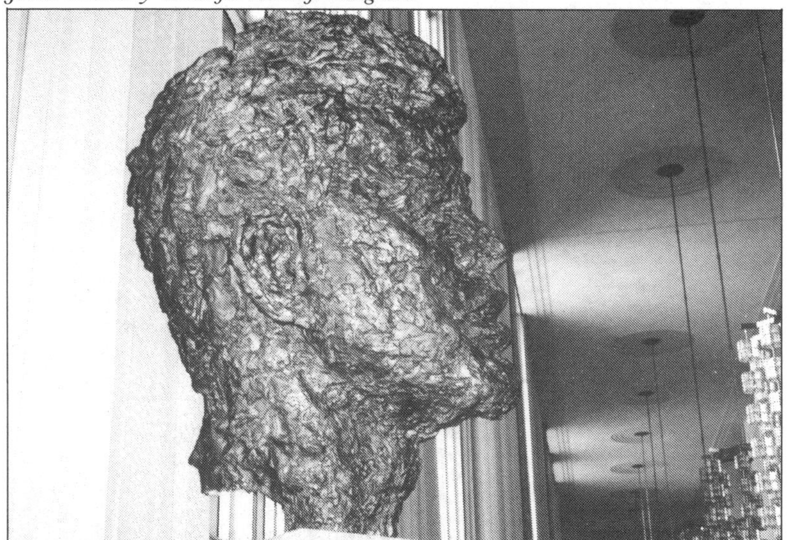

stationed at the memorial to tell you about it and Mr. Lincoln. They are able to bring to your attention the important details of the monument and the President's career.

Whiz Tips

❢ Lincoln knew not a day of peace during his terms as President. Seven states (South Carolina, Mississippi, Florida, Alabama, Georgia, Louisiana and Texas) had already seceded from the Union by the time he made his inaugural speech. Unlike his lame-duck predecessor, Buchanan, Lincoln couldn't, nor wouldn't let the problem of secession solve itself. As he said to the seceding states in his Inaugural Address: "You have no oath registered in Heaven to destroy the government, while I shall have the most solemn one to 'preserve, protect and defend' it." During his two terms, he issued the *Emancipation Proclamation* and the *Homesteaders Act* (see Homestead NM, NE). Most of all, he is regarded for the healing words he chose to define the aftermath of the Civil War. "With malice toward none; with charity for all; with firmness in the right, as God gives us to see the right, let us strive on to finish the work we are in; to bind up the nation's wounds." These words are etched in the walls at the memorial.

❢ While most of us find it convenient to visit the memorial during the day, the best pictures of the alabaster statue are taken at night as the lights add a heavenly haze about the President's countenance.

Kids' Stuff

★ Lincoln, of all the country's leaders, seems the most accessible to children of all ages because of his seemingly inherent humanitarianism. This is a must for kids who have studied Lincoln.

Access: At 23rd. St NW btwn. Constitution & Independence Ave. near downtown Washington. **Days/Hours:** Daily 8-12 midnight (clsd. Dec.25). **Camping:** Greenbelt Park (175 sites) & Prince William Forest Park (80 sites). **For info.:** Superintendent, Lincoln Memorial, National Capital Parks-West, 1100 Ohio Dr., SW, Washington, DC 20242. 202/485-9880.

Mary McLeod Bethune Council House National Historic Site

The headquarters for the National Council of Negro Women is an affiliated site. Established by Mary McLeod Bethune, founder of Florida's Bethune-Cookman College in 1935, the site commemorates her leadership in black women's rights movements.

Access: In Washington, DC. **Camping:** Greenbelt Park (175 sites) & Prince William Forest Park (80 sites). **For info.:** Mary McLeod Bethune Council House National Historic Site, 1318 Vermont Ave., NW, Washington, DC 20005.

Potomac Heritage National Scenic Trail

Washington, DC is the terminus for this trail that parallels the Potomac River on both banks beginning at the river's mouth and travelling 704 miles. While much of the trail which passes through parts of Virginia, Maryland and Pennsylvania, is not yet developed, 184 miles of it coincide with the Chesapeake and Ohio Canal Towpath (see Chesapeake and Ohio Canal NHP, MD).

For info.: Potomac Heritage National Scenic Trail, c/o National Capital Region, 1100 Ohio Dr., SW, Washington, DC 20242.

Rock Creek Park

Allow: 1 day *FREE*

Like an artery giving life to the

nation's capital, Rock Creek Park runs through to the heart of the city. One of the country's oldest (over 100 years) and largest (1700 acres) city parks, Rock Creek is managed by the park service. In a city renowned for its man-made monuments and stifling humidity, Rock Creek offers a natural sanctuary and at least 10 degrees cooler temperatures. The park is also responsible for the administration of several Civil War forts.

Highlights

★ When you ask at other Washington parks about children's programs, they all recommend Rock Creek. The nature center alone takes 4 hrs. to peruse. On weekends, there's a full slate of interpretive programs for you and your family. You can learn about the local Indians, the park's flora and fauna and take in the planetarium shows.

Whiz Tips

❢ Pierce Mill is a functioning grist grinding mill with park interpreters, volunteers and a machinery operator who presents interpretive tours of the mill and costumed demonstrations of grinding corn and wheat into flour and mill. The mill is open W-Su 8-4:30.

❢ The Old Stone House is the sole surviving pre-Revolutionary stone building left in D.C. From Wed.-Sun., demonstrations of spinning, candlemaking, cooking and needlework can be seen. On weekends, special programs include woodworking and walks in the garden around "Old Georgetown."

Kids' Stuff

★ Each summer there's a Jr. Ranger program where children have an opportunity to perform work just like real rangers.

★ The Nature Center tailors its planetarium offering so children can grasp the complexities of the universe. Its discovery room is a great place for youngsters to see and touch stuffed and live park creatures. There are also special activity days, like the one at Pierce Mill when children can make 18th century "doodads" and play "old-timey" games.

Access: Nature Center, S of Military Rd & Oregon Ave. at 5200 Glover Rd.NW. **Days/ Hours:** The Nature Center, Pierce Mill

Lincoln Memorial COURTESY JIM MILLER

and Old Stone House W-Su 9-5 (clsd. fed. holidays). **Camping:** Greenbelt Park (125 sites) & Prince William Park (80 sites). **Special Events:** Fort Stevens, the only fort in the vicinity to experience an attack during the Civil War, an encampment; Sept. 30, Rock Creek Park Day, interpretive programs, living historians, environmental presentations and musical productions. **Teacher's Package:** Available. **For info.:** Superintendent, Rock Creek Park, 5000 Glover Rd., NW, Washington, DC 20015. 202/426-6829.

Sewall-Belmont House National Historic Site

This historic house, now an affiliated site, was damaged by the fire the British set when they captured the nation's capital in the War of 1812. Since 1929, it has been the headquarters of the National Woman's Party. It serves to remind us of the exploits of Alice Paul, the party's founder and a leader in the women's suffrage movement.

Access: In Washington, DC. **Camping:** Greenbelt Park (125 sites) & Prince William Park (80 sites). **For info.:** Sewall-Belmont House National Historic Site, 144 Constitution Ave., NE, Washington, DC 20002.

Thomas Jefferson Memorial

Allow: 1 hr. *FREE*

"Nature intended me for the tranquil pursuits of science, by rendering my supreme delight. But the enormities of the times in which I have lived forced me to take part in resisting them, and to commit myself on the boisterous ocean of political passion."

Thomas Jefferson

The Jefferson Memorial sits in juxtaposition with the Washington Monument and the Lincoln Memorial in the nation's capital. The observatory-like monument to the nation's third president contains a statue of Jefferson and some of his famous quotations carved in the marble walls. Rangers are on duty to help interpret the memorial for you.

Thomas Jefferson Memorial

Highlights

★ Be sure and ask the rangers to give you an introduction to the memorial and a briefing on Thomas Jefferson. You'll discover that Jefferson's interests went beyond his belief in personal freedom.

Whiz Tips

❢ In spite of Jefferson's service as the nation's leader and his political influence over his successors, he remains best known as the primary author of the Declaration of Independence. His own tombstone for which he drafted the inscription reads, "Here was buried Thomas Jefferson, Author of the Declaration of Independence, of the Statue of Virginia for Religious Freedom, and the Father of the University of Virginia." Jefferson's legacy also includes the Louisiana Purchase (see Jefferson NEMem, MO), the Lewis and Clark expedition (see Fort Clatsop NM, OR), the Embargo Act (see Salem Maritime NHS, MA), the American monetary decimal system, the end of international slave trade and the invention of the swivel chair, an adjustable (architect) table and a plow moldboard (tilled soil more efficiently).

❢ Despite regard for personal freedoms, he was less than supportive of initiatives for the rights of African Americans, Native Americans and women. A man of his times he said, "The appointment of a woman to office is an innovation for which the public is not prepared, nor am I." In 1983, an historian's poll ranked Jefferson the 4th most effective of the nation's presidents, the last of the so-called "great" presidents. His visage is one of the four presidents so honored at Mt. Rushmore National Memorial, SD.

Kids' Stuff

★ For children who have studied the Declaration of Independence and Thomas Jefferson, this trip personalizes their knowledge of one of America's greatest philosophers, a true Renaissance Man.

Access: South bank of the Tidal Basin near downtown Washington. **Days/Hours:** Daily 8-midnight. **Camping:** Greenbelt Park (175 sites) & Prince William Forest Park (80 sites). **For info.:** Superintendent, Thomas Jefferson Memorial, National Capital Parks-Central, 900 Ohio Dr.SW, Washington, DC 20242. 202/485-9880.

Vietnam Veterans Memorial

Allow: 1 hr. *FREE*

The smooth black granite V-shaped plates recessed into the earth are covered in the names of the dead lost in Viet Nam. The brain-child of Maya Ying Lin, the sculpture was designed to point to the Lincoln and Washington Monuments. Maya Ying Lin was a student when she entered her proposal in the competition for the memorial. Immediately after she had finished her work, some felt it wasn't sufficient. Today, few question the elegance and emotional impact the edifice has on visitors. It has become the premier symbol of the grievous loss the nation suffered.

Highlights

★ It's hard not to be drawn to the piece. Even if your connections to this episode of American history are tenuous at best, you still find yourself scrutinizing the names.

★ Sculptor Frederick Hart's nearby depiction of three young men dressed as they would have been in "Nam," is a riveting piece. His life-like figures echo the contrast between the killing equipment they carry so casually and their youth. We are acutely aware that 58,132 young men like these have been reduced to names inscribed on black marble.

Whiz Tips

❢ Perhaps it should come as no surprise that Mother's Day is the most heart-rending day on which to experience the memorial. Each year, mothers from across the nation pay homage to their "babies" who died in the service of their country. With 58,132 names listed, unfortunately, there are many mothers and fathers who are less impressed with the artistry of the structure and more focussed on their children's names and their memories.

! Even today the controversies surrounding the Vietnam period surface. Veterans are concerned with the memorial becoming a tourist mecca. In order to comply with these feelings, the park service has established an information kiosk a respectable distance from the monument.

Kids' Stuff

★ Students who have studied the Viet Nam conflict will find the wall of interest. The mark this conflict has left on the American psyche has reverberated in every conflict since then. Older students must continually refer to Viet Nam in their social studies classes.

Access: Constitution Ave. & 23rd St. near downtown Washington. **Days/Hours:** Daily. **Camping:** Greenbelt Park (175 sites) & Prince William Forest Park (80 sites). **For info.:** Superintendent, Vietnam Veterans Memorial, National Capital Parks-Central, 900 Ohio Dr., SW, Washington, DC 20242. 202/485-9880.

Washington Monument

Allow: .5 hrs. *FREE*

This towering obelisk dominates the National Mall like no other structure. It is 555 ft. 5 1/8 in. high and weighs 90,854 tons or 18,170,800 lb. When it was finished in 1885, it had cost $1,187,710. Alone on the knoll in the middle of the governmental green, it beckons visitors to its base. Nobody asks why it was built, but rather, why it took so long to build a fitting monument to the nation's first president, George Washington.

Highlights

★ The view from the top provides a marvelous panorama of the city. When you're down on the ground

Vietnam Veterans Memorial

wandering from granite block-size building to granite block-size building you can quickly lose your perspective. The wait is short, the elevator quick and the view worth it.

Whiz Tips

❢ Historians credit George Washington with using his popularity to create a democracy rather than a monarchy. He knew that every act he performed set a precedent for his successors "Many things which appear of little importance in themselves and at the beginning, may have great and durable consequences from their having been established at the commencement of a new general government." To his credit he deflected his lionization and was most judicious in his decisions. In 1983, historians ranked him the country's 3rd most effective leader behind Lincoln and FDR.

❢ It wasn't until 1833 that the Washington National Monument Society, a citizens group, got fed up with indecisive politicians and undertook the task of building a monument for Washington. It took them 14 years before they had accumulated $87,000. The next year the cornerstone was laid. In 1854, the project bogged down and went into a stupor for 22 years. President Grant put the government back in the drivers seat in '76, but it took 4 more years before work began again. The Corps of Engineers completed the task with the capstone being placed on Dec. 6, 1884. The public was to wait 4 more years before it could view it.

Kids' Stuff

★ Little kids find the elevator ride to the top and the resulting view thrilling. There are platforms at each side for kids to stand on to see the view.

Access: In National Mall btwn. 15th & 17 Dr. SW near downtown Washington. **Days /Hours:** Daily 9-5 (clsd. Dec.25), summer 8 a.m.-12 midnight. **Camping:** Greenbelt Park (175 sites) & Prince William Forest Park (80 sites). **For info.:** Superintendent, The Washington Monument, Mall Operations Office, 1100 Ohio Dr. SW, Washington, DC 20242. 202/485-9880.

White House

Allow: 1-2 hrs. *FREE*

Visiting the White House at 1600 Pennsylvania Ave. is more the moment than the act. Much like the Statue of Liberty, the building is more than its parts. It is history. Each piece, each room has played some role in the making of the nation. The staff are congenial and informative but they sure aren't inviting. Bristling with physical and armed capabilities, you can't help feeling scrutinized and with good reason. The president and his family are but a wall or two away.

Highlights

★ Being there. Sure, in the off-season you can stand in line for quite a while being bombarded by cannon-

Washington Monument

COURTESY JIM MILLER

ading spiels telling you the history of the building or during summer, you have to get there early for a ticket with a specific time. Then it seems as though you're finished almost before you thought you were started. As you walk down the driveway towards the gates, you feel sure you'll be back again for a closer look, perhaps as a guest. Wouldn't that be grand! (Don't be discouraged by the seemingly long lines. Things move fairly quickly and the rangers will let you know how long you'll have to wait.)

Whiz Tips

Although Washington conceived the capital's design, including the White House, he never got to live in it. The original White House was burned by the British in 1814 in retaliation for a similar occurrence perpetrated by the U.S. in Canada. The practice of opening the house each morning to visitors, started by Jefferson, remains in practice. The White House we see today was completed in 1817, with James Monroe its first occupant.

In 1829, Jackson furnished the East Room and opened it to the public. In '33, running water and an indoor bathroom were added. By '48, Polk could read by gaslight. In '53, Pierce could warm his tootsies by central heating and, in '57, he could relax in a glassed conservatory on the west terrace. 1865 saw its first assassinated president on view in the East Room. In 1881, assassinated President Garfield became the second. '86 brought happier tidings, as Grover Cleveland became the only president to use the house to hold his wedding. In 1891, Benjamin Harrison was the first resident to turn on electric lights.

Teddy Roosevelt formally adopted the popular name "the White House," thus burying the official name, the Executive Mansion. It was also during his two terms that the White House underwent extensive refurbishing and expansion, including the 1909 addition of the West Wing and the Oval Office. The three story look came about in 1927. Given the length of F.D.R.'s presidency and the size of his own Hyde Park home, it's not surprising that he enlarged the West Wing, built the East Wing and an air raid shelter, then put a movie theater in the east terrace.

White House

Truman, ever the country gentleman, added a balcony in '48. However, at this time it was clear the home needed a complete facelift. It wasn't until '52 before Harry and Bess Truman would sleep beneath its roof. All changes since then have been in the interior decorating. On Oct. 13, 1992, the White House will celebrate its bicentennial.

Kids' Stuff

★ Sure, the stuff inside isn't of much interest to the kids BUT this is the White House. The build-up and anticipation are the excitement here. Children don't complain about the lines...much.

Access: 1600 Pennsylvania Dr., near downtown Washington (wheelchair entrance is at NE gate); closest Metro (subway stop is McPherson Sq. **Days/Hours:** Tu-Sa 10-12 noon (clsd. some holidays & special functions); from Memorial Day-Labor Day tickets are issued beginning at 8 with specific times so visitors don't have to stand in line. **Camping:** Greenbelt Park (175 sites) & Prince William Forest Park (80 sites). **Special Events:** April and Oct. selected wknds., Garden tours available; Dec., Candlelight tours; Easter Monday; traditional Easter Egg Roll. **For info.:** Park Manager, President's Park, National Park Service, National Capital Region, 1100 Ohio Dr., SW, Washington, DC 20242. 202/755-7798/472-3669.

FLORIDA

Big Cypress National Preserve

Allow: 2-3 hrs. *FREE*

"In none of the forty-eight states does life leap so suddenly, in an hour's motor drive, from the suburban snooze to the primeval ooze."
Alistair Cooke
One Man's America

This is but one of the places in southern Florida preserving the ooze from the bulldozer. Big Cypress Swamp, not truly a swamp, covers 2,400 sq. mi. of marshes, sandy islands, dry and wet prairies populated by gators, panthers, bears and bald eagles. The forest includes trees such as the namesake cypresses, both dwarf and bald varieties, slash pines and sable palm trees. This preserve was established because of the threat of a jetport and to protect the watershed for adjacent Everglades National Park.

Highlights

★ The preserve has few visitor conveniences. The Tamiami Trail (US 41) is a one-hour drive cutting through the preserve. Make sure you stop in at the Oasis Visitor Center for its orientation AV and exhibits explaining the area.

Whiz Tips

The pressure on Florida marshlands has been intense. With the growth in population, the demand for water has threatened the plant and wildlife in this region.

Mid-fall through to mid-spring are the ideal times to visit as there's less humidity and fewer bugs.

Kids' Stuff

★ While there are no programs specifically developed for children, a tour through this area will provide kids with an insight into this unique and valuable ecosystem.

★ You can fish the canals for catfish, bass and bluegill.

Access: 35 mi. E of Naples or 30 mi. W from Miami on US 41. **Days/Hours:** Visitor center, daily 9-4. **Camping:** Park has undeveloped roadside camping; nearby Everglades NP (403 sites); Collier-Seminole State Park (111 sites). **For info.:** Superintendent, Big Cypress National Preserve, S.R.Box 110, Ochopee, FL 33943. 813/695-2000.

Biscayne National Park

Allow: .5 days *FREE (Fee boat)*

"In variety, in brilliance of color, in elegance of movement, the fishes may well compare with the most beautiful assemblage of birds..."

Louis Agassiz, 19th century French naturalist

Discover a truly unique national park that is 95% water. Biscayne National Park, just 21 mi. east of Everglades National Park, was created to protect the mainland mangrove shore, the underwater coral reefs and Biscayne Bay's flora and fauna. The park has preserved a marvelous marine area in what has become a recreation mecca, the Florida Keys. Visitors can see this natural wonder aboard a glass-bottom boat, their own craft or by taking scuba/snorkeling excursions.

Highlights

★ Enter a world where it truly seems as though "no man has gone before." Brilliant blues, shimmering shapes and courtly coral are constantly changing with the ebb and flow of the tides. Some of our most enjoyable hours have been spent hovering over reefs, transfixed by the creatures that played out their lives before us. Don't miss an opportunity to study this underwater Garden of Eden. However, like all great things in nature, it suffers most from our wanting to get too close and from our wanting to capture it for our own personal collections. Recent studies have demonstrated we are loving

Gator at Everglades National Park COURTESY NPS

coral reefs to death. Besides souvenir hunters taking away samples of reefs, well-intentioned people walk on them, boats bang into them, while even touching them can harm them.

Whiz Tips

Coral reefs are the result of thousands of years of tiny creatures called "polyps" anchoring themselves to their ancestor's skeletons to feed, die and support a new generation. The coral gradually builds to form reefs which prove to be attractive habitats for all manner of undersea life. At Biscayne, over 200 species of fish have been noted.

Less compelling to sight-seers but no less important to the Bay and its lifeforms are the coastal mangroves. Their grotesque root systems perform a number of services. They are a nursery to the young who can hide here until they are able to fend for themselves. They are the rope that holds the mainland together against the ocean's storms. They are the sieve that grasps the pollution from entering the crystal clear waters.

Kids' Stuff

★ The park conducts interpretive programs aboard the glass-bottom boats. This is an excellent way for families with small children to see this place and to learn a great deal. For families with older children, the boat operator offers family snorkel/scuba trips. The mainland Convoy Point Visitor Center has "hands-on" exhibits of marine life for kids to fondle.

Access: Park H.Q. 9 mi. E of Homestead. Park accessed by private or concession operated boats only (reservations recommended). **Days/Hours:** Daily 8-sundown. **Camping:** Nearby Everglades NP (403 sites). **Special Events:** Columbus day weekend, the Regatta, a two day sailboat race from Miami to Elliott Key. **For info.:** Superintendent, Biscayne National Park, P.O.Box 1369, Homestead, FL 33090-1369. 305/247-2044.

Canaveral National Seashore

Allow: 1-2 days *FREE*

About half way down Florida's

Biscayne National Park COURTESY BISCAYNE NP, NPS

Atlantic coast is a place we normally associate with the numbers 10,9,8,7,6,5,4,3,2,1-- We have a lift-off! NASA's Kennedy Space Center was established on the land north of Cape Canaveral in the early 60s as the spring board for Project Apollo's journey to the moon. NASA uses about 105 of its 140,000 acres of land and water for its space operations. Virtually all the buffer zone is managed by Department of the Interior's Merritt Island Wildlife Refuge and the Canaveral NS. Canaveral has two recreation areas where you can swim, fish, boat, hike and loll about in the sun. In addition, the wildlife refuge protects 315 species of birds, 25 mammals, 117 fishes and 65 amphibians and reptiles. The refuge supports 22 endangered and threatened species, more than any other refuge in the country.

Highlights

★ Canaveral has beaches where you can enjoy the company of others and beaches where you can be alone. The sand is fine and the waters are warm, but the ocean undertow can be dangerous at times.

Whiz Tips

There are year-round interpretive programs including beach walks, hammock hikes, history talks, skills demonstrations and wildlife programs.

The Turtle Mound trail is a boardwalk leading to a Timucuan midden which has centuries-worth of clam and oyster shells. The Timucuans spent their winters hunting and fishing in the area. Numbering about 40,000 before Europeans arrived, they, like most Native Americans, proved susceptible to European diseases, and in a little over 200 years their numbers had been reduced to a handful. They have since disappeared as a distinct culture.

Local birds are divided into four classifications: wading birds - like the great blue heron, the great egret and the white ibis; shore birds - like the laughing gulls, sandpipers and plovers; soaring birds like the turkey vulture, bald eagle and osprey; and waterfowl - like the American coot and pied-billed grebe.

The endangered manatee, a large aquatic plant-eating mammal, is found in these waters. Man is this

Canaveral National Seashore

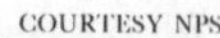
COURTESY NPS

gentle giant's greatest enemy. The manatee which can reach over 12 ft. long and 1,200 lbs. can be scarred and sometimes killed by the propellers of speeding boats. Spring and fall are the best times to see manatees in this area. On warm summer days, you might see alligators sunning themselves along the canals in the park/refuge's southern portion. On summer nights giant loggerhead sea turtles nest on the beaches along the seashore. To protect the endangered turtles, visitors must view them during a ranger-led program.

Kids' Stuff

★ The summer interpretive schedule includes programs specifically designed for children ages 6-12. By attending programs from three categories: lagoon, wildlife and ocean and completing a special project, kids can earn a Jr. Ranger patch and certificate.

★ We're talking miles of beaches here. Kids can build gigantic castles or play in the surf. In the northern area of the park, there are several short walks that you can take; all are less than a mile long. In cool winter months the walks are perfect for families with small children.

★ You can try your luck in the lagoon for sea trout, mullet, redfish and snook. Surf anglers can catch mackerel, bluefish, pompano and whiting.

Access: Off US 1, I-95, S of Daytona Beach & N of Kennedy Space Center. **Days/ Hours:** Daily, spring & summer 6-8 & fall & winter 6-6 (clsd. Dec.25 & Jan.1). **Camping:** Permit backcountry camping throughout park's North District. **Special Events:** April 22, Earth Day, June and July, Turtle Watch, the giant loggerheads come ashore to lay their eggs (reservations, 8-mid-night & children should be at least 8); Sept., Coastal Clean-up Campaign. **For info.:** Superintendent, Canaveral National Seashore, 2532 Garden St., Titusville, FL 32796. Manager, Merritt Island National Wildlife Refuge, P.O.Box 6504, Titusville, FL 32782. 305/267-1110.

Castillo de San Marcos National Monument

Allow: 1 hr. *Fee*

"...a part of St. Augustine lingers as the Southeast's most tangible relic of the Spaniards' bid for power."

Harnett T. Kane
Gone Are the Days

Battered but unbroken, the fortress of Castillo de San Marcos stands as the oldest stone fort in the country. For two centuries this was the Spanish northern stronghold against covetous France and England. St. Augustine was a key harbor on the eastern Florida coast and as such, was a much-prized possession for any country with plans to control the sea lanes. To protect it, the Spanish constructed not just this formidable bastion but a wall of palm logs which enclosed their city, making it one of only a few walled towns in the U.S. Visitors can tour the Castillo and learn about the time when Spanish galleons ruled these waters.

Highlights

★ As we draw to the close of the twentieth century, it's a pleasure to see a story-book fortress. Sidled next to Matanzas Bay, the Castillo has a water-filled moat protecting its other flanks. Each corner is specially designed to allow cannons to protect the walls from being scaled, and there's a ravelin attached by a drawbridge for an extra line of defence. The design proved itself against repeated attacks and was so formidable that Carolinian invaders took their frustrations out by burning St. Augustine when they couldn't capture the fort.

Whiz Tips

❢ The rangers give interpretive talks about the fort and St. Augustine's history. If you visit on wknds., you may be fortunate enough to see a cannon firing demo (make sure your kids cover their ears as the pressure created by the explosion can cause discomfort to some people).

❢ Founded in 1565 by Pedro Menendez de Aviles (see Fort Caroline NMem. & Fort Matanzas NM, FL), St Augustine saw 9 wooden forts built before this bulwark was started in 1672. The material, a shell-rock called coquina, was quarried from Anastasia Island, which is just across the bay from the stronghold. Over time, the Spanish, British, Spanish again and the Americans added their own embellishments.

Kids' Stuff

★ Children really love visiting this storybook-like fort surrounded by a moat with a drawbridge and cannons. Although few of us are willing to admit children love the idea of fighting, our kids really enjoy visiting forts and seeing weapon-firing displays.

★ People have been known to catch bass, salmon and trout off the seawall.

Access: Downtown St. Augustine. **Days/ Hours:** Daily, 9-5, summer extended hrs. (clsd. Dec.25). **Camping:** Nearby Anastasia State Recreation Area (139 sites, elec. & shwrs.). **Special Events:** 3rd. Sat. in June, Spanish Nightwatch celebration; 1st Sat. in Dec., British Grand Illumination; several open-house programs throughout the year. **Teacher's Package:** Available. **For info.:** Superintendent, Castillo de San Marcos National Monument, 1 Castillo Dr., E, St. Augustine, FL 32084-3688. 904/829-6506.

De Soto National Memorial

Allow: 1 hr. *FREE*

Just south of Tampa Bay is a park commemorating Hernando De Soto, an intrepid Spanish entrepreneur/explorer. With images of the vast stores of riches found to the south, De Soto invested his money in outfitting a troop and led them in search of gold. For four years they marched through parts of Florida, Georgia, South Carolina, North Carolina, Tennessee,

Castillo de San Marcos National Monument COURTESY NPS

Alabama, Mississippi, Louisiana, Arkansas and Texas. The memorial re-creates aspects of this enterprise and interprets the incredible journey.

Highlights

★ During winter, the park presents living-history programs demonstrating the lives of the early Spanish conquistadors. They dress in period clothing, including armor, and fire cross-bows and arquebus, a matchlock musket. Throughout the year, visitors can see the memorial's introductory AV.

Whiz Tips

When De Soto landed in Tampa Bay, he had the good fortune to find a survivor of an earlier expedition, Juan Ortiz, who had been living with the Florida natives for 12 years. Ortiz proved invaluable throughout their travels as an interpreter. Of the 600 Spaniards who left the Gulf shores in 1539, 322 reached Mexico in 1543. De Soto was not among them. He died, some said of fever, alongside the Mississippi and was laid to rest beneath the great river's waters. While they hadn't found gold, they did find pearls and they investigated a significant portion of the New World.

De Soto National Memorial

COURTESY NPS

Kids' Stuff

★ The park's AV and interpretive offerings are winners for children. Unlike most American history sites, this one portrays a far earlier period of European exploration. The Spanish influence in this region of the world is long-standing and their efforts on this escapade demonstrated their commitment to investigating the fullness of this strange land.

Access: On Tampa Bay 5 mi. W of Brandenton. **Days/Hours:** Daily 8-5:30. **Camping:** S at Sarasota, Myakka River State Park (76 sites, elec. & shwrs.). **For info.:** Superintendent, De Soto National Memorial, P.O.Box 15390, Bradenton, FL 34280-5390. 813/792-0458.

Everglades National Park

Allow: 1 day *Fee*

"What flows in from the north is the national park's lifeblood."

John G. Mitchell
American Heritage

At the southern tip of Florida sits an enormous natural park (second only to Yellowstone in the lower 48) which is slowly dying. For millennia, the Everglades served as the drainage of Florida. Countless creatures used the watery land to breed and feed. Today, even though the land has been set aside to protect those that remain, the waters that feed the land and ultimately its dependents, are being siphoned off by the growing numbers of bipedal sun-seekers. Today, you can still see many of this World Heritage Site's wildlife, but for how long?

Highlights

★ Winter, the park's dry season, is the best time for visitors to avoid the worst of the tiny flying blood-suckers and reap the bonus of wildlife sightings as the creatures collect at the remaining waterholes. There are gators, crocs, turtles, manatee and the rare Florida panther. The park's proliferation of bird species makes it a favorite for birders.

★ Although there are walks to take, the main attraction is the park's waterways. There's the 99-mile-long Wilderness Waterway which connects Everglades City to Flamingo or lesser trips you can take by boat. There are boat-accessible Chickee platforms with picnic tables and places to put your tent. Here you can enjoy the unique experience of dining while watching the water flow beneath your feet.

Whiz Tips

As you would expect, winter is the peak season. This is true of the interpretive offerings. Essentially, there are four main areas where you can join a ranger-led program. Shark Valley sports bike and tram tours, talks, walks and swamp stomps. Everglades City has the 10,000 Island and Kingston Key Boat Tours as well as a 5-6 hrs. canoe (reservations) journey. At Royal Palm, you can find out about the park's ecosystem and alligators. Birders love Flamingo, where they can bike, canoe or walk to see the feathered "exotica" of the 'glades.

Kids' Stuff

Although no specific children's programs are scheduled, most of the interpretive programs can be and are tailored by the rangers to meet the needs of the smaller of our species. If your kids are up to it (6 yrs. or older & able to swim), we'd recommend the canoe trip so they can get out on the water and really see what this park is about.

Most of the walking trails are over boardwalks, which place little demand on families other than making sure your kids don't climb off.

You can rent boats and houseboats at Flamingo if you want to go out on the water on your own. Everglades has an abundance of freshwater and saltwater fishing available. Bass and bluegills are the prime freshwater species, while the estuaries harbor snook, bonefish, tarpon, redfish and snapper.

Access: Main visitor center 12 mi. SW of

Everglades National Park COURTESY NPS

Homestead on Rte. 9336. **Days/Hours:** Shark Valley entrance 8-6; visitor center, winter 8-5. Visitor centers 8-5; excpt. Shark Valley 8:30-5:15. **Camping:** Park's Long Pine Key & Flamingo campgrounds (403 sites). **For info.:** Superintendent, Everglades National Park, P.O.BOX 279, Homestead, FL 33030. 305/247-6211.

Florida National Scenic Trail

Running north from Everglades National Park through Big Cypress National Preserve and several national and state forests is a 1,300 mile trail which has seen some development for public use.

For info.: Florida National Scenic Trail, Director, Recreation Management, U.S. Forest Service, P.O.Box 2417, Washington, DC 20013.

Fort Caroline National Memorial

Allow: .5 days *FREE*

On Jacksonville's eastern flank lies a reconstructed 16th century French fort and 35,000 acres of wetlands (Timucuan Ecological & Historic Preserve). The fort's history details the troubled relations between Spain and France in the 16th century as they each vied for territorial claims in the New World (see Castillo de San Marcos NM & Fort Matanzas NM, FL). The Huguenots, French Protestants, established the fort as part of their search for a place where they could practice their beliefs without persecution. The wetlands were vital to the Timucuan Indians' way of life.

Highlights

★ At Fort Caroline you can learn about this unusual chapter in French /Spanish relations. There were territorial disputes, religious differences and pirate attacks.

★ The Spanish Pond has an inter-

Nature Walk at Everglades National Park

pretive facility and trail to explain its natural and human history. Another interesting stop is the Ribault Monument, which commemorates Jean Ribault the leader of the Huguenots' attempts to colonize Florida.

Whiz Tips

❢ Fort Caroline was the Huguenots' second attempt to colonize the New World. When a small group of Fort Caroline's men mutinied and escaped south to raid Spanish vessels, they alerted Spain to the new intruders. A second group of mutineers further enraged the Spanish as they also attacked their vessels. Fearing Spanish vengeance, the Huguenots prepared to return home, but Ribault arrived with supplies and men. Feeling his oats, Ribault decided to attack the Spanish first. His attempt was doomed by a storm that swept his fleet south and destroyed it, leaving the fort open to an overland attack by the Spanish from St. Augustine. The Spanish showed no mercy as they slaughtered the unguarded residents. Ribault and his men were to meet a similar fate at Fort Matanzas (see Fort Matanzas N.Mem.). While France was abhorred by this blood-letting, it did nothing. Two years later a French Catholic, Dominique de Gourgues who had once been a Spanish galley slave, achieved revenge by leveling the renamed San Mateo settlement.

Kids' Stuff

★ The park has three nature trails, all of which are accessible to families. On weekends, tours are given which add background to a sometimes forgotten era of American history.

Access: 10 mi. E of Jacksonville on FL 10. **Days/Hours:** Daily 9-5 (clsd. Dec.25 & Jan.1). **Camping:** N near St. Marys, GA, Crooked River State Park (60 sites, elec. & shwrs.). S near St. Augustine, Anastasia State Recreation Area (139 sites, elec. & shwrs.). **For info.:** Superintendent, Fort Caroline National Monument, 12713 Fort Caroline Rd., Jacksonville, FL 32225. 904/641-7155.

Fort Jefferson National Monument

Allow: .5 days *FREE (boat or air: fee)*

Proof that massive defense spending on outmoded systems is not just a recent phenomenon, rifled cannon rendered Fort Jefferson ineffective (see Fort Pulaski NM, GA). It was to be the largest such 19th century fortification in the nation, with 8 ft. thick walls standing 50 ft. high and housing 450 guns and 1,500 men. Visitors to this national monument archipelago marvel at its sheer immensity, then take in the natural pleasures of surf and sea. The small islands are excellent rookeries for sea-going birds and their waters, pristine habitats for coral reefs chock full of marine life.

Highlights

★ There's a snorkeling area just off the fort's moat. There you can see "forests" of staghorn coral, sea ferns, sponges and colorful fishes.

★ A rare but still seen sight is a member of the area's namesake, three species of sea turtle: hawksbill, green & loggerhead.

Whiz Tips

❢ Rangers are available to assist you when you visit here.

❢ The atoll formation is known as the Dry Tortugas because of the lack of fresh water and the presence of turtles (tortuga). The Keys harbored pirates whose tales of buried treasure still excite imaginations. The buccaneers' presence became untenable when the U.S. took possession in 1821 and civilization in the form of a lighthouse took their place.

Kids' Stuff

★ The park brochure designates which waters are better for fishing, snorkeling and scuba diving. Many of the snorkeling areas are in waters less than 6 ft., prime places for children to learn the skill and pleasures of snorkeling.

Access: Air or boat. **Days/Hours:** Daylight. **Camping:** Park's Garden Key Campground. **For info.:** Superintendent, Fort Jefferson National Monument, c/o Everglades National Park, P.O.BOX 279, Homestead, FL 33030. 305/247-6211.

Fort Matanzas National Monument

Allow: 1 hr. *FREE*

Just south of St. Augustine, visitors can tour the remains of Fort Matanzas, a 1742 Spanish stone fortification. Matanzas, Spanish for slaughter, was named for two bloody massacres which occurred here almost two centuries before. The fort can be reached by a three minute FREE boat ride. The monument also contains a .5 mi. nature boardwalk and 1 mile of beach.

Highlights

★ The fort was built by Spaniards, desperate to thwart expansionist British aims. They realized their wooden works would not withstand an attack by the Georgian colonists and would leave St. Augustine in peril. The stone fort apparently served its purpose because after its completion, it never suffered an attack.

Whiz Tips

The area has a history of continental powers disputing territorial claims. Each tried to establish colonies to substantiate its ownership. In 1565, national and religious differences led to a horrible end for 245 French Huguenots. The Protestant Huguenots were besieged within France. France supported the Huguenots' desire for their own settlement because it would establish a French beachhead in Florida (see Fort Caroline NM) while relieving disputes at home. The Spanish, who, like French Catholics, viewed the Protestants as heretics, wanted to demonstrate their prior claim to this territory and felt justified in eradicating non-believers. The Huguenots under Jean Ribault decided to remove the Spanish threat by attack-

Biscayne National Park COURTESY BISCAYNE NP, NPS

ing St. Augustine. A tropical storm doomed their attempt and wrecked their fleet, leaving their settlement unprotected and them vulnerable. Somehow, the shipwrecked Huguenots got split up and created the opportunity the Spanish needed. Convinced the Spanish would beat them in a battle, the first group of 126 surrendered. The Spanish bound them then slaughtered all but 15, who claimed they were Catholic. The second group fell prey to the same strategy and 134 were executed, including Ribault, with the Catholics again being spared. Thus the French incursion in Florida was ended.

Kids' Stuff

★ Kids will fancy the brief boat ride and exploring the stone tower. The beach is another great place for children to frolic.

Access: 14 mi. S of St. Augustine on FL A1A. **Days/Hours:** Daily 8:30-5:30. **Camping:** N, near St. Augustine, Anastasia State Recreation Area (139 sites, elec. & shwrs.); S 15 mi. Flagler Beach State Recreation Area (34 sites, elec. & shwrs.); W. 15 mi. Faver-Dykes State Park. **For info.:** Superintendent, Fort Matanzas National Monument, 1 Castillo Dr., St. Augustine, FL 32084. 904/471-0116.

Gulf Islands National Seashore

Allow: 3-4 days *Fee*

Gulf Islands National Seashore has many unique features. It spans two states (Mississippi & Florida) while skipping one (Alabama). As you would expect of the nation's largest national seashore (150 mi.), it has excellent sandy beaches. It also includes five different fortifications, the nation's first tree preserve (1828) and the only bayou in the park service.

Highlights

★ For all its unique features, the most common use of the park is its beaches. The gently sloping shoreline is composed of gleaming, fine white sand that has been likened to "spun sugar."

★ Mississippi has one fort and Florida has two (out of four) you can visit. The park rangers conduct daily tours of the three forts (Fort Pickens & Barrancas year-round and Advanced Redoubt summer).

★ The Naval Live Oak Area was set aside by John Quincy Adams as a tree farm. The wood from this area makes an ideal building material for ships as it resists disease and decay and tolerates the salt water.

★ For many visitors the highlight of their stay is a visit to Davis Bayou to see its wealth of wildlife. The park puts on boat tours of the salt marsh on weekends.

Whiz Tips

! The rangers demonstrate fishing techniques, give nature talks and walks, demonstrate weapons firing and have history tours.

! Fort Pickens was built large enough to accommodate infantry to repel a land attack. Ironically, Mississippi's Fort Massachusetts was being completed at the same time as it was being made irrelevant by rifled cannons (see Fort Pulaski GA).

Kids' Stuff

★ Both sections of the park have a Jr. Ranger program allowing children to earn a special decal and certificate by completing specific educational tasks. On summer Saturdays, Mississippi puts on a one-hour environmental program specifically tailored to the wee ones.

★ This park has great beaches, boat rides, surf fishing, nature trails and forts to explore; a full slate for any child.

Access: MS park islands boat access only; Davis Bayou, off US 90. FL Johnson Beach SW on FL 292 from Pensacola; mainland forts off FL 295 at main entrance of Pensacola Naval Air Station; Fort Pickens & Naval Live Oaks on US 98 from Pensacola. **Days/Hours:** Daily (clsd. Dec.25). **Camping:** Davis Bayou, MS (51 sites, elec. & shwrs.); near Fort Pickens, FL (200 sites, elec. & shwrs.). **Teacher's Package:** Available. **For info.:** Superintendent, 3500 Park Rd., Ocean Springs, MS 39564. Superintendent, 1801 Gulf Breeze Pkwy., Gulf Breeze, FL 32561. FL: 904/934-2600, MS: 601/875

GEORGIA

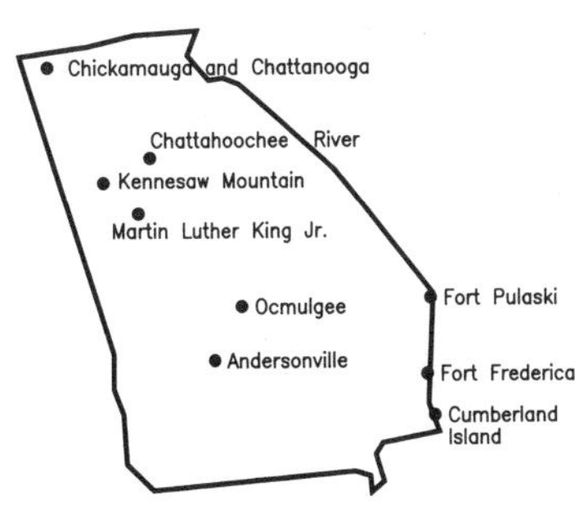

Andersonville National Historic Site

Allow: 1-2 hrs. *FREE*

Andersonville was a Confederate prisoner-of-war camp, designed to hold no more than 10,000 prisoners. During its infamous 14 months of existence, 45,000 Federal soldiers were confined here; close to 13,000 never walked out its gates. Like the rest of the Civil War, the tragedy seems so much greater because it was committed by people of one nation, one heritage and, in many cases, one blood. The park contains recreated remnants of the prison camp, a national cemetery and a memorial to American prisoners of war and MIAs.

Highlights

★ The reconstructed stockade corner and makeshift prisoners' tents demonstrate the futility of housing over 30,000 men. The overcrowding and subsequent collection of human waste caused rampant health hazards. The post-war trials indicated the Confederate keepers were so lax that prisoner lawlessness between the walls was unparalleled. Packs of ruthless prisoners preyed on the weak. Prisoners formed their own vigilante groups to restore order. Captain Henry Wirz, the prison commandant, was the first war crimes defendant hanged for his cruelty to prisoners through his lack of action.

★ Because Andersonville epitomizes such callous treatment of prisoners-of-war, it has become the shrine for all American prisoners-of-war. There's a museum devoted to all those courageous unfortunates.

Whiz Tips

In order to get the most from your visit here, start at the visitor center where you can get a FREE audio guide tape and see an introductory AV and exhibits.

Prisoner-of-war camps of this scale were a new phenomenon. Prior convention was to require prisoners to swear an oath to withdraw from fighting. The Confederates, in particular, were desperate for men and couldn't afford this luxury. Also, the Confederates would not honor these conventions with African Americans. They either gave them no quarter when they tried to surrender or forced them into slavery. As a result of these factors, General Grant refused to exchange prisoners-of-war. With the discontinuance of prisoner exchanges, prisoner-of-war camps had to be built and captured prisoners suffered greatly in both north and south camps.

❢ Clara Barton, the "Angel of the Battlefield," continued her humanitarian efforts after the Civil War by trying to identify Andersonville's dead. She felt their families could live in peace if they knew what became of them. Clara went on to found the American Red Cross (see Clara Barton NHS, D.C.).

Kids' Stuff

★ Depending on how much of the world's cruelty and inhumanity you feel your children can handle, Andersonville is certainly informative. If nothing else, it shows people were willing to address the problem by establishing conventions or rules for the treatment of prisoners.

Access: SW of Macon on I-75 & Rte. 49 or SE of Columbus on Rte. 49. **Days/Hours:** Daily 8-5. **Camping:** Andersonville City Campground (20 sites, elec. & shwrs), Whitewater Creek Park, & Georgia Veterans State Park (25 mi.). **Special Events:** Feb.'s last wknd., Opening of Camp Sumter re-enactment; Aug., Dedication of Cemetery re-enactment; Memorial Day programs. **Teacher's Package:** Available. **For info.:** Superintendent, Andersonville National Historic Site, Rte.1, Box 85, Andersonville, GA 31711. 912/924-0343.

Chattahoochee River National Recreation Area

Allow: 2 days *FREE*

"Son, don't be fooled by her beauty. She looks pretty and she is. She babbles like gossip and giggles like a girl. If you didn't care for beauty, looking at her way up here, you might be callin' her a piddlin' river. But, son, she ain't. I've seen her come out of the mountains like a wild stallion with logs in his mane."

Ralph McGill

The South and the Southerner

Andersonville National Historic Site

The National Park Service maintains over a dozen places along a 48 mi. stretch of the Chattahoochee for day use recreation. Floaters, hikers and anglers cart their gear here to take part in a natural pilgrimage to escape Atlanta's heat.

Highlights

★ As a Class I and II waterway, the river provides excellent waters for less-skilled kayakers, canoeists and rafters to test their mettle. During the various seasons, the floaters take in the multitude of rich colors the neighboring thick forests afford.

★ For landlubbers, the Cochran Fitness Trail has a 3 mi. activity path with 22 exercise stations challenging people of all levels of fitness. Some of the park units have large open fields which folks use for games, kite-flying and picnics.

Whiz Tips

Year-round interpretive programs on the area's cultural and natural history are offered at several units. Rangers give guided walks on a regular basis along the Paces Mill Loop Trail, at Palisades West and Powers Island.

An important part of the park's Summer Outreach Program is a rafting trip down a segment of the river rich in educational prospects.

Kids' Stuff

The park has a number of family nature trails. Jones Bridge, Island Ford, Vickery Creek, Gold Branch, Palisades, Cochran Shoals and Johnson Ferry have developed trails networking through them. At Palisades, kids can visit sandy beaches and see views of the river gorge. At Sope Creek in Cochran Shoals and at Vickery Creek, your children can see evidence of man's earlier settlements and industrial efforts. Kids find plenty of fishing (trout), rafting and canoeing opportunities.

Access: NE of Atlanta. **Days/Hours:** Daily. **Camping:** Red Top Mountain State Park (286 sites, elec. & showers) N off I-75; Lake Sidney Lanier 50 mi. N of Atlanta; Stone Mountain Park E off I-285. **For info.:** Superintendent, Chattahoochee River National Recreation Area, 1978 Island Ford Parkway, Dunwoody, GA 30350. 404/394-7912/8335/8324 or 952-4419.

Chattahoochee River National Recreation Area COURTESY NPS

Chickamauga & Chattanooga National Military Park

Allow: 1 day *FREE*

On the mountainous border of Tennessee and Georgia the armies of the North, first under General Rosecrans and then under General Grant and the armies of the South under General Braxton Bragg were to meet and meet again until a final account could be arrived at. The park encompasses the two major battlefields, Chickamauga, the Confederate victory and Chattanooga, the Federal victory.

Highlights

★ Chickamauga and Chattanooga were the first battlefields to enlist both northern and southern interests to establish memorials and to have legislation supporting their preservation. The result is more than 600 monuments, 700 plaques and 255 cannons. The most recognizable of these monuments is the 85 ft. Wilder Tower which has a well-used observation tower.

Whiz Tips

During the peak tourist season, the park has living history demonstrations and puts on car caravan tours.

Chickamauga, ironically, Creek for "River of Death," was a particularly bloody battle. The Confederates were able to breech and break the Federal lines. General Rosecrans acted on unconfirmed reports of a gap in his lines and ordered men from another area thus creating a gap in his lines which the Rebels flooded through. While the South was able to claim the battlefield, they suffered over 18,000 casualties to the North's 16,000, horrible numbers for both sides. President Lincoln had more to mourn than the Union loss at Chickamauga. His brother-in-law, Confederate General Benjamin Hardin Helm, died in the fighting.

Chattanooga launched General Grant as commander of all the Federal armies, pitting him against the formidable General "Bobby" Lee. Grant began his attack against Bragg's seemingly impregnable

Chickamauga & Chattanooga National Military Park

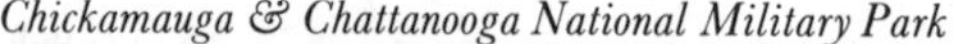

mountain stronghold by having his soldiers, dressed in their finest, march at the foot of the hills as though they were in some great parade. They then wheeled and charged up the slopes, gaining a foothold against the surprised defenders. Even during the heat of battle Bragg remarked, "There are not enough Yankees in all Chattanooga to come up here. Those are all my prisoners." At the battle's end, Bragg narrowly escaped becoming their prisoner.

Kids' Stuff

★ Like so many battlefields, this one is a great bicycling area as you and your family see and read about the events that took place here. The park has recently introduced a dramatic orientation program on the Battle of Chickamauga that kids really enjoy.

Access: S of Chattanooga, TN off I-75 on US 27. **Days/Hours:** daily, winter 8-4:45 & summer 8-5:45 (clsd. Dec.25). **Camping:** Tennessee's Harrison Bay State Park and Georgia's Cloudland Canyon State Park. **Special Events:** Late Sept. and late Nov., Anniversary Civil War programs; encampments during the year. **For info.:** Superintendent, Chickamauga & Chattanooga National Military Park, P.O.Box 2128, Fort Oglethorpe, GA 30742. 404/866-9241.

Cumberland Island National Seashore

Allow: 2-3 days *FREE (Ferry fee)*

Just north of the Florida border is Cumberland Island National Seashore. Visitors are limited to 300 at any one time. Once the almost exclusive territory of the super-rich Carnegies of Pittsburgh, the park service now manages most of the 16 mi. long island.

Highlights

★ This is truly a natural getaway. Although there are still a few residents motoring around, most of the island is designated as a wild area. There is sunbathing, beachcombing, hiking and even fishing to be found.

Whiz Tips

The mainland visitor center has an introductory AV and exhibits. On the island, there's another visitor center with more exhibits which help to orient you. The island is home to 227 animal species, most of which are birds, although alligators and Loggerhead sea turtles are among those who lay their eggs here.

The island has a surprisingly notable history. Colonel James Oglethorpe, who tried to capture St. Augustine from the Spaniards, is the first recognizable historic character to figure in the island's mythology. Brigadier Nathanael Greene, the Revolutionary War hero, bought part of the island but never lived to see out his plans.

Kids' Stuff

★ Certainly a visit is an adventure. The ferry ride and the island's remoteness are exciting. There is a lot to explore, but the beaches have no lifeguards, so proper caution should be exercised.

Access: E from I-95 on GA 40 to St. Marys River bank. Ferry: summer, daily & winter Th-M. **Days/Hours:** Daily 8-4:30. **Camping:** Reservation camping only (16 allowing up to 60 overnighters) (showers); near St. Marys, Crooked River State Park (60 sites, elec. & shwrs.). **Special Events:** On the first Sunday of every month, there are tours to visit Plum Orchard, Carnegie's 30 room mansion. **For info.:** Superintendent, Cumberland Island National Seashore, P.O.Box 806, St. Marys, GA 31558. 912/882-4335.

Fort Frederica National Monument

Allow: 1-2 hrs. *Fee*

This is the most northern of a string of national park forts which played key roles as French, English, and

Spanish interests battled for control of this part of the New World (see Florida's Fort Matanzas NM, Castillo de San Marcos NM, & Fort Caroline NMem). The Spanish came first and their hold was tenacious. After they had vanquished the French, the English colonies begun by James Edward Oglethorpe became their new concern. Oglethorpe founded Savannah and built Fort Frederica to protect her southern flank. At the fort you can see the remains of the military town which succeeded in its mandate and ended any threat of Spanish invasion.

Highlights

★ For most of us, the time before the American Revolution is a little-known period of American history. Yet, in the "Deep South," a colony was started that forbade slavery and rum and accepted peoples of differing religions and nationalities. The people were given equal-sized plots to farm and made their living supplying the soldiers posted there. As you wander the remains of the town, you can picture the orderliness that existed. For 12 years all was right in the universe. Unfortunately, the fort's success led to its eventual downfall.

Whiz Tips

❢ The park provides ranger-led walks explaining the life and times of the fort. In summer, there are living history presentations.

❢ The Georgia settlements were funded to relieve the poor conditions that existed in Britain by offering many a chance in the New World. Hoping to check Spanish incursion from spreading northward, the Crown granted Oglethorpe permission to set up Savannah and southern colonies. Realizing the more southward his towns were placed, the more likely the Spanish would object, Oglethorpe made sure he was properly defended. The Carolinians were becoming upset with the Spanish because run-away slaves were gaining freedom by fleeing south and converting to Catholicism. Hostilities broke out and Oglethorpe, ever the man of action, precipitated the fight by taking it to the Spanish at St. Augustine. Turned back by the formidable fortress, Castillo de San Marcos, he was forced to then defend Fort Federica. In July of 1742, 50 ships containing 2,000 Spanish soldiers attacked and were turned back. Another force was ambushed at Bloody Marsh and the dispute between the two powers dissipated.

Kids' Stuff

★ Our children love to see the living historians outfitted in clothes their forefathers wore. Besides being colorful, the uniforms always have a number of accouterments that children can't hear enough about and the costumed guides never tire of revealing.

Access: 12 mi. from Brunswick on St. Simons Island on Us 17 & Brunswick-St. Simons Causeway. **Days/Hours:** Daily 8-5. **Camping:** Near St. Marys, Crooked River State Park (60 sites, elec. & shwrs.). **For info.:** Superintendent, Fort Frederica National Monument, Rte. 9, Box 286-C, St. Simons Island, GA 31522. 912/638-3639.

Fort Pulaski National Monument

Allow: 1-2 hrs. *Fee*

Just east of Savannah lies Fort Pulaski, named for Casmir Pulaski, a Polish Count and Revolutionary War hero. Built in anticipation of war with Britain, the fort was part of a coastal system of defense meant to ward off foreign aggressors. Indeed these masonry forts were built so well that nearly all of the so-called Third System fortifications still stand (see Fort Jefferson NM, FL; Fort Point NHS, CA; Fort Washington Park, MD; Fort Sumter NM, SC and Gulf Islands NS, FL & MS). Fort

Pulaski's importance over these other forts was that it was the first masonry fort to prove vulnerable to rifled cannons. This military technological advance made these forts obsolete.

Highlights

★ The fort is still fascinating because it seems so formidable with its high brick walls, encircling moats filled with water and drawbridges with solid iron gates.

Whiz Tips

In the 1820s, America was concerned about possible European attacks and decided to fortify its coastal waters. Over the next 30 years, 30 forts were constructed along the Atlantic and Gulf coasts. Ironically, they were completed just in time for the Civil War, and in the case of Fort Pulaski, just in time to be occupied without a shot by Confederate troops. The Federal troops returned to Fort Pulaski in February the following year. With them they brought 10 experimental rifled cannons. Prior to these experimental weapons, gun barrels were smooth-bored. By cutting spiral grooves within the gun barrel (rifling), it was discovered that a bullet or cannon ball would acquire a spin, which enabled it to cover over twice the distance with a great deal more accuracy. These new engineering marvels were able to break down the walls that were once described by the U.S. Chief of Engineers as like trying to "bombard the Rocky Mountains." After only 30 hours, the South surrendered the fort and it remained in the North's hands for the remainder of the war.

Kids' Stuff

★ Kids love the look of this fort. The water moat and drawbridges stir up images of castles and great battles. There are plenty of rooms to investigate and the ramparts can be scaled for a look at the terrain.

Access: 15 mi. E of Savannah on US 80. **Days/Hours:** Daily 8:30-5:30 (summer extended hrs.) (clsd. Dec.25). **Camping:** Skidway Island State Park, just southeast of Savannah. **Teacher's Package:** Available. **For info.:** Superintendent, Fort Pulaski National Monument, P.O.Box 30757, Savannah, GA 31410-0757. 912/786-5787.

Fort Pulaski National Monument

Kennesaw Mountain National Battlefield Park

Allow: 2 hrs. *FREE*

"There is a boy here today who looks on war as all glory, but boys, it is all hell."
General William T. Sherman

On the northern outskirts of Atlanta sits sentinel-like Kennesaw Mountain. The Army of Tennessee fortified the hill in its attempt to halt General Sherman from advancing to the Confederate States' supply house - Atlanta. The park preserves the key points of the battle and by doing so serves as a wildlife sanctuary and scenic watch tower.

Highlights

★ The park is an excellent place to hike past the Kennesaw Mountain battle sites. As you trek through the hills, you get a real feeling for how difficult it must have been to attack. The hills are steep affording the defensive forces a winning advantage. A bonus for today's visitor is the view from the hilltops of Atlanta and the valleys below.

Whiz Tips

After Grant defeated the Army of Tennessee at Chattanooga, General William Tecumseh Sherman took over the drive south. By a series of flanking maneuvers, Sherman had pushed General Joseph E. Johnston's rebels back to the very environs of Atlanta. Sensing the Southern lines were thinly stretched, Sherman decided to see if he could break through them at Kennesaw Mountain and Cheatham Hill. Some feel this is the biggest mistake Sherman ever made as he lost 3,000 men unnecessarily. Returning to his successful flanking action, he caused the rebels to abandon their mountain fortress in order to defend Atlanta. Confederate President Davis replaced Gen. Johnston for timidness and placed General Hood in command. Hood promptly attacked Sherman, suffering damaging defeats. Sherman then took Atlanta and began his march through the South.

Kids' Stuff

★ Kennesaw Mountain Battlefield is somewhat unique among the many

Kennesaw Moutain National Battlefield Park–Overlook of Atlanta

national park battlefields because it is on a mountain. Most battles fought in the Civil War were fought on relatively flat surfaces. Few armies were willing to charge up so steep an incline to dislodge the enemy. The mountain's a great place for kids. They can expend their seemingly unending energies clambering through these hilly wilds looking for plaques explaining the events of 1864.

Access: 20 mi. NW of Atlanta off I-75. **Days/Hours:** Daily 8:30-5 (clsd. Dec.25 & Jan.1) **Camping:** Red Top Mountain State Park (286 sites, elec. & showers) N off I-75. **Teacher's Package:** Available. **For info.:** Superintendent, Kennesaw Mountain National Battlefield Park, P.O.Box 1610, Marietta, GA 30061. 404/427-4686.

Martin Luther King, Jr., National Historic Site

Allow: 2-3 hrs. *FREE*

"I have a dream that my four little children will one day live in a nation where they will not be judged by the color of their skin, but by the content of their character...When this happens, when we let it ring, we will speed the day when all God's children, black men and white men, Jews and Gentiles, Protestants and Catholics, will be able to join hands and sing in the words of the old Negro spiritual: 'Free at last, free at last, thank God Almighty, we're free at last'."

Martin Luther King Jr.

Located just east of downtown Atlanta is the very orderly neighborhood where Martin Luther King Jr. grew up and used as his home base for much of his life. The area was an enclave for upper middle class Americans of African descent. The park service preserves many of the furnished homes and buildings to show how they appeared during Reverend King's childhood. In addition, there are several modern architectural triumphs that have been erected to honor Martin Luther King Jr.

Highlights

★ The birth home of young M.L., as he was called, is available for touring with a park ranger. His home is very similar to any middle-class home of the era. Young M.L., according to the park service, was a very typical boy. He loved sports, was close to his sister and incurred the usual amount of parental discipline.

★ The Center for Non-Violent Social Change acts as a museum for the site. There is a heart-rending Time-Line exhibit here detailing Martin Luther King's accomplishments and the civil rights events of the era. Month by month, year by year, you see the legal battles, the human struggles, the protests and sadly, the deprivations committed as a group of people struggle to achieve equality in the "Land of the Free." The center also has an AV presentation on Reverend King.

Martin Luther King, Jr., NHS

COURTESY NPS

Whiz Tips

Whether by chance or design, it is clear that, although Martin Luther King's childhood was unremarkable, he was destined for greater things. A year after Reverend King accepted a pastoral position in Montgomery, Alabama, Rosa Parks was arrested for refusing to move to the back of the bus so a white man could sit. As Ramsey Clark, former Attorney General, said; "If Rosa Parks had not refused to move to the back of the bus, you and I might never have heard of Dr. Martin Luther King." King was chosen to head the protest group defending Ms. Parks and boycotting the bus company. From that day on, Martin Luther King Jr. devoted himself to leading a non-violent struggle for African American equality. He achieved a Ph.D. in theology and studied Gandhi's teachings of non-violence in India so he could better accomplish his goal. It was while pursuing this goal that he was assassinated in Memphis, Tennessee on April 4, 1968. While it is impossible to measure the cumulative effects of his efforts, he received a Nobel Peace Prize for his efforts. Since his death, the nation honors Dr. King with a national holiday and it is the rare large city in the union that does not have a street or boulevard named for him.

Martin Luther King, Jr., NHS

COURTESY NPS

Kids' Stuff

★ It's difficult to determine at which age children should be introduced to the depressing conditions in which Americans of African descent were subjected. For those children who are aware of Dr. Martin Luther King Jr. and the civil rights movement, visiting here by can be a stirring and highly educational trip.

Access: E of I-75 & I-85 in downtown Atlanta. **Days/Hours:** Birth home, Daily, summer 10-6 & winter 10-5. King Center, daily, summer 9-8 & winter 10-5:30. Ebenezer Baptist Church, M-F 9-4. **Camping:** Red Top Mountain State Park (286 sites, elec. & showers) N off I-75. **Teacher's Package:** Available. **For info.:** Superintendent, Martin Luther King, Jr., National Historic Site, 522 Auburn Ave., NE, Atlanta, GA 30312. 404/331-3920.

Ocmulgee National Monument

Allow: 2 hrs. *Fee*

"[The Cherokee Indians] are as ignorant as we are, by what people or for what purpose those artificial hills were raised."

William Bartram, from his study of Ocmulgee in 1773-1777.

On the southeast outskirts of Macon, Georgia, is the most comprehensive example of 12,000 years of continuous Native American habitation in the U.S. Looking much like a slightly wild city park, the site includes a reconstructed earthlodge and two unique hillocks, the Great Temple Mound and Lesser Temple Mound.

Highlights

★ The earthlodge represents a ceremonial chamber used by the Mississippian culture in AD 1000. Inside, an audio accompaniment transports you back in time to explain the facets of the structure.

Whiz Tips

One of the great American mysteries of the last century was who built these large mounds. It was widely assumed that the Native Americans had not reached this level of sophistication (see Mound City Group NM, OH & Effigy Mounds NM, IA).

The film "People of the Macon Plateau" explains the stages of Native American habitation of the region. The early peoples are delineated primarily by their diets. Paleo-Indians were hunter/gatherers and the Archaic culture supplemented their diets with seasonal plants and shellfish. Around 1000 BC, the Woodland people began farming squash, gourds, corn and beans. They were pushed aside by the flourishing Mississippian people, who had complex villages, social structures and sophisticated farming techniques. It was at this stage that the earthlodges and large mounds were built for formal ceremonies. After the Mississippian culture waned (perhaps from succeeding crop failures), the Lamar culture, which Hernando de Soto met, occurred. The Lamar people incorporated farming and hunting and built a palisaded town. The last Native Americans to live here were the Creeks, a great civilization that used the town as a trading center with the British until they were defeated in the Yamassee War (see Horseshoe Bend NMP, AR).

Kids' Stuff

There are a number of short trails which, taken together, make for an interesting walk with kids (just make sure you're mosquito-proofed). You wind past the Temples, a trading post, the village site, swamps and prehistoric trenches.

Access: E Macon on US 80. **Days/hours:** Daily, 9-5 (clsd. Dec.25 & Jan.1) **Camping:** Bibb County operates the nearby Tobesofkee Recreation Area. **Special Events:** In March, Torchlight Tours (reservations). **Teacher's Package:** Available. **For info.:** Superintendent, Ocmulgee National Monument, 1207 Emery Hwy., Macon, GA 31201. 912/752-8257.

Ocmulgee National Monument

Trail of Tears National Historic Trail

Beginning June 1838 through March 1839, 15,000 Cherokee Native Americans were marched from their ancestral homelands in North Carolina, Tennessee, Georgia and Alabama to the so-called "Indian Territory" in what is now Oklahoma and Arkansas (see Horseshoe Bend NMP, AL). Their route is marked for visitors to follow.

For info.: Trail of Tears National Historic Trail, Southeast Region, National Park Service, 75 Spring St., SW, Atlanta, GA 30303.

GUAM

American Memorial Park

Located in the Northern Mariana Islands is a combination recreational park and memorial for those who died in the Marianas Campaign of WW II. The affiliated site offers swimming, picnicking, jogging, sports and boating.

Access: N of Garapan Village in Tanapag Harbor on the island of Saipan. **Days/Hours:** Daily. **For info.:** American Memorial Park, P.O.Box 198 CHRB, Saipan, CM 96950.

War in the Pacific NHS

COURTESY NPS

War in the Pacific National Historical Site

Allow: .5 days *FREE*

Like a bull's-eye in the center of the Japanese-controlled Pacific, Guam shared the devastations of World War II with its Asian neighbors. The park retains the debris of the fighting and exhibits films, photos and memorabilia detailing the events at seven sites on the island's western flank. Like most places, Guam was to experience the trauma of invasion at least twice. With lightning quickness, the Japanese occupied most of the Pacific Islands and facing mainlands shortly after crippling the U.S. fleet at Pearl Harbor (see USS Arizona NMem., HI). For almost three years the Japanese ruled Guam. On July 21, 1944, U.S. forces invaded, and by Aug. 10 the island was reclaimed.

Highlights

★ The Asan Units have most of the elements reflecting the American invasion. Sunken remains of American military equipment are found by divers offshore. Entrenched Japanese fortifications are hidden in the hills. At the museum you can learn more about the Pacific theater of operations.

★ Hiking to the Piti Guns has a two-fold reward: three Japanese coastal defense guns and scenic overlooks.

Whiz Tips

❢ Ranger-led tours of the museum exhibits are available upon request. The park seeks to factually relate the events of the War in the Pacific, including those events that precipitated it. The Guamanians were poorly treated during Japanese occupation and severely punished for noncompliance of strict regulations. During the 1944 fighting on Guam, the Americans suffered 7,000 casualties while the Japanese force of 18,500 men had 17,500 casualties, roughly 95% of their complement.

❢ Guam was under Spanish rule until the Spanish-American War at the end of the last century. With Puerto Rico, it became a U.S. territory in 1898. Since 1950, it has been under the guidance of the Dept. of the Interior. It has a governor and a single legislature.

Kids' Stuff

★ The park is suitable for children who have studied WW II's Pacific campaign. There are "hands-on" demos of products made from endangered species, like turtle-shell jewelry, crocodile purses, stuffed birds and sea turtles in the visitor center. Another "hands-on" experience is to carefully examine deactivated WW II weapons. Parents should be cautious because live ammunition is still found on the park grounds and can explode if tampered with.

Access: By plane. **Days/Hours:** Daily, M-F 7:30-3:30 & S&S 8:30-2 (clsd. Thanksgiving, Dec.25 & Jan.1). **Camping:** The Government of Guam has its own camping facilities. **Special Events:** On July 21st, liberation celebration. **For info.:** Superintendent, War in the Pacific National Historical Site, P.O.Box FA, Agana, Guam 96910. 671/472-7240.

War in the Pacific National Historical Park COURTESY NPS

HAWAII

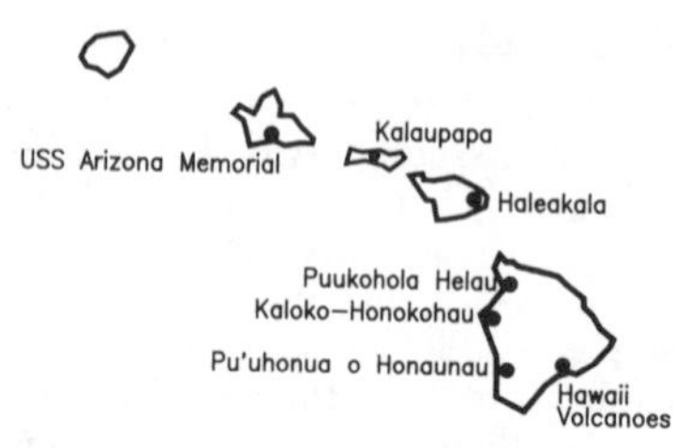

Haleakala National Park

Allow: 1-2 days *Fee*

"The dormant volcano at Haleakala, on the island of Maui, is a majestic bowl of copper, black and purple volcanic matter punctuated by monumental cinder cones."

Francine du Plessix Gray
Hawaii: The Sugar Cane Fortress

Towering 29,000 feet above the ocean floor and 10,000 feet above sea level, Haleakala Crater National Park has two areas visitors can visit to see the effects of recent volcanic activity. Both have risks. Visitors who take the switchbacks up 7,000 feet to the Crater District hope for a clear day. While those who skirt around to the east on the dramatic, twisty coastal road, pray for the spectacular waterfalls of Kipahulu to be brimming.

Highlights

★ The Crater District is often windy, rainy and 30 degrees F. cooler than the beach, so leave the flip-flops at the hotel. However, if the visibility is optimal, expect panoramic views of Maui and the opportunity to gaze at or journey down into the 19-sq. mi. volcanic crater. This region features endemic vegetation and colorful Hawaiian birds like the 'i'iwi, 'apapane and 'amakihi. Interestingly, although the mountain-top receives a considerable amount of rain, much of its vegetation is adapted to desert conditions because the cinder surface can't retain the falling water. The

Haleakala National Park

plants must store rainwater when it falls as they can't rely on their roots to soak it out of the earth.

★ Kipahulu is a conundrum. Each twist and turn offers lush, wild, mountainous coastal scenery but at a price. This road ranks as one of the most difficult we have ever tackled. Unfortunately, the best time to see the waterfalls (incorrectly known as the "Seven Pools") is during or immediately following a rainstorm when they are in their prime. We say "unfortunately," because the road is very treacherous when wet and slippery.

Whiz Tips

❢ The park staff regularly schedules talks or takes people on hikes, explaining the park's geology, native plants and birds and Hawaiian legends.

❢ The prognosis for Haleakala is that it is a dormant and soon-to-be extinct volcano. As the Pacific Plate slides the Hawaiian Islands northwestward away from the volcanic fissure in the earth's crust, the possibility of an eruption becomes increasingly remote. Haleakala's last volcanic activity was two centuries ago (very recent in geologic time). Currently, the big island, Hawaii is over a "hot spot" and at Hawaii Volcanoes NP, you can envision what Haleakala went through. The islands of Oahu and Kauai were formed earlier than Maui and serve as examples of what Maui will become.

Kids' Stuff

★ At Haleakala Crater, families can hike into the crater on the Sliding Sands and the Halemau'u trails. You'll be trekking over rugged ground at over 7,000 ft. above sea level, so dress accordingly. A favorite outing for visitors is to come to the Crater District for sunrise. Families find that catching the setting sun instead can be equally rewarding, warmer and more in tune with their children's daily routines. Families should carry food and drink as there is not even a pop machine up at the park.

★ There are many short child-size loop trails in the Kipahulu District. The park cautions all visitors to be very careful around the freshwater pools because of rapid water level changes and submerged rocks.

Access: On Maui island. **Days/Hours:** House of the Sun Visitor Center, daily sunrise-2:45; H.Q. Visitor Center, daily 7:30-4; Kipahulu, daily limited hrs. **Camping:** Park's Hosmer Grove Campground (25 persons) and Oheo Campground. **For info.:** Superintendent, Haleakala National Park, P.O.Box 369, Makawao, Maui, HI 96768. 808/572-7749.

Hawaii Volcanoes National Park

Allow: 2-3 days *Fee*

"The Sandwich Islands remain my idea of the perfect thing in the matter of tropical islands. I would add another story to Mauna Loa's 16,000 feet if I could, and make it particularly bold and steep and craggy and forbidding and snowy;"

Mark Twain
More Tramps Abroad

Covering 344 sq.mi. of the "Big Island", Hawaii Volcanoes National Park preserves three active craters and threatened indigenous plants and wildlife. Although it's hard to tell, Mauna Loa is one of the tallest mountains on earth. It begins 15,000 ft. below the water's surface and rises 13,680 ft. above sea level, totaling almost 30,000 ft.

Highlights

★ By taking the Crater Rim road, you can see the aftermath of volcanic activity. Rain Forests that have gained footage in the soil stand next to areas still devastated from the spillage of molten rock. The Chain of Craters area has huge craters and lava flows. The drive has pull-outs for overlooks and parking areas for hikers. The best way to see the park is to don thickly treaded boots and a backpack.

★ Late afternoon is the time to visit Hilina Pali for a great view of the coastline. To get a closer look, HI 13 takes you along the brink to Puu Loa past a large concentration of petroglyphic art.

Whiz Tips

The park has evening programs and interpretive walks to help explain the park. Typical day programs include Thurston Lava Tube, walking Crater Rim and eruption interpretation at a live lava flow site. The Thomas A. Jagger Museum is not to be missed.

Although all the Hawaiian Islands are products of volcanic activity, the more northern an island is, the older is its formation. All are produced by shield volcanoes which produce relatively gentle slopes and less explosive eruptions. It is estimated the lava flowing up out of the caldera might be travelling as far as 35 mi. from the earth's depths. When the force is unable to push the molten lava to the surface, either because it has lessened and/or the volcano has grown so far from the source, the volcano will be still and is deemed dormant. A dormant volcano could still explode if the force increases. In the northern islands, the volcanoes are deemed to be extinct because the Pacific Plate has moved them from the source of the pressure.

Lava Flow

COURTESY GARY MAUSER

Because of their relative isolation and recent (in geological time) formation, the Hawaiian Islands hosted only those flora and fauna that were borne by wind and wave. These few specimens evolved at their own pace and design. It wasn't until the coming of the Polynesians that any mammal other than bats populated these shores. Since that time, Polynesians and others have introduced a host of plants and animals which have for the most part displaced the original owners of the land. Here at Hawaiian Volcanoes, you can still see some of the original plants and birds the first Hawaiians encountered.

Kids' Stuff

★ This is an exciting place for kids to visit. Children can see the effects of recent volcanic activity and appreciate the nature's power. The evidence is not just in the devastating lava flows and explosive craters but the ability of life to catch hold where there appears to be nothing to support it.

Access: 29 mi. SW of Hilo off HI 11 on Island of Hawaii. **Day/Hours:** Daily 8:30-4:30. **Camping:** Park's 3 FREE drive-in campgrounds; Kipuka Nene, Namakani Paio and Kamoamoa. **Special Events:** Jan., the Kilauea Volcano Wilderness Marathon and Rim Runs; Ho'ola'ulea ma Kamoamoa, a one-day Hawaiian cultural festival. **Teacher's Package:** Available. **For info.:** Superintendent, Hawaii Volcanoes National Park, P.O.Box 52, Hawaii, HI 96718-0052. 808/967-7311.

Kalaupapa National Historical Park

Allow: .5 days *FREE (tour fee)*

The physical and social impacts of Hansen's Disease, or leprosy, took Hawaiians over a century to comprehend. Fear for their own safety led people to shun and denigrate those who had fallen ill. Kalaupapa is Hawaii's story of how they dealt with the problem. It is not a story to be proud of. However, there are heroes, those who came voluntarily to help the ill and the ill themselves as they strived to maintain their dignity and make of life what they could. A special colony was set aside and the ill were brought by boat and abandoned to their own wiles. Food was lowered over the cliff to them but they had to establish their own social order to survive. By special permit from the Hawaii State Dept. of Health and the park service, people over the age of 16 can visit this "melancholy landing." (Robert Louis Stevenson).

Highlights

★ Some of the afflicted still reside here. Through them, the exhibits and the rangers who interpret the community, you can learn about man's struggle for humanity.

Whiz Tips

So strong was the fear of leprosy, that the people who contracted the disease came to be known by the disease and were called "lepers." The term evolved to denote individuals whom people didn't want to be around as in "social leper." This pejorative is frowned on today like all slurs that take away the individuality of a person and replaces it with a stigma. Leprosy or Hansen's Disease was found to be an infectious disease in 1873, shortly before Father Damien, a Belgian priest, decided to go to the colony and help the people who had been banished there. Father Damien eventually contracted the disease even though the odds of doing so are about 5%. Like others with leprosy, it is assumed the disease greatly shortened his life. His courage in attending these people encouraged others like Mother Mari-

Hawaiian Nene (goose)

anne and Brother Dutton who also came to help.

Kids' Stuff

★ It is illegal for persons under the age of 16 to visit the park. The settlement can be viewed from the overhanging cliffs of Palaau State Park.

Access: Windward coast of the Island of Molokai. **Days/Hours:** n/a. **Camping:** Palaau State Park. **For info.:** Superintendent, Kalaupapa National Historical Park, Kalaupapa, HI 96742.

Kaloko-Honokohau National Historical Park

The park preserves the site of an important pre-European arrival Hawaiian settlement. Legend has it that King Kamehameha I (the Great), the first Hawaiian king, is buried here. There are over 200 archaeological features within the park. It also includes coastline, 3 large fishponds and a house site. It remains without visitor facilities.

For info.: Superintendent, Kaloko-Honokohau National Historical Park, c/o Pu'uhonua o Honaunau NHP, P.O.Box 128, Honaunau, Kona, HI 96726. 808/328-2326.

Pu'uhonua o Honaunau National Historical Park

Allow: 1 hr. *Fee*

On the big island, Hawaii, is a park detailing the social and religious culture of the original Hawaiians. This is where the great kings lived, died and were placed. It is their spirits which provided the aura allowing wrong-doers and sanctuary seekers a new life. The tall coconut palms serve to restore the historical scene. The buildings and images have been reconstructed according to accounts while the three pu'uhonua temple foundations are authentic. Living history "Polynesians" practicing the duties of the day are very willing to explain their tasks and other aspects of the park.

Highlights

★ The Americanization of the islands often leaves visitors with a sense of loss. At this park you can get a real appreciation of how the strict social structure and religious practices melded. Sure, the punishments were harsh. In war, all the defeated people were killed. In peace, lawbreakers faced only one punishment, death. But there was a way to survive. If the threatened could reach a place of sanctuary, a pu'uhonua, they could undergo a cleansing and begin their lives anew. Near the pu'uhonua are the chiefs' quarters, where the bones of at least 23 Hawaiian leaders (ali'i status) are interred in Hale-o-Keawe Temple. Their position was protected by the harsh laws restricting commoners from entering the grounds. The huge wall between the pu'uhonua and their living quarters provided another measure of safety.

Whiz Tips

❢ Try to catch the talks at the visitor center, which are held at 10, 10:30, 11, 2:30, 3 & 3:30 or listen to the taped audio presentations. The interpretive plaques and traditionally-dressed rangers introduce visitors to another way of life, another language. You learn about "mana", a special power embodied by the ali'i, his possessions and even the ground he walked upon. When a chief died his bones were placed in the "heiau," or temple where his "mana" remained. It was the collection of chiefs' bones here that gave this pu'uhonua such great power. Breakers of "kapu," the religious rules, could avoid death by outrunning the angry people or by swimming the bay and reaching here. The reason why death was proscribed is that the people believed the crops took revenge if the people didn't. Therefore, forgiven misdeeds, which have not been sanctified by the priests, would result in life-threatening volcanoes or tidal waves or some other natural disaster.

Kids' Stuff

★ At the visitor center, you can pick up a copy of the rules for "konane," a Hawaiian game similar to checkers. There's a stone "board" along the nature trail where you can play "konane" with your kids. Keone'ele Cove has a swimming beach.

Access: 30 mi. S of Keahole Airport on HI 160, Island of Hawaii. **Days/Hours:** Daily 7:30-midnight, visitor center 7:30-5. **Camping:** Hawaii Volcano NP & Spencer County Beach Park (415/392-8173). **Special Events:** Wknd. closest July 1st, FREE 3 day Hawaiian cultural festival includes a royal procession, participatory arts & crafts, hula performances, food tasting, canoe rides and a hukilau in the cove. **For info.:** Superintendent, Pu'uhonua o Honaunau National Historical Park, P.O.Box 129, Honaunau, Kona, HI 96726. 808/328-2326.

Puukohola Heiau National Historic Site

Allow: 1 hr. *FREE*

This is a place where legend and fact mingle. Under the waters of the bay are the remains of Hale O Ka Puni Heiau, a temple to the shark god whose minions can still be seen cutting through the surface. Mailekini Heiau temple predates King Kamehameha, the first ruler of all the Hawaiian Islands. Its foundations are all that remain. The famed Pu'ukohola Heiau which Kamehameha constructed at the bidding of priests who said this was the first step to his supremacy, was also destroyed. Today, you can see a reconstructed temple (the temples are restricted to native Hawaiians for religious purposes).

Highlights

★ This park designates the genesis of Hawaii as one nation. Although peopled by Polynesians, each region was a state of its own, villages bat-

Puukohola Heiau National Historic Site COURTESY NPS

tled, formed allegiances, inter-married, shared social and religious beliefs but resisted bowing to one leader.

Whiz Tips

Kamehameha the Great's rise to rule all the islands was foreordained. According to legend, before his birth there was a prediction that a "killer of chiefs" was to be born. Other chiefs heard this and tried to kill him but his mother had sent him away to safety. Whatever his beginnings, he grew to be a feared warrior. He controlled the northeastern section of Hawaii and warred on the other chiefs. The famous prophet, Kapoukahi, predicted Kamehameha would prevail if he built a temple honoring the war god, Ku-ka'ili-moku on Pu'ukohola, the hill of the whale. Kamehameha had to battle the other Hawaiian chiefs while trying to complete this task because they believed in the power gained from such a feat. His main Hawaii Island rival, Keoua, lost many of his men in a volcanic eruption as he sought to attack Kamehameha. True or not, Keoua voluntarily came to the temple's initiation ceremonies knowing he would be killed and end up as the sacrificial offering. Within four years, Kamehameha subdued the rest of the islands fulfilling the prediction. After his death, his son renounced the traditional Hawaiian beliefs and destroyed the temples.

Kids' Stuff

★ The story about this place fascinates children. We're talking warring chiefdoms, volcanoes and magical powers. There's enough color in this story to keep any child's attention and fire their imaginings. For those children who like reality, show them black or white tipped reef sharks circling in the bay.

Access: NW shore on the Island of Hawaii. **Days/Hours:** Daily 7:30-4. **Camping:** Nearby Spencer County Beach Park (415/392-8173). **Special Events:** Second Aug. wknd., FREE Pacific Asian American Heritage Day includes a cultural festival, a royal procession, hula presentations and participatory arts and crafts. **For info.:** Superintendent, Puukohola Heiau National Historic Site, P.O.Box 44340, Kawaihae, Hawai'i, HI 96743. 808/882-7218.

U.S.S. Arizona Memorial

Allow: 1-2 hrs. *FREE*

"We were about to change an island of dreams into a living hell."

Tatsuya Ohtawa, Japanese pilot at Attack on Pearl Harbor's 40th anniversary

Separated by the Pacific Ocean, culture, language and race, two rising world forces, Japan and America, chose war as a means of settling their differences. Recognizing their economic and resource deficiencies in such a battle, the Japanese sought to gain the upper hand by crippling the larger foe. On that fateful December Sunday, the Japanese launched an air and naval attack on the still-sleeping Pearl Harbor Naval Base, killing 2403 people and smashing 347 aircraft and 21 ships while only losing 129 men, 6 subs and 103 aircraft. This memorial while acknowledging all losses, is especially dedicated to the entire crew of the U.S.S. *Arizona* who went down with the ship.

Highlights

★ The U.S. Navy shuttles visitors across the water to the gleaming white Memorial where you can see down into the water where the battleship rests. The names of the 1,177 sailors and marines who went to their watery graves are engraved on a Vermont marble wall within a shrine chamber.

Whiz Tips

The rangers provide an introductory talk and show an AV about the attack. The visitor center has a museum explaining the events leading

up to December 7, 1941 and its aftermath (see War in the Pacific NHP, GU).

Interestingly, the Japanese Military School had been preparing its forces for almost a decade by quizzing its graduating students on how they would conduct a surprise attack on Pearl Harbor. Luck was on the Japanese side. From the time their fleet left northern Japan on November 26, they were protected from discovery by storms and fog. Early December 7th, they were in position, 240 mi. north of Oahu, to launch their attack. Aircraft and midget submarines were sent to Pearl Harbor to wreck havoc. With the cry of "Tora, Tora, Tora" to signal the onslaught, they certainly accomplished their mission but the damage they caused was short-lived as the American fleet was quick to recover. Admiral Yamamoto, the Chief of Japanese Combined Fleet, put it best when he said they had "awakened a sleeping giant and filled him with a terrible resolve."

Kids' Stuff

The children enjoyed the boat ride over to the memorial and seemed to grasp its importance. Parents shouldn't underestimate the kids pleasure at seeing "real" sailors up close. For students who have studied WW II, particularly the Pacific Campaign, the memorials' presentations and artifacts are an excellent way to reinforce their learning.

There used to be a restriction to children over 45 in. It has been removed.

Access: Just W of Honolulu International Airport. **Days/Hours:** Daily 7:30-5. **Camping:** Off SR 92 from Honolulu, Sand Island. **For info.:** Superintendent, USS *Arizona* Memorial, Honolulu, HI 96818. 808/422-0561.

U.S.S. Arizona Memorial

COURTESY NPS

IDAHO

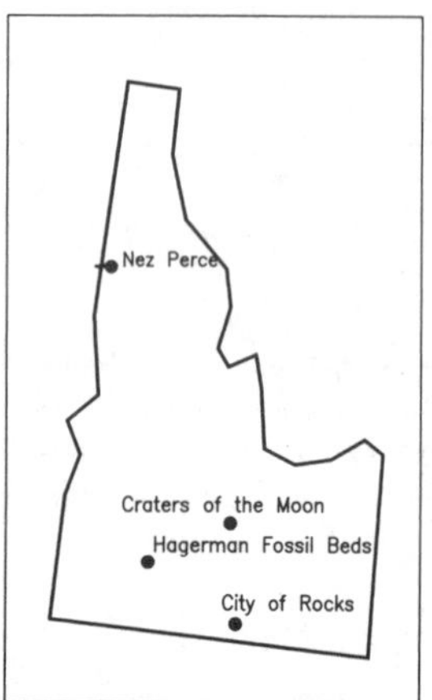

City of Rocks National Reserve

Recently designated, the reserve oversees scenic granite spires and remnants of the California Trail. Idaho's City of State Rocks State Park which has facilities is within the reserve.

For info.: City of Rocks National Reserve, 2647 Kimberley Rd. E, Twin Falls, ID 83301.

Craters of the Moon National Monument

Allow: 1-2 days *Fee*

"But for those who know it and have stood within its strength, it is a splendid and limitless area upon which thousands of centuries will leave almost no mark of change; and they love its caves and craters and the wild terracing of its scene."

The Federal Writers Project of the WPA
Idaho: A Guide in Word and Picture

About the time of Christ's birth, the land calmed after 13,000 years of primordial screaming. Geologists call the remaining pained expression; cinder cones, fissure vents, lava flows, volcanic cones and lava caves. They also wait, expecting another outburst of volcanic activity to once again mutilate the earth's surface. While most people associate lava and craters with a volcano, volcanic action often manifests itself in fields of fissures and openings rather than one large mountain. This is the case here.

Highlights

★ The 7 mi. loop road takes you into the prime points of interest. North Crater Flow Trail wends its way through the lava leading you to a volcano vent. An added feature to Devils Orchard is the June/July blossoming of dwarf monkeyflowers. The Inferno Cone Viewpoint offers visitors a view of Big Cinder Butte, one

Craters of the Moon NM

COURTESY JIM MILLER

of the world's biggest basaltic cinder cones. The Spatter Cones look like baby volcanoes. At the Tree Molds you can see how trees encased in lava left a mold when they rotted away. The last stop takes you to the four lava caves: Dewdrop, Boy Scout, Beauty & Surprise and Indian Tunnel.

Whiz Tips

Summer interpretive programs understandably emphasize the monument's geology. Cave walks are popular programs.

The monument has three kinds of lava: "aa," "pahoehoe" and lava bombs. The aa, Hawaiian for "hard on the feet" can easily cut boot soles. Pahoehoe, Hawaiian for "ropy" is relatively smooth. The lava bombs are quite literally balls of lava that have been launched by the volcano, hardening as they fall.

Lava tube caves are formed by a lava flow when the exterior cools and hardens, providing a tube through which the molten lava can still flow. Eventually, the river of lava dissipates, leaving the hollow tunnel.

Kids' Stuff

★ Our children enjoy visiting these strange landscapes. Their imaginations are captured by the earth's spewing forth of molten rock, ash and cinders. Exploring lava caves has also proven to be another winner. Our children enjoy the suspense of exploring in the dark with only a flashlight to guide them.

Access: 18 mi. W of Arco on US 20, 26 & 93. **Days/Hours:** Daily, summer 8-6 & winter 8-4:30 (clsd. Thanksgiving, Dec.25 & Jan.1). **Camping:** Park's Lava Flow Campground (52 sites). **Teacher's Package:** Available. **For info.:** Superintendent, Craters of the Moon National Monument, P.O.Box 29, Arco, ID 83213. 208/527-3257.

Hagerman Fossil Beds National Monument

A recent addition to the park service holdings, the park preserves an extraordinarily rich finding of fossils embedded along the banks of the Snake River. The monument allows paleontologists to conduct research

Craters of the Moon National Monument COURTESY JIM MILLER

for display and interpretation of their finds.

For info.: Hagerman Fossil Beds National Monument, 2647 Kimberley Rd. E, Twin Falls, ID 83301.

Nez Perce National Historical Park

Allow: 1-2 days *FREE*

"This isn't scenery. It is desperate grandeur. It is remorseless manifestation. It is wild water and wild stone, wild beyond the reach of belief, and it is beautiful."

A.B. Gutherie Jr.
American Panorama: West of the Mississippi

And it was the Nez Perce's land when Lewis and Clark came calling in 1806. It was never ceded to the United States by a most of the Nez Perce people. When the Nez Perce tried to enforce their right to their lands, they were chased across the Rockies almost to the Canadian border before succumbing to the government's will. The park traces the tribe's historical boundaries and noteworthy places, including 24 sites along 400 miles of road. Most visitors begin at the Spalding Visitor Center and plan their stops with the aid of the rangers.

Highlights

★ The Spalding Visitor Center exhibits Nez Perce artifacts. In town, are the Indian Agency, the grist mill, the sawmill and the Spalding Mission, as well as Watson's Store, Lapwai mission and the Presbyterian church. Nearby Fort Lapwai still has an 1883 officer's quarters. St. Joseph's Mission was the first Roman Catholic mission for the Nez Perce. Two sites, Ant and Yellowjacket and Coyote's Fishnet, represent traditional Nez Perce legends. The Lenore archaeological site provided evidence of over 10,000 years of habitation.

★ At White Bird Battlefield, the Nez Perce demonstrated their ability to fight the U.S. Army on equal terms (U.S. losses 34, Nez Perce 0). The one-way loop trail has interpretive markers detailing the encounter.

Nez Perce National Historical Park COURTESY NPS

Unfortunately for the Nez Perce, their's was a battle of attrition and the U.S. government had the numbers.

Whiz Tips

! During summer, the rangers give daily interpretive programs on the Nez Perce traditional art forms and tipi pitching. Another regular feature is the afternoon cultural demonstrations on traditional beadworking, leatherwork and cornhusk-weaving.

! When Lewis and Clark came over the mountain passes from Montana, it was the Nez Perce who hosted them and helped them to reach the coast. It wasn't long after that Donald MacKenzie set up his fur trading post.

Kids' Stuff

★ The tipi pitching demonstration is a great one for the kids as the audience gets to lend a helping hand. This exercise demonstrates the rigors the nomadic Nez Perce had to endure.

★ Much of the drive is through the Nez Perce Indian reservation. Our kids have always had a real fascination with visiting the lands of our native people. We've tried to make it a point that they understand the special role these people had in the country. It was their land. Native peoples took what they needed, not what they wanted. They left enough so they wouldn't suffer next year. Society is beginning to understand the importance of living in balance with nature.

Access: From the twin cities of Lewiston, ID/Clarkston, WA, take Hwys. 12 or 95. **Days/Hours:** Spalding visitor center, daily, summer 8-6 & winter 8-4:30 (clsd. Thanksgiving, Dec.25 & Jan.1). **Camping:** National Forest and state (Hells Gate State Park 4 mi. S of Lewiston; Winchester Lake State Park 20 mi. S of Spalding on US 95; Chief Timothy State Park 6 mi. W of Clarkston on US 12; Fields Spring State Park 32 mi. S of Clarkston on WA 129 & Wallowa Lake State Park 6 mi. S of Joseph). **Special Events:** Last Aug. wknd., Cultural Day with speakers & tribal dances, Spalding. **For info.:** Superintendent, Nez Perce National Historical Park, P.O.Box 93, Spalding, ID 83551. 208/843-2261.

Nez Pierce National Historic Site

COURTESY NPS

Nez Perce National Historic Trail

In 1877, many of the Nez Perce tribe fled from northeastern Oregon as the U.S. Army pursued them. Their trail took them through Idaho (see Nez Perce NHP, ID) into eastern Montana (see Big Hole NB, MT) criss-crossing the Continental Divide bisecting Wyoming's Yellowstone National Park and moving up through the plains of central Montana close to the Canadian border. It was at the foothills of the Bear Paw Mountains that the army finally subdued them.

For info.: Nez Perce National Historic Trail, Nez Perce National Forest, 319 East Main St., Grangeville, ID 93530.

ILLINOIS

Chicago Portage National Historic Site

Cook County administers this affiliated site preserving a portion of the portage discovered by the French explorers Jacques Marquette and Louis Joliet. The portage was a vital link to trade between the Great Lakes and the Mississippi River.

Access: W side of Harlem Ave. .5 mi. N of I-55. **For info.:** Chicago Portage National Historic Site, c/o Cook County Forest Preserve, Cummings Sq., River Forest, IL 60305. 312/366-9420.

Illinois and Michigan Canal National Heritage Corridor

This affiliated site is the core of a number of community parks and recreational areas. In 1848, the canal and railroads that paralleled it were key transportation systems to the opening up of the west and Chicago's growth.

For info.: Illinois & Michigan Canal National Heritage Corridor, 30 North Bluff St., Joliet, IL 60435.

Lincoln Home National Historic Site

Allow: 1 hr. *FREE*

"A bronzed lank man! His suit of ancient black,
A famous high top-hat and plain work shawl
Make him the quaint great figure that men love,
The prairie-lawyer, master of us all."

Vachel Lindsay
Abraham Lincoln Walked at Midnight

In the city that he helped make the state capital, Lincoln spent his middle years, almost half his life. It was his career in government that brought him to Springfield and it was his career in government that took him away. Visitors can tour his home and hear about his dual career as lawyer and politician.

Highlights

★ Unfortunately, many of Lincoln's furnishings were lost in a fire. However, as you tour the house, you can see that while he wasn't a poor man, neither was he a rich one.

Whiz Tips

Abe was a 28-year-old state representative when he first moved to Springfield. About a year and a half later, he became acquainted with 21-year-old Mary Todd. Within three years, they were determined to be married against Mary's socially-conscious family's opposition. The family reluctantly agreed to sanction the bonding. Lincoln withdrew from running for state offices at this time and limited his political activity to party politics for about 5 years. In 1847, he went to Washington as a congressman, but his unpopular stance against the Mexican War doomed him to lawyering once more, a job he excelled at. In 1856, the issue of slavery brought Lincoln back to the national scene. He had recently aligned himself with the newly-formed Republican party and was chosen by them to run for the U.S. Senate. Although Lincoln failed to win this election, a series of debates with opponent Stephen Douglas won him national acclaim that launched him to the presidency. Other national parks related to Lincoln's life are: Lincoln Memorial, DC; Ford Theatre, DC; Lincoln Boyhood NMem, IN; Abraham Lincoln Birthplace NHS, KY; Gettysburg NMP, PA.

Kids' Stuff

★ This site is an excellent place to familiarize children who have studied Lincoln's pre-presidential adult life. From age 25 through 50, Lincoln started a family, made a successful law practice and continued to play a role in the governing of his country. Political setbacks did not deter his belief in influencing the process. His philosophies and ambition ultimately won him the country's leadership but left him to confront a problem "greater than that which rested upon Washington." That he succeeded so admirably is a blessing to the country today.

Access: Downtown Springfield. **Days/Hours:** Daily 8:30-5 (clsd. Thanksgiving, Dec.25 & Jan.1). **Camping:** Riverside Park (387 sites, elec. & shwrs.). **For info.:** Superintendent, Lincoln Home National Historic Site, 413 S. 8th St., Springfield, IL 62703. 217/492-4150.

INDIANA

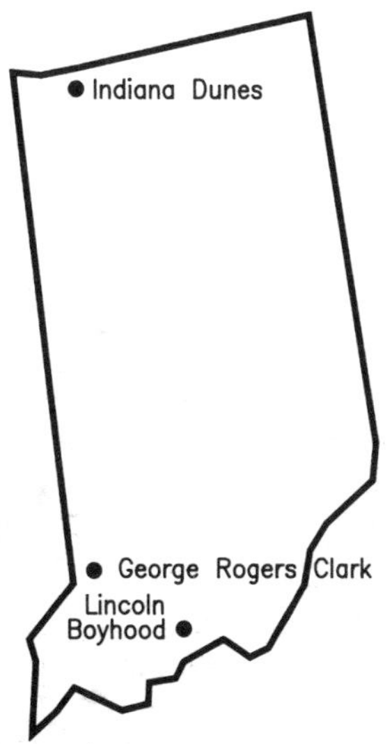

George Rogers Clark National Historical Park

Allow: 1-2 hrs. *Fee*

"Great things have been effected by a few men well conducted,"

George Rogers Clark

When the roll is called for famous American families, only a few will recognize Clark. Were it not for the brothers Clark, Canada might well have bordered Mexico. Although George has this park dedicated to his Revolutionary heroics, it's his younger brother who is best remembered. And yet, George's money, motivation and moxie paved William's (and Meriwether Lewis') way to fame.

Had it not been for George, the American west may have remained the Appalachians. In Vincennes, at the Indiana/Illinois border, he successfully concluded one of the most courageous feats of combat seen in any American war. In the dead of winter, he led his band of Kentuckians some 180 miles through flooded country. Although they had to wade through ice-cold rivers up to their shoulders, Clark was able to keep their spirits up until they reached their destination. The shocked and out-numbered forces of British Lt. Governor Hamilton surrendered their fort, which Clark was able to control for the remainder of the hostilities.

Highlights

★ Start with the film dramatizing Clark's exploits in the visitor center, then visit the Clark Memorial, the largest of its kind east of Washington, DC. It is an imposing piece of work, reminiscent of the kind of structures protecting Lincoln and Jefferson from the elements.

Whiz Tips

❢ Clark lobbied for funding and official support so he could raise a force to harry the British in the Ohio Valley and secure the territory for the new republic. Unfortunately, although Clark told his men "Our cause is just...our country will be grateful," his country wasn't that grateful. Clark used his own money to pay his "army." Unfortunately, Clark, like so many Revolutionary financial supporters, discovered his efforts were considered "donations" to a good cause. Clark was to flounder financially until his death.

Kids' Stuff

★ Although Disney and others haven't seen fit to put this early American hero on a pedestal, his efforts dwarf most who have enjoyed such exposure. Initiative, leadership, courage and daring weren't just words to this transplanted Virginian, but facts of life. While others gave lip service, Clark gave effort. Children who have studied the War for Independence can learn more about the western battles which receive too little attention.

Access: Downtown Vincennes. **Days/Hours:** Daily, 9-5 (clsd. Thanksgiving, Dec.25 & Jan.1). **Camping:** 3 mi. N. of

George Rogers Clark National Historical Park

Vincennes, Knox County Ouabache Trails Park. **Special Events:** Memorial Day wknd. Sat. & Sun., Spirit of Vincennes Rendezvous Revolutionary War encampment. **For info.:** Superintendent, George Rogers Clark National Historical Park, 401 S. 2nd St., Vincennes, IN 47591. 812/882-1776.

Indiana Dunes National Lakeshore

Allow: 2-3 days *FREE*

"The Dunes are to the Midwest what the Grand Canyon is to Arizona and Yosemite is to California. They constitute a signature of time and eternity."

Carl Sandburg

Located on the southern tip of Lake Michigan wedged between Gary and Michigan City, are 25 miles of beaches, sand dunes, bogs, forests, a functioning 1890s farm and an early French homestead.

Highlights

★ Continually on the move and hosting a multiplicity of plants and animals, the dunes are truly living things. Interestingly, their progress can be traced through the type of vegetation they sport. Mt. Baldy is a must for dune-watchers.

Whiz Tips

You can participate in a full program of activities year-round. Daily summer interpretive offerings include walks, open houses (Bog), talks, lifeguard demos, campfires, living history presentations, cultural festivities, star-gazings and special films. Participants can learn about dunes, wildlife, the lake, pioneering, farming, fire fighting and local history. A recurring feature is traditional and folk singing, part of their "Music Heritage Series.".

Almost 300 species of birds have been spotted within the bounds of the park. Many of them use the area as a migratory lay-by.

Although the Paul H. Douglas Center for Environmental Education's primary task is to assist organized groups, it has Sunday open house. The center has AV programs, computers, live animals and other innovative activities.

Kids' Stuff

★ The Jr. Ranger program is primarily for local kids with once-a-month meetings. Special children's presentations (puppet show & storybook time) are occasionally part of the scheduled interpretive programs. The visitor center has "hands-on" exhibits which cater to the wee ones.

★ Kids love visiting here. There's plenty to explore, lots of things to do including fishing and usually plenty of other kids to play with. There's also a veritable feast (45 mi.) of hiking trails, like Miller Woods, Inland Marsh, West Beach, Little Calumet and Ly-co-ki-we trails. In summer, the gently sloping sandy beaches are a haven for families. Children can swim, splash in the shallows, dig sandcastles and run up and down, all within walking distance of mass transit.

Access: 60 mi. E of Chicago on I-94, I-80 & I-90, US 12 & 20 or IN 49. **Days/Hours:** West Beach , daily, summer 9-sunset & winter 8-sunset. Visitor center, daily, summer 8-6 & winter 8-5. **Camping:** In 1992, national lakeshore will have campground (shwrs.); adjacent Indiana Dunes State Park (reservation-219/926-4520). **Special Events:** Late Sept., Duneland Harvest Festival, a turn-of-the-century folk shindig; mid-March, Maple Sugar Time. **For info.:** Superintendent, Indiana Dunes National Seashore, 1100 N. Mineral Springs Rd., Porter, IN 46304. 219/926-7561.

Lincoln Boyhood National Memorial

Allow: 2-3 hrs. *Fee*

" All that I am or hope to be, I owe to my angel mother."

Abraham Lincoln

As Abraham Lincoln's family made its way westward through Kentucky, Indiana and Illinois looking for more productive lands, it settled here for 12 of Abe's boyhood years. It was, however, the last stop for Abe's mother, Nancy. She died of "milk-sickness," caused by drinking the milk of cows who had eaten a weed called white snakeroot. After his mother died, Abe was fortunate that his father married the widow Sarah Johnston. Abraham said of his step-mother, "she proved to be good and kind." The park has a large visitor center and a living history pioneer farm.

Highlights

★ The visitor center has an AV about Lincoln's boyhood narrated by Senator Everett Dirkson, a hall devoted to Nancy Hanks Lincoln and a large collection of family photos and pictures. Nancy Hanks Lincoln is buried on a wooded knoll near the visitor center.

★ The living history farm is an operating reproduction of 1816 farmstead Thomas Lincoln carved from "a wild region, with many bears and other wild animals." Costumed "pioneers" carry out family and farming activities from mid-Apr. through mid-Oct. The farm has a cabin, a smoke house, a barn, a corn crib, a chicken coop, a thriving garden, a carpenter shop and farm animals.

Whiz Tips

Although Lincoln was born in a log cabin, his family was not poor. They always had land holdings and his father was a respected member of his community. In Indiana, Thomas owned 100 acres of land outright. He was a farmer and an excellent carpenter and cabinet-maker. Abe's mother Nancy taught him to read and spell. His humor and story-telling abilities are attributed to his father. Some historians credit Thomas' search for better lands as the legacy

Lincoln Boyhood National Memorial COURTESY NPS

left with Lincoln that was to result in the *Homesteader's Act* of 1862 (see Homestead NM, NE).

Other national parks related to Lincoln's life are; Lincoln Memorial, DC; Ford Theatre, DC; Lincoln Home NHS, IL; Abraham Lincoln Birthplace NHS, KY and Gettysburg NMP, PA.

Kids' Stuff

★ Children who have studied Abraham Lincoln will find the Living farm very interesting. The farm is particularly instructive for kids who are accustomed to today's homes, packaging and labor-saving devices. In the cabin, they'll find dried spices hanging from the rafters ready for use. The "pioneers" guides take great pains to accurately duplicate the domestic and farm work and are only too pleased to demonstrate daily chores. The farm is "hands-on" so kids can closely examine the 1800's implements.

★ Nearby Lincoln State Park holds the remains of another important influence on Lincoln, his sister, Sarah who died giving birth. The state park hosts the *Young Abe Lincoln Musical Outdoor Drama*, a presentation covering Abe's Indiana years.

Access: In Lincoln City, 8 mi. S of I-84 on IN 162. **Days/Hours:** Daily 8-5 (clsd. Thanksgiving, Dec.25 & Jan.1). **Camping:** Adjacent Lincoln State Park (322 sites & shwrs.). **Teacher's Package:** Available.

For info.: Superintendent, Lincoln Boyhood National Memorial, Lincoln City, IN 47552. 812/937-4541.

IOWA

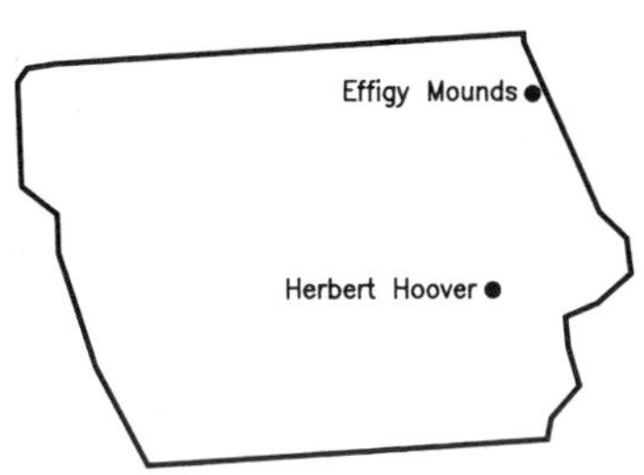

Effigy Mounds National Monument

Allow: 1-2 hrs. *Fee*

"So mythical Mound Builders of non-Indian blood had to be invented by the white man, and as fabulous tales woven about them, while outraged Hopewell specters glowered in silent fury."

Robert Silverberg
And the Mound Builders Vanished from the Earth

Although much debated in the last century, archaeologists believe the mounds are the work of a number of Native American cultures (see Ocmulgee NM, GA & Mound City Group NM, OH). The mounds were used as burial places and most probably in ceremonies. At this northeastern Iowa national monument, three major groups of mound-builders are represented: the Red-Ocher, Hopewell and Effigy cultures. The monument is named for the Effigy culture because these people fashioned their mounds in the images of birds or animals.

Highlights

★ By taking a one-hour walk along the Fire Point Trail, you can see all aspects of the cultures who resided here. There are interpretive markers and exhibits along the way explaining the monument's many facets.

Whiz Tips

During summer, rangers lead interested parties along the trails providing commentary on the mounds.

❢ About 12,000 years ago, nomadic people used the region. Over time, more permanent settlements were evidenced. Then about 2,500 years ago, the people we call the Red Ocher culture started building mounds. The major changes distinguishing this culture from its successor, the Hopewell, is the style of pottery and the increased use of materials from all over the continent. Appalachian mica, Rocky Mountain obsidian, Gulf of Mexico seashells and Lake Superior copper were found in the mounds constructed from 100 B.C.-A.D. 600. The Effigy culture appears to have overlapped the Hopewell. Beside their different mound configurations, Effigy peoples used copper for tools rather than as ornaments, and buried their dead with fewer offerings.

Kids' Stuff

★ There are a number of national park sites demonstrating the widespread trade that took place between the prehistoric native peoples (see Knife River Indian Villages NHS, ND, Salinas Pueblo Missions NM, NM, Pecos NHP, NM, Pipestone NM, WI & Alibates Flint Quarries NM, TX). The importance of these sites for children is that they present industry and commerce, a little known side of these people. Trade was as important to them as it was to the Europeans.

Access: 3 mi. N of Marquette on IA 76. **Days/Hours:** Daily, summer 8-7 & winter 8-5 (clsd. Dec.25). **Camping:** Yellow River State Forest on SR 13 (100 sites) & Pikes Peak State Park on SR 40 (75 sites, elec. & shwrs.) **For info.:** Superintendent, Effigy Mounds National Monument, RR 1, Box 25A, Harpers Ferry, IA 52146. 319/873-3491.

Herbert Hoover National Historic Site

Allow: 1-2 hrs. *Fee*

"Twenty million people are starving. Whatever their politics, they shall be fed!"

Herbert Hoover

Just off I-80, next to historic West Branch, are Herbert Hoover's birthplace cottage, his gravesite, a replicated blacksmith shop, a one-room schoolhouse, a Quaker Meetinghouse, the Herbert Hoover Presidential Library-Museum (fee) and twenty other historic structures. For his work helping the starving people of Europe and Russia, Hoover was variously known as "The Great Humanitarian," "The Knight of the Lean Garbage Can" and "The Friend of Helpless Children." The thirty-first President, Herbert Hoover had the misfortune to be in office at the rise of the Great Depression.

Highlights

★ The park is an excellent example of a mid-American town, circa 1880s. Hoover's birthcottage has some of the original furniture. In summer, you can see how Herbert's father practiced his early trade as living history guides demonstrate the art of blacksmithing. The Meetinghouse and Schoolhouse are original 1850s buildings transplanted here.

Whiz Tips

❢ Herbert lost his father at age six and his mother at nine. He was raised in Oregon by an uncle who was both a physician and a business man. Herbert went to a private school run by his uncle and was in the first graduating class of engineers from Stanford. Through wise investments and fortuitous career moves, he became a multi-millionaire by age 40. His first public duty occurred at the outbreak of WW I, when he assisted stranded Americans in England to get back home. He then directed efforts to feed the newly invaded Belgians. With the U.S.'s entry into the war, he was assigned by President Wilson to head the country's Food Administration. He balanced the soldiers' needs with the people back home so well, he avoided rationing. After the war, he headed the American Relief Administration (again for free) to aid the millions starving in Europe and Russia. The introductory quotation was his response to criticism that he was aiding Bolsheviks. His career successes as a superb administrator, food relief specialist and Secretary of Commerce, would seem to have prepared him better than any man to cope with the Great Depression. However, his failure to deal with this national crisis is blamed on his conservative policies. His popularity was so low that shanty towns were named "Hoovervilles." In a 1983 poll of 900 historians, Herbert Hoover was ranked 21st out of 36 president's in effectiveness.

Kids' Stuff

★ The site is of particular interest to children who have studied President Hoover or the late 19th century. Kids also enjoy the living history guides and wandering around historic West Branch.

Access: 10 mi. E of Iowa City or 40 mi. W of Davenport on I-80. **Days/Hours:** Daily 9-5 (clsd. Thanksgiving, Dec.25 & Jan.1). **Camping:** Several campgrounds nearby. **Special Events:** Closest wknd. to Herbert's birthday (Aug.10), Hooverfest; Oct., Cider Days; Christmas, special programs. **For info.:** Superintendent, Herbert Hoover National Historic Site, Box 607, West Branch, IA 52358. 319/643-2541.

Herbert Hoover National Historic Site

COURTESY NPS

KANSAS

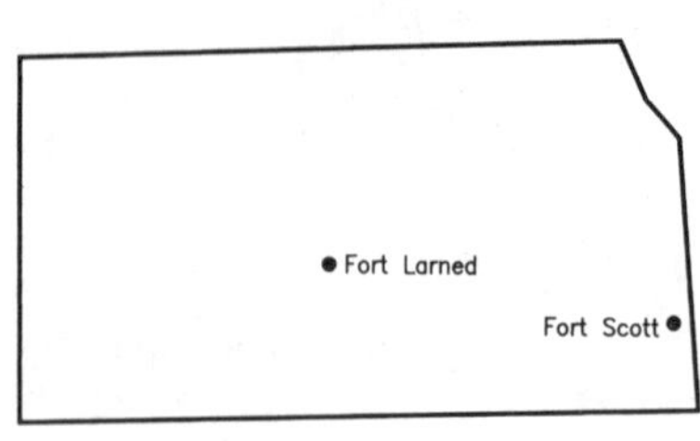

Fort Larned National Historic Site

Allow: 1 hr. *Fee*

Northwest of Wichita, near where the Pawnee River joins the Arkansas, Fort Larned NHS has ten historic structures relating its past. The fort guarded as far west as Colorado and New Mexico including the famed Santa Fe Trail from 1859-1872 when the railroad replaced the wagon trains. Today's stone and wood structures replaced the original adobe buildings in 1868 and serve to remind us of the strained relations between the indigenous people and the advances of western society. The fort later served as an agency for the Indian Bureau distributing annuities to the plains tribes. Its last gasp was to serve as a protectorate for the railroad builders whose work made the Santa Fe Trail redundant. The fort was finally closed in 1878.

Highlights

★ As we toured the army forts of the Old West, we were always surprised at the number without enclosing walls. Even without walls Native Americans rarely attacked these garrisons. This fort has many furnished rooms within its structures which show us how the inhabitants lived. The park has let the prairie recover to its previous state. White-tail deer, coyotes, badgers and ground squirrels are some of the animals who once again use the tall grasses for safety.

Fort Larned National Historic Site COURTESY NPS

Whiz Tips

❢ On summer weekends the park rangers conduct interpretive programs, including living history demonstrations explaining fort life.

❢ Fort Larned had a hand in one of the more infamous ambushes in the west. In 1868-69, several plains tribes, notably the Kiowas, Comanches and Arapahos were asserting their rights. Lt. Colonel George A. Custer and the 7th Cavalry were sent to Fort Dodge, for a campaign into Indian territory. Custer managed to find a Cheyenne tribe under Chief Black Kettle who had already been a victim in the 1864 Sand Creek Massacre. Black Kettle, who was at peace with the whites, must have had a terrible sense of deja vu just before he died. Custer and the 7th joined Black Kettle in hereafter when they encountered a more readied group of natives at Little Bighorn (see Custer Battlefield NM).

Kids' Stuff

★ The fort is an excellent place for children to learn about the Santa Fe Trail and how the soldiers who protected it lived in the 1860s. The furnished buildings and the guided programs make this period of American history real.

Access: 6 mi. W of Larned on KS 156. **Days/Hours:** Daily 8-5 (clsd. Thanksgiving, Dec.25 & Jan.1). **Camping:** N on I-70 at Ellis, Ellis Campground (38 sites, elec. & shwrs. **Special Events:** Large living history events & occasional candlelight tours. **For info.:** Superintendent, Fort Larned National Historic Site, Rte. 3, Larned, KS 67550. 316/285-6911.

Fort Scott National Historic Site

Allow: 1 hr. *Fee*

On the Missouri/Kansas border lies early frontier Fort Scott. Although geographically isolated, the fort was designed as part of a picket-fence of fortifications along the Indian Territory. The Military Road ran north from Fort Jessup, LA to Fort Towson on the Texas border to Fort Smith (see Fort Smith NHS, AR), on to Fort Scott and extending to Fort Snelling, MN. The fort's thirteen re-

Fort Scott National Historic Site COURTESY NPS

stored/reconstructed structures accurately reflect the 1840s.

Highlights

★ As you tour the grounds, you can see how the soldiers lived, what they wore and how they spent their time. The visitor center has an AV providing background information and displays exhibits pertinent to the fort.

Whiz Tips

During the summer, the park rangers provide weekend interpretive tours and presentations. Some of the living history demonstrations include enlisted men's and laundresses' daily lives, weapons firing and a retreat ceremony.

This era of the American military is particularly colorful. Fort Scott was occupied by dragoon and infantry regiments during the 1840's. Dragoons, the elite fighting men, were trained to fight from the saddle and on foot. The rule of dress appears to have been the more decorative the better. The dragoons were so particular that the horses had to be color-coordinated. Each dragoon in a particular company had to have a horse of a certain color. For example, everyone in "G" company had gray horses while everybody in "B" had chestnuts.

Although their principal function was to maintain peace among the newly-moved eastern tribes, the local settlers and the plains tribes, the action around the fort was non-existent. In 1845, Stephen W. Kearney took his dragoons on a 99-day, 2200-mile whirlwind exploration of the plains. Two companies, "A" and "C", were also involved in the Mexican War.

While the fort was abandoned in the 1850s, the anti-slavery/pro-slavery Kansas conflict brought violence to the town of Fort Scott and the return of the army to maintain peace. During the Civil War, Fort Scott was to be one of the first forts to house African American troops, the 1st Kansas Colored Infantry.

Ranger & Kids

COURTESY NPS

Kids' Stuff

★ If you can time your visit to the interpretive programs, your children will enjoy the costumed historians. These guides are well-schooled in answering questions and imparting details you usually don't get from self-interpretive visits.

Access: 90 mi. S of Kansas City in Fort Scott. **Days/Hours:** Daily, summer 8-6 & winter 8-5 (clsd. Thanksgiving, Dec.25 & Jan.1). **Camping:** Fort Scott city park-Gunn Park; Farlington State Park (15 mi.). **Special Events:** In May, Civil War encampment; June's first wknd., Good Ol' Days; early Sept., Mexican War Encampment; late Sept., American Indian Weekend & Mountain Man Rendezvous; Nov.30 & Dec.1, 1845 Frontier Candlelight Tour (reservations). **Teacher's Package:** Available. **For info.:** Superintendent, Fort Scott National Historic Site, Old Fort Blvd., Fort Scott, KS 66701. 316/223-0310.

KENTUCKY

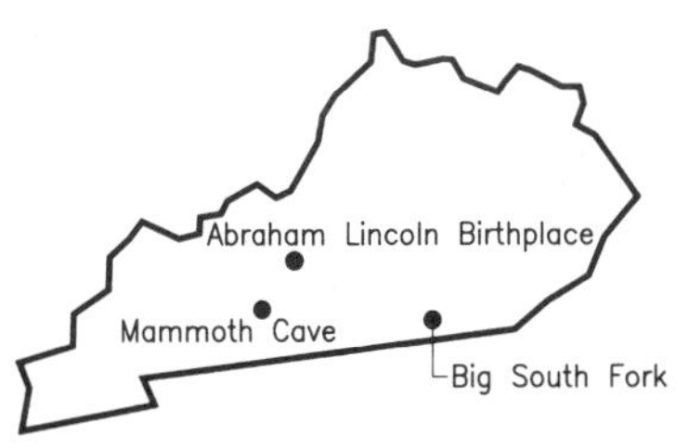

Abraham Lincoln Birthplace National Historic Site

Allow: 1 hr. *FREE*

"He was not a born king of men...but a child of the people,"

Horace Greely

Midway between Louisville and Mammoth Cave stands the log cabin that was probably Lincoln's birthplace. Through the efforts of famous benefactors, novelist Mark Twain, Democratic presidential candidate William Jennings Bryan, labor leader Samuel Gompers and publisher Robert Collier, Lincoln's birthplace was not only preserved but funds for a suitable monument to contain it were raised. The park encompasses these structures on the land that Thomas and Nancy Lincoln tilled.

Abraham Lincoln Birthplace NHS

COURTESY NPS

Highlights

★ The climb up the 56 steps (one for each year of his life) to the granite and marble neoclassical memorial predates the Washington, DC tribute which bears a close resemblance. However, instead of the aged visage of a leader receiving his people, we find a roughly hewn house of wood enclosed in the stone monument.

Whiz Tips

During summer, the park has interpretive programs explaining the Lincolns' early days and life on the farm. Although Abe was born in a log cabin, his father owned two farms, livestock and several townsites. While the log cabin we see today may seem a poor residence, it was typical for the times. Sinking Spring farm was Abe's home until he was two. Other national parks related to Lincoln's life are: Lincoln Memorial & Ford's Theater NHS, DC; Lincoln Boyhood NMem, IN; Lincoln Home NHS, IL; Gettysburg NMP, PA.

Kids' Stuff

★ For children who have studied Lincoln, this is a memorable stop. The interpretive programs explaining early pioneer farming are real eye-openers for children who believe putting their plates in the dishwasher is manual labor.

Access: 3 mi. S of Hodgenville on US 31E/KY 61. **Days/Hours:** Daily, spring & fall 8-5:45, summer 8-6:45 & winter 8-4:45 (clsd. Dec.25). **Camping:** Near Bardstown (27 mi.), My old Kentucky Home State Park (39 sites, elec. & shwrs.); Mammoth Cave NP (50 mi. S, 111 sites & shwrs.). **Special Events:** Late Jan., Musical Tribute to Dr. Martin Luther King; Feb. 12, Lincoln's birthday, Wreath Laying at Birthplace Cabin; July 13 & 14, a founder's day celebration; Dec. 12, Christmas in the Park. **Teacher's Package:** Available. **For info.:** Superintendent, Abraham Lincoln Birthplace National Historic Site, 2995 Lincoln Farm Rd., Hodgenville, KY 42748. 502/358-3874.

Cumberland Gap National Historical Park

Allow: 1 day *FREE*

"... bits of scenery wherein rocks and streams, mountain-ferries, quaint old-fashioned mills, farmhouses and cabins perched like birds among the clefts of hills, lovely perspectives, wildflowers and waving grain,"

F.G. De Fontaine's, 1875
Picturesque America

Little has changed. This is the land of Daniel Boone, mountain feuds and moonshine stills. Sure, the mountain ferries have been retired with a super highway bridging the Gap but the quaint dwellings are still to be found in the wooded hills.

Highlights

★ Most visitors drive up to the Pinnacle, an overlook of the Gap, and stop by the remains of Civil War forts nearby.

★ The park has a shuttle (fee) taking visitors back into these Appalachian highlands to Hensley Settlement. Abandoned hard-scrabble homesites and beleaguered hamlets are all that's left of the rugged souls who came, settled and left for better. Living history farmers introduce life in the hill country.

Whiz Tips

At Cumberland Gap some 250,000 people followed the trail Daniel Boone made famous. They came seeking the rich lands of Kentucky, Tennessee and the Ohio Valley. Their settlements put pressure on the people who felt they had a prior claim: the French, then the English and always the Native Americans. Daniel Boone was neither the first European to discover the Gap nor the first to establish a town. But his exploits were widely circulated, popularizing the blue grass of Kentucky and the wealth of animals and fertile land. He built the first road through and lost two sons to Indian attacks. Although he has achieved lasting fame, he suffered many financial losses over disputed land claims and never achieved a comfortable life. Oh yeah, contrary to Walt Disney's projected image of Boone in a coonskin cap complete with tail, he wore a wide-brimmed beaver hat.

Kids' Stuff

★ The Cumberland Gap is maintained as a wild area. There are good hiking trails in the park and, of course, the trip back into Hensley is worthwhile for children.

Access: US 25E from KY & TN or US 58 from VA. **Days/Hours:** Daily, summer 8-6 & winter 8-5 (clsd. Dec.25); Hensely shuttle 5 days/wk. in summer & wknds. in Sept. **Camping:** Park's Wilderness Road Campground (160 sites). **Teacher's Package:** Available. **For info.:** Superintendent, Cumberland Gap National Historical Park, P.O. Box 1848, Middlesboro, KY 40965. 606/248-2817.

Mammoth Cave National Park

Allow: 1-2 days @$ = Fee

Located in central Kentucky, about mid-point between Louisville and Bowling Green, is the world's longest cave. At a known 300-plus miles and an estimated 500 miles in length, Mammoth is by far the world's longest cave. Russia's Optimistitscheskaya, the second longest cave, is "only" 90-plus miles long. Aside from its great length, Mammoth is renowned for its diversity of wildlife, including 30 eyeless species. There are two species of eyeless fish, an eyeless crayfish and the endangered eyeless cave shrimp. Visitors see only about 15 miles of the area mapped beneath the surface.

Highlights

★ Where to begin? This is the question facing every visitor who wishes to enter the cave. During summer, there are at least 8 different scheduled tours. While some overlap, many cover completely different sections of the cave. The Historic Tour interprets two miles of the cave which early Native Americans and the first known Europeans explored. Another tour, the Frozen Niagara, is more scenic featuring stalactites, stalagmites, and flowstone formations. The most strenuous of the year-round tours, the Half-Day Tour, is a geological highlight package exploring various types of cave passages (elliptical, canyon and massive areas of breakdown). On this tour you see a wide variety of cave formations such as gypsum, stalactites, flowstones and draperies. Some exotic tours offer an underground boat trip, a lantern tour or a crawling, climbing adventure called a "Wild Cave Tour."

Whiz Tips

💡 Mammoth Cave is protected by 50 feet of sandstone which acts like a roof. The cave has been literally sculpted by underground streams carving their way through the limestone layer. Mammoth is the world's longest cave because the limestone runs fairly horizontal. The slightly acidic water dissolves the limestone and drains into the Green River. As the Green River works its way lower, the cave water seeks lower and lower levels of bedded limestone, gradually creating this enormous intestine-like cave. Although there are several examples of stalactites, stalagmites and flowstone, Mammoth is not as regarded for its calcite formations as are some of the park service's western caves (see Jewel Cave, NM &

Mammoth Cave National Park

COURTESY NPS

Wind Cave NP, SD; Timpanogos Cave NM, UT). As early as 2000 BC, pre-Columbian Indians mined the cave for its minerals. This early evidence of man, the wealth of animal life and the cave's sheer size has earned the cave recognition as a World Heritage Site, one of only a dozen in the United States.

Kids' Stuff

★There are five tours we would recommend for children. The shortest and best one to test whether or not caving is for them is the Travertine Tour. It lasts a little more than an hour, goes only 1/4 of a mile and covers the most scenic portion of the cave. Longer but very interesting trips are the Historic and Frozen Niagara Tours. For us the Echo River Tour has the most "kid appeal" as visitors get to take boat trip 360 feet underground, a once-in-a-lifetime ride. More limited in availability is the "kids only" Trog Tour. Here the more adventuresome children (8-12 yrs.) get to don lighted helmets and crawl through segments of the cave unseen by the rest of us. As a bonus, they get to keep their helmets. For still bigger kids (13-15 yrs.), there's the Explorer Tour which requires kneepads, helmet and headlamp.

★Mammoth Cave has a Jr. Ranger program. The program is structured by age group, 6-9 & 10-13. They must attend two interpretative programs, see the park film, and walk a nature trail to qualify.

Access: I-65 traveling S take EXIT 53 at Cave City, then KY 70 W 9 mi.; I-65 traveling N take EXIT 48 at Park City, then KY 255 W 8 mi.; Western Kentucky Pkwy exit at Leitchfield onto Ky 259 S to Brownsville, then KY 70 E. **Days/Hours:** Daily, summer 7:30-7, spring & fall 7:30-6 & winter 8-5:30 Central Time. **Camping:** Park's 3 campgrounds; Headquarters Campground (111 sites), Houchins Ferry (FREE 12 sites) & Dennison Ferry (FREE 4 sites). **For info.:** Superintendent, Mammoth Cave National Park, Mammoth Cave, KY 42259. 502/758-2328/2251.

LOUISIANA

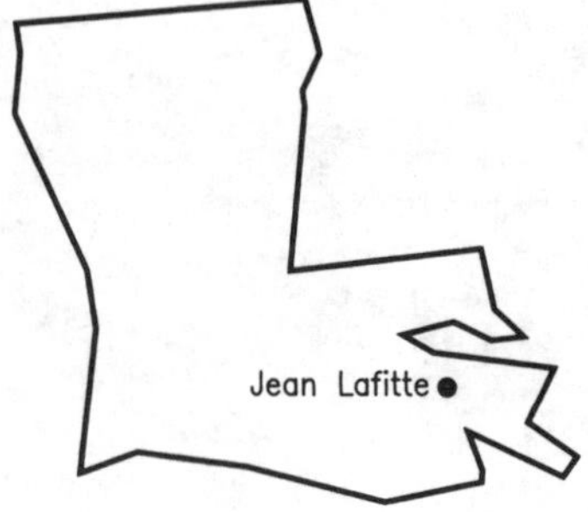

Jean Lafitte National Historical Park & Preserve

Allow: 1 day *FREE*

"New Orleans is the most cosmopolitan of provincial cities. Its comparative isolation has secured the development of provincial traits and manners, has preserved the individuality of the many races that give it color, morals, and character,"

Charles Dudley Warner, 1889
Studies in the South and West

The park consists of three entities in and around the city of New Orleans. The downtown section seeks to relate that exotic neighborhood called the French Quarter. The Chalmette Unit tells of the great triumph over the British, which came two weeks after the peace treaty was signed. The third portion, the Barataria, encompasses the cultural diversity of the Mississippi Delta.

Highlights

★ Chalmette has, magnificent antebellum mansion which was built after the historic battle that was fought here. There's an obelisk honoring the victory and a national cemetery.

★ The Isleno Cultural Center, 7 mi. SE, is part of the Chalmette Unit. Encouraged by the Spanish, Canary Islanders came to this area to settle. They fought with Spain against the British. The Islenos established lifestyles very similar to the Cajuns. This center shows visitors what's distinctive about their culture.

Whiz Tips

The battle won at Chalmette has historic significance because it clearly foretold of a new age and a new power. The British were devastated by American fire. In 30 min. over 2,000 Redcoats were dead or wounded, compared with 13 American dead. Jean Lafitte, for whom the park is named, was a pirate leader who was wooed by both sides. He received an American pardon for his help. However, he ended his career leading over 1,000 buccaneers. Andrew Jackson parlayed his victory into the nation's highest post. The rangers time their interpretive programs to the tour ferries (fee) arriving from downtown New Orleans.

Kids' Stuff

Most Sat. mornings the Chalmette site puts on living history demonstrations showing how the armies of 1815 would have gone about their daily routine.

Access: Chalmette Unit, 6 mi. E from New Orleans; French Quarter Unit, downtown New Orleans on Decatur St.; Barataria Unit, S on Rte.90 to LA 45 from New Orleans about 40 min. **Days/Hours:** Chalmette, daily 8:30-5 & Isleno Cultural Center, daily 9-5 (clsd. Dec.25 & Mardi Gras Day emid-Feb.f). **Camping:** St. Bernard State Park, 8 mi. SE from Chalmette Unit on Hwy. 39 (elec. & shwrs.). **Special Events:** On wknd. closest Jan. 8, Chalmette Unit, anniversary of the Battle of New Orleans, complete with an encampment, weapon firing demos and special ceremonies; March's last week, Isleno Cultural Center, Museum Days with craft demos, storytelling, music, dance and contests. **For info.:** Superintendent, Jean Lafitte National Historical Park & Preserve, 419 Decatur St., New Orleans, LA 70130. Chalmette 504/589-4428, Isleno 504/682-0862.

Poverty Point National Monument

A recent addition to the park service, the remains of the largest and most intricate Native American geometrical earthwork. Since its construction 3,000-4,000 years ago, the structure has fallen prey to erosion and agriculture.

For info.: Poverty Point National Monument, c/o Poverty Point State Commemorative Area, P.O.Box 248, Epps, LA 71237.

MAINE

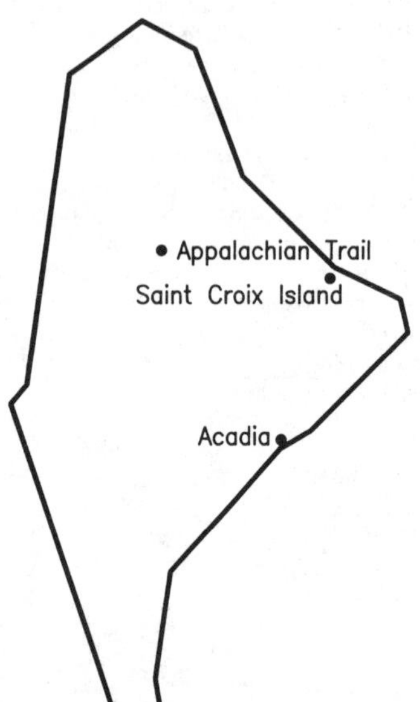

Acadia National Park

Allow: 2-3 days *Fee*

"Maine is not just the land. It is also the sea. There is an eternal struggle between the two. Neither quite wins, neither quite loses."

Pearl S. Buck,
America

Could there have been a more appropriate piece of ground to symbolize the rugged Maine coastline and preserve it for posterity? Encompassing part of a mountain island rift with inlets and points, this wild coastal shoreline of Northern Maine has opportunity after opportunity to show its stuff. But Acadia is more than this.

Highlights

★ There are some who take advantage of the warmer mountain lakes and ponds for a swim, a boat ride or to wet a line; there are others who spend their time cycling the carriage

Tide Pool at Acadia National Park

roads; there are many who hike the hills or walk the trails; there are those who study the lighthouses and New England architecture; but all seek solace with the sea. Whether it be the rocky promontories with their gliding gulls, the sand beaches with their children playing or the pebbled stretches with the sea's donation of shells and plants, each of us inhales the water's salty breath as though it were Ponce de Leon's dream of the "fountain of youth."

★ The carriage roads criss-crossing the park are a tremendous boon for families with small children. Relatively level, you can have a relaxing country outing.

Whiz Tips

Check the park's newspaper carefully and focus on those guided trips close to your home base as some programs overlap each other. The interpretive programs include; nature hikes, bird walks, campfire programs, geology talks, photo workshops (incl. a Kodak representative), marine life and historical cruises.

The park was the brainchild of George Dorr, who convinced his rich acquaintances (principally John D. Rockefeller Jr.) of the idea. He gradually acquired lands which he lobbied the government to protect. Some 4,000,000 people each year can thank George for his good works. The park has a guided tour of the foundation of George's parents' summer retreat.

Bar Harbor and Acadia have vestiges of the time of millionaires. Before that insidious blight called income taxes, industrialists reaped great fortunes from monopolies, combines and an over-supply of labor. They gained not just riches but a more vital commodity, leisure time. They built large mansions and hiking trails among these wooded hills. Acadia is the only national park formed exclusively by donations from private citizens.

Saint Croix Island International Historic Site 120 mi. N of the park is administered by Acadia on the Maine/New Brunswick border. However, it is a rare visitor who makes the pilgrimage to this island

Acadia National Park

commemorating the founding of New France. There is no ferry service to the island and access is by private boat only.

Kids' Stuff

★ There's a Jr. Ranger program that rewards successful participants with a pin. You are advised to reserve for children's programs like The Island's Edge and Nature's Way which are participatory in nature.

Access: 47 mi. SE of Bangor on ME 3. **Days/Hours:** Visitor center daily, summer 8-6 & May & Oct. 8-4:30. **Camping:** Park's 2 campgrounds, Blackwoods (310 sites, Ticketron-summer) & Seawall (212 sites); near Ellsworth, Lamoine State Park (61 sites). **For info.:** Acadia National Park, Bar Harbor, ME 04609. 207/288-3338.

Roosevelt Campobello International Park

Located on Campobello Island in New Brunswick, Canada is the summer home Franklin D. Roosevelt used from his childhood until he was stricken with polio. This is the first international park to be administered by a joint commission. You can tour (FREE) the large (34 room) summer cottage, see an orientation AV and many exhibits.

Access: 1.5 mi. from border at Lubec on NB 774. **Days/Hours:** Memorial Day-mid-Oct., 9-5. **Camping:** Provincial campground at Herring Cove; Cobscook Bay State Park at Whiting, ME. **For info.:** Superintendent, Roosevelt Campobello International Park, P.O.Box 97, Lubec, ME 04652. 506/752-2997.

MARYLAND

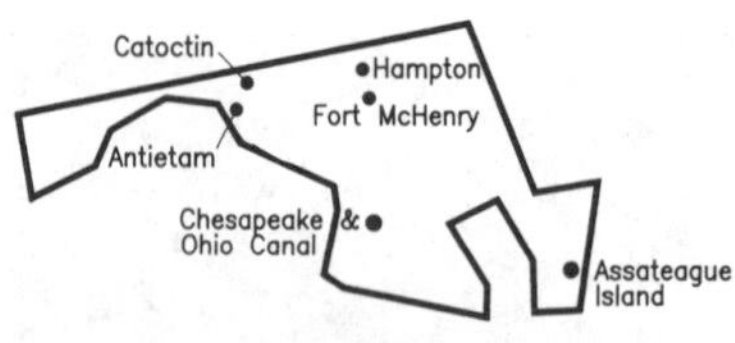

Antietam National Battlefield

Allow: 1-2 hrs. *Fee*

"The truth is, when bullets are whacking against tree trunks and solid shot are cracking heads like egg-shells, the consuming passion in the breast of the average man is to get out of the way."

Pvt. David L. Thompson, Company G, 9th New York Volunteers

This, the bloodiest day of the war, launched a presidential candidate. Considered a draw by most, it was viewed as a Federal moral victory. By all accounts, this battle along the Maryland/West Virginia border was the second most important battle of the Civil War. After hearing the outcome, Britain, which was close to recognizing the Confederacy, didn't, while Lincoln, feeling he had enough support to sign the *Emancipation Act*, did.

Highlights

★ The 8.5 mi. long auto tour allows you to see that the battlefield was farm fields, scant protection from rifle and cannon shot. Federal General Hooker tells of his army's fire into a cornfield occupied by "Stonewall"

Jackson's Confederate troops; "...every stalk of corn...was cut as closely as could have been with a knife, and the slain lay in rows precisely as they had stood in their ranks a few moments before."

Whiz Tips

23,110 soldiers were dead or wounded between dawn and dusk. When the North threatened to cut off a Rebel retreat, Jackson's troops, fresh from victory at Harpers Ferry, (see Harpers Ferry NHP, WV) arrived to save the day. McClellan, the Union leader, kept 33,000 troops out of the fight. He could have routed the Confederates had he chosen to force the issue the next day. Many feel either action by McClellan might have ended the war, then and there. Lincoln, having reached the end of his tether with McClellan's lack of initiative, replaced him. McClellan became Lincoln's opponent in the 1864 presidential campaign.

About a dozen times each year the park presents living history days when visitors can take a step back in time.

Antietam, the North's name for the battlefield, is named for the small creek there. The South named their battlefields for the closest towns and called this one Sharpsburg. Why the difference? Fashion.

Like all things, battles are very much subject to single-mindedness. Leaders get it into their mind to do something and ignore all evidence that would lead them to different (better) decisions. For example, the battle's best known landmark, Lower Bridge, is regarded as the cornerstone of McClellan's failure to win the battle outright. General Burnside repeatedly ordered his men to take the bridge but they were held at bay by a few hundred Georgia sharpshooters. A local resident, Henry Kyd Douglas, was to write his dismay at the Union's actions. "Go look at it and tell me if you don't think

Antietam National Battlefield

Burnside and his corps might have executed a hop, skip and a jump and landed on the other side. One thing is certain, they might have waded it that day without getting their waist belts wet..." After scrutinizing the spot, we'd have to agree with Mr. Douglas.

Kids' Stuff

★ This is another battlefield ideal for cycling with the roadway mostly one-way and not part of the highway. There are trout to be found in the "crick." Kids under 16 don't need a license to try their luck.

Access: 11 mi. S of Hagerstown off MD 65. **Days/Hours:** Daily; summer 8-6 & winter 8:30-5 (clsd. Thanksgiving, Dec.25 & Jan.1). **Camping:** 20 mi. N of Antietam, C & O Canal NHS' McCoys Ferry (14 sites); N Maryland's Fort Frederick State Park (28 sites). **Special Events:** June, 10K *Run Through History*; mid-Sept., battle's anniversary with 100 full costumed interpreters & Torchlight Tour; Dec.'s 1st wk., Illuminary Tour; mid-Dec., Civil War Christmas. **Teacher's Package:** Available. **For info.:** Superintendent, Antietam National Battlefield, P.O. Box 158, Sharpsburg, MD 21782. 301/432-5124.

Chincoteague NWR

COURTESY CHINCOTEAGUE NWR

Assateague Island National Seashore

Allow: 2-3 days *Fee*

Assateague Island National Seashore is but one of three agencies sharing the island. Assateague State Park and Chincoteague National Wildlife Refuge provide different services for the 30,000,000 people who live within a 4 hr. drive. Another unique aspect of this island is that it spans two states, Maryland and Virginia, with the state line separating the national wildlife refuge from the national seashore. Both national facilities have visitor centers and interpretive programs.

Highlights

★ Originally, the seashore was set aside for recreational usage, and that's still its prime function. Most visitors come for the beaches and mild surf. However, the island is a habitat for some 225 kinds of birds.

★ The island is known for its wild horses or ponies, not truly wild but rather "feral," meaning they have returned to the wild. In summer, the beach and Old Ferry Landing are good spots to see them, while the salt marshes are favored places in the off-seasons. In Virginia, their stomping grounds are limited to protect the other wildlife. They can occasionally be seen on the "Safari" tour or from the Woodland observation platform.

Whiz Tips

❢ Maryland's Barrier Island Visitor Center features an aquarium and programs such as surf fishing and shellfishing demos, canoe trips, bird walks, salt marsh explorations and beach trips. Toms Cove Visitor Center in Virginia also has an aquarium and its programs focus on the natural wonders. Some programs like the bird walk require advance reservations.

❢ The beach parking fills up quickly in summer so you should plan on getting there early if you want to make a day of it beaching.

❢ The Chincoteague National Wildlife Refuge also has its own programs and a wildlife loop in addition to its extensive hiker/biker trails.

Kids' Stuff

★ There are Seashore Ranger programs for kids aged 6-11. By attending two of the naturalist-led programs and completing a small questionnaire, children can receive a certificate and decal.

★ There are special interpretive programs targeted at the kids. Past offerings have been a Bay Discovery trip and a Beach Discovery walk.

★ Chincoteague NWR also has children's programs like "Kid's n' Critters", their own Jr. Refuge Manager, plus a teacher's package.

Access: 150 mi. from Baltimore, MD or Washington, DC on US 50 or 140 mi. from Philadelphia, PA or 90 mi. From Norfolk, VA on US 13 & 113. **Days/Hours:** Assateague Island NS-Toms Cove, daily 8-6 & Barrier Island, daily 8:30-5:30; Chincoteague NWR-daily. **Camping:** In Maryland, 2 campgrounds (150 sites-Ticketron); Assateague State Park (311 campsites, shwrs. & some sites reserved 1 week. min). **Special Events:** During Thanksgiving week, Chincoteague NWR, Waterfowl Week. **For info.:** Superintendent, Assateague Island National Seashore, Rte.611, 7206 National Seashore Ln., Berlin, MD 21811. Toms Cove 804/336-6577. Barrier Island 301/641-3030/1441. Refuge Manager, Chincoteague National Wildlife Refuge, P.O.Box 62, Chincoteague, VA 23336. 804/336-6122.

Catoctin Mountain Park

Allow: .5 days *FREE*

Just south of Gettysburg and the Pennsylvania border is hill country that plays host to the world's leaders. Hidden deep in the woods is the presidential retreat, Camp David. The area's main attractions are its recreational opportunities and its cool mountain air. The park which looks much as it did when the first European settlers arrived, has over 20 mi. of hiking trails and 2 trout streams.

Chincoteague National Wildlife Refuge

COURTESY CHINCOTEAGUE NWR

Highlights

★ As recently as the early '30s, this area was homesteaded and stripped of it riches to make charcoal leaving a fairly denuded land. Since coming under the park service's care, it has literally blossomed into a hardwood forest which the founding fathers would recognize, proving that sub-marginal land can be restored through time and proper management.

★ Some of the special features of the park are remnants of man's passing. There are the Blue Blazes Whiskey Still, a sawmill, a blacksmith shop and a trail telling the story of charcoal-making.

Whiz Tips

The park's interpretive programs focus on both the natural and cultural history. In summer, programs rotate between the stories of moonshining, sawmills and blacksmithing. Weekend walks include spring Wildflower Walks, Fall Color Walks and summer nature walks.

The park is close enough to Washington, DC for campers to commute and see the capital's wonders while enjoying a natural setting. It proved ideal for us as we were able to use it as a central base for visiting Gettysburg (.5 hrs. N); Baltimore (1 hr. E); Washington, DC (1 hr. S); Harpers Ferry (45 min. S) and Antietam (1 hr. W).

Kids' Stuff

★ Interpretive trails have either printed brochures or signs to help you learn about the various facets of the park. In this way, you can help your children learn about the woods and its history while getting plenty of good exercise. Good family trails include: Deerfield Nature Trail Loop, Brown's Farm Trail, the Whiskey Still Trail, the Falls Nature Trail and the Charcoal Trail. The Spicebush Nature Trail, an easy .5 mi. loop, is paved with benches making it ideal for wheelchairs and baby strollers.

Access: 3 mi. W of Thurmont & Rte.15 on MD 77. **Days/Hours:** Visitor center, daily 10-4:30 (clsd. some holidays). **Camping:** Park's Owen's Creek Campground (51 sites, Apr.-Oct.); Cunningham Falls State Park, Houck Area (148 sites, & shwrs) & Manor Area (31 sites). **For info.:** Superintendent, Catoctin Mountains Park, Thurmont, MD 21788. 301/663-9388.

Catoctin Mountain Park

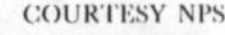

Chesapeake & Ohio Canal National Historical Park

Allow: 1 Wk. *FREE (canal boat-fee)*

"Attend all ye drivers, I sing of my team;
They're the fleetest and strongest that ever was seen....
The three altogether in motion outdo
Any team of their age, the whole canal through."

Canallers' song

As America steamed pell mell toward the twentieth century on the backs of locomotives, a quieter, more environmentally friendly mode of transportation was all but forgotten, the canal boats. From 1850 to 1924, the boats plied along 184.5 miles of the Potomac. They maneuvered through 74 lift locks that raised them 600 ft. to deliver goods from the interior to Washington. Ultimately, technology passed them by and they almost disappeared from memory. Today, you can tour the locks and even ride on a canal boat.

Highlights

★ Whether walking alongside the canal or placidly floating atop them, few can help but realize the appeal they hold. Time is something to be treasured, not to worry about. The air feels fresher, the sounds clearer, the smells subtler. There's a neighborliness that pervades everyone, a sort of shared goodwill that transcends differences and reminds one and all of the famed small-town America.

★ Beginning at the canal's terminus, the Cumberland Visitor Center, you'll find a feeder dam, a guard lock and the Paw Paw Tunnel. Hancock Information Center about 1/4 of the way downriver, has two locks and an aqueduct. The Four Locks area has four locks, a lockhouse, a dam, a mule barn and a mill. Both Great Falls and Georgetown have the canal boats, in addition to their working lock systems. The still-standing Great Falls Tavern was an inn for travelers on the system.

Whiz Tips

💡 Mule-driven, the canal boats proceeded at a stately 2 miles an hour,

Chesapeake & Ohio Canal National Historical Park

while the crew picked up extra change for ridding the dikes of ground hogs. The bordering farmers worked out a compromise to protect their produce from constant foraging by allowing the canal boat operators to cull the land immediately adjacent to the canal. The boats weighed about 21 tons and had to be continually maintained each spring because of ice damage. Locks and dikes also had to undergo constant repair. In fact, the same rains that caused the Johnstown Flood (see Johnstown Flood NMem., PA) so wrecked the dikes that the company went bankrupt trying to repair them.

Kids' Stuff

★ The canal boat ride is great for children after they've used some of their energies walking the pathways. They can also fish in the canal.

Access: Georgetown Visitor Center, downtown Georgetown, DC; Great Falls, Potomac, MD; Hancock Visitor Center, downtown Hancock, MD. **Days/Hours:** Daily (clsd. Dec.25). **Camping:** Over 25 primitive camping sites along the canal, some walk-ins. **For info.:** Superintendent, Chesapeake & Ohio Canal National Historical Park, Box 4, Sharpsburg, MD 21782. 301/739-4200. Canal Boat info.: (Georgetown) Foundry Mall, 1055 Thomas Jefferson St. NW, Washington, DC 20007. 202/472-4376. (Great Falls) Great Falls Tavern, 11710 MacArthur Blvd., Potomac, MD 20854. 301/299-2026

Clara Barton National Historic Site

Allow: 1 hr. *FREE*

"You have never known me without work, and you never will."

Clara Barton

Adjacent to Glen Echo Park is Clara Barton's 3 story combination home/office/warehouse. Clara Barton toiled throughout the Civil War, gaining fame as the "Angel of the Battlefield." She wasn't a supporter of war trying to repair the wounded so they could participate again; rather her view was: "Men have worshipped war till it has cost a million times more than the earth is worth..." She went on to found the American Red Cross in 1881.

Highlights

★ Clara Barton's home was originally constructed in 1891 with the floor plans of a hotel. It was first used as a warehouse for American Red Cross disaster relief supplies. When she converted it to living and office space, Clara made sure she could still store Red Cross supplies by having hidden closets built.

Whiz Tips

❢ "I believe I must have been born believing in the full right of women to all privileges and positions which nature and justice accord her common with other human beings." With the onset of the Civil War, Clara, a sometime school teacher and patent clerk, devoted herself to the care of the sick and wounded. After the war's conclusion, Secretary of War Stanton requested she work to locate the 100,000-plus Union soldiers who remained missing (see Andersonville NHS). In 1869, Miss Barton became involved with the International Red Cross during the Franco-Prussian War. Returning to the States, she campaigned to have the U.S. participate in the Treaty of Geneva and form its own arm of the Red Cross. In 1881, she formed her own Red Cross Society and in 1882, Congress ratified the Geneva Convention. One of the American Red Cross's first efforts was at Johnstown following the flood of 1889 (see Johnstown Flood NMem). The organization has helped people in need world-wide. Clara Barton is credited with her compassion, her work in times of war and disaster, founding the American Red Cross, her work on behalf of women's rights and her outspoken views on all of the above.

❢ The American Red Cross continues to conduct its humanitarian efforts in a number of ways. Besides providing disaster relief and a national blood bank, it conducts preventative training programs in First Aid, Water Safety and Cardio-Pulmonary Resuscitation. It aids the armed forces by providing surgical supplies, sending workers to cheer the wounded and visiting prisoners of war with gifts from home. Its members even include first aid prisoners in correctional institutes who tend to the wounds of prisoners when officials won't venture for fear of their own safety.

Kids' Stuff

★ The tour of the house traces Clara Barton's career and notes how the house reflects her unusual personality. Children can see how a determined individual, even if granted less than equal status, can rise above the social framework and accomplish a great deal. Tours before noon tend to be smaller, permitting greater interaction.

Access: Just N of Washington, from I-495 take Exits 40 or 41. **Days/Hours:** Daily 10-5 (clsd. Thanksgiving, Dec.25 & Jan.1). **Camping:** Greenbelt Park (175 sites) & Prince William Forest Park (80 sites). **For info.:** Superintendent, Clara Barton National Historic Site, 5801 Oxford Rd., Glen Echo, MD 20812. 301/492-6245.

Fort McHenry National Monument and Historic Shrine

Allow: 1-2 hrs. *Fee*

"O! say can you see by the dawn's early light' What so proudly we hailed at the twilight's last gleaming,"

Francis Scott Key
"The Star-Spangled Banner"

Wherever these words are sung in the "Land of the Free and the Home of the Brave," Fort McHenry is remembered in deed, if not by name. The star-shaped fort was typical of Early American fortifications. During the War of 1812, Fort McHenry withstood the continual bombardment from a British fleet that was still covered with soot from the burning of the nation's capital. This act of

Fort McHenry National Monument & Historic Shrine COURTESY NPS

stubborn courage saved Baltimore from a similar fate.

Highlights

★ Touring the fort provides visitors with a colorful description of what transpired on Sept. 13-14, 1814. Interestingly, the fort was initially built due to fears of war with France.

Whiz Tips

❢ Francis Scott Key watched from an American vessel while British ships conducted a cacophonous symphony. Some have questioned the "rockets red glare" phrase in the song. However, the British had successfully used rockets to frighten troops in their attack on Washington, DC. Baltimore was pre-warned of this tactic and the rockets had little effect. The British had forced some of the 15,000 American militia back to Baltimore. However, they lost their general in the opening skirmish of the Battle of Baltimore and faced a new entrenchment at the city's east side and at Fort McHenry. The fleet gave up its quest when they failed to reduce and neutralize the fort after bombarding it for 25 hours. The fort unfurled its huge (30 by 42 ft.) flag on the morning of Sept. 14 as the British sailed away. Given the fact that Baltimore was a "nest of pirates" that used the conflict to prey on British merchants, it's surprising that the British fleet gave up after just a day of bombing.

❢ During the Civil War, the fort which became known as the "Baltimore Bastille" was the scene of an ironic event. Before Maryland's government could vote to secede, Lincoln had them arrested. On Sept. 14, 1861, Frank Key Howard, a pro-slavery, pro-secessionist newspaper editor was incarcerated at Fort McHenry. Mr. Howard was Francis Scott Key's grandson.

Kids' Stuff

✯ The park has a Jr. Ranger program. By completing a qualifying fact-finding hunt, children can get a certificate and a small prize.

✯ The fort is a great place to explore. Several of the rooms have exhibits which have audio explanations. On summer weekends, children really enjoy the Fort McHenry Guard dressed in 1814 uniforms.

Access: In Baltimore on I-95 take Exit 55. **Days/Hours:** Daily 8-5 (clsd. Dec.25 & Jan.1). **Camping:** Patapsco Valley State Park, 2 locations; Hollofield-60 sites & Hilton-24 sites (both shwrs.); Greenbelt Park on beltway (175 sites). Special Events; June 14, Flag Day involves nationwide Pledge of Allegiance; Sept.'s 2nd Sun., Defenders' Day and the writing of "The Star-Spangled Banner" commemorated. **Teacher's Package:** Available. **For info.:** Superintendent, Fort McHenry National Monument and Historic Shrine, Baltimore, MD 21230-5393. 301/962-4299.

Fort Washington Park

Allow: 1 hr. *Fee*

About an hour southeast of Washington, DC, is an early 1800s fort built to protect the nation's capital. At the time of its construction, navies used wooded vessels armed with smooth-bore cannons. The first fort to occupy the site, Fort Warburton, proved of little use in the War of 1812, as the British merely landed downstream, marched around the fortification and burnt Washington. During the Civil War, the existing Fort Washington became outmoded when rifled cannons were introduced (see Fort Pulaski NM, GA). Visitors can tour this large masonry fortification and marvel at its obsolescence.

Highlights

★ It's hard to believe such a formidable fortress proved so useless when challenged. The walls seem so strong, the moat so impassable and yet it can only threaten the ill-informed.

Whiz Tips

❢ The park service conducts guided tours of the fort on weekends.

❢ After Washington, DC fell to the British and President Madison and his cabinet had escaped to the backwoods, the commander of Fort Warburton decided to destroy the structure rather than let it fall into enemy hands. Twelve days later, the French engineer, Maj. Pierre L'Enfant was commissioned to rebuild it. From 1815-1824, the fort was slowly constructed. L'Enfant was fired and a young officer named Robert E. Lee was brought in to assist. Lee never got to challenge his work because the Federal navy quickly defeated the Confederate naval effort.

Kids' Stuff

★ The fort is a great place to explore. The fort has deep interior ditches, doors leading out the base of the walls to the river bank, parapets from which to scout the countryside and cannons.

Access: 4 mi. S of the Beltway on MD 210 to Fort Washington Rd then right 3 mi. **Days/Hours:** Fort daily; summer 7:30-8 & winter 9-5 (clsd. Dec.25) **Camping:** Cedarville State Forest (130 sites & shwrs.). **Teacher's Package:** Available. **For info.:** Superintendent, Fort Washington Park, National Capital Parks-East, 1900 Anacostia Dr., SE, Washington, DC 20020. 301/763-4600.

Greenbelt Park

Allow: .5 days *FREE*

Primarily a green reserve (1,110 acres) in a highly urbanized region, Greenbelt Park provides a natural recreation area. At the turn of the century, this was abandoned farmland. Today, it's conveniently located just 12 miles from downtown Washington, DC. The park offers nature trails, camping, picnicking and interpretive programs.

Highlights

★ The nature trails allow you to see the full extent of life's recuperative powers. The growth that has flourished is typical plant life found in this region when Native Americans were the only residents. Visitors relax at

Fort Washington Park

their shaded campsites or take to the trails.

Whiz Tips

The park rangers put on summer campfire talks and conduct weekend nature walks. The topics they present range from sightseeing in the nation's capital to wildlife, Native Americans and cultural history.

Kids' Stuff

★ For city families, the park provides a nice convenient place for an outing (12 mi. of nature trails). For out-of-towners, the close proximity of a well-priced camping facility is a boon.

Access: Just off the jct. of the Beltway and the Baltimore/Washington Pkwy. **Days/ Hours:** Daily, sunrise-sunset. **Camping:** Park's campground (178 sites). **Special Events:** May, Kid's Day includes Fire Department demonstrations & Park Police presentations; fall, Take Pride in America Day. **For info.:** Area Manager, Greenbelt Park, Greenbelt, MD 20770. 301/344-3948.

Hampton National Historic Site

Allow: 1-2 hrs. *FREE*

Just north off of Baltimore's beltway, lies the country estate of the Ridgelys, a rich, slave-owning family. Much like the Vanderbilt NHS, NY, the Ridgelys' summer home epitomizes the lifestyle of this era's wealthy. What they accomplished in terms of history is minimal compared to the material goods they left for us to comprehend their lives. The Georgian 33-room mansion is one of the largest and most ornate in the country. The overseer's house, slave quarters and other plantation structures demonstrate the social order.

Highlights

★ Georgian style dictated symmetry as an ideal, so the rooms mirror one another in layout. While not all the artifacts on display were the Ridgelys, they are representative of what they owned. Each room reveals aspects of the wealthy's daily pastimes (for they clearly did not work).

Greenbelt Park COURTESY NPS

Musical instruments are in evidence in the social rooms as music was the prime entertainment of the day. For all the riches to be found here, it is interesting to note this was only the summer house and rarely, if ever, occupied during winter.

Whiz Tips

❢ Make sure to explore the grounds. On the other side of the road lie the homes of the workers and the storage buildings.

❢ For over 200 years, the Hampton estate was a working plantation. Most of the hard labor was done by slaves up until 1864 (ironically, while the 1863 *Emancipation Proclamation* freed the slaves in the states in rebellion, it didn't free slaves in Union states). Once the farm had to depend on paid labour, it struggled as did the family's fortunes. The lands also had an iron foundry which was a key supplier of weapons for the Revolutionary Army in the 1780s.

Kids' Stuff

★ The grounds prove more interesting for kids than the many gilded antiques inside. They can see "real" slave quarters and a spring house which served as the farm's refrigerator.

Access: From I-95 take Exit 27 N, then right onto Hampton Lane. **Days/Hours:** Daily, mansion tours-hourly; grounds tours-summer Tu, Th & Sa. **Camping:** Patapsco Valley State Park; Hilton Unit (24 sites& shwrs.) & Hollofield Unit (60 sites & shwrs.) **Special Events:** Early May, Heritage Festival, craft demos & children's activities. **For info.:** Site Manager, Hampton National Historic Site, 535 Hampton Lane, Towson, MD 21204. 301/962-0688.

Oxon Hill Farm

Allow: 2 hrs. *FREE*

Just south of the nation's capital is a quick fix for urban blues, a real farm. There are cows, horses, chickens, ducks, pigs, goats, sheep and turkeys. In order to house these "critters'" there are barns and coops. Fields grow the food used to feed the farm's residents. This is the ultimate family getaway.

Hampton National Historic Site

Highlights

★ The FREE hayride is a fun way to become acquainted with the grounds. Other chores you can try your hand at are: milking a cow, collecting eggs, pressing apple cider or shelling corn in season.

Whiz Tips

The "farmers" put on demonstrations of the many seasonal chores they have to perform. You can learn how to shear sheep, (something that doesn't come up too often in Washington, DC's office settings), make corn husk dolls, spin or carve wood. The workers are more than happy to interrupt their daily toil to answer questions.

Kids' Stuff

★ Beside the occasional hay ride, kids like to get involved in the action. Cow milking, egg collecting and feeding chickens are enjoyable chores done daily.

★ The Woodlot Trail has an interesting accompanying brochure to keep your children involved as they complete the circuit.

Access: Just S of Washington, from I-95 take Exit 3-A. **Days/Hours:** Daily 9-5. **Camping:** Greenbelt Park (175 sites) & Prince William Forest Park (80 sites). **For info.:** Superintendent, Oxon Hill Farm, National Capital Park-East, 1900 Anacostia Dr., SE, Washington, DC 20020. 301/839-1177.

Piscataway Park

Allow: 1-2 hrs. *FREE (fee colonial farm)*

Just south of Fort Washington is a park that owes its existence to the fact it is opposite George Washington's Mount Vernon home. Land developers and industrial interests were evaluating the property when interested parties realized the idyllic view George enjoyed was about to change drastically. The result of their efforts was the creation of the park, the National Colonial Farm and Hard Bargain Farm.

Highlights

★ National Colonial Farm (accepts the Golden Eagle Pass) has living history guides who can tell you what it was like to work the land during

Oxon Hill Farm

Piscataway Park

the nation's colonial period. The farm grows produce and raises farm animals typical of the 1700s. Their efforts to recreate the past have succeeded so well that their seeds are bought by other historic farms so they too can provide historically correct settings.

Whiz Tips

Hard Bargain Farm, an environmental education center is open to the public only a few times each year. Its primary service is to educate, on a reservation basis, thousands of children to the river environment.

Kids' Stuff

The park has a couple of picnic sites. Kids can explore the river marsh or enjoy seeing the rare Red Devon cattle, Dorset Horn sheep or razorback hogs at the colonial farm.

Access: From Beltway take Exit 37s to Rte.210S 10 mi. to Accokeek then right on Bryan's Point Rd for 4 mi. **Days/Hours:** Daily, dawn-dusk. **Camping:** Cedarville State Forest (130 sites & shwrs.). **For info.:** Superintendent, Piscataway Park, National Capital Parks-East, 1900 Anacostia Dr., SE, Washington, DC 20020. 301/283-0112.

MASSACHUSETTS

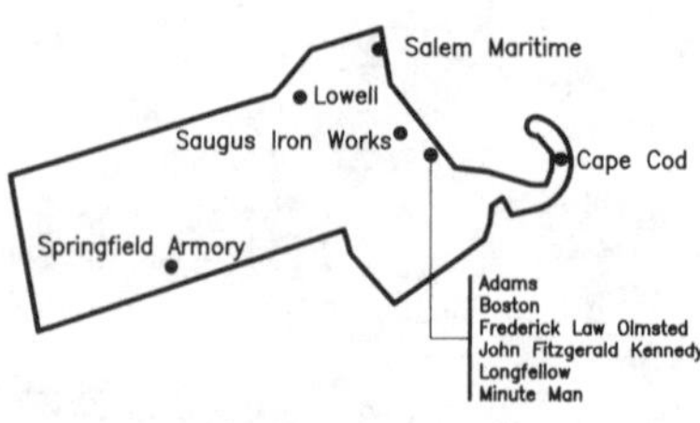

Adams National Historic Site

Allow: 2 hrs. *Fee*

The Adams family, one of the leading families in American history, lived just south of Boston in what is now Quincy. The park consists of the Adams' mansion and accompanying property and the two homes in which the only father/son American presidents, John and John Quincy Adams, were born. By visiting these buildings you can see the heights to which the Adams family rose and maintained well into the 20th century.

Highlights

★ At the birth homes, you can see that while the Adamses were landowners, they weren't moneyed. Once John became one of the country's leading lawyers, John and Abigail Adams moved into the mansion in 1788 and it served the Adams family for almost another 150 years. The ranger-led tour of the home accents the many Adams' significant careers (politicians, writers, scholars, historians and diplomats).

Whiz Tips

Ironically, John Adams conducted the successful defense of the British soldiers charged in the so called "Boston Massacre." Serving in the Continental Congress, he performed so admirably that he was referred by some as the "Atlas of American Independence." Noted for

Adams National Historic Site

his writings, including his assistance in drafting the Declaration of Independence, it was his political acumen which steered the document through the Congress. During the Revolution, Adams' service as ambassador to France brought them into the conflict, swaying the tide in America's favor. After independence, he was the American envoy to Great Britain, where he helped to heal the political wounds. It was during these diplomatic missions that his son, John Quincy Adams, was to gain an unparalleled education in foreign affairs. John described his job as George Washington's vice-president, as "...the most insignificant office that ever the invention of man contrived or his imagination conceived." As president, John was plagued by conflict with his vice-president and major political opponent, Thomas Jefferson. Ironically, on July 4, 1826, exactly 50 years from the signing of the Declaration of Independence, both John Adams and Thomas Jefferson, probably the most important men in the drafting and acceptance of this document, died. Although they had been political opponents, in their later years they enjoyed lively written correspondence.

❢ John Quincy Adams was said to have inherited his father's traits, both good and bad. At 14, he was so well-educated that he was enlisted in the foreign service as interpreter in Russia. During his diplomatic career, he negotiated some of the most important agreements in American history. The Treaty of Ghent, ending the War of 1812, is credited as one of America's most favorable settlements. He also handled the acquisition of Florida and wrote the Monroe Doctrine. In 1824, while Andrew Jackson had received the most votes, Adams, who placed second, gained the office with the aid of Henry Clay. Needless to say, the Jackson people were irritated and John Quincy's term would be beleaguered by dissension much like his father's. In 1828, he suffered the same fate as his father: defeat. However, unlike his father, he returned to politics and spent his remaining 18 years as a formidable Congressman leading the fight for civil liberties to repeal the so-called "gag rules" which prevented Congress from hearing petitions against slavery. Although both Adams presidents were unable to win re-election, an historians' poll in 1983 placed John as the 9th most effective president and John Quincy as the 16th (out of 36).

❢ Abigail Adams, John's wife and John Quincy's mom, clearly felt every bit John's equal. Her influence on the two Adams presidents helped shape this country. Other Adams progeny includes a stellar group. Charles Francis Adams, who ran unsuccessfully as Martin Van Buren's vice-president, served as the Union's Minister to Great Britain during the Civil War and is credited with preventing England from aiding the Confederacy. Charles Adams II, who served as a brigadier general in the Civil War, became a scholar exposing the corruption in railroading. He then became the president of the Union Pacific Railroad. His brother, John Quincy Adams II, was a politician, and another brother, Brooks Adams, was a writer. The fourth brother, Henry, became perhaps the greatest 19th century American historian.

Kids' Stuff

★ The Adamses were not the charismatic leaders that most children learn about in school. Rather, the family displayed their prodigious intellectual gifts. The homes prove interesting because they serve as examples of homes for the period. Our 12-year-old nephew had studied this talented family and was very focussed during the visit.

★ The Adamses' mansion makes a special attempt to help kids better understand the site by providing a children's package. In addition, there's a Jr. Ranger program in the works.

Access: S from Boston on I-93 take Exit 8 to 135 Adams St. or 133-141 Franklin St., Quincy. **Days/Hours:** Daily Apr.19-Nov.10, 9-5. **Camping:** Wompatuck State Park at Hingham S take Exit 14 (400 sites, elec. & showers). **Teacher's Package:** Available. **For info.:** Superintendent, Adams National Historic Site, P.O.Box 531, Quincy, MA 02269. 617/773-1177.

Blackstone River Valley National Heritage Corridor

The industrial miracle that became the most powerful nation in the world began here along the 40 some miles of river and canals joining Worcester, MA to Providence, RI. Today the affiliated mills, villages and transportation networks relate the industrialization of America.

For info.: c/o Blackstone River Valley National Heritage Corridor Commission, National Park Service, 15 State St., Boston, MA 02109.

Boston African American National Historic Site

Allow: 2-3 hrs. *FREE*

Beacon Hill homes that sell for millions were first built and owned by the elite of Boston's African Americans and known as "behind the beyond." Beginning at Boston Common, you follow an urban ranger along the Black Heritage Trail past homes to schools ending at the African Meeting House. During the tour, you learn about these historic residents and the anti-slavery movement.

Highlights

★ Boston Common's Augustus Saint Gaudens' (see Saint Gaudens NHS, NH) statue depicts the Massachusetts' 54th, the first African American regiment to fight in the Civil War, whose exploits were described in the film, *Glory.* Ironically, this monument, dedicated to remind us of this courageous group of men, originally honored only the white officers lost in the war. It was not until

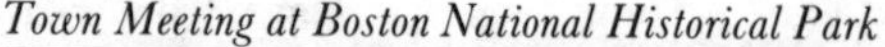

Town Meeting at Boston National Historical Park

much later that the names of the heroic dead African Americans were carved into the stone.

★ The African Meeting House which serves as the terminal for your tour, played a unique role in binding the community. Like an African American Faneuil Hall (see Boston NHP, MA), the building mixed godly worship with political angst. It is the oldest African American church still standing in the United States.

Whiz Tips

Boston was a hot-bed of anti-slavery rhetoric, and the Beacon Hill area became a haven for runaway slaves and a major depot in the Underground Railroad. In 1832, the historic "Declaration of Anti-Slavery Sentiments" were read from the pulpit of the African Meeting House.

The Boston NHP visitor center across from the Old State House can give you the times for the tour.

Kids' Stuff

★ Children who have studied the Civil War and are aware of African American slavery will greatly enhance their knowledge on the tour. The Black Heritage Trail demonstrates that early 19th century free African Americans were able to forge a good life and made schooling a priority for their community.

Access: Downtown Boston. **Days/Hours:** Daily. **Camping:** Wompatuck State Park at Hingham has 400 sites S on Rte. 3-Exit 14 (elec. & showers). **For info.:** Superintendent, Boston African American National Historic Site, 46 Joy St., Boston, MA 02114. 617/742-5415.

Boston National Historical Park

Allow: 1-2 days *FREE*

"Full of crooked little streets; but I tell you Boston has opened and kept open more turnpikes that lead straight to free thought and free speech and free deeds than any other city..."

Oliver Wendell Holmes
The Professor at the Breakfast Table

Boston has painted the town red creating the Freedom Trail. As you follow the 2.5 mi. red line/paving

Boston African American National Historic Site

stones, you discover not just historic Boston but an energetic urban cornucopia. At one end of the red line is the Shaw Memorial, a tribute to the African American Massachusetts 54th regiment. At the other, Bunker Hill Monument marks the 1775 battle against the British redcoats. In between are public buildings where colonials gathered to debate the issues of the day, Paul Revere's home and noteworthy sites. You can tour these sites on your own or with a park ranger.

Highlights

★ A good place to start your journey is at the visitor center near the Old State House and the marker designating the site of the Boston Massacre. Inside you can get the lowdown on all the sites, tours and talks that are available.

★ The Charlestown Navy Yard is home to USS *Constitution*, (*Old Ironsides*), and USS *Cassin Young*, a destroyer representative of the product this same yard produced in WW II. Naval tour guides proudly regale visitors with *Constitution*'s accomplishments. Volunteers staff *Cassin Young* and rangers lead tours of *Cassin Young*.

Boston National Historical Park

COURTESY NPS

★ Boston's "Cradle of Liberty," Faneuil Hall, has rangers on hand giving regular talks about its place in history. The hall became a place for colonists to vent their frustrations over the actions of the distant crown.

★ Breed's Hill, not Bunker Hill, is the site of Bunker Hill Monument, a stone obelisk with 294 steps to a view of the Boston area. The name confusion appears to have transpired when the revolutionary forces erected their fortifications here instead of on the taller Bunker Hill as they planned (the reason still seems to be in doubt). The British won the battle but at a great cost. The "winners'" losses were 1,054 casualties versus the "losers'" at 441.

Whiz Tips

❢ If Paul Revere has been overly acclaimed thanks to Longfellow's poetry, the national parks in Boston certainly clarify his role. At Minute Man NHP, Longfellow NHS and the Freedom Trail, rangers explained how Revere was only one of two riders (William Dawes, was the other) who conveyed the news of British troop movement to others, who in turn passed the message along. Revere never even reached Concord. At the time of the Revolution, he was more renowned for his silver impression of the so-called Boston Massacre, another over-dramatized incident.

❢ The Boston Massacre is marked by a stone in a road divider. Five locals were shot and killed during a staged riot against British rule. The British soldiers, grossly outnumbered, were being assaulted with rocks. The upshot of the "massacre" was that John Adams (see Adams NHS) successfully defended the soldiers but the colonists were enflamed by the exaggerated stories of the event.

Kids' Stuff

★ Our kids enjoyed scrambling over the destroyer and visiting the *Constitution.* They loved exploring the Freedom Trail as we wandered from pillar to post, but their "bestest" thing was the Town Meeting where they got to throw their "two bits" into the debate. Not an everyday event, rangers dress up in 1770s togs and collect in front of the Old South Meeting Hall. There, they enlist the audience to debate the actions they should take against the crown. Even our little ones got to contribute. The Meeting Hall was the scene of the post-Massacre march demanding and getting British soldiers removed from Boston proper. It also served as the jumping-off point for the revelers partaking in the famous Boston Tea Party.

Access: Downtown Boston. **Days/Hours:** Visitor center summer M-F 8-6 & wknds. 9-6 & early June & Sept. M-F 8-5 & wknds. 9-5. Faneuil Hall daily 9-5. U.S.S. Constitution daily 9:30-3:50 & U.S.S. Cassin Young 9:30-5. Bunker Hill daily 9-5. **Camping:** Wompatuck State Park at Hingham has 400 sites S on Rte. 3-Exit 14 (elec. & showers). **Teacher's Package:** Available. **For info.:** Superintendent, Boston National Historical Park, Charlestown Navy Yard, Boston, MA 02129. 617/242-5642.

Cape Cod National Seashore

Allow: 2-3 days *Fee*

"A first glimpse of the great outer beach of Cape Cod is one of the most memorable experiences in all America."

Henry Beston
intro. to Thoreau's *Cape Cod*

Like a beckoning finger, the cape extends out from the mainland curling northward toward Boston. Its proximity to the heavily populated northeast has made it a brand name for chips and sweaters. Its seashore towns are almost as recognizable: Hyannis Port and Provincetown. The Cape is sand, salt air, waves breaking, converted fishing villages-cum-artist colonies, solitary silhouettes sand-strolling, seagulls skirmishing for scraps and bathing beauties baking their bodies. It's the place where you join everybody else to get away from it all. As Henry Da-

Cape Cod National Seashore

vid Thoreau said in his book *Cape Cod*, "A man may stand here and put all America behind him." Mind you, sometimes they are right behind him.

Highlights

★ The beaches along the Cape are great places for a family outing. Kids cavort along the seashore, making sand castles, running into the surf and collecting their salty treasures. Try to get there early as parking is limited and easy access to the beaches will be closed when the lots fill.

★ Visiting Marconi's Wireless Station dramatizes how far we've come in this century. How commonplace it seems to watch live broadcasts from around the world. How difficult it must have been to imagine such a thing when overseas communication took a week by boat.

★ As odd as it may sound, take one of the swamp trails. Because swamps offer protection for smaller critters, they make great places to explore for wildlife.

Whiz Tips

The park has an outstanding selection of interpretive programs in the peak months. Each of their ecosystems can be examined with an able ranger-guide. Because Cape Cod caused so many boating mishaps, lighthouses and life-saving programs had to be developed and maintained. The rangers explain the importance of these functions.

The mile-high glaciers scoured the Great Canadian Shield, ground up the rocks and left enormous mounds of sand which the ocean is continually re-distributing like some Atlantic City faro dealer.

There are 9 self-guiding nature trails open all year. Salt marshes teem with life serving as nurseries for ocean bound creatures. Birds use the still waters to rest on their longitudinal journeys. The sandy shores and dunes nurture crabs, sand dollars, skates, gulls, beach grass and poison ivy.

Off-shore are the migratory waters of the great Atlantic whales. While the park doesn't have much involvement with these marine mammals, the nearby towns run tours at better prices than the mainland because of their proximity.

Kids' Stuff

There are several programs tailored to kids. Our crew attended one children's program which coupled mask-making with a blind-man's bluff seashore treasure hunt. They were forced to use their non-visual senses to determine where they were and what the objects they fondled might be.

For a small fee, children can attend two programs and perform some park clean-up to achieve a Jr. Ranger badge.

Our children had a ball here exploring the waterfront, swimming in the saltwater and constructing sand developments. There are also three well-developed bicycle trails ideal for family use.

Access: Salt Pond Visitor Center in Eastham on Rte. 6 & Province Land Visitor Center in Provincetown on Race Pt. Rd. **Days/Hours:** Salt Pond Visitor Center, daily, Mar.-Dec., summer 9-6 & winter 9-4:30. Province Lands Visitor Center, daily mid-Apr.-Thanksgiving, summer 9-6 & 9-4:30. **Camping:** Nearby East Brewster, Nickerson State Park (400 sites & shwrs.); Bourne Scenic Park; Scusset State Beach Reservation (100 sites, elec. & shwrs.); Shawme Crowell State Forest (260 sites & shwrs.). **Teacher's Package:** Available. **For info.:** Superintendent, Cape Cod National Seashore, South Wellfleet, MA 02663. 508/349-3785 or 487-1256 or 255-3421.

Frederick Law Olmstead National Historic Site

Allow: 1-2 hrs. *FREE*

Frederick Law Olmstead is credited as being the founder of American landscaping. He helped design New York's Central Park, was a key element in the establishment of Yosemite as a national park and planned or influenced a number of North American city parks. Visitors can tour "Fairstead," his Brookline home and see the many elements of landscaping.

Highlights

★ For most of us, city parks are commonplace. We don't think about their design a great deal unless we're concerned with finding parking. At "Fairstead," you can see how each facet of a park is planned and learn why.

Whiz Tips

❢ The rangers introduce you to Olmstead and his work with an AV. They then show his lithographs, maps, plans and photographs.

Kids' Stuff

✱ Children can learn about the "how" and the "why" of parks.

Access: 99 Warren St. (& Dudley) in Brookline. **Days/Hours:** F-Su 10-4:30 (clsd. Thanksgiving, Dec.25 & Jan.1). **Camping:** Wompatuck State Park at Hingham has 400 sites S on Rte. 3 take Exit 14 (elec. & showers). **For info.:** Superintendent, Frederick Law Olmstead National Historic Site, 99 Warren St., Brookline, MA 02146. 617/566-1689.

John Fitzgerald Kennedy National Historic Site

Allow: .5-1 hr. *Fee*

"...ask not what your country can do for you ask what you can do for your country"

President John F. Kennedy

In the Boston suburb of Brookline is the birthhome of the nation's 35th president. Although both Joseph and Rose Kennedy, his parents, came from relatively well-to-do parents,

John F. Kennedy National Historic Site

this home is decidedly middle class, a well-built structure suited to its neighborhood. The family lived in the house for seven years before they moved to larger quarters to house their growing family. John was four years old at the time. The house was restored by Rose Kennedy and looks today as she remembered it did in 1917 when JFK was born. Visitors can tour the home and learn more about the Kennedy mystique.

Highlights

★ During the guided tour, you see the importance John's mother Rose had in shaping the family. Rose felt strongly about providing her children with a sense of community responsibility and the need to excel. The park also offers walking tours (spring-fall) of the Kennedy neighborhood.

Whiz Tips

❢ For any parent wishing to create an environment in which their children will excel, this is a mandatory stop. The oldest son, Joe, died a war hero but was felt by all to be the most likely to succeed. Bobby and Teddy became senators and both were presidential candidates. John's career reads like a storybook. He wrote his first book as a junior at Harvard from which he graduated "cum laude." He was a genuine Second World War hero in the Pacific when he led his PT 109 boat crew to safety after it was sunk by the Japanese. He progressed from the House of Representatives to the Senate by age 36. He won a Pulitzer Prize in history for his book, *Profiles in Courage*. In 1960, he became the nation's youngest elected President at age 40. He also was the first Roman Catholic to attain the office. While he only served three years, his charismatic presence and moving speeches have made him a figure to which other candidates are compared. The 1983 poll of 900 historians placed JFK as the 13th most effective president out of the 36 considered.

Kids' Stuff

★ Perhaps Kennedy's legend is more telling in how children react to his name. Although its been almost 30 years since his death, pre-teen children still know a great deal about him.

★ The house tour is relatively short and the articles are recent enough that most kids, no matter how small, recognize most of the furnishings.

Access: Downtown Brookline. **Days/Hours:** Daily 10-4:30 (clsd. Thanksgiving, Dec.25 & Jan.1). **Camping:** Wompatuck State Park at Hingham has 400 sites S on Rte. 3 take Exit 14 (elec. & showers). **Special Events:** Wknd. closest May 29, JKF's birthday; 2nd. wknd. in Dec. **Teacher's Package:** Available. **For info.:** Superintendent, Olmsted, Longfellow, Kennedy National Historic Sites, 83 Beals St., Brookline, MA 02146. 617/566-7937.

Longfellow National Historic Site

Allow: 1-2 hrs. *Fee*

Near Harvard Square is the estate of America's most popular 19th century poet, Henry Wadsworth Longfellow. The large mansion reflects Longfellow's taste as well as the lifestyles of his era's well-to-do. Longfellow, whose popularity has begun to dim with time, remains the only American poet to have a bust in Westminster Abbey's Poet's Corner.

Highlights

★ While the house reflects the ostentation of new-found wealth, there is a homeyness about it. As a student border in the home, Longfellow learned George Washington had used the place as his Boston headquarters. The poet liked this bit of history and desired the home. Fortunately, he married "up" so-to-speak, and was able to gain possession of the building when he came to Harvard to teach. Longfellow's friends included such luminaries as Senator Charles Sumner, the famous abolitionist, novelist, Nathaniel Hawthorne and philosopher, Ralph Waldo Emerson.

Whiz Tips

Longfellow was educated, then taught at Maine's prestigious Bowdoin College. His class has to have been one of the most illustrious in American history. He went to school with Nathaniel Hawthorne and the nation's 14th president, Franklin Pierce. Longfellow travelled to Europe to broaden his horizons and displayed an amazing gift for language acquisition. Not only did he master the major European tongues, but he also learned Icelandic and Finnish. His most famous pieces include *Evangeline, Hiawatha* and *Paul Revere and his Midnight Ride.* He became so famous throughout the western world that, in 1885, when he published the *Courtship of Miles Standish,* his first day sales were 15,000.

Kids' Stuff

Longfellow had a special affinity for his children and wrote for them. One of his most famous children's writings is *The Children's Hour.*

The tour of the house was a little much for our smaller children, but they got a kick out plucking a poem from the Poet Tree (poetry) and hearing their poem which they could take with them. On the other hand, our 12-year-old nephew, who had studied Longfellow, was quite interested in seeing his home.

Access: Just W of Harvard Square or downtown Cambridge. **Days/Hours:** Daily (clsd. Thanksgiving, Dec.25 & Jan.1). **Camping:** Wompatuck State Park at Hingham has 400 sites S on Rte. 3 take Exit 14 (elec. & showers). **Special Events:** Throughout the summer, Longfellow Poetry Reading Series & Garden Concert Series. **For info.:** Superintendent, Longfellow National Historic Site, 105 Brattle St., Cambridge, MA 02138. 617/876-4491.

Lowell National Historical Park

Allow: .5 days Fee

"...the only city in the United States with

Longfellow National Historic Site

factory stacks rising higher than its church steeples."

Jack Kerouac, graduate of Lowell High School *On the Road*

Not far from Boston near the New Hampshire border is the industrial town of Lowell. In 1824, this small city started an industrial revolution America is still experiencing. Making use of Pawtucket Falls and the Merrimack River, investor Francis Cabot Lowell came to the hamlet of East Chelmsford and built cotton mills. Since then, the town's fortunes have risen and fallen with the factories'. The park maintains historic mills, canals, trolley lines, worker housing, a visitor center and the Boott Cotton Mills Museum.

Highlights

★ There are a variety of interpretive tours available. Most entail the trolley ride, canal boat rides and tours of the Suffolk Mill. Others include walking tours of Lowell, boat rides to Pawtucket Falls and a Sunset Cruise along the Merrimack. Each seeks to introduce you to what Anthony Trollope called in his 1862 *North America* book, "...the realization of a commercial Utopia." Were it so.

Whiz Tips

❢ Francis Cabot Lowell put his photographic memory to good use when he toured England's industrial plants. When he returned to America, he was able to build his own power looms and cotton mills. Water drove the big machines, washed the material and unfortunately, contaminated the people who worked there. Lowell, famous for his paternalism, relied on women from rural areas. He built chaperoned boarding houses so they could remain respectable, a trait society felt was an anomaly for a "working" woman.

❢ The industrialization of cotton milling created a tremendous drop in the product's price because of oversupply. Plant owners who had invested heavily in buildings and machinery sought to compete by lowering wages. By hiring new immi-

Lowell National Historical Park COURTESY JIM HIGGINS

grants and women, these industrial "leaders" exploited cheap labor. The working conditions in the mills got so bad that 60-year-old workers were a rarity. Subject to deafness and acute emphysema, the workers also suffered the "Kiss of Death," tuberculosis, when they pulled threads through shuttles using their mouths after infected workers had already done the same.

Kids' Stuff

★ The park advises the shorter tours for children, but we have to disagree. The continual changes in settings on the full tour keeps it interesting and enjoyable. Our children loved the canal ride, didn't seem to recognize how short the trolley ride was and were totally entranced with the living historical mill worker, Sarah Page.

Access: Downtown Lowell. **Days/Hours:** Daily 8:30-5 (clsd. Thanksgiving, Dec.25 & Jan.1); boat tours (July 1-Columbus Day) & walking tours (Oct.-June). **Camping:** Nearby N. Andover, Harold Parker State Forest (129 sites, showers). **Special Events:** Early Apr., Thoreau's Portage Whitewater Invitational Slalom; late July, Lowell Folk Festival; early Sept., Annual Banjo & Fiddle Contests; end of Oct., Great Pumpkin Halloween Festival; Nov.30/Dec.1, City of Lights Holiday Festival & Toys for Tots Telethon. **Teacher's Package:** Available. **For info.:** Superintendent, Lowell National Historical Park, 169 Merrimack St., Lowell, MA 01852. 508/459-1000.

Minute Man National Historical Park

Allow: 2-3 hrs. *FREE (fee at Wayside)*

"By the rude bridge that arched the flood, their flags to April's breeze unfurled, here once the embattled farmers stood, and fired, the shot heard round the world!"

Ralph Waldo Emerson

On the western outskirts of Boston along a heavily used commuter road, is the path the retreating British army followed back from Concord. The famed Minute Men, those Revolutionary figures of mythic portions, gained their fame at the Battle of Concord when they chased the "lobster-backs" back to Boston. The park embraces many important sites along this path including the grounds where the famous shot was fired.

Highlights

★ The Concord Unit hardly seems the place where farmer and merchant took up arms against their mother country. After finding a small quantity of the weapons and munitions they heard were hidden there, the British burned them. The patriot militia hiding across the river saw the smoke and became enraged, thinking the British were burning the town. Charging back toward the town, the famous shot was fired. Major Buttrick said "Fire, fellow soldiers, for God's sake, Fire!" These were the first shots fired into the ranks of British soldiers by the colonists.

★ At Battle Road Visitor Center, the duck pond, rolling hills and comely woods stand in contrast to the scenes that were played here in 1775. From behind farm houses and barns, fences and trees, men fired upon the authorities. Although they had limited firepower, they humiliated the King's finest and demonstrated their displeasure with British rule.

★ Dissociated with the Revolutionary War, the Wayside was the home of three generations of authors, including Amos Bronson Alcott, young Louisa May Alcott, Nathaniel Hawthorne and Harriet Lothrop (Margaret Sidney).

Whiz Tips

❢ The sites have special interpretive programs throughout the summer. Some of these include a 1774 Town Meeting, Paul Revere, the man behind the myth and the British Soldier.

This action more than any other defines the start of the American Revolution. The Boston Tea Party was but a form of protest. The Boston Massacre proved to be a footnote. After the fighting at Lexington and Concord, every colony prepared for rebellion.

Minute Men were formed from a long-standing British colonial practice. Each month, villagers were required to train so they would be prepared to fight in event of an Indian or French attack. Rebel leaders initiated a more rigorous training program requiring volunteers to train at least once a week and to keep their weapons close by so they could react within a minute's notice. Both minute men and militia only fought so long as they had ammunition. Once they were out of bullets, they went home.

Kids' Stuff

★ Each site has costumed rangers who give the talks and demonstrate the loading and firing of their weapons.

★ At the North Ridge Visitor Center, there's a "dress-up" room on the second floor where kids can put on colonial clothes to see how they would have looked in the late 1700s.

Access: North Bridge off Liberty St. in Concord; Battle Road off Rte.2A in Lexington. **Days/Hours:** Daily 8:30-5, winter only North Bridge Visitor Center open; the Wayside, summer tours F-Tu. **Camping:** Nearby N. Andover, Harold Parker State Forest (129 sites, showers). **Teacher's Package:** Available. **For info.:** Superintendent, Minute Man National Historical Park, Box 160, Concord, MA 01742. 617/862-7753 or 508/369-6993.

Salem Maritime National Historic Site

Allow: .5 days *FREE*

"The seaports of Massachusetts have turned their backs to the element that made them great, save for play and fishing..."

Samuel Eliot Morison
Maritime History of Massachusetts

When one thinks of Salem, Mass., one thinks of witches. However, Salem's story is one of industry, inter-

Minute Man National Historical Park

national trade, foreign ports, pirates and meddling federal policies. Once the sixth largest city in the country, Salem accounted for 14% of the nation's entire tax base. What happened to this national treasure trove? The park uses historic buildings and interpretive programs to trace Salem's rich and storied business life.

Highlights

★ The remaining wharf, Custom House, and Derby residences are but vestiges of Salem's glory days. The town once boasted over 50 wharfs and Salem's sailors travelled from the Baltic Sea to Africa and on to the far east leaving natives in these climes with the mistaken impression that "Salem" was a rich country in its own right.

Whiz Tips

The nation's 3rd oldest settlement began as a fishing village. During the Revolutionary War, Salem was one of the few coastal ports to shake off British chains and to conduct privateering raids capturing 450 British vessels.

This early prowess at sea allowed Salem to capitalize on its new found trading freedom. Called the "Venice of the New World," Salem may have been the place where the term "Yankee Ingenuity" was coined. Discovering the Dutch were monopolizing the supply of coffee and pepper, the Salem traders usurped their supplies by buying direct, extracting a 700% profit from pepper alone. To demonstrate how much impact these Yankee traders made in their short reign (3 decades), until very recently, Australians referred to pepper as Salem pepper. Two acts in the early 1800s caused Salem's decline as a seaport. In 1807, Thomas Jefferson almost caused the secession of the New England states when he put an embargo on trade because a small number of American vessels were being attacked by Barbary pirates or were being confiscated by warring France and England. During the War of 1812, larger clipper ships which Salem's harbor couldn't hold became the trading vessels of choice. Forced to change its focus, Salem built mills and shipped in raw materials to feed its new industry. Like most American mill towns, it suffered when too

Salem Maritime National Historic Site

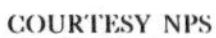
COURTESY NPS

many competitors entered the market.

Kids' Stuff

★ Almost all of the interpretive programs take young visitors into consideration. The programs incorporate costumes for children to wear and "hands-on" materials including how to build a ship.

Access: Downtown Salem. **Days/Hours:** Daily, summer 8:30-6 & winter 9-5 (clsd. Thanksgiving, Dec.25 & Jan.1) **Camping:** Nearby N. Andover, Harold Parker State Forest (129 sites, showers). **Special Events:** June's first weekend, Maritime Festival with many activities for kids; end of Oct., Haunted Happenings with children's dress-up events. **Teacher's Package:** Available. **For info.:** Superintendent, Salem Maritime National Historic Site, 174 Derby St., Salem, MA 01970. 508/745-1470.

Saugus Iron Works National Historic Site

Allow: 2 hrs. *FREE*

North of Boston is a picturesque site dedicated to recreating a 17th century ironworks. Down in the valley, water drives huge wooden wheels, which in turn work giant-sized bellows and gears. This was America's first successful ironworks and one of the first places where colonists were allowed to make a finished product from raw materials. As you tour this recreated industrial facility, you can learn how iron is made and how it is shaped into useful items.

Highlights

★ Saugus Iron Works is more than quaint rustic buildings; it's the American story in miniature. An entrepreneur saw the potential for making money by supplying people who were desperate for iron. He raised the capital and brought in skilled craftsmen. Heck, he even went so far as to make a little less than an above-board deal for some captured Scottish rebels. He created a whole community to run this operation. Sure, he struggled and there were worker problems but the iron works survived for 22 years.

★ The Iron Works House is the only structure remaining from the 17th century. Five rooms are open to viewing and contain furnishings.

Whiz Tips

💡 Make sure you tour the Works with the ranger so you get the full story and the blacksmith's demonstration. Iron was made with "bog myne" (iron ore) from the marshy Saugus River, "rock myne" (gabbro) from the Nahant peninsula and charcoal from the nearby forests. Under tremendous heat, the iron ore was added to the charcoal and gabbro. The gabbro acted to remove the impurities in the iron ore, thus purifying the final product. The slag or impurities floated to the top and were removed. Once or twice daily, the molten iron was tapped and allowed to run out into a sand trough where it hardened into a bar called a sow

Saugus Iron Works National Historic Site

(hence the term pig iron). The finer quality iron was run into molds for pots, kettles and other finished products. The remaining pig iron continued to be worked. Although Saugus failed because of mismanagement and high production costs, it provided the spark which caused other iron works to flame.

Kids' Stuff

★ While the workings of the enterprise are a challenge to most adults, the site nevertheless intrigues children. Just seeing the waterwheel drive the bellows causes kids to "oh" and "ah." The blacksmith took his time to explain each part of the workings and gave our kids free 17th century style nails he made on the spot.

★ There's a 1/2 mi. marsh and woodland nature trail you can explore using an interpretive pamphlet.

Access: In town of Saugus at 244 Central St. **Days/Hours:** Daily, summer 9-5 & winter 9-4 (clsd. Thanksgiving, Dec.25 & Jan.1). **Camping:** Harold Parker State Forest near N. Andover (129 sites, showers). **Teacher's Package:** Available. **For info.:** Superintendent, Saugus Iron Works National Historic Site, 244 Central St., Saugus, MA 01906. 617/233-0050.

Springfield Armory National Historic Site

Allow: 1-2 hrs. *FREE*

"Marooned on a rocky soil, Massachusetts men had to be ingenious to survive, and they early became skilled at devising shrewd 'notions,' commercial and intellectual."

Ray Bease
Massachusetts

Starting life as a depository for the nation's weapons to be utilized in times of need, Springfield Armory grew to capitalize on some of the 'notions' of these shrewd New Englanders. The Springfield site which saw three different centuries of use as a combination armory, arsenal and magazine, preserves its buildings, small arms exhibits and armament innovations.

Highlights

★ The small arms collection displayed in the Main Arsenal is re-

Springfield Armory National Historic Site

COURTESY NPS

garded as the world's largest. Visitors can see how these weapons were manufactured and why changes occurred.

★ An unusual highpoint is the free-standing spiral staircase. How it supports its own weight let alone others, is an engineering feat.

Whiz Tips

To facilitate your learning experience, the newly renovated museum has "hands-on" displays and station monitors with computer graphics and short AVs explaining the history of American arms production.

The Springfield Arsenal (Armory) played a key role in a little-known American revolution just after the well-known American Revolution. Folks in Massachusetts were very concerned about taxes and farmers losing their property because of debts. Daniel Shays, a destitute farmer and Revolutionary army captain, directed 1200 men to capture Springfield Armory and arm themselves. The newly raised state government forces dispersed the unruly force and hunted them down. This encounter accelerated the adoption of a federal constitution.

The armory is credited with a number of inventions. Thomas Blanchard produced a lathe which could crank out identical gun stocks. Master Armorer Erskine Allin came up with the 1903 Springfield which introduced breech-loading into outmoded muzzle-loaders. Later products included the M1 and M14s.

Kids' Stuff

★ The park suggests children over the age of 10 are better able to understand the arms and the production exhibits.

Access: In Springfield. **Days/Hours:** Daily 9-5 (clsd. Thanksgiving, Dec.25 & Jan.1). **Camping:** Granville State Forest W on MA 57 (39 sites). **Teacher's Package:** Available. **For info.:** Superintendent, Springfield Armory National Historic Site, 1 Armory Sq., Springfield, MA 01105. 413/734-8551.

MICHIGAN

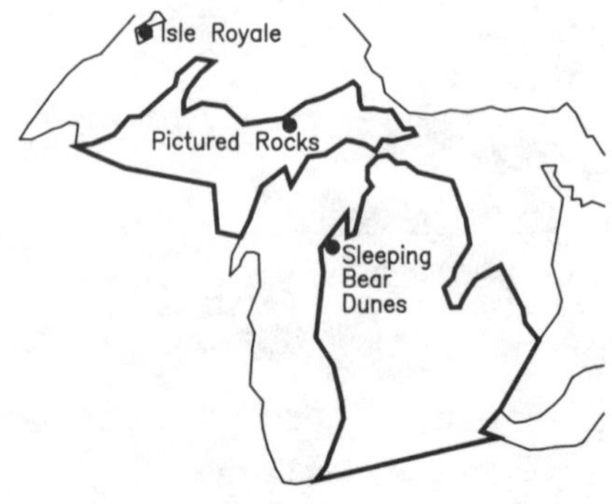

Father Marquette National Memorial

One of the first Europeans to venture this far west in the 17th century was Father Jacques Marquette. The French priest and explorer founded a Jesuit mission at this affiliated site in 1671 and was buried at it in 1678.

For info.: Father Marquette National Memorial, Parks Div., Michigan Dept. of Natural Resources, P.O.Box 30028, Lansing, MI 48909.

Isle Royale National Park

Allow: 1 week *FREE*

Isle Royale is 4.5-6 hrs. by boat from either Grand Portage, MN or Houghton or Copper Harbour, MI. A sanctuary for the eastern timber wolf and moose, 99% of the park is legally designated a wilderness. True, it has 166 mi. of trails, but it is the adventuresome who take to them. The park includes the island sitting just inside the U.S./Canadian border and much its bordering Lake Superior waters.

Highlights

★ Pocked with bright blue lakes and shimmering rivers amid rich green forests, the island is a nature lovers Nirvana, a quiet natural temple in which to worship the mother who tends it.

Whiz Tips

One of the most interesting facets of the island is its large mammal wildlife. Although both moose and wolf are today's residents, they weren't to be found here at the turn of the century. By tracing their beginnings, scientists have been able to see how and why certain species exist and adapt in isolation. The moose came first, probably putting their considerable swimming skills to use. Wolves likely came across the frozen ice from Canada in the winter of 1948-49. Before the wolf came, the moose population experienced extreme swings as they either ate themselves out of "house and home" and were subsequently so reduced in numbers that the abundant plant life allowed them to feast. With the introduction of the wolf, a natural predator, both animals have maintained balanced populations.

The park visitor/information centers offer interpretive programs. One topic they cover is the early copper mining that Native Americans did on the island. The copper they mined has been found throughout the Mississippi River valley.

Kids' Stuff

Like most wilderness parks, it's difficult to cater for children (there are no phones and very few facilities). For families who do visit, you can rent canoes to explore the island's lakes (the park warns against going out on Lake Superior - something about 6 ft. high swells and 50 degrees F. waters). There is fishing in all the waters.

Access: Boat or float plane. **Days/Hours:** Summer season. **Camping:** Permit backcountry camping. **For info.:** Superintendent, Isle Royale National Park, Houghton, MI 49931. 906/482-0984.

Pictured Rocks National Lakeshore

Allow: 1-2 days *FREE*

"The lake country of Michigan handsome as a well-made woman, and dressed and jeweled."

John Steinbeck
Travels with Charley

The first national lakeshore comprises 40 miles of Michigan's Lake Superior shoreline, almost half of which consists of the famed "pictured rocks." Multi-hued layers of sandstone have been carved by the lake waters into turrets and towers, caves and coves, arches and angles. The lakeshore includes Twelvemile Beach, a sand and pebble playground.

Highlights

★ With 50 degree F. water temperature, Lake Superior is noted more as a boating and fishing recreation spot than as a swimmer's delight. The lakeshore has over 100 mi. of hiking trails leading to several waterfalls or overlooks.

Whiz Tips

❢ During summer there are daily ranger-led interpretive programs. Past offerings have included strolls through Grand Sable Dunes, walks from Miners Castle, hikes along Twelvemile Beach up to the Au Sable Light Station, wildflower searches, swamp jaunts and nature treks. In winter the park offers limited programs featuring local people describing their life and work in the region.

Kids' Stuff

★ In addition to the regular interpretive programs which cater to families, on summer Saturdays the park puts on special children's programs such as; dunes hiking, beachcombing or cultural demonstrations.

★ There are few park hikes that overtax an active family. Most are less than 2 miles round-trip and provide ample opportunity for little ones to explore the great outdoors.

Access: 2 mi. E of Munising & 2 mi. W of Grand Marais off Cty.Rd.H-58. **Days/ Hours:** Munising visitor center, summer, daily 8-6; spring & fall, daily 9-4:30 & winter, Tu-Sa 9-4:30. **Camping:** Park's Twelvemile Beach (37 sites), Little Beaver (8 sites) & Hurricane River (21 sites). **For info.:** Superintendent, Pictured Rocks National Lakeshore, P.O.Box 40, Munising, MI 49862. 906/387-3700.

Sleeping Bear Dunes National Lakeshore

Allow: 1-2 days *FREE*

According to Chippewa legend, a mother bear and her pair of cubs were escaping a fire in Wisconsin by swimming across Lake Michigan. After reaching the shore, she lay down to await her cubs. They never made it. The mother continues to wait as Sleeping Bear Dune, while the Manitou Islands are the drowned cubs. This national sea-

Sleeping Dunes National Lakeshore COURTESY NPS

shore alongside Lake Michigan's northeastern shores contains islands, dunes, inland lakes and miles of sandy beach.

Highlights

★ Sleeping Bear Dune rises 500 feet above the lake, offering marvelous vistas for those who trudge to the top. The pine and hardwood forests encroaching upon the shoreline and stretching off into the distance present different appearances with each season. The Pierce Stocking Scenic Drive is another great way to see the sights of the area.

★ Visiting the Manitou Islands is a unique experience. North Manitou, the larger of the two, has a lake, dunes and several miles of trails covering its 15,000 acres. South Manitou offers park interpretive programs about the lighthouse and the U.S. Life-Saving service. The ferry service provides vehicle tours of the island.

Whiz Tips

During the peak summer season, the rangers conduct a host of guided walks and campfire talks. Visitors who tag along can learn about birds, wildflowers, deer, beavers, early settlers and the environment.

The Sleeping Bear Point Coast Guard Station Maritime Museum details an era most of us have forgotten. The Great Lakes were a key transportation element in the development of America's north country. Ships plied the waters carrying raw goods out and finished product in. Life-savers, the forerunners of the Coast Guard, manned the shores of these huge bodies of freshwater the same as they did the nation's saltwater shores. The museum lovingly presents these bygone days.

Kids' Stuff

★ Kids can earn a park patch by completing the Junior Ranger program. In summer, the daily Heroes of the Storm program is tailored especially for the wee ones. They can participate

Sleeping Bear Dunes National Lakeshore COURTESY NPS

in a ship rescue and see how it was done.

★ Children can swim, fish (lake or river), play on the dunes, hike, bike, boat, canoe, cross-country ski, snowshoe or just enjoy the great outdoors.

Access: Park H.Q. & visitor center in Empire. **Days/Hours:** Empire Visitor Center, daily 9:30-4 & summer extended hrs. (clsd. Thanksgiving & Dec.25). **Camping:** Park's D.H Day Campground (89 sites) & islands backcountry camping; nearby state campgrounds (ask at the park for a camping map). **Special Events:** Early Aug., Coast Guard Day (rescue equipment displays); mid-Aug., annual Perseid Meteor Shower at Glen Haven; late Aug., Maritime Heritage celebration, (exhibits, tours, demos, boats and special offerings). **For info.:** Superintendent, Sleeping Bear Dunes National Lakeshore, P.O.Box 277, 9922 Front St. (Hwy.M-72), Empire, MI 49630. 516/326-5134.

MINNESOTA

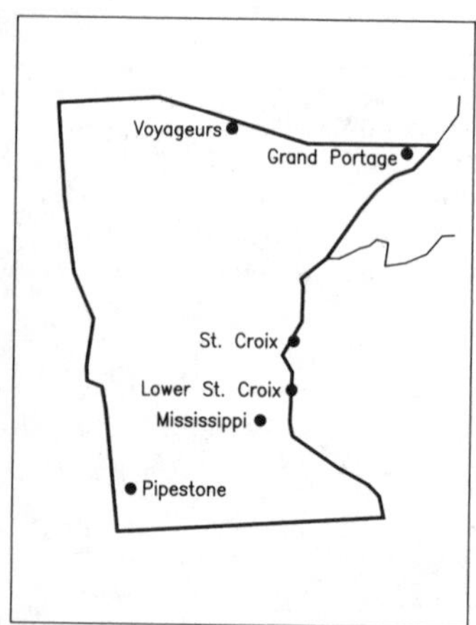

Grand Portage National Monument

Allow: .5 days *Fee*

"The northeastern tip of this part of the state is called the arrowhead, which suggests both its shape on the map and the Indians who once had the place to themselves."

George Moses
Minnesota In Focus

In the mid-1600s, the local Cree and Ojibwa met the first French traders. The French introduced them to wool blankets and iron implements while learning about survival in the wilderness including hunting and water transportation. One such waterway was Pigeon River which becomes unnavigable forcing canoeists to lug their 90 lb. packs over 9 mi. of backcountry to Ft. Charlotte on the Pigeon River. The monument focuses on the North West Co.'s gateway to fur trade with three reconstructed buildings, a .5 mi. nature trail and

Grand Portage National Monument

COURTESY NPS

the 9 mi. historic Grand Portage. In summer, it also serves as a ferry (fee) terminus to Isle Royale National Park.

Highlights

★ As you tour the grounds, you relive the days when the stockade was bustling with activities. Grand Portage was the crossroads for the North West Company. Supplies from Montreal and furs from the interior would intersect here. The Great Hall is furnished to show you life in the early 1800s. The adjacent kitchen is a good place to see how their sustenance was prepared. Outside the stockade you can see two authentic birchbark canoes, which were the choice mode of transportation. Fragile-looking, they carried tons of goods thousands of miles through whitewater and seemingly endless lakes. By canoe, a top voyageur could cover up to 80 mi. a day, a darn site better than walking 20.

★ The Mount Rose nature trail climbs 300 ft., providing an excellent overview of the magnificent lake scenery.

Whiz Tips

Throughout the summer, the park rangers conduct interpretive programs on archaeology, historic gardening, birch bark canoes, the people and cooking.

For over 200 years, Europeans and Native Americans engaged in the business of trade. Grand Portage, the "Great Carrying Place" served as a vital link in this enterprise. While all warm furs were desired by northern Europe, beaverskins used to cover top hats, were prized as status symbols for men of station. The trade was so brisk that if silk hadn't supplanted beaver as the material of choice, the beaver might be extinct.

The North West Co. and rival Hudson's Bay Co. vied in often stormy battles for control of the continent's fur trade. Their voyageurs paddled deep into the wilderness to get the prime furs first. They had to be physically strong, capable of winning the natives' confidence and able to get along with their compatriots during isolated winters (canoes generally required 4-6 men or 8-10 for the larger Montreal canoes). In 1803, the British-operated compa-

Grand Portage National Monument COURTESY NPS

nies abandoned this location for Fort William when they learned they were on American soil. In 1821, the two companies merged.

Kids' Stuff

★ Children can dress up in period clothing and handle objects from the fur trading days. Our children love to climb up into the lookout towers of these wooden fortifications. The rangers encourage the kids to participate during their interpretive presentations.

Access: 36 NE of Grand Marais on US 61. **Days/Hours:** Mid-May through mid-Oct., daily 8-5. **Camping:** Park's backcountry camping (2 sites) at the end of the portage; Grand Marais Recreation Area (300 sites, elec. & shwrs.); 4 national forest campgrounds, East Bearskin Lake (33 sites), Flower Lake (35 sites), Kimble Lake (11 sites), Two Island Lake (38 sites); Judge C.R.Magney State Park (40 sites). **Special Events:** 2nd Aug. wknd. historic two day fur trade rendezvous (FREE); local Ojibwa tribe (the park was part of the Grand Portage Indian Reservation until the tribe donated it to the government) sponsor a traditional pow wow. **For info.:** Superintendent, Grand Portage National Monument, P.O.Box 668, Grand Marais, MN 55604. 218/387-2788.

Mississippi National River & Recreational Area

Recently established, the park includes 69 miles of the mighty Mississippi from Dayton to Hastings. Boaters can see a variety of landscapes and cultural features.

For info.: Mississippi National River & Recreational Area, c/o Midwest Region, National Park Service, 1709 Jackson St., Omaha, NE 68102.

Pipestone National Monument

Allow: 2-3 hrs. *Fee*

The plains Indians felt the stone taken from these quarries was valuable for more than its soft yet resilient qualities. They believed (and some still believe) it held spiritual powers. As a result, the Yankton

Voyageurs National Park COURTESY NPS

Sioux made sure any treaty settlements included their stewardship of the area. Today, this 300-year-old quarry of valuable rock still has reserves of pipestone. Could Euro-American stewardship make a similar claim?

Highlights

★ The self-guiding 3/4 mi. Circle Trail takes you to the important sites. At the Upper Midwest Indian Cultural Center, you can see the crafting of the ornamental pipes which came to signify that most important state of being, "peace."

Whiz Tips

❢ Although Native Americans had been utilizing pipes for almost 2,000 years, it wasn't until shortly before the white man's arrival in this area that the quarry was first mined. The Sioux operated a monopoly of the precious red and pink stone, trading it for goods with the other plains tribes. The product of this quarry has been found in wide distribution throughout the Great Plains, indicating the Sioux had a very good thing going. The rock is taken from a strata of pipestone which angles eastward beneath a hard and thickening layer of quartzite. As part of their mining, the Indians would leave small tokens for the quarry to ensure the supply of stone didn't run out. So far these gifts have proven their worth.

Mayfly Hatching

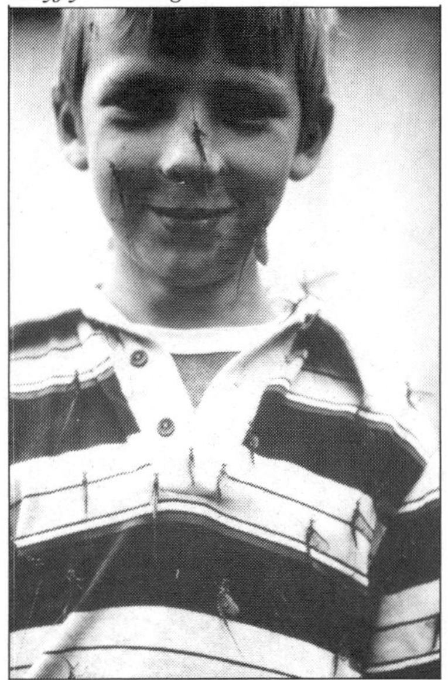

Kids' Stuff

✱ Like some other Native American national park sites, this one shows a degree of industry and artistry among the native populations which popular stereotyping has thus far ignored. A visit to any of these sites demonstrates to children that bareback riding and bow-and-arrow marksmanship were not the sole occupations of these people.

Access: Just N of Pipestone on MN 23 or MN 30. **Days/Hours:** Daily 8-5 (clsd. Dec. 25 & Jan.1). **Camping:** 8 mi. S on SR 23, Split Rock Creek State Park (28 sites, elec. & shwrs.) & near Luverne on US 75, Blue Mounds State Park (78 sites, elec. & shwrs.). **For info.:** Superintendent, Pipestone National Monument, P.O.Box 727, Pipestone, MN 56164. 507/825-5464.

Voyageurs National Park

Allow: 1 week *FREE*

It shouldn't be surprising to find that this is primarily a water park. Voyageurs, French fur traders, lived most of their lives upon the water. They paddled the lakes, rivers and streams of the Canadian Shield in search of people to trade with (see Grand Portage NM, MN). Within the boundaries of the park are over 30 lakes and countless bogs, marshes and beaver ponds.

Highlights

★ Most visitors don't chance upon Voyageurs; rather, they make it a goal. They bring their motorboats or canoes, their fishing equipment, their hiking shoes and a bathing suit. It's vacation time! And the park provides a natural getaway few other places in the lower 48 can equal. It's not unusual for people to see bald eagles, ospreys, loons or cormorants. With over 3,000 beavers, you can almost hear the ghosts of Voyageurs calculating their take. Along with sister park, Isle Royale (see Isle Royale NP, MI), it is the only place in the continental U.S. where you can hear the howl of eastern timber wolves. They prey on the park's moose and deer.

Whiz Tips

The park naturalists have several daily programs during summer. One of the favorite guided tours is the North Canoe Voyage where costumed rangers take visitors aboard a replica of a voyageurs' 26 ft. birchbark canoe on Rainy Lake. Kabetogama Lake also has canoeing programs and Ash River has a beaver pond nature walk.

The park's rocks are the oldest on the planet, est. 2.7 billion yrs. old. Four different ice ages with glaciers up to two miles deep covered the region. Picture ice as high as 100 of the park's tallest trees standing on top of each other.

Kids' Stuff

★ The park has dedicated specific interpretive programs to children. They have puppet shows which help explain facets of the region. The "Kids Explore Voyageurs," a 7 to 12 yr. olds offering, takes the kids on a ride in the 26 ft. long "Duck" (boat) in search of beavers or on a ranger-led hike.

★ If you're going after the succulent walleye, plan on one fish per four hours of fishing. The park suggests you consider increasing your chances of a catch to include bass, crappies and pike, which are terrific sport fish. Our kids are still into quantity.

Access: Park interior by boat, plane, hiking, snowmobile or cross-country skiing. Park borders on US 53 from Duluth, Cty. Rte. 23/24 from Orr, Cty. Rte.129, Cty. Rte. 122 S of International Falls. **Days/ Hours:** Rainy Lake Visitor Center, daily, summer 9-7 & winter reduced hrs. Summer only, Kabetogama Lake Visitor Center 9-5 & Ash River Visitor Center 12-5. **Camping:** Park's 120 boat-in-only campsites; Ash River State Park; Kabetogama State Forest, Woodenfrog Campground (59 sites). **For info.:** Superintendent, Voyageurs National Park, International Falls, MN 56649. 218/286-5258.

Voyageur National Park Courtesy NPS

MISSISSIPPI

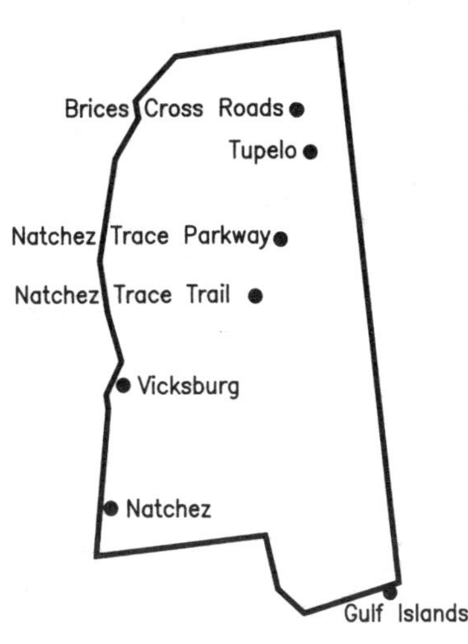

Brices Cross Roads National Battlefield Site & Tupelo National Battlefield

Allow: .5 hrs *FREE*

"...get there first with the most men."
Major General Nathan Bedford Forrest

Certainly the "first" was the case at Brices Cross Roads, when Forrest and his Confederate forces out-raced the Federals to the location, then beat them badly in battle. However, later in the summer of '64, it was the Federals under Smith who got to Tupelo "first," holding off Forrest's forces before conducting an orderly retreat. Brices Cross Roads is in a rural setting just north of Tupelo and the Natchez Trace Parkway. Both sites have a granite memorial, two cannons, an interpretive marker and map.

Highlights

★ For Confederate Civil War fans, these two battlefields are noteworthy because they demonstrate the resolution of the Southern forces.

Whiz Tips

Brices Cross Roads is counted among the most brilliant victories in the Civil War as Forrest executed a startling rout of an army twice as big. With his army firmly entrenched, he was able to stop the Federal forces, attack them before they could catch a breath, and so confuse them that their retreat turned into a shambles. His men captured over 1,500 as the Federals fled back to Memphis. Unfortunately, while he captured Sherman's attention, he didn't succeed in cutting Sherman's supply lines, which was his intent.

At Tupelo, the Federals took advantage of the undefended town. They forced the Confederates to try and free-up their own supply lines. While the Federals who were supposed "to follow Forrest to the death," didn't complete the task, they did succeed in exacting greater Southern casualties.

Noted Civil War novelist, Shelby Foote, recounts a conversation with Forrest's granddaughter in which he told her the Civil War produced two geniuses, her grandfather and President Lincoln. The granddaughter paused, then said that while she appreciates the compliment about her granddaddy, her family still didn't think too highly of Mr. Lincoln. Forrest, while regarded as a military genius, has had his reputation tarnished over two incidents. At Fort Pillow his troops overwhelmed a lightly defended Federal force killing over 200 northern troops, most of whom were black. The Federals claimed the black soldiers were killed while they were trying to surrender. After the Civil War, the Ku Klux Klan chose Forrest as their first Grand Dragon. Although he later renounced the post, claiming he was unaware of the organization's goals and means, his name is still linked to the notorious racist society.

Kids' Stuff

★ There's little to occupy children at either site unless they are very familiar with the Civil War.

Access: Brices Cross Roads 6 mi. W of Baldwyn on MS 370. Tupelo NB in Tupelo 1 E of Natchez Trace Pkwy. **Days/Hours:** Daily. **Camping:** E of Tupelo, Tombigbee State Park (showers). **For info.:** C/O Superintendent, Natchez Trace Parkway, R.R.1, NT-143, Tupelo, MS 38801. 601/842-1572.

Natchez National Historical Park

Allow: .5 hrs. *Fee*

"People always want to come back to Natchez. We've boomed economically, but we haven't gone hustle-bustle modern. With 40 or so old mansions right in Natchez, we could hardly dare go garish."

Tom Byrne, Natchez Mayor-1971

This newly created park has acquired one property, the Melrose plantation. Residence of John T. McMurran, a Pennsylvania lawyer, the house represents the antebellum architecture so prevalent in the South when cotton was king. However, Melrose never served as a cotton plantation, rather it was a food-producing farm. Natchez National Historical Park is planning future developments to fulfill its mandate "to preserve and interpret the history of Natchez, Mississippi as a significant city in the history of the American South."

Highlights

★ Tours of the mansion introduce visitors to many of the original furnishings that McMurran used. The estate still has a number of the first buildings used on the farm.

Whiz Tips

Natchez was a major trading center along the Mississippi River. The original inhabitants were the tribe for whom the town is named. In 1716, France settled the region only to pass it to England, then Spain. In 1798, it was the capital of the Mississippi Territory and later became Aaron Burr's H.Q.s for his new republic in the Southwest. Burr was arrested for treason but later acquitted. The first half of the 18th century was the town's hey-day, as river traders and cotton plantation owners reaped the harvest of slave labor.

Kids' Stuff

★ Natchez reflects an important era in American history. Many believe the Civil War was as much a battle between lifestyles as a dispute about states rights or slavery. The South was heavily agricultural while the North was an industrial juggernaut. The cultures reflected their economies.

Access: Melrose within Natchez on Melrose-Montebello Pkwy. off Sergeant Prentiss Dr. **Days/Hours:** Daily, grounds 8:30-5 & house 9-4. **Camping:** Natchez State Campground 13 mi. on US 61 (28 sites & elec.). **For info.:** Park Manager, Natchez Trace Parkway, P.O.Box 1086, Natchez, MS 39121. 601/442-7047.

Natchez Trace National Scenic Trail

The trail runs parallel to the existing parkway (see Natchez Trace Parkway, MS) from Nashville, TN to Natchez, MS.

For info.: Natchez Trace National Scenic Trail, Southeast Region, National Park Service, Richard B. Russell Building, 75 Spring St., SW, Atlanta, GA 30303.

Natchez Trace Parkway

Allow: 2-4 days *FREE*

"The old Natchez Trace has sunk out of use; it is deep in leaves. The river has gone away and left the landings. Boats from Liverpool do not dock at these empty crags. The old deeds are done, old evil and old good have been made into stories,"

Eudora Welty
Some Notes on the River Country

From the evidence uncovered at the Mound Builders and other Native American sites, we know extensive trade was carried out throughout the continent. Natchez Trace was one of the key routes these prehistoric travelers used. Running from the mighty Mississippi River (today's Natchez, MS) northeast to the Tennessee Valley, a path was worn which "Kaintuck" boatmen and others tramped along. It wasn't until the Mississippi River could be traversed by steam that this historic American roadway would fall into disuse. Today, there are 400 mi. (proposed 444 mi.) of paved highway taking visitors from Nashville, TN, to Natchez, MS.

Highlights

★ As you can imagine, there are many sites to see over such a long roadway. The park service alerts you to the noteworthy at each of its information centers. Mount Locust (15.5), a restored 1810 stand (inn), has interpretive rangers. Cypress Swamp Nature Trail is a short stroll through a cypress swamp with 22 interpretive stops. The Tupelo Visitor Center and nearby Confederate gravesites and Old Trace areas are not to be missed. While traveling the Tennessee portion of the trace, Meriwether Lewis (see Fort Clatsop NM, OR & Thomas Jefferson NEMem., MO) came to a mysterious end. His grave can be seen at mi. 385.9.

Whiz Tips

The Mississippi portion of the parkway takes you past seven locations (six of which are identified) where the Mound Builders left their mark. The Native Americans who built these particular mounds are referred to as the Mississippian Culture (see Effigy Mounds NM, IA; Mound City Group NM, OH and Ocmulgee NM, GA.) and were prob-

Natchez Trace National Scenic Trail Courtesy NPS

ably the ancestors of the historic tribes: Natchez, Creek, Choctaw and Chickasaw. Beginning at Natchez, you pass Emerald Mound, the 2nd largest in the country; Magnum Mound, Boyd Mounds, Bynum Mounds, Pharr Mounds (the largest and a very important archaeological site in the South) and finally, Bear Creek Mound at milepost 308.8.

Kids' Stuff

★ Of the 20-plus trails along the parkway, the longest is 3.5 mi. Most are less than a mile, ideal lengths for families with small children. At Rock Spring (330.2), kids can see an abandoned beaver dam.

Access: Begins at Natchez, MS and ends at Nashville, TN. **Days/Hours:** Tupelo Visitor Center, daily 8-5 (clsd. Dec.25), Mount Locust, daily, Feb.-Nov. 8:30-5. **Camping:** Parkway's 3 campgrounds; Rocky Springs (54.8), Jeff Busby (193.1) & Meriwether Lewis (385.9); Natchez State Park (8.1), Grand Gulf State Park (41.1), Trace State Park (259.7), Tombigbee State Park (263.6), Tishomingo State Park (303.9) and David Crockett (369.9) (state-shwrs.). **For info.:** Superintendent, Natchez Trace Parkway, R.R.1, NT-143, Tupelo, MS 38801. 601/842-1572.

Vicksburg National Military Park

Allow: 2-3 hrs. *Fee*

Vicksburg still sits guarding the Mississippi River. It's easy to see its importance in the Civil War. Supplies and men could move freely as long as you controlled the major gun placements. Almost impregnable from the north and south because of the swamps and bayous, Vicksburg was a daunting fortress. Visitors can relive the campaign by touring the battle lines where both sides dug in, the visitor center, the Shirley House, the National Cemetery and the USS *Cairo* Museum.

Highlights

★ As you tour the park's 16 mi. route, you can see why it took so long for Grant to subdue the Confederates. Vicksburg's landscape works to the defenders' advantage.

★ The restored ironclad river gunboat, the USS*Cairo* has proven to be

Natchez Trace Parkway Courtesy NPS

of invaluable historic importance. The first vessel to be sunk by an electrically detonated mine, she sank with all gear on board. When recovered, historians were able to piece together how she was outfitted, providing new insights into Civil War naval life.

Whiz Tips

- During summer, the park features rifle and cannon firing demonstrations as part of its living history presentations.
- Only two Confederate battlements, Vicksburg and Port Hudson, remained on the Mississippi River. Grant chose Vicksburg as the first and most concerted assault because of its size and position. Thwarted in his amphibious attempt through the bayous, Grant marched his men down the Louisiana side of the river below the city, then struck eastward to Jackson and the railroad. Of the second of his two frontal assaults, one of his soldiers would say, "Twenty thousand muskets and 150 cannon belched forth death and destruction...The charge was a bloody failure." Grant abandoned direct attack and dug in. Union boats bombarded the city, driving many inhabitants to seek shelter in caves. As one resident put it, "Hardly any part of the city was outside the range of the enemy's artillery..." In the end, the Confederates surrendered with favorable terms of surrender, thus retaining their freedom with a pledge to desist hostilities.

Kids' Stuff

- The USS *Cairo* Museum with its restored ironclad has all kinds of neat things for kids to see. The ironclads were the fore-runners of the great battleships we see today.
- Families can make this a real recreational outing by cycling the park.

Access: In Vicksburg on US 80 1 mi. from I-20. **Days/Hours:** Visitor center, daily 8-5 & museum, daily 9-5. Both extended summer hrs. (clsd. Dec.25). **Camping:** E Rocky Springs (22 sites) on Natchez Trace Parkway. **Special Events:** In July, there's a Vicksburg Civil War Reenactment. **For info.:** Superintendent, Vicksburg National Military Park, 3201 Clay St., Vicksburg, MS 39180. 601/636-0583.

MISSOURI

George Washington Carver National Monument

Allow: 1-2 hrs. *Fee (Apr.-Oct.)*

"There is no short cut to achievement. Life requires thorough preparation..."
George Washington Carver

In southwestern Missouri, not far from the Oklahoma/Arkansas borders, is a small peaceful farm with a pond, a spring, a cemetery and a simple house. Walnut and persimmon trees grow and a stream wanders past the restored prairie. It was into this rural setting that George Washington Carver was born a slave. An insatiable curiosity drove George to leave home at age 12 to attend a segregated school. He went on to make outstanding contributions in the development of products from soybean, sweet potato and peanuts, which ultimately led to the diversification of the South's agricultural base.

Highlights

★ As you tour the Carver Nature Trail, you can't help but wonder how this boy became a superlative researcher and teacher. As a baby he was kidnapped along with his mother by Confederate bushwhackers. Rescued at the behest of his master, George never saw his mother again nor knew his father. Slave-owners-turned-guardians, Moses and Susan Carver raised George and his brother, Jim. His guardians weren't worldly or wealthy. Their own home was not the house that exists today, which was built well after George had left. Rather it was little more than the slave cabin George and his family had shared.

George Washington Carver NM

COURTESY NPS

Whiz Tips

Although Carver was renowned as a botanist, agronomist, artist and educator, this monument pays dutiful homage to his sacrifices. He left a good job at Iowa Agricultural College to help Booker T. Washington establish Tuskegee Institute (see Tuskegee Institute NHS, AL) as a viable post-secondary educational institute for African Americans. While there, he recognized the South had been rapidly depleting its agricultural lands by relying on cotton. He devoted his efforts to helping "the man furthest down." He demonstrated the values of crops like soybeans, peanuts and sweet potatoes. For example, he published a list of 150 different uses for peanuts, including medicines, dyes, cosmetics and beverages.

On weekends there are interpretive programs ranging from Ozark craft demonstrations to films.

Kids' Stuff

★ The monument has a Jr. Ranger program for 10-12 yrs. olds on summer Sat. mornings. The children learn about natural sciences, history, archaeology and their environment.

Access: 3 mi. W. from Diamond on MO V. **Days/Hours:** Daily 8:30-5. **Camping:** Roaring River State Park about 1 hr. SE (192 sites, elec. & shwrs.) and Mark Twain National Forest about 45 min. S. **Special Events:** Feb., Black History Month; June, "Airing of the Quilts"; 2nd July Sun., "Carver Day"; "Prairie Day". **Teacher's Package:** Available. **For info.:** Superintendent, George Washington Carver National Monument, P.O.Box 38, Diamond, MO 64840. 417/325-4151.

Harry S Truman National Historic Site

Allow: 1-2 hrs. *Fee*

"Within the first few months, I discovered that being a President is like riding a tiger. A man has to keep on riding or be swallowed."
Harry S Truman

Near downtown Independence, now a suburb of Kansas City, is the home where the "buck" truly stopped. Harry returned home after his tour of duty at the White House. Like so many of the president's homes, Harry's is a reflection of his public image. Known for plain speaking, he lived plainly. His house is no more and no less than what you would expect of a moderately successful middle-American.

Highlights

★ "I tried never to forget who I was and where I'd come from and where I was going back to." (Harry S Truman). Your tour begins at the visitor center in downtown Independence. There you are introduced to the president's home life and arrange for a ticket to view the home. The large frame home was built by Bess's (Harry's wife) grandfather. Nailed-down linoleum, lumpy sofas and a simple kitchen table attests as much to the family's frugality as their unpretentiousness. Although Bess' Mom always felt she'd married "beneath" herself, Truman lived peaceably with her for the duration of her long life. In fact, he lived with Bess' siblings as his closest neighbors as they built their homes in the backyard of the original holdings. It was a rare day they didn't share a meal or a coffee.

Whiz Tips

When Franklin D. Roosevelt died in office, Truman faced the unenviable task of having to prove himself a worthy successor to probably the country's most popular president since Washington. He had WW II to wrap-up and the vestiges of the less than favorable wartime agreements the West had struck with Russia. What can be said about his closure of the war? Almost as many Japanese people, civilians, women and children, were killed by the atomic bomb as America lost in both Europe and

Harry S Truman National Historic Site Courtesy NPS

the Pacific. Historians will be forever split on whether the end was justified by the means. Perhaps the world needed some terrible demonstration of this weapon, which has yet to be used in anger. To the people of Hiroshima and Nagasaki, this is small consolation.

❢ Republican Senator Kenneth Keating once said: "Roosevelt proved a man could be President for life; Truman proved anybody could be President; and Eisenhower proved you don't need to have a President." If "anybody could be President," then what of the 28 other president's whom historians, in 1983, rated as performing below him (Harry was ranked 8th). Oh yeah, Harry wasn't quite the nobody either he or others would lead us to believe. His lineage can be traced to at least one previous president, President John Tyler, his great-uncle.

❢ There's no mistake that the "S" in the President's name doesn't have a period. It's not an initial rather it is a full name. The family couldn't agree which "S" name to call him and the letter was a compromise.

Kids' Stuff

★ "By the time I was thirteen or fourteen years old, I had read all the books in the Independence Public Library." (Harry S Truman). If there is one lesson which seems resoundingly clear after we toured accomplished people's homes, it is that reading is the key to success. Harry's home has over 1,000 books.

★ Children who have studied the presidents, can learn more about a Democrat whose style has proven so resilient that recent Republican presidents have praised him.

Access: Downtown Independence. **Days/ Hours:** Daily, 8:30-5 (clsd. winter Mon. & some holidays). **Camping:** Fleming Park Lake Jacomo Campground on Hwy. 50 (60 sites, elec. & shwrs.) & Longview Campground on Hwy. 350 (120 sites, elec. & shwrs.). **For info.:** Superintendent, Harry S Truman National Historic Site, 223 N. Main St., Independence, MO 64050-2804. 816/254-7199.

Jefferson National Expansion Memorial

Allow: .5 days *Fee*

"Only remember West of the Mississippi it's a little more look, see, act. A little less rationalize, comment, talk."

F. Scott Fitzgerald

The most memorable symbol in middle America, is the great arch over St. Louis. Gateway to the West, this arc of silver could just as easily be a gigantic staple holding the north to the south. Eero Saarinen designed the 630 ft. stainless steel arch to stand over the Museum of Western Expansion. Also within the park's administration are the Old Courthouse and Old Cathedral, living testimonies to St Louis' colorful past.

Highlights

★ The Gateway Arch is truly a marvel of engineering. It is the nation's tallest monument, beating the Washington Monument by 75 ft. and more than doubling the Statue of Liberty. The *Monument to a Dream* film is a riveting drama that shows each step in the erection of this remarkable structure. The planners calculated 13 construction workers would be killed but not one life was lost. Bad planning; great execution!

★ The Museum of Western Expansion creatively incorporates period exhibits to entice visitors back through time. Like tree-rings, each platform represents successive decades detailing their events which culminated in a nation stretching from "sea to sea."

Whiz Tips

❢ The park has rangers stationed in the viewing area of the arch to answer questions. They also provide interpretive tours of the Museum of Western Expansion. In the Old Courthouse, they guide visitors through its four museums explaining everything from the building's architecture to its historic moments.

In 1803, Jefferson concluded the Louisiana Purchase. Initially, Jefferson's emissaries were to purchase Florida and New Orleans, and negotiate travelling rights on the Mississippi. Napoleon offered the whole territory. Meriwether Lewis and William Clark set off from St. louis on their historic journey to the Pacific (see Fort Clatsop NHS, OR).

The Old Cathedral stands on the property put aside for it in 1764, when the Village of St. Louis was founded. The Old Courthouse, which dominates the entry to the city from the Gateway Arch, was the scene of the famous Dred Scott case. Dred Scott was a slave who travelled with his owners from Missouri to Illinois, a free state. He claimed that living four years in a state prohibiting slavery entitled him to freedom. The local court maintained his position but the State Supreme Court overrode it. The U.S. Supreme Court, led by the son of a slaveowner, issued a contentious decision stating Dred Scott had no rights under the law because he was a slave. Many feel this decision was a contributing factor in bringing about the Civil War.

Kids' Stuff

★ The four-minute ride to the top of the arch and the thrill of being atop the Great Plains is a real winner with children.

★ The Museum of Western Expansion's exhibits are so well presented that with very little help your kids can see how the various stages in the settlement of the country occurred and how they differed.

Access: Under the Arch in St. Louis. **Days /Hours:** Daily, summer 8-10 & winter 9-6. **Camping:** Dr. Edmond A Babler Memorial State Park 20 mi. W on SR 109 (77 sites) & NE (IL) Horseshoe Lake Recreation Area (48 sites). **Special Events:** Feb., Black Heritage Month; March's 2nd wk., Women's History Week; May's 1st wk., St. Louis Storytelling Week; Nov's. 2nd wk., Native American Week; Dec., Victorian Christmas at the Old Courthouse & A World of Christmas featuring Christmas Trees from throughout the world. **Teacher's Package:**

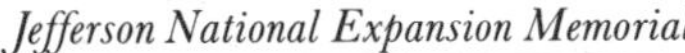
Jefferson National Expansion Memorial

Courtesy NPS

Available. **For info.:** Superintendent, Jefferson National Expansion Memorial, 11 N. 4th St., St. Louis, MO 63102. 314/425-6010.

Ozark National Scenic Riverways

Allow: 2-3 days *FREE*

"Under the Ozarks, domed by Iron Mountain,
The old gods of the rain lie wrapped in pools."

Hart Crane
The Bridge

The old gods are still there. Woodsmen have altered their river banks; farmers have used their waters and moved on; but they remain. The soft sweep of wooden paddles caresses them. Fishing line reaches down to titillate their neighbors. And still the old gods of the rain remain. They may rage as they have in recent years, causing great flooding and creating new homes for themselves. They may lie peaceably, slumbering beneath the summer sun. Visitors must give them their due or pay the price. For the most part, the park entails just the 134 mi. of water of the Current and Jacks rivers and their banks.

Highlights

★ While the Ozark Trail cuts through the park, it alone serves hikers. This place is for those who paddle or motor to their chosen goals. This part of the Ozarks is rapidly returning to its previous state while maintaining historic vestiges of human intervention.

★ A must-see for most visitors is Big Spring, one of the largest springs in the U.S. In summer, cultural demonstrations, including quilting and building Ozark johnboats, are part of the interpretive offerings at this locale.

Whiz Tips

The rangers take people on tours of Alley Mill and Round Spring cave during the summer season. The mill is a historic roller mill, circa 1890. Visitors learn about life in the turn-of-the-century Ozarks and how corn is ground. Other interpretive pro-

Ozark National Scenic Riverways

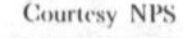
Courtesy NPS

grams include canoe trips, talks on the river's geology, biology and history.

Kids' Stuff

★ Visiting these rivers is a wonderful outing for any family with outdoor interests. The fishing and boating are truly first class. Large and smallmouth bass, trout and goggle-eye are the choice inhabitants. The interpretive programs are a bonus, with the cave tour the highlight for most children.

Access: 175 mi. S of St. Louis. **Days/Hours:** Aley Mill, daily 8-5. **Camping:** Park has 7 campgrounds; Akers (81 sites), Pulltite (55 sites), Round Spring (60 sites), Two Rivers (12 sites), Powder Mill (10 sites), Big Spring (195 sites & reservations-Ticketron) & Alley Spring (187 sites). **Special Events:** Memorial Day wknd., Big Springs Arts & Crafts Festival. **For info.:** Superintendent, Ozark National Scenic Riverways, Van Buren, MO 63965. 314/323-4236.

Wilson's Creek National Battlefield

Allow: 1-2 hrs. *Fee*

Wilson's Creek was the second major Civil War battle and the second Southern victory (see Manassas NB, VA). It seemed proof of the Confederacy's supremacy and gave hope they could win the war. However, it became apparent that Northern Brigadier General Nathaniel Lyon's brave death was not in vain. His union soldiers had valiantly held their own against overwhelming Rebel numbers and regrouped to deter further Southern advancement into Missouri. You can drive, bike, walk or jog the 5-mile one-way loop road through the battlefield.

Highlights

★ There are 8 historic stops along the route. The Ray House, which served as a post office during the war, still stands. The most famous landmark is Bloody Hill where Lyon and 4,000 Union soldiers held off repeated attacks until Lyon, who had already been hit twice, was hit again for the final time and the Union forces had to retreat.

Whiz Tips

❢ On summer weekends, the park puts on living history demonstrations. Soldiers dressed in period clothing show visitors what their life was like during these difficult times.

❢ At the outbreak of the Civil War, Missouri was a state of divided loyalties. Ostensibly a slave state, its ruling governor, Clairborne F. Jackson, was sympathetic to the South and attempted to secede. Then Captain Nathaniel Lyon overcame a vanguard of southern sympathizers who had banded together to overtake the federal arsenal in St. Louis. Governor Jackson set up a provisional government near Wilson's Creek. Unaware that the South had also assembled a force exceeding 12,000 men, Lyon set forth with 6,000 troops to rout the enemy. The first engagement caught both sides by surprise, but the Union troops held the day. However, even though Lyon had figured out he was outnumbered, he decided to surprise the Rebels by attacking. His initial charge at Wilson's Creek benefited by his risk-taking, but the larger Southern force inevitably slowed his progress and the tide turned in its favor.

Kids' Stuff

★ Kids really enjoy seeing the "soldiers" and women dressed in Civil War fashion. The equipment excites their curiosity and encourages even the shyest of children to ask about its use.

★ The park road is divided into pedestrian traffic and auto traffic. Biking families should feel comforted at an outing here.

Access: 3 mi. E of Republic & 10 mi. W of

Springfield on MO ZZ. **Days/Hours:** Daily, summer 8-8 & winter 8-5. **Camping:** S on O 76 Cape Fair (86 sites, elec. & shwrs.). **Special Events:** Memorial Day, July 4, Aug. 10 and Labor Day. **For info.:** Superintendent, Wilson's Creek National Battlefield, Rte. 2, Box 75, Republic, MO 65738. 417/732-2662.

MONTANA

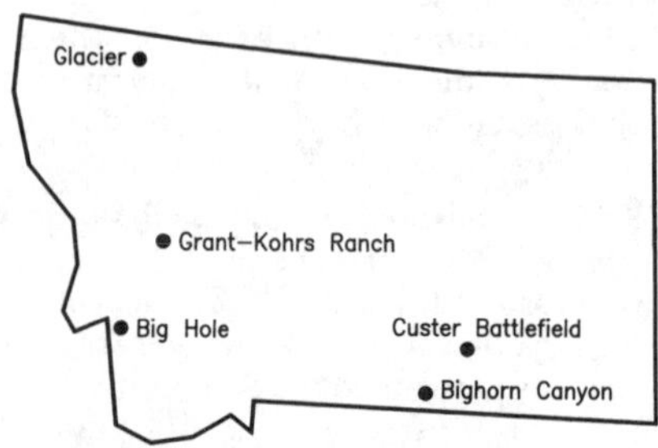

Big Hole National Battlefield

Allow: 2-3 hrs. *Fee (May-Sept.)*

"Hear me, my chiefs. I am tired; my heart is sick and sad. From where the sun now stands I will fight no more forever."

Chief Joseph, Nez Perce

Located in S.W. Montana is the site of one of the major battles fought between the fleeing Nez Perce Indians and the U.S. Army in 1877. Almost 1,200 miles of mountainous terrain were crossed in flight as the Nez Perce sought sanctuary. Big Hole was mid-point in their journey and their fortunes. The battlesite relates the events that transpired here. While the tribe fought its way free from a surprise attack by a greater force, its fate was sealed. Defeat awaited the Nez Perce at today's Chief Joseph Battlefield of the Bear's Paw State Monument, MT, 30 miles from freedom in Canada. Thus ended what was perhaps the most compelling search for life, liberty and freedom in the country's history.

Highlights

★ As you take one of the three self-guiding trails, you're hard-pressed to remain objective. A well-armed force of men charge out of the misty dawn randomly shooting a beleaguered village where almost 9 out of 10 are women and children. Worn out from two months of trudging through hill country and constantly looking over their shoulders, the Nez Perce valiantly regroup and repel the larger force. Even in the face of a howitzer, they gain the upper-hand and besiege the ambushers. What courage, what desperation they must have displayed.

Whiz Tips

❢ Talk about "added value," descendants of the Nez Perce help interpret the site. You learn about the tribe's daily life, culture and perspective on the battle. You also hear from living history guides about the soldier's lot.

❢ The Nez Perce in this battle had never ceded the lands the government took from them. They had never agreed to relocate to the smaller reservation upon whose land their brethren had always lived. Yet, when the army pushed them to live on the reservation, they only asked a reasonable amount of time to collect their stock and complete their journey in safety. The U.S. proved unsympathetic. The tribe began the move, but hot-headed vengeful warrior youths satisfied their pride by killing some white settlers who had killed or cheated their families. The flight began. Perhaps Custer's fate made the army cautious, because it attacked the Nez Perce at Whitebird (see Nez Perce NHP, ID) and withdrew. The soldiers also retreated at Big Hole and failed to encounter the straggling village for much of the chase. The Shoshone and Crow, whom the Nez Perce went to for help, were very leery about the government's revenge and refused to help. An interesting side note is that tourists visiting Yellowstone National Park at that time actually saw the fleeing Nez Perce.

Kids' Stuff

★ Each of the trails is less than 1.5 mi., a good distance for wee ones. The park has two FREE children activity brochures you can use to help interpret the park with your kids.

★ The demonstrations of Nez Perce crafts, tipi pitching and soldier uniforms are biggies with kids.

★ This is a story of much bravery against overwhelming odds. The Nez Perce story is one few are familiar with. It epitomizes the overall treatment of our Native peoples. Children should recognize that even great nations make mistakes.

Access: 10 mi. W of Wisdom on MT 43. **Days/Hours:** Visitor center, daily, summer 8-8 & winter 8-5 (clsd. Thanksgiving, Dec.25 & Jan.1). **Camping:** The National Forest's May Creek Campground 7 mi. on MT 43. **Special Events:** Early Aug., one of the most moving events you'll ever witness, Anniversary Memorial, military living historians and Nez Perce tribal members gather to relate life in 1877, Nez Perce also give talks and perform traditional songs, drumming and dances. **For info.:** Superintendent, Big Hole National Battlefield, P.O.Box 237, Wisdom, MT 59761. 406/689-3155.

Bighorn National Recreation Area

Allow: 2-3 days *FREE*

The park's main feature is the water recreation bonanza offered by 70-mile-long Bighorn Lake. Created by the Yellowtail Dam (summer tours), the lake can be visited from either the north (Montana) or south (Wyoming) ends. Most visitors come for the water's superb fishing and boating.

Highlights

★ Getting out on the water is a

Big Hole National Battlefield Courtesy Jock Whitworth & NPS

must for any visitor. If you don't have your own boat, you can rent or take a boat tour. The lake is enclosed by winding steep canyon walls with each bend offering colorful vistas. The lake features brown and lake trout and walleye. The streams flowing in offer good fly-fishing for brown, rainbow, brook and cutthroat trout. The Bighorn River is classified as a blue ribbon trout fishery (highly recommended).

★ For camera buffs and scenery-lovers the Om-ne-ah trail (north) and Devils Canyon (south) overlook are musts.

Whiz Tips

The visitor center in Lovell, is partly run from its solar collectors which utilize a small pond to reflect more sunlight. They will be pleased to demonstrate how it works upon request.

Both visitor centers have campfire programs on F & Sa from Memorial Day to Labor Day. Topics include Crow Indian culture, geology, fishing, wildlife and pioneers. Yellowtail Dam has summer tours.

What would Bighorn Canyon be without its namesake? Man's attempts to reintroduce the famed sheep have failed. However, a wandering herd has repopulated the base of the Pryor Mountains on the nation's only National Wild Horse Range and is succeeding at rates rarely found within managed herds. Some of the wild horses that can be seen on occasion from the Trans-Park highway, have markings (dorsal stripe & striping) which are common among the truly wild horses of Russia and Outer Mongolia.

Kids' Stuff

★ While the South District visitor center at Lovell has more hands-on exhibits, the North district center at Fort Smith also has an activity center for kids.

Access: 43 mi. from Hardin S via MT 313 or 13 mi. from Lovell via WY 14A & WY 37. **Days/Hours:** Visitor centers, daily summer 9-6 & winter 8-5 (clsd. Thanksgiving, Dec.25 & Jan.1). **Camping:** Park's Horseshoe Bend Campground, S., (126 sites) & Barry's Landing Campground, N., (20 sites). **For info:** Superintendent, Bighorn Canyon Recreation Area, P.O.Box 458, Fort Smith, MT 59035. 406/666-2412.

Bighorn Canyon National Recreation Area Courtesy NPS

Continental Divide National Scenic Trail

Trying to follow the invisible line called the Continental Divide, the trail runs from the Canadian border through Montana, Idaho, Wyoming, Colorado and New Mexico to Mexico.

For info.: Continental Divide National Scenic Trail, Director, Recreation Management, U.S. Forest Service, P.O.Box 2417, Washington, DC 20013.

Custer Battlefield National Monument

Allow: 2 hrs. *Fee (summer only)*

Is there a more famous western battle? There are over 900 paintings, countless songs and stories, each offering different perspectives on what occurred during the two hours it took the Indians to obliterate Custer and the 262 7th Cavalrymen with him. Even today the park service links the Vietnamese conflict to society's changing opinions of the massacre. Who exposed to this event in their early years has not adopted an interpretation of the account? Who, while visiting the site today, will not wonder how in such a small place, Custer's U.S. 7th Calvary could not readily see the enormous numbers of its Indian foes? Who will not question Custer for forcing the issue? The mystique began with Custer, the dashing Civil War hero who apparently had political ambitions and dreamed of the Presidency. It continues because of the evolving recognition that the Native American was victim of a greedy and growing nation which kept asking for more. The monument is located in southeastern Montana on I-90.

Highlights

★ Without the park, this would be just another rolling foothill. When you see the actual battlefield and the approach to the Indian encampment you wonder how anybody could have continued an attack on what was an extremely large gathering (recent studies by the National Geographic Society have confirmed at least 1,500

Custer Battlefield National Monument Courtesy Custer Battlefield NM

well-armed warriors). It all looks so harmless and placid. How frightening it must have been to be surrounded by so many deadly enemies?

★ The visitor center has displays concerning the troop and Indian movements during the skirmish. Narrated topographical models using different colored lights recreate the movement of the participants.

Whiz Tips

❢ For those less familiar with the events, you are taken back to an historic point-in-time, Sunday, June 25, 1876, shortly before the Nation's Centennial celebration. Nearby Yellowstone has been a national park for four years. You are introduced to the climate leading up to the event as well as told about the fateful day and its aftermath. For those who are more familiar with the events, it is interesting to compare your awareness with what the monument presents. We obviously were surprised at how visible the huge Indian encampment would have been to the 7th Cavalry. From atop the hills, it's clear Custer and his troops could see the river valley and the vast Indian encampment. Our previous impression was the Indians surprised Custer by their numbers. There's no way that was the case. He must have decided his soldiers could hold their own against such a vast force.

❢ There is an area in the exhibition hall that has been dedicated to the Indians. For many years the Indians believed the monument's purpose was to glorify Custer and vilify the Native Americans. Today, the park service and its information pieces present a more objective analysis of the event.

❢ Drive out to the Reno-Benteen Entrenchment Trail where the troops under these sub-officers rallied while Custer and his men were being annihilated, so you see firsthand what the lay-of-the-land is like. Apparently, because of the prevailing wind, these soldiers didn't even hear the slaughter.

Kids' Stuff

★ The audio-visual presentation, "Red Sunday," is dramatically narrated, making it a very good introduction for the uninitiated, particularly kids.

Access: S 15 mi. from Hardin on I-90. **Days/Hours:** Visitor center daily, summer 8-8, spring & fall 8-6 & winter 8-4:30. (clsd. Thanksgiving, Dec.25 & Jan.1). **Camping:** 57 mi. Big Horn Canyon NRA After Bay Campground at Fort Smith (34 FREE sites). **For info.:** Superintendent, Custer Battlefield National Monument, P.O.Box 39, Crow Agency, MT 59022. 406/638-2621.

Glacier National Park

Allow: 2-3 days *Fee*

There is an International Park comprising Glacier National Park (U.S.) and Waterton National Park (CAN.) saddling the Alberta/Montana border. It honors the longstanding peaceful coexistence between Canada and the United States which share 4,000 miles of border. Set in the heart of the Rocky Mountains, this 9 million acre Glacier still provides ample wilderness for the grizzly to claim lordship over. You can hope to see moose, elk and, recent emigrants, wolves living in the wild. With barren stone peaks reaching skyward and crystal clear mountain lakes nestled beneath, Glacier preserves the true grandeur of the Rocky Mountains.

Highlights

★ The Going-to-the-Sun Road is one of the premiere drives in North America. Bracketed by two large mountain lakes is one of the most stunning mountain passes in the country. If you feel like some international travel, you can literally walk on a relatively flat trail from the pass into Canada (mind you it'll take a day or so).

★ Two Medicine Lake and Many Glacier roads both offer vistas worth the trip. Each would be worthy of its own national status if it weren't part of this sizable international treasure.

★ Canada's Waterton Lake is often depicted as the backdrop for the magnificent Canadian Pacific Hotel. Travelers familiar with the European Swiss Alps must feel they've made a U-turn and landed in Europe when they first encounter this setting.

Whiz Tips

Depending on your interests and capability, each of the eight major areas of interest offer a full range of activities and interpretive programs throughout the summer. The programs cover nature, geology, topography, orienteering, birds and aquatic life. Five of the areas have guided boat rides (fee) and hikes.

Time your drives for sunrise or sunset so you can benefit from better photographic light. As a bonus you stand a far greater chance of seeing wildlife.

Wolves, the largest of the dog family, have been slaughtered throughout the contiguous U.S.. Today, timber (gray) wolves can still be found in the deep forests of Minnesota; Mexican wolves can be seen in some remote deserts in the Southwest; the red wolf is being reintroduced in Great Smoky Mountains National Park. Recently, Glacier National Park has had a small pack of wolves moving back and forth from Canada. The debate as to their place in the scheme of things still rages. Conservationists argue they have a natural right and actually do considerable good by controlling other wildlife populations. Ranchers and farmers respond that wolves are effective predators; they hunt those prey most easily caught: domestic animals. Is there a place for wolves in our world? Who will pay for farmer and rancher losses? These are all questions left to be answered.

Upon arriving at the park, you'll see bear warnings. Pay attention! Both grizzly and black bears inhabit the park. While the park service is quick to respond to bears who take a liking to frequenting campgrounds, they aren't always there when you'd

Glacier National Park Courtesy Jim Miller

like them to be. Remember the best way of dealing with bears is to spot them before they see you and retreat. It is far more likely that you will spot black bears than the famed grizzly. These large, carnivorous mammals have no enemies save man and other bears. Yet their need for a large territory has led to frequent unhappy encounters with man which in turn has led to their dwindling numbers. Black bears weighing about 300 lbs. and measuring almost 5 ft. in length, have been known to set up quarters in tree holes 60 ft. up. Grizzlies, standing up to 10 ft. high and reaching weights of 1600 lbs., have been known to run down horses.

Kids' Stuff

★ Both the Canadian and U.S. parks offer Jr. Naturalist programs. In addition, Canada's Waterton also has puppet shows at its Heritage Center. Children's familiarity with electronic entertainment like the T.V. and videos doesn't seem to have lessened their enjoyment of a "live" puppet show.

Access: On US 2 & US 89. **Days/Hours:** Visitor centers, daily 8-4:30. **Camping:** Glacier has 8 developed campgrounds plus 5 primitive areas. Waterton has 3 main campgrounds; Townsite (elec.). **For info.:** Superintendent, Glacier National Park, West Glacier, MT 59936. 406/888-5441.

Grant-Kohrs Ranch National Historic Site

Allow: 2 hrs. *Fee*

"In Montana, you're never quite comfortable, you know; a little too hot in the sun, a little too cool in the shade."

Montana rancher
Touring the Old West

At Deer Lodge, within site of the interstate is a wonderful trip back in time to the days of the great cattle herds. The original buildings are still intact providing visitors with a glimpse of life on a big ranch. The place owes its name to its founder, Johnny Grant who started operations around the 1862, and a butcher who bought him out, Conrad Kohrs. Kohrs turned this holding into the headquarters of an enormous ranching operation (1 million acres). By using an additional 9 million of open range, his cattle wandered a land mass equal the size of Switzerland. He brought his herds to market by conducting large roundups and trail drives overcoming stampedes and rustlers. Visitors can tour the very nicely furnished "big house" and immediate ranch yard.

Highlights

★ The guided tour of the main house provides a comprehensive explanation of the ranch, its former inhabitants, the furnishings and the area. Each stop illuminates your understanding of cowboy history and the times these people struggled through. The obvious luxuries are a tribute to Conrad Kohrs' business acumen.

Whiz Tips

You can learn about life on a ranch and see the furnishings and the tools of the times. The major technological change effecting ranching was the invention of barbed wire which proved to be the end of the free-roaming range cattle as ranchers were limited to lands they owned or leased.

Kids' Stuff

★ Grant-Kohrs Ranch Jr. Ranger Program is divided into 2 age groups: 4-7 & 8-12. Each group has a question sheet to complete successfully and upon ranger approval, the kids get a certificate.

★ Kids enjoy the huge Belgian draft horses and farmyard fowls. There's bunk house where the cowboys slept, a chuck-wagon which served them their meals on the trail during roundup and the "big" house.

Access: W edge of Deer Lodge. **Days/ Hours:** Daily, summer 9-5:30, winter 9-4 (clsd. Thanksgiving, Dec.25 & Jan.1). **Camping:** 2 national forests campgrounds within 30 min. **Special Events:** Third July wknd., Birthday celebration with livestock branding, chuckwagon cooking, games & special events particularly appealing to kids. **For info.:** Superintendent, Grant-Kohrs Ranch National Historic Site, P.O.Box 790, Deer Lodge, MT 59722. 406/846-2070.

NEBRASKA

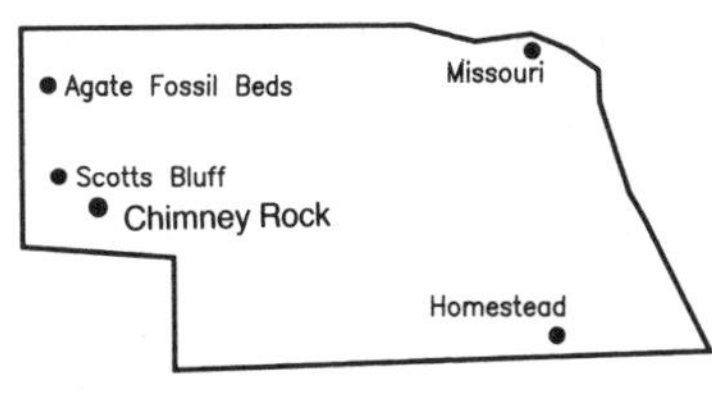

Agate Fossil Beds National Monument

Allow: 2-3 hrs. *FREE*

Agate Fossil Beds National Monument, in western Nebraskan preserves an excellent collection of prehistoric mammal remains. The fossil site was brought to the attention of the scientific world by Captain James H. Cook. In 1891, the scientific community began examining the ranch and by the turn of the century, there were competing scientific factions rooting in the hills on the ranch. Today you can see exhibits of these fossils and during summer, you may be fortunate to see paleontologists at work.

Highlights

★ The self-guiding trails leading to the exposed fossils explain the stratifications. The exhibits in the visitor center go beyond the explanation of the fossils as they detail a good deal of the goings-on at the digs.

Whiz Tips

So often we think of fossilized remains in terms of dinosaurs. However, this monument shows the variety of mammals that came after the dinosaurs only to share their fate. Two common creatures uncovered at the site were the "menocerus," a two-horned rhinoceros who was smaller than a Shetland pony and the "stenomylus," a deer-like beast standing less than two feet high. Probably the most ferocious animal was the seven-foot-tall "terrible pig." Another big mammal was the "moropus," who had the head of a horse, the body of a tapir, rhinoceros-like front legs and bear-like back legs. The Devil's Corkscrew was the fossilized burrow of the "palaecastor," a small beaver-like animal. Like dinosaurs, these animals probably disappeared when their means of survival no longer fit the time. Perhaps some died off because of more efficient predators or competitors. Others may have expired because of climatic changes caused by the periodic global warming and cooling or by meteorites that crashed into the earth. What caused the extinction of the animals represented at Agate is not really known and may never be.

Kids' Stuff

★ The large mural in the visitor center shows a very different world than we see today. The colorful reproduction fascinates kids although they find it difficult to reconcile the bones left embedded in the dirt to the world pictured in the mural.

Access: 23 mi. S of Harrison or 26 mi. N of Mitchell on NE 29. **Days/Hours:** Visitor center, daily 8:30-5:30 & winter, wknds. 8-5. **Camping:** N Fort Robinson State Park (150 sites) or S Lake Minatare State Recreation Area (152 sites) (both elec. & shwrs). **For info.:** Superintendent, Scotts Bluff National Monument, P.O.Box 27, Gering, NE 69341. 308/436-4340

Chimney Rock National Historic Site

Allow: .5 hrs. *FREE*

Of all the landmarks the western-bound pioneers noted and passed along to would-be-travelers, none was mentioned so often as Chimney Rock in southwestern Nebraska. In the over 700 personal accounts, diaries and journals written by the passing pioneers, almost all make special note of the spire rising up out of the prairie. Besides its importance as a landmark, Chimney Rock has a spring with fresh, clear water which was greatly welcomed by the travel-weary. While the North Platte River was the highway the migrants followed across the prairie, it was a muddy river which one pioneer referred to as "a moving mass of pure sand." Imagine these travelers' relief at finding clean spring water.

Highlights

★ Today, although 50-100 feet shorter, this geological wonder still dominates the landscape rising some 470 feet from a flat plain.

Whiz Tips

Composed of Brule clay, mixed with volcanic ash and Arickaree sandstone, the conical mound has withstood the weathering of time while the more easily eroded clay surrounding it has been washed away. The additional height and the thousands of pioneer inscriptions that were carved into the Chimney have disappeared into the rubble at its base.

Kids' Stuff

★ In summer, there's a information trailer set up here where kids can learn about their hardy fore-fathers.

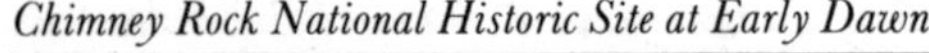

Chimney Rock National Historic Site at Early Dawn

Access: W of juncture of US 26 & NE 92. **Days/Hours:** Summer, daily. **Camping:** N Lake Minatare State Recreation Area (152 sites) (both elec. & shwrs). **For info.:** Superintendent, Chimney Rock National Historic Site, P.O.Box 27, Gering, NE 69341. 308/436-4340.

Homestead National Monument

Allow: 1-2 hrs. *FREE*

"In Nebraska, as in so many other states, we must face the fact that the splendid story of the pioneers is finished, and that no new story worthy to take its place has begun."

Willa Cather
These United States

In the southeast corner of Nebraska in a sea of unbroken prairie sits a park commemorating the settlers who came to this bleak land to claim their 160 acres granted by the *Homesteader Act*. The park consists of a 124-year-old log cabin, a restored country school and the farming implements used to turn the Great American Desert into the world's bread-basket.

Highlights

★ The park's film describes the life these hardy people had to endure to succeed. It follows the composite letters from a pioneer woman to her eastern sister. Slowly, the land works its magic. Features that appeared dull are viewed differently as the lady learns to see the land's nuances and it becomes her home.

Whiz Tips

During summer, park rangers dress up on weekends becoming living homesteading historians.

In 1862, President Lincoln, whose family had continually pioneered westward, signed a bill near and dear to his heart, the *Homestead Act*. The act provided 160 acres of free prairie land so long as the person agreed to work the land for five years. The intent of the bill was to ensure the land the Americans had negotiated and fought wars for, remained theirs. The migrants consisted of easterners, Civil War veterans and thousands of immigrants

Homestead National Monument Courtesy NPS

who couldn't dream of owning land in their home countries. Of course, there were people who took advantage of the open offer to secure large tracks of land, but overall, the bill succeeded in providing people with their first homestead. The pioneers endured the harsh weather, the unforgiving land, drought and pestilence and learned what grows and what doesn't. New strains of wheat from the Russian Steppes found their way to the Great Plains and ultimately, man triumphed.

Kids' Stuff

★ Your children can participate in the Jr. Pioneer program and earn a patch by visiting at least 10 stops at the monument and completing 3 other activities in their Jr. Pioneer booklet.

★ Children will enjoy comparing their schools to the Freeman School, which is furnished as it was in 1870. A great "hands-on" exhibit is the pioneer truck with reproduced tools, toys and utensils which can try out as well as clothes they can try on.

Access: 5 mi. NW of Beatrice or 40 mi. S of Lincoln on NE 4. **Days/Hours:** Daily 8:30-5. **Camping:** Beatrice's Chautauqua Park (elec. & showers) & Riverside Park (elec.) (4 mi.), Rockford Lake State Recreation Area (14 mi.) & Rock Creek Station State Historical Park (22 mi.). **Special Events:** Late June, Homestead Days & mid-Dec., Christmas on the Homestead. **Teacher's Package:** Available. **For info.:** Superintendent, Homestead National Monument, Rte.3, Box 47, Beatrice, NE 68310-9416. 402/223-3514.

Lewis and Clark National Historic Trail

The trail follows almost 4,500 miles of water routes, trails and marked highways that approximate the outbound and return routes of the 1804-1806 Lewis and Clark Expedition. Meriwether Lewis and William Clark set out from St. Louis (see Jefferson National Expansion Memorial, MO) across the prairies (see Knife River Indian Villages NHS, ND) over the Rockies to Idaho (see Nez Perce NHP, ID) to the Columbia River and on to the Pacific Coast where they wintered (see Fort Clatsop NMem, OR). They then retraced part of their path on their journey back.

For info.: Lewis and Clark National Historic Trail, Midwest Region National Park Service, 1709 Jackson St., Omaha, NE 68102.

Missouri National Recreational River

The park comprises the 59 mile free-flowing stretch of "Big Muddy" that runs from Gavins Point Dam near Yankton, SD to Ponca, NE. Boaters can expect to see a dynamic river that reflects its nick-name and presents shifting islands, bars, chutes and snags as each season (or rain) sculpts a new look.

For info.: Missouri National Recreational River, c/o Midwest Region, National Park Service, 1709 Jackson St., Omaha, NE 68102.

North Country National Scenic Trail

Nebraska is the terminus of the 3,200 mile trail (approx. 1,000 mi. are open for public use) which begins at Crown Point, NY.

For info.: North Country National Scenic Trail, Midwest Region, National Park Service, 1709 Jackson St., Omaha, NE 68102.

Scotts Bluff National Monument

Allow: 1-2 hrs. *Fee*

Spurred by the depression of 1837, the stories of free lush farmlands and no snow, people began to dribble to California and Oregon. During the 1840s, over 150,000 people and a million head of livestock took part in one of the greatest migrations in the history of man. They spent months plodding across the "Great American Desert." Slowly peeking over this seemingly endless prairie was Scotts Bluff, a landmark signalling the beginning of the West. Today, the Nebraska panhandle monument serves to remind us of the spirit and vision of these brave souls.

Highlights

★ To get the most from your visit, see the audio-visual orientation program and spend some time in the exhibit area before going atop the bluff for the view.

Whiz Tips

There are special Thursday Night Programs from mid-June to mid-Aug. Every summer, the monument presents living history demonstrations. Costumed pioneers make camp and tell you about their trials and tribulations, their dreams and hopes and their daily chores and lives.

The Oregon and California Trails were so well travelled that at the monument you can still see depressions carved in the earth 8 ft. deep. On the river's north bank, some 16,000 Church of Jesus Christ of Latter-Day Saints, fleeing persecution, created the Mormon Trail as they journeyed to the Salt Lake Valley.

Scotts Bluff was named for a fur trapper, Hiram Scott, who, according to legend, was left for dead by his companions in an Indian attack. Scott eventually died but only after he'd pulled himself from the river bed up to the base of the bluff. The Indians called the bluff, "the-hill-that-is-hard-to-go-around."

Kids' Stuff

★ Your children will enjoy the liv-

Scotts Bluff National Monument

ing history portrayals. They will learn about the Mormons who travelled the north river trail in a religious exodus and the southern route travelers who weren't fleeing but rather chasing their dreams of fortune. What better way to teach your children about an important era of American history?

Access: 45 mi. S off I-80 on NE 71 or 92. **Days/Hours:** Daily 8-5. **Camping:** Nearby Lake Minatare State Recreation Area and Wildcat Hills Recreation Area require a permit; both Gering & Scottsbluff have city campgrounds. **Teacher's Package:** Available. **For info.:** Superintendent, Scotts Bluff National Monument, P.O.Box 27, Gering, NE 69341. 308/436-4340.

NEVADA

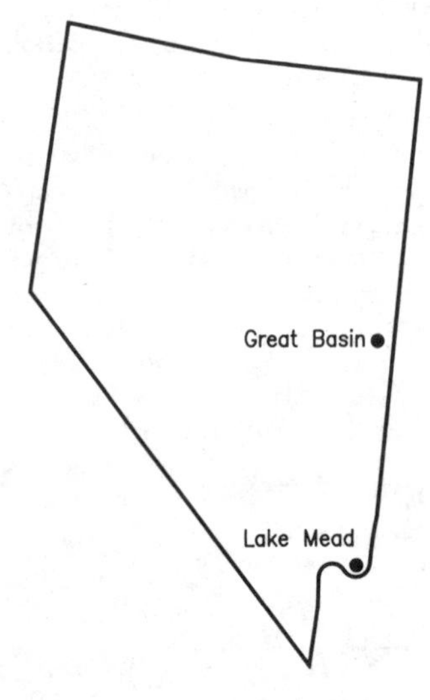

Great Basin National Park

Allow: 2-3 days *FREE (cave tour fee)*

"...asked what he knows about Nevada, he will usually mention the Great Basin-envisioned as a huge hollow bowl...That the state is a mountainous region with flora rivaling that of California in richness and variety, comes to him as astonishing news."

The Federal Writers Project of the WPA

Nevada: A Guide to the Silver State

There are few places in the lower 48 as remote as this recently created national park along the Nevada/Utah border. Initially preserved as a national monument because of its remarkably ornamented Lehman Caves, the park encompasses sagebrush and mountain country unique to the Great Basin.

Highlights

★ No visit to the park would be complete without touring the 1/4 mi. long Lehman Caves, really one cavern consisting of winding tunnels connected to larger vaulted rooms. The underground openings were formed by carbon dioxide-laden water seeping into rock cracks and dissolving the more soluble marble. As the environment became more arid, the water gradually ran off. As the water evaporated, it left the calcite and calcium carbonate cave formations. The cave is noted for its palettes or shields, stalactites, stalagmites, helictites, popcorn and argonite.

★ For picturesque vistas, you can take the Wheeler Peak Drive, which leads you to a campground at almost 10,000 ft. above sea level. You can hike past Stella and Teresa lakes on your way to the 13,000 ft. high summit. The park's only glacier lies nearby.

Whiz Tips

❢ The main interpretive programs are the campfire talks and cave tours. The evening chats focus on the region's wildlife, history or geology.

In addition to the regular ranger-led 1.5 hr. cave tour (dress warmly as it's 50 degrees F. in the cave), every summer evening there's a Candlelight Tour. On weekends, there are more adventurous Spelunking Tours.

Great Basin bristlecone pines are found in three groves here. The bristlecone's size gives little hint to its longevity. Ironically, the oldest tree in the world (4,900 yrs. old), a bristlecone, was cut down near Wheeler Peak to measure how old it was. In California, a bristlecone named "Methuselah" is 4,600 years old and thought to be the current age record-holder.

Kids' Stuff

★ Most children enjoy cave tours. Occasionally, a child will balk at going underground. You're wise not to force the issue; claustrophobia or fear of the dark are difficult to overcome. Our kids love exploring caves; if they get to see fantastic formations, so much the better.

★ The park has a nature trail at the visitor center that is ideal for families. Many people take their kids on some of the trails at Wheelers Peak.

Nature Hike

COURTESY NPS

Lake Mead National Recreation Area

COURTESY JIM MILLER

Access: 10 mi. from US 6-50 on NV 487 & 488, 480 mi. from Salt Lake City, UT or 286 mi. from Las Vegas on I-15 to US 6-50. **Days/Hours:** Daily 8-5 (clsd. Thanksgiving, Dec.25 & Jan.1). **Camping:** Park's 4 campgrounds (104 sites & pit toilets). **For info.:** Superintendent, Great Basin National Park, Baker, NV 89311. 702/234-7221.

Lake Mead National Recreation Area

Allow: 1-2 days *FREE*

It's almost as if the people responsible for building everything bigger and better than Reno decided to outdo Reno's nearby Lake Tahoe by damming the Colorado. The result is lakes Mead and Mohave. Arizona and Nevada share the lakes as their border line. Lake Mead reaches back to the Grand Canyon with one arm, while its second points north into the Virgin Mountains. Lake Mohave follows the river bed down through the lows the river bed down through the Black Canyon towards the Gulf of California. Water-lovers have been reaping their pleasures from the area since 1935, when the Hoover Dam was completed.

Highlights

★ Surrounded by desert country, the 274 sq. mi. lake is where it's at. Boaters can sightsee, water ski, sail, troll for fish and find plenty of places far from the madding crowd.

★ Two exciting boat trips for photo buffs are the narrow channels of Black Canyon in Lake Mohave and Lake Mead's Iceberg Canyon.

Whiz Tips

Rangers provide interpretive programs throughout the year. You can also join a guided tour of Hoover Dam or take a self-guided tour of Davis Dam.

These huge bodies of water belie the general weather conditions for the region. Temperatures can rise to 110 degrees F and less than 6 in. of rain falls each year. The wildlife and vegetation have adapted over the millennia to cope with these conditions. The existence of the lakes has also resulted in changes in the mix of creatures in the area. For example, the game fish inhabiting the clear lakes are different from the fish previously found in the muddy Colorado. Trout and bass have replaced bottom-feeders, like squawfish. In addition, migrating waterfowl now make regular stops here whereas the previously swift-running river and arid land were avoided.

Kids' Stuff

★ There are summer interpretive programs for children at Boulder Beach and Katherine Landing.

★ The water in much of the lakes reaches as high as 78 degrees F, an excellent swimming temperature. The park has two designated swimming areas: Boulder Beach on Lake Mead and Lake Mohave's Katherine Beach.

Access: 4 mi. NE of Boulder City. **Days/Hours:** Daily. **Camping:** Park has 8 campgrounds. **For info.:** Superintendent, Lake Mead National Recreation Area, 601 Nevada Hwy., Boulder City, NV 89005-2426. 702/293-8907.

NEW HAMPSHIRE

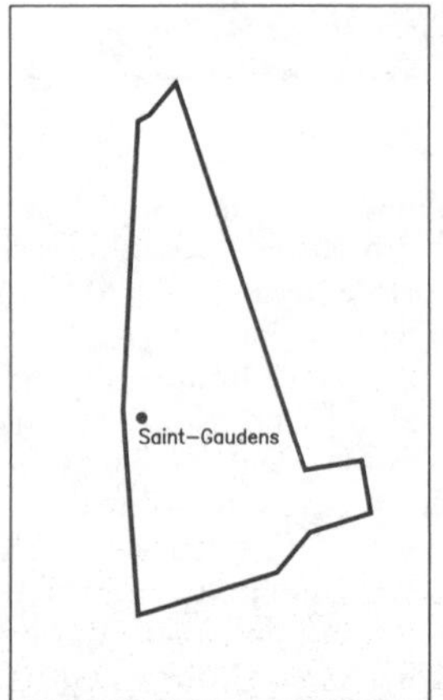

Saint-Gaudens National Historic Site

Allow: 2-3 hrs. *Fee*

"It is New Hampshire out there,
It is nearly the dawn.
The song of the whippoorwill stops
And the dimension of depth seizes everything."

Galway Kinnel
Flower Herding on Mount Monadnock

The final home of America's most famous sculptor, Augustus Saint-

Gaudens, is nestled along the New Hampshire/Vermont border. A city boy, he was uncertain about the country but perhaps his visits here convinced him the rural life would add a "dimension of depth" to his work. Several of the artist's works can be seen on the grounds and gardens, which Saint-Gaudens tended with almost as much care as his art. The buildings included in the site include his home, the little studio, the stable, the ravine studio, the temple, the picture gallery and the new gallery.

Highlights

★ The best way to appreciate the scope of this great American is to try and time your visit to the ranger-led tours. Start by seeing the introductory AV program, then link up with one of the many house tours and top it off with the 2 p.m. grounds tour.

★ The park has two self-interpretive walks taking you through the beautiful New Hampshire forest. Each trail has its own pamphlet detailing the spots of interest.

Whiz Tips

Augustus Saint-Gaudens' family fled the 1848 Irish Potato Famine. They settled in New York, where it became clear that young Augustus possessed artistic talent. At age 19, he attended France's famous Ecole des Beaux-Arts. A beneficiary of early patronage, he worked in Rome for five years. His first triumph was the Admiral David Farragut statue which resides in New York's Madison Square. From that point on, Saint-Gaudens had more work than time. Yet, he continued to teach and give time to his favorite causes. His legacy includes some of the most memorable works in America: what some regard as his masterpiece, the Shaw Memorial in Boston (see Boston African American NHS, MA), the Standing Lincoln in Chicago, the Adams Memorial in Rock Creek Cemetery and the Sherman on New York's Fifth Ave. near Central Park. While residing here, he launched the Cornish Colony of artists where the rich and talented intermingled.

Kids' Stuff

★ The park has children's interpre-

Saint-Gaudens National Historic Site

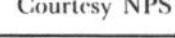
Courtesy NPS

tive programs which explain sculpting. Whether it's their details, their artistic flair or their very size, children love to see Saint-Gaudens works. Much of his efforts were directed toward Civil War monuments which offered fertile ground for dramatic images. Coin collectors marvel over his creations for President Theodore Roosevelt.

★ The nature trails are great places to take the family as the longest is 2 mi.

Access: In Cornish off of NH 12A, 9 mi. N of Claremont, NH & 2 mi. from Windsor, VT. **Days/Hours:** Buildings, daily, May-Oct 8:30-4:30, grounds 8-dusk. **Camping:** Mt. Ascutney State Park (49 sites & shwrs.) & Wilgus State Park (22 sites & shwrs.), both near Ascutney, VT. **Special Events:** July & Aug., Sunday concerts (2 p.m.). **Teacher's Package:** Available. **For info.:** Superintendent, Saint-Gaudens National Historic Site, RR #3, Box 73, Cornish, NH 03745-9704. 603/675-2175.

NEW JERSEY

Edison National Historic Site

Allow: 2 hrs. *Fee*

"Genius is 1% inspiration, 99% perspiration."

Thomas Alva Edison

Oh, for that 1%! Your kids may ask "What gives?" as you take-in this antiquated factory in West Orange, a satellite city of Newark. There's nothing terribly scenic about this National Park nor is there a singular sculpted monument in which its story is self-evident. No, this site is dedicated to the mind not the senses. Thomas Alva Edison was all mind. He lived to think. This collection of rambling, shambling factory buildings represents to American civilization what the now classic ruins were for the Greek and Roman empires. These were the places where great thinkers gathered to flesh out ideas to achieve cultural, social and economic success. Visitors can learn about both the 1% and 99% that Edison put into everything he did.

Highlights

★ The exhibit hall, the films and the tour of Edison's complex act in concert, allowing visitors to recognize the depth and breadth of Edison's accomplishments. As you tour, it becomes clear that the setting is more than the sum of its parts. True, many innovative things were invented here, but a big part of why they could be invented was that Edison had invented one of his greatest concepts, a Research & Development Center.

★ On weekends, you can visit Edison's up-scale Glenmont estate. The original furnishings still fill the 23-room mansion.

Whiz Tips

Thomas Edison was the ultimate WHIZ KID. With virtually no formal education, he was self-taught. Until his death, it was clear his mind never stopped trying to absorb as much as it could. He truly felt, "We don't know a millionth of one per cent about anything." And he wanted to expand that. Edison is still the all-time record holder of patents in the United States with 1,093. Second place isn't even close. He recognized a basic economic rule early in life. If he was to continue to invent, he had to invent things that people would pay him money for. His first invention was an electronic voting machine that nobody wanted. From then on, every invention had to first satisfy a market. Edison is best known as the man who invented the light bulb. He didn't! He did, however, invent the first commercially viable light bulb. Edison recognized the need for an electrical system, so he invented electrical generation, transferring, switching and house systems. He went on to invent the record and motion picture industries along with countless equipment inventions that these industries still use. At one point, Thomas Edison ran 34 companies all producing goods and services for the world. Unlike today's mega-corporate leaders, Edison was creating new industries and new jobs where none had existed before.

Kids' Stuff

Older children can really appreciate the degree of Edison's accomplishments, although it's difficult to comprehend a world lit by gas lamps so rapidly changing into a world of moving pictures and sound travelling through the air. The minimum age for children to get the most from the tour is around 10, but our kindergarten kids really enjoyed the visitor center with its films and exhibits.

Access: Main St. at Lakeside Dr. in West Orange just N off I-280. **Days/Hours:** Lab tours W-Su 9:30-3:30; Glenmount Sa & Su 11-4. **Camping:** Wawayanda State Park, Cheesequake State Park (53 sites & shwrs.) & Stephen Saxon Falls State Park (resvns.). **Special Events:** Mid-Jan., Black Maria Film and Video Festival; early Feb., Pre-

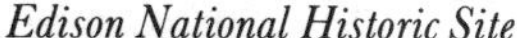

Edison National Historic Site

senting...Movie Night at the Edison Labs; early Mar., Edison's home life; mid-Apr., Focus on the Phonograph; late Apr., Victorian Gardens; late Oct., Casting Call...The Great Train Robbery; Dec., Concert at Glenmont & Christmas at Glenmont. **For info.:** Superintendent, Edison National Historic Site, Main St. & Lakeside Ave., West Orange, NJ 07052. 201/736-5050.

Morristown National Historical Park

Allow: 2-3 hrs. *Fee*

Perhaps Washington's greatest strength as a leader was his ability to hold an army together through horrendous winter encampments. Morristown, 30 miles from New York, may have been extremely strategic in terms of its defensibility but it proved a hard place to winter. The park consists of Washington's H.Q., the Ford Mansion located in the town proper, Jockey Hollow Encampment and Fort Nonsense. The theme is the desperate struggle the Continental Army underwent to survive Morristown's coldest, most miserable winter, a winter which made Valley Forge's look balmy (see Valley Forge NHP, PA).

Highlights

★ At Jockey Hollow you can see the AV reenactment of the winter encampment. You can visit with a costumed park ranger at the Wick House. Active families like to walk or pedal around the grounds to see the soldier's huts, the Grand Parade field.

★ As you tour Ford Mansion, you're told how Washington struggled to hold his army together during the brutal winter. It's hard to reconcile Washington's quarters with the rough-hewn huts at Jockey Hollow.

Whiz Tips

❢ If the winter encampment during 1777-78 in a Pennsylvania valley forged Washington's army, the winter of 1779-80 tempered them. That year Morristown experienced 20 major snow storms; the Hudson River froze over, as did New York Bay all the way out to today's Liberty Island. The 1st Connecticut Brigade, who had already experienced Valley Forge, mutinied because of lack of

Morristown National Historical Park Courtesy NPS

food. The 10,000 men who began the winter were decimated by death (86) and desertion to less than 9,000.

Morristown first entertained the Continental Army in the winter of 1776-7. They constructed an earthen fort to protect their military storehouse. Because the fort was never attacked, 19th century people said Washington had his men build the fort to keep them busy and jokingly referred to it as Fort Nonsense.

Kids' Stuff

★ At Jockey Hollow, families can bike around the one-way loop roads or take to hills on foot as they explore this beautiful forested park land. Several groups of deer were feeding in the meadows when we visited. The "soldiers" kept the kids enthralled with explanations of their "lives" here.

Access: In Morristown, off I-287, southbound take Exit 32 & northbound take Exit 32A for Washington's H.Q.; for Jockey Hollow, southbound use Exit 26B & northbound take exit for Rte.202. **Days/Hours:** Washington's H.Q., daily, 9-5 (clsd. Thanksgiving, Dec.25 & Jan.1); Jockey Hollow, daily May-Oct. 9-5, limited winter schedule. **Camping:** Round Valley State Park (116 sites), Spruce Run Recreation Area (70 sites & shwrs.) & Voorhees State Park (33 sites). **Special Events:** Wknd. closest St. Patrick's Day, a reenacted encampment; last Aug. wknd., Colonial Fair. **For info.:** Superintendent, Morristown National Historical Park, Morristown, NJ 07960. 201/539-2085.

NEW MEXICO

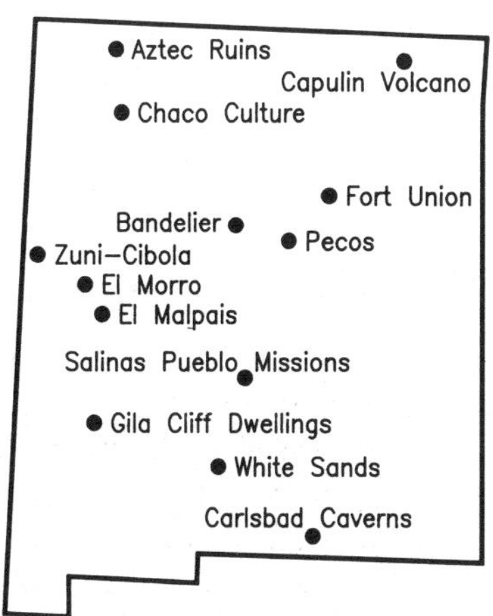

Aztec Ruins National Monument

Allow: .5 days *Fee*

Located in northwestern New Mexico, in the town of Aztec, is a gem of a national monument. Anasazi, not Aztecs, were the people who lived in these buildings for centuries. What's interesting about these ruins is that two different periods of occupation are evident. The first inhabitants were related to the Chaco Anasazi, possibly connected by the "Great North Road" to what is now Chaco Culture National Historic Park (70 miles to the south). After they abandoned the site, people more closely influenced by the Mesa Verde culture (see Mesa Verde NP, CO) moved in only to abandon the site around AD 1300.

Highlights

★ A remarkable feature of the park is a completely restored Great Kiva, the only one in existence. After seeing ruin after ruin, it was fascinating to go inside this elegant structure and more fully imagine what took place there. Purists recoil at the possible loss of historical information during the reconstruction of this building. Apparently, even though restoration tries to recreate what existed, it inevitably alters the site. Also, reconstruction is based on what is known and assumed at a point in time which later may prove incorrect. The trade-off at this attraction does provide the visitor with a greater understanding of the complexity of this culture.

Whiz Tips

❢ There's a self-guiding trail guide to the ruins, a small museum and an introductory AV. Make sure you catch the ranger talks at the Great Kiva which can range from the Kiva to the Anasazi.

Kids' Stuff

★ Our oldest children became engrossed in their Junior Ranger Program. As we wandered around the ruins, they were busy learning the necessary information to successfully complete their worksheet and earn a badge.

Access: Just N of Aztec. **Days/Hours:** Daily, 8-5 (clsd. Dec.25 & Jan.1). **Camping:** Navajo Lake State Park E on US 64 & SR 511 (61 sites, elec. & shwrs.). **Teacher's Package:** Available. **For info.:** Superintendent, Aztec Ruins National Monument, P.O.Box 640, Aztec, NM 87410. 505/334-6174.

Bandelier National Monument

Allow: 1 day *Fee*

Up in the hills just west of Santa Fe is one of New Mexico's delights, Bandelier National Monument. Throughout our visits to the Southwest's ruins, we continued to be somewhat put off by the reference to the cliff-dwellers having lived in caves. Like our children, we kept expecting to see large dark caverns but instead we were told the terraces in the rock were caves. Well, at Bandelier, they have real caves. They're dark, spooky and received four small children's stamp of approval as authentic.

Highlights

★ Frijoles Canyon has several caves including a Cave Kiva and a Ceremonial Cave. The trip to Ceremonial Cave is thrilling or frightening de-

Aztec Ruins National Monument

pending on your acrophobia quotient as you climb a series of Indian-style ladders taking you high over the valley. At the top you are rewarded with a wonderful view and you can enter a roofed kiva, a rare treat.

★ You may have the good fortune, as we did, of seeing native artists at work behind the visitor center. They were very willing to answer questions about their art and its significance within their culture. There is also an extensive nature trail and a beautiful museum at the park.

Whiz Tips

❢ It was particularly interesting to see how these ancient Americans, the Anasazi, adapted their architecture and settlement to different areas. At Bandelier, unlike many of their other locations, there is a fairly reliable source of flowing water. Whether this source of water altered their building is in question, but there are many more ruins in the bottom of the canyon than we saw at other settlements.

Kids' Stuff

★ The caves, ladders and relatively easy hiking make this a good kid's spot. The park's natural resources, including a mountain stream, have allowed the park service to develop picnic and camping facilities which make it a recreation destination for tourists and locals alike.

★ They have a Junior Ruins Ranger Program which requires kids to complete 7 of the listed activities. In addition, the park puts on specific programs for children when its staffing allows it.

Access: 46 mi. N on US 285 & W on NM 4 from Santa Fe or NE on NM 44 & NM 4 from Albuquerque. **Days/Hours:** Daily, summer 8-6, winter 8-4:30 (clsd. Dec.25). **Camping:** Park's Juniper Campground (60 sites). **For info.:** Superintendent,Bandelier National Monument, Los Alamos, NM 87544. 505/672-3861.

Bandelier National Monument

Capulin Volcano National Monument

Allow: 2-4 hrs. *Fee*

In New Mexico's northeastern extremes is a dormant volcano. Although 7,000 years old, scientists still classify this as a potentially active volcano. With this in mind, you feel a tinge of excitement as you approach Capulin's cone. Somehow the parking lot in the volcano's cone and the relatively short hike to peek into the crater vent don't quite offer all the assurance of home.

Highlights

★ The rim trail hike provides panoramic views of the surrounding countryside which includes four states: New Mexico, Colorado, Oklahoma and Texas.

★ Just walking into the cone of a volcano is an experience all of its own. Curiosity about these fiery phenomena led to a number of deaths when oft-warned visitors and residents of Mount St. Helen's ignored that volcano's signals. Fortunately, here we have cause to believe the possibility of a Capulin eruption is pretty remote.

Whiz Tips

❢ The site itself is an excellent example of a cinder-cone volcano and the visitor center has audio-visual material and exhibits which explain volcanoes. Most of us still believe the interior of the earth is hot molten rock which spews forth when a fissure occurs in the earth's crust. "T'ain't so." The earth is solid rock throughout. When an opening occurs in the earth's crust giving vent to molten lava, it is the tremendous pressure surrounding this crack that causes the rock to liquefy. The pressure creates enormous heat resulting in flames, smoke and explosions until the aperture is sealed. Why the crack occurs, is still a mystery.

Capulin Volcano National Monument Courtesy NPS

Kids' Stuff

★ Imagine Show & Tell when your kids tell their classmates they were inside the cone of potentially active volcano.

Access: 33 mi. E from Raton & 57 mi. W from Clayton on US 64/87 & NM 325. **Days/Hours:** Daily, summers 8-5:30 & winter 8-3:30. (clsd Dec.25 & Jan.1). **Camping:** Sugarite State Park (35 mi. W) and Clayton State Park (65 mi. E). **For info.:** Superintendent, Capulin Volcano National Monument, Capulin, New Mexico 88414. 505/278-2201.

Carlsbad Caverns National Park

Allow: .5 days *Fee*

At the southern reaches of New Mexico, a hop, skip and jump from West Texas, Carlsbad Caverns National Park draws a phenomenal number of tourists to this barren country. Huge, colossal, awesome, frightening...this strange and wonderful "other" world quickly becomes your reality. Like Jonah, we were swallowed by its enormous seemingly-bottomless mouth, spiralling ever downward, deep into the throat and then forsaken in the dark. Fortunately, we have electric lights to guide our way through the bowels of this whale-like, land-locked reef. Earlier visitors lowering themselves into the cave by rope depended on candlelight to guide them.

Highlights

★ There are two self-guided tours, the red and the blue. The red tour involves taking the elevator both ways and is limited to the Big Room. The Big Room is so big it can hold the nation's capitol building and is as long as 14 football fields. Unless you have health considerations or are claustrophobic, take the blue tour which encompasses all of the cave open to the general public. Descending into the natural cavity and having the daylight gradually disappear is a remarkable experience. The tour also includes several of the smaller, more picturesque caverns like Green Lake, King's Palace, Queen's Chamber and Papoose Room.

★ The bat exodus each evening

Cave at Bandelier National Monument

complete with the ranger's narration is a special treat. Early residents in the area thought the colony was the evidence of a huge fire or explosion. Darkening the sky in total chaotic unison, the bats rush out to begin their night of foraging. Each fall, they leave the cave as one and migrate to Mexico. Each spring, they return in dribs and drabs to take up their summer residence.

Whiz Tips

At the Top of the Cross in the Big Room, the rangers give interpretive talks about the cave. Also, rangers are assigned to places along the cave routes to answer questions you might have about stalactites, stalagmites, flowstone, columns and draperies. Both the cave and these formations were formed by water leaking down into the rock and dissolving the limestone components. Scientists speculate that the process was accelerated when this rainwater mixed with a residue of remaining saltwater to create sulfuric acid, a very corrosive agent. This would account for the enormous size of the chambers. The rainwater continued to seep downward dissolving the limestone left above the cave. This mixture slowly dripped into the cave leaving small particles of calcite which gradually built one upon another until after millions of years they had created the fantastic formations we see today. It is estimated that it takes hundreds and, in some cases, thousands of years to add one inch to a stalactite's length. Think of how many thousands of years it took to create Carlsbad's formations. Heed the park's warnings and don't touch them.

Although there is some signage in the caves, we would strongly recommend renting (minimal cost) an audio phone that plays recordings on the displays as you pass them. The audio program explains how the cave was made, the special formations and the history of exploration of the cave.

At the visitor center, you can ask to see a film on the bats of Carlsbad, a preview of the evening bat outing (bats are only present spring through fall).

There is a limited availability lantern-led tour allowing you to see the so-called "new" cave.

Kids' Stuff

★ Make sure you take the blue tour with the kids. They love descending into the cave via the paved switchbacks even if it is 91 stories, mostly down, and almost two miles of walking.

★ The recent success of Batman may have kindled greater interest in the small flying rodents, but kids have always been fascinated with these critters.

Access: 20 mi. W from Carlsbad or 150 mi. E from El Paso on US 62-180. **Days/ Hours:** Park open daily (clsd. Dec.25). Visitor center daily, summer 8:30-7, winter 8-5:30; Carlsbad Cavern Tour, summer 8:30-3:30, winter 8:30-2; Big Rom Tour daily, summer 9-5, winter 8:30-2; New Cave Tour, summer twice daily, winter wknds only (reservations). **Camping:** Brantley Lake State Park, Guadalupe Mountains National Park & Lake Carlsbad Campground (municipal). **For info.:** Superintendent, Carlsbad Caverns National Park, 3225 National Parks Hwy., Carlsbad, NM 88220. 505/785-2232.

Chaco Culture National Historical Park

Allow: 1 day *Fee*

In a remote area of northwestern New Mexico rests the remains of a magnificent civilization. Chaco Culture National Historical Park preserves the ruins of the center of the Chacoan world and perhaps the Anasazi's. At the end of a long dirt road is evidence of several large Chaco communities, a subset of the people we now call Anasazi. With a splendid museum adorned by Chacoan masonry, the visitor center also offers excellent orientation films.

Highlights

★ It is interesting to compare the large Anasazi settlements on the northern side of the canyon with the small villages across the wash. Of particular note are the three large structures, Pueblo Bonito, Pueblo del Arroyo and Chetro Ketl which were built within shouting distance of each other. The Great Kiva at Casa Rinconada is the largest religious/social edifice in the region. Many archaeologists believe the large size of these structures indicates Chaco served as the religious, cultural and social center for all Anasazi peoples.

★ Pueblo Bonito is truly one of the most formidable structures built in the pre-European U.S.. Built and remodeled over 3 centuries, it reached five stories high and had over 650 rooms in a fascinating, almost capital D shaped construction.

★ Although unnoticeable at ground level, aerial photographs of Chaco reveal intricate roadwork leading between each Chaco village including far-off Aztec (approx. 70 miles N.). Scientists continue to ponder why the Chacoans built roads as straight as arrows when they never used the wheel. In addition, some roads had formal curbing, flagstone or sherd "pavement," and wide stairways up and down the suckrock escarpments.

Whiz Tips

The Chacoan Anasazi appear to have been the master builders of their era. Structures were preplanned and made use of thousands of timbers gathered in the distant (60 mi.) mountains. They built their structures by fitting together shaped rocks, relying very little on mortar to hold their works together. The museum uses the different eras of masonry style to showcase their associated artifacts.

Recent discoveries lead us to believe the Chacoans clearly understood both solar and lunar cycles. In an area closed to the public, there is a combination stone formation and spiral petroglyph which precisely mark the arrival of the seasons. This evidence of Anasazi's astronomical knowledge has placed new light on the sophistication of their culture.

Chaco Culture National Historical Park

❢ The park's interpretive programs include petroglyph hunts, examining the daily lives of the Anasazi and exploration of the many ruins.

Kids' Stuff

★ The hike up to Una Vida and the petroglyphs were a hit. We skirted through Indian ruins, then wound our way up the mesa-side on a narrow path until we reached the murals of ancient rock art.

★ On the path between Pueblo Bonito and Chetro Ketl there's a great echo. We couldn't get our little crew to leave as they kept trying out different sounds. In Pueblo Bonito, your kids can crawl through doorways and passages connecting to its deep inner rooms.

Access: 36 mi. S of Blanco off NM 44 or 60 mi. N from Thoreau off I-40 on NM 57. **Days/Hours:** Daily, summer 8-6 & winter 8-5. **Camping:** The park has 46 sites which are typically filled by 3 p.m. during the peak season. **For info.:** Superintendent, Chaco Culture National Historical Park, Star Route 4, P.O.Box 6500, Bloomfield, NM 87413. 505/988-6716.

El Malpais National Monument

Allow: 1-2 days *FREE*

These New Mexican "badlands" or the Spanish El Malpais are the result of volcanic eruptions over 3 million years. The lava flows and cinder cones replaced the typical valley scene with something "unworldly." There is evidence to suggest the Native Americans saw at least the last known volcanic activity in the region. Nevertheless, they remained and the monument preserves the region partly to ensure their legacy is not lost.

Highlights

★ Either of the park's two roads (53 or 117) will lead you to awe-inspiring scenery. Most visitors who take 117, hike to the Bureau of Land Management's La Ventana Natural Arch, the largest accessible arch in New Mexico or to the sandstone bluffs overlook. NM 53 winds past the Zuni Acoma Pueblo Indian trade route, El Calderon with its cave, cra-

National Park Passports

ters and cinder cone and the soon-to-be-included Bandera Crater and Ice Caves.

Whiz Tips

On summer weekends, the rangers lead interpretive walks and cave tours. The focus is on the region's unique geology and wildlife and cultural history.

Kids' Stuff

★ Families who come prepared with flashlights (3 are recommended) can visit some of the lava caves. Care should be taken not to intrude in the bat cave in the El Calderon area, as it upsets the bats.

Access: S of Grants off I-40 16 mi. on NM 53 or 10 mi. 117 (high clearance advised). **Days/Hours:** Grants' Info. Center at 620 E.Santa Fe Ave., daily, summer 8-5 & winter 8-4:30 (clsd. winter fed. holidays). **Camping:** El Morro NM Campground (9 sites) & Bluewater Lake State Park, 7 mi. W of Grant. **For info.:** Superintendent, El Malpais National Monument, P.O. Box 939, Grants, NM 87020-0939. 505/285-5406.

El Morro National Monument

Allow: 2-3 hrs. *Fee*

South of Grants and Gallup near the Navajo Indian Reservation and close to the Zuni Indian reservation is a 200-foot-high rock upon which man has noted his passing. El Morro, or Inscription Rock, bears witness to Native American etchings called petroglyphs, Spanish adventurers' poems and American camel drivers' signatures. Signing the rock is now illegal as the park service attempts to preserve the historical scripts of previous passers-by.

Highlights

★ El Morro was a significant landmark for the people who populated this region. The natives utilized the water at its base for centuries before Spaniards came seeking the "seven cities of Cibola." Once the "El Estanque del Penol" Pool by the Great Rock was discovered by the European interlopers, it became a favored stopover. The signatures and notes that have been carved in the rock recall times when men seeking riches stayed to save souls and later travelers paused for a moment on their way to greener pastures in California.

★ To get to the top of the mesa and a rewarding view, you pass through a picturesque box canyon.

Whiz Tips

The rock has been called "one of the most significant documents of Southwestern history." Dates and names have been correlated with other historical papers to provide us with proof of past doings. The site relates the history of this region from before Europeans arrived to the Spanish conquest through Mexican administration to the U.S. ownership.

Kids' Stuff

★ In the museum, there is a "hands-on" table and, on the back patio, a "pretend you are an archaeologist" box. Parents should be aware, the 2 mi. trail to the mesa top has some sheer drop-offs and carrying water is recommended.

Access: 56 mi. SE of Gallup or 42 mi. W of Grants on NM 53. **Days/Hours:** Daily, summer 8-7 & winter 8-5. **Camping:** Park FREE 9 site campground. **Teacher's Package:** Available. **For info.:** Superintendent, El Morro National Monument, Rte. 2, Box 43, Ramah, NM 87321-9603. 505/783-4226.

Fort Union National Monument

Allow: 2 hrs. *FREE*

Guarding Santa Fe and its famed trail against the eastern plains' raiders, the Comanche and Kiowas, the fort's ruins seem fitting somehow. The fort served more as a holding station for troops than an effective barrier. Three times it was built and three times the buildings were abandoned. Not because of battles, as one would suppose of a fort, but because of poor placement (the first and second) and obsolescence (second and third).

Highlights

★ The fort comes alive in the summer with living history presentations. Rangers and volunteers dress and work as though they were the fort's early inhabitants.

★ The stroll around the fort ruins is surprisingly interesting with audio stories. Each conversation you eavesdrop on is a piece of fabric making up the quilt that constituted a day in the life of the fort.

Whiz Tips

❢ Fort Union was the largest fort in the southwest and like all western garrisons never experienced an attack. After all, what opponent would attack such a well-armed garrison! It's interesting to see how inadequate even well-equipped fixed garrisons are in the face of foes who are extremely mobile. The Indians were able to choose their battlefields as they attacked small parties of travelers and soldiers. Then they dispersed into the wilderness disappearing like the smoke from a burning wagon.

❢ The first fort was badly situated making it an easy target for opponents who might attack it from the hills nearby. During the Civil War, the second star-shaped fort was threatened. The Colorado volunteers under the soon-to-be infamous Major Chivington (the "Slaughterer at Sand Creek") visited there on their way to defeat a Confederate force under Fort Union's previous commander, Major Henry Sibley. This earthen fort was abandoned after the Confederate threat was eliminated. The third fort was by-passed by the railroad.

Kids' Stuff

★ The kids love the living history presentations. You've never seen children listen as well as when their instructor is dressed up in a costume.

Access: 9 mi. N of Watrous off I-25 on NM 477. **Days/Hours:** Open daily, summer 8-6, winter 8-5 (clsd. Dec.25 & Jan.1). **Camping:** Nearby Storrie Lake State Park. **Special Events:** Late June, Santa Fe Trail-Freighting for Uncle Sam; late July, Soldiering on the Santa Fe Trail; late Aug., An Evening at Old Fort Union (reservations). **For info.:** Superintendent, Fort Union National Monument, Watrous, NM 87753. 505/425-8025.

Gila Cliff Dwellings National Monument

Allow: .5 days *FREE*

The prized jewel in an already opulent crown, Gila Cliff Dwellings National Monument sits high in the Gila National Forest (whose rangers administer the park). A little-known southwestern New Mexican recreational paradise, the national forest is rift with picture postcard valleys, glittering lakes, glistening rivers and gleaming mountain peaks. It's no wonder that, with the wealth of wildlife, the Mogollon Indians built their elaborate cliff dwellings here.

Highlights

★ To visit these magnificent cliff dwellings is a rare pleasure. As you walk among the ruins, you look out over the mountain valleys and feel a small degree of the peace these people knew.

★ The park has a natural hot springs within a .5 mi. of the visitor center.

Whiz Tips

❢ Common thought on the rationale for these dwellings has turned away from the protective theory, i.e. they built cliff dwellings to protect themselves from other Indians. There has been no supportive evidence for the theory of "Threat" and the dwellings would be next to useless if besieged. Without basis, one could as easily speculate they built them for aesthetic reasons.

❢ If most guesses about the fate of the Mogollon and Anasazi cliff-dwellers are correct, then some of the current Southwestern Pueblo Indians are their descendants. This could account for the differences in language between the current Pueblo Indians.

❢ First the good news: the roads to this monument are paved. However, put on your rally flags, as you'll be putting your vehicle through its handling paces. Twisting and turning over hill and dale, you'll be lucky to average 20 m.p.h.

Kids' Stuff

★ The ruins are on a self-guided one mile long trail with caves to explore and ladders to climb, sort of a prehistoric playground.

★ Beside the immense fun of traipsing in and around the ruins, the Gila National Forest is a recreational treasure-trove. Camping, fishing, hiking and exploring are the order of the day here.

Access: 44 Mi. N on NM 15 from Silver City. **Days/Hours:** Cliff Dwellings daily, summer 8-6, winter 9-4. Visitor center daily 8-5 summer & 9-4:30 winter (clsd. Dec.25 & Jan.1). **Camping:** Nearby 2 FREE developed national forest campgrounds. **For info.:** Gila Cliff Dwellings National Monument, Rte. 11, Box 100, Silver City, NM 88061. 505/536-9461.

Pecos National Historical Park Courtesy NPS

Pecos National Historical Park

Allow: 1-2 hrs. *Fee*

Just to the southeast of Santa Fe is the remains of what was once the largest pueblo in the Southwest, Pecos Pueblo. Pecos, a Spanish adaptation of the Keresan word for "watering place," dominated the major trading route between the farming Pueblo Indians and the hunters of the Great Plains. It housed over 2,000 people, long before the Spanish came seeking the fabled Seven Cities of Cibola and stayed to bring Christianity, disease and change to the Pueblo's way of life. Finally, the Comanches ravaged Pecos, forcing the native population to abandon the site. The park is important because of its rich Native American and Spanish archaeological remains.

Highlights

★ The ruins are fairly extensive, demonstrating the size of the pueblo and the workmanship that went into constructing the churches. At Pecos, the large fortress church, the only one of its kind to be found north of Mexico City, was a casualty of the Pueblo Indian Revolt of 1680. The pueblo and a smaller church were rebuilt. However, the population continued its swift decline and the decimated people of Pecos straggled northward and joined the Jemez Pueblo which still celebrates Pecos' feast day on Aug. 2nd. With the influx of Americans over the Santa Fe Trail, the pueblo was put to use as a landmark to mark the way.

Whiz Tips

❢ Stereotypical images of Native Americans portray tribes as overwhelmed by European trinkets, ready to give up valuable furs and craft work for beads and buttons. Rarely do we get a picture of any degree of commerce. Yet, at Pecos, and further to the south at Salinas, we find large settlements established on trade routes. Clearly these people had developed sophisticated inter-tribal business relations.

Kids' Stuff

★ While the ruins lack the thrill of climbing in and around the cliff dwellings of the more ancient ancestors of these people, they do serve to remind us and our children how civilizations flourished because of commerce. We can picture Native American Marco Polos travelling across the plains trading goods not just with New Mexico but with the Aztecs of Mexico and the coastal Indians of California.

Access: 25 mi. SE on I-25 from Santa Fe. **Days/Hours:** Daily, summer 8-6, winter 8-5 (closed Dec.25 & Jan.1). **Camping:** 8 Santa Fe National Forest campgrounds within 21 miles. **Special Events:** First Aug. Sun., Feast Day Mass. **For info.:** Superintendent, Pecos National Historical Park, P.O.Drawer 418, Pecos, NM 87552. 505/757-6414/6032.

Salinas Pueblo Missions National Monument

Allow: 1 day *FREE*

Southeast of Albuquerque are three ruins whose occupants were separated by miles of country and language. They have been placed together as one National Monument because it was thought they were abandoned Spanish mission pueblos. Further excavation has shown that although their abandonment occurred at the same time, these pueblos existed long before the Spaniards arrived in the Americas. The Tompiro people who occupied Gran Quivira and Abo have the unfortunate distinction of extinction as a culture. The Quarai peoples were the most southerly of the Tiwa-speaking Pueblos.

Highlights

★ Abo and Quarai are the smaller ruins. Both used red sandstone as their primary building material. The church architecture of each, however, was very different. At Abo the builders used a highly sophisticated buttressing technique which allowed them to construct much thinner walls. Abo has tall church towers remaining and large unexcavated ruins. Quarai is noteworthy because its church ruins are the best preserved.

★ The largest pueblo, Gran Quivira, is truly a dominating structure. It differs not just in the size of the pueblo but in the use of gray limestone as the building material. Gran Quivira has undergone extensive study and you can see the results of this work in excavated pueblo sections as well as the two churches at the site.

★ The visitor center which is in the town of Mountainair, has an interesting exhibit hall with a series of imaginative paintings.

Whiz Tips

Like Pecos to the north these pueblos were trading centers for the Plains and Pueblo Indians. It is interesting to note that these pueblos failed after the Spanish took over their administration. In fact, it is pretty clear that the bad relations between the nomadic Plains tribes and the Spanish had devastating results on those Pueblo Indians most visibly aligned with the "foreigners." Being "border" communities, Pecos and the Salinas Pueblos reaped benefits when relations were productive but bore the brunt of ill feelings.

Kids' Stuff

★ The sites provide a context where your children learn about the history of the Indians and the Spanish in this part of the world.

Access: From Mountainair: Gran Quivira 26 mi. S on NM 14; Quarai 8 mi. N on NM 14 & Abo 9 mi. W on US 60. **Days/Hours:** Daily 8-5 [Ruins 9-5] (clsd. Dec.25 & Jan.1). **Camping:** Near Quarai, Manzano Mountain State Park (35 sites) & Cibola National Forest. Near Gran Quivira's, Na-

Salinas Pueblo Missions National Monument Courtesy NPS

tional Forest sites in the Gallinas Mountains. **Special Events:** Late Aug., Native American Feast Day at Gran Quivira. **For info.:** Superintendent, Salinas National Monument, P.O.Box 496, Mountainair, NM 87036. 505/847-2585.

Santa Fe National Historic Trail

Following the historic overland pathway from Arrow Rock, MO through Kansas, Oklahoma and Colorado, this trail commemorates the importance commerce played in the settlement of the west.

For info.: Santa Fe National Historic Trail, Southwest Region, National Park Service, P.O.Box 728, Santa Fe, NM 87504.

White Sands National Monument

Allow: .5 days *Fee*

In south central New Mexico is a truly remarkable scene. If you were to be awakened in an air-conditioned car in the middle of this gypsum desert, you could very well believe you were in the middle of some fierce winter snow storm. The wind whips the snow-like sand particles in swirling spires. The alabaster particles are so fine, they seem as though they could melt in the harsh New Mexican sun. This geologic phenomenon, the world's largest gypsum dune field, presents a surreal picture that fascinates many. Surprisingly, the seemingly-lifeless dunes host a number of interesting plants and animals.

Highlights

★ Don't come to look from afar and leave. Drive out into this sea of shifting sand and marvel at the earth's forces. This curiosity is truly unexpected and even in retrospect, unbelievable. Never could we imagine particles of the earth so white, so minute, or so smooth. To see them forming moving dunes silhouetted against canvas-colored mountains is awe-inspiring.

★ Big Dune Trail, a self guiding 1 mi. trail, has a booklet explaining the dunes' flora and fauna.

White Sands National Monument Courtesy NPS

Whiz Tips

❢ The visitor center has an interesting light and sound show explaining how erosion has left this desert of pure white gypsum sand. The narrated three-dimensional program explains each step in the process.

❢ In summer, there are daily nature walks and evening programs. Special programs are presented on nights when there's a full moon.

Kids' Stuff

★ The rangers cater to families on the nature walks and during their talks so kids can better appreciate the area.

★ Letting the little ones get out and play in this sand is a once in a lifetime treat. Better than any sandbox, we're talking sand so fine you'll be finding it in the bottom of your washer for weeks to come.

★ The park is working to have a Jr. Ranger program in place.

Access: 15 mi. SW of Alamogordo on US 70-82. **Days/Hours:** Dunes drive, summer 7am-10pm, winter 7 to .5 hrs. after sunset; visitor center daily, summer 8-7, winter 8:30-4:30 (clsd Dec.25). **Camping:** Oliver Lee Memorial State Park 25 mi. S (showers); Lincoln National Forest 35 mi. E.; Aguirre Springs Recreation Area 35 mi. W. **For info.:** Superintendent, White Sands National Monument, Box 458, Alamogordo, NM 88311-0458. 505/479-6124.

Zuni-Cibola National Historical Park

The 1700-year history of the Zuni Tribe is preserved and protected with this recent 800 acre, non-federal addition to the park service. Many scientists believe the Zuni have descended from the Anasazi, Mogollon and Hohokam peoples, and this heritage is to be interpreted. The collision of cultures when Cortez's Expedition met the Zuni people will also be interpreted.

For info.: Zuni-Cibola National Historical Park, c/o Southwest Region, National Park Service, P.O.Box 728, Santa Fe, NM 87504-0728.

NEW YORK

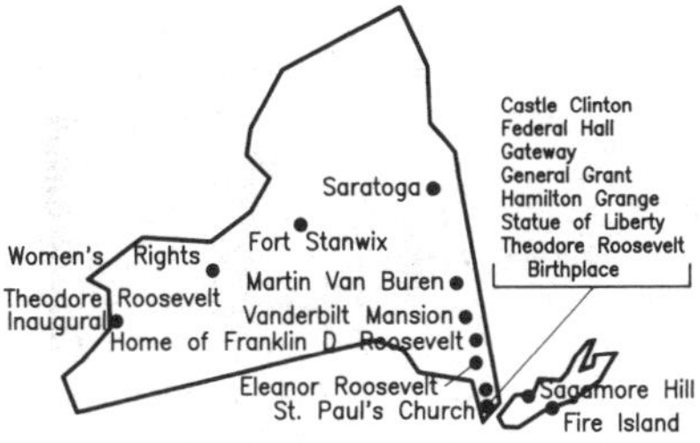

Castle Clinton National Monument

Allow: 1 hr. *FREE*

At the tip of Manhattan Island is an aged structure now known as Castle Clinton National Monument. Like most things in the Big Apple, the term "castle" is an over-promise. The structure was originally built as a defensive fortification in the period just before the War of 1812. Called the Southwest Battery, it was one of five built to protect the country's fastest growing city. It was renamed Castle Clinton in honor of a New York mayor who became governor, DeWitt Clinton. Today, although it serves more as a ferry terminus for the Statue of Liberty and Ellis Island, its park rangers offer an interesting collection of interpretive talks explaining the structure's history.

Highlights

★ While Ellis Island has recently enjoyed a renewed fame as the place where so many Americans can trace their ancestors' arrival, few realize that Castle Clinton then known as Castle Gardens pre-dates Ellis Island as the prime entry point. From 1850-1890, thousands of new immigrants streamed through its gates.

Whiz Tips

From 1896-1941, it became the New York City Aquarium. Competing for the ever-fickle entertainment dollar, the aquarium had to close its doors as Coney Island grew in popularity.

DeWitt Clinton, called Magnus Apollo because of his enormous size, was a U.S. Senator and an unsuccessful presidential candidate (1812). His major accomplishment was the planning and completion of the Erie Canal.

Kids' Stuff

★ While the monument doesn't have programs expressly oriented to children, its varied history recounted by enthusiastic rangers makes an interesting visit for anybody.

Access: Southern tip of Manhattan. **Days/ Hours:** Daily 8:30-5:30. **Camping:** Fahnestock State Park (83 sites), Carmel, NY; Harriman State Park (220 sites), Stony Point, NY; Hither Hills State Park (165 sites), Montauk, NY; Wildwood State Park (322 sites), Wading River, NY; Fire Island National Seashore's Watch Hill Campground (20 sites). **For info.:** Superintendent, Castle Clinton National Monument, C/O Manhattan Sites, 26 Wall St., N.Y., NY 10005. 212/344-7220.

Eleanor Roosevelt National Historic Site

Allow: 1-2 hrs. *FREE*

"I think somehow, we learn who we really are and then live with that decision."

Eleanor Roosevelt

On a remote corner of Franklin D. Roosevelt's family estate, Eleanor Roosevelt finally got a home she could call her own, Val-Kill. The park includes Eleanor's original stone cottage retreat and the converted Val-Kill furniture manufacturing plant which served as Eleanor's home after Franklin passed away. In addition, there's a country pond complete with sunfish, a tennis court and a doll house so large it was used as the nanny's living quarters.

Highlights

★ Eleanor's residences are very consistent with her public image. They are homes that most of us could imagine growing up in: comfortable chairs, cozy reading nooks and clutter. Interestingly, most of the furniture was made in Eleanor's own Val-Kill factory. The furniture shop was just one way Eleanor tried to be her own person.

Whiz Tips

Eleanor Roosevelt's early life gives little hint to who she really would become. Orphaned at an early age, she was raised by her grandparents. Demonstrating no laudable skills in her youth, she blossomed to become as President Harry S Truman named her, "First Lady of the World." The process was gradual as she was exposed to her husband's career. It accelerated when Franklin was stricken with polio. From then on she became her husband's ambassador-at-large, trooping around the world collecting firsthand knowledge she could pass along to him. At first her trips were within the country during the Great Depression. Then in WW II, she visited the boys overseas. After Franklin's death in 1945, it was assumed she would drop from the spotlight but her overwhelming humanitarian concerns came to the fore. She was the driving force behind the United Nations' Universal Declaration of Human Rights, which many regard as the world equivalent of the Declaration of Independence. In her later years she played king-maker in the Democrat party as office seekers would visit to gain her support.

Kids' Stuff

★ This is a homey place for children to visit. Too often historic sites recount the accomplishments of the many great men of the nation. Eleanor Roosevelt is rightly honored by having her home included in the national park offerings. No women and few men so dominated the American psyche and have fared so well in historical retrospects. All children should recognize the efforts this great human being made to make this world a fairer, kinder place. Here was a person whose words and actions were in concert.

Access: Off SR 9G. **Days/Hours:** Daily May-Oct. & wknds. Nov, Dec, Mar. & Apr., 9-5. **Camping:** Just N of Hyde Park, Margaret Lewis Norrie State Park (45 sites & shwrs.). **For info.:** Superintendent, Roosevelt/Vanderbilt National Historic Sites, 249 Albany Post Rd., Hyde Park, NY 12538. 914/229-9115.

Federal Hall National Memorial

Allow: 1 hr. *FREE*

On April 30, 1789, New York witnessed the first inauguration of a duly-elected president: George Washington. Dressed in a brown suit made of good Connecticut cloth, Washington stood on the second floor of then converted city hall and took the oath of office. Although that building, which served as the first capitol, had earlier hosted the first Congress and the first Senate, is not the building of today, the location is historic. Today's structure is the 1800s U.S. Customs Building. Inside, there are exhibit halls with austere pictures of historic leaders.

Eleanor Roosevelt National Historic Site

Highlights

★ The Wall St. steps of Greek-influenced Customs Building complete with Doric columns and a huge statue of Washington is claimed as one of the most photographed spots in the world.

Whiz Tips

In 1735, the first seeds of liberty were set here during the libel trial of John Peter Zenger (see Saint Paul's Church NHS, NY). Zenger had unleashed criticisms of the New York governor in his paper, the *New York Weekly Journal*, for which he was jailed on the charge of "seditious libel." Zenger's attorneys chose an unorthodox defense and argued that it was Zenger's duty to print truthful criticism of the government. The jury bought it and set him free. 56 years later, freedom of the press was incorporated in the constitution as the First Amendment under the Bill of Rights.

Kids' Stuff

★ The cartoon AVs of Zenger's trail and Washington's inauguration facilitate children's understanding of the importance of this historic site.

Access: Wall St. & Nassau, downtown Manhattan. **Days/Hours:** Daily 8:30-5:30. **Camping:** Fahnestock State Park (83 sites), Carmel, NY; Harriman State Park (220 sites), Stony Point, NY; Hither Hills State Park (165 sites), Montauk, NY; Wildwood State Park (322 sites), Wading River, NY; Fire Island National Seashore's Watch Hill Campground (20 sites). **For info.:** Superintendent, Federal Hall National Memorial, C/O Manhattan Sites, 26 Wall St., N.Y., NY 10005. 212/344-7220.

Fire Island National Seashore

Allow: 1 day *FREE*

"Christened with a name that has come to be the color of its reputation, clasped in the bosom of Long Island and yet, closer to the South Seas than the South Shore."

Alfred Aronowitz
NY Post

Fire Island is a barrier island lying on the Atlantic side of Long Island. For "out-of-towners," it's difficult to reconcile the seascapes of sand-swept Fire Island with the cement jungle so close at hand. The national seashore constitutes about 1/3 of 32-mile-long Fire Island. It is interlaced by small communities harboring "artist colonies," nature lovers and "summerlings." And yet it encompasses the only designated wilderness area in the Empire State.

Highlights

★ As always, the ocean beckons. Visitors come for the beach. They play in the surf, build castles and cavort in the sand. They explore the shifting dunes and watch migrating waterfowl rest before continuing their seasonal journeys.

★ The Sunken Forest is one of these havens of plant life guarded by the hilly dunes. The twisted trees, holly and sassafras forming vertical beds for poison ivy and wild grape actually grow beneath sea level.

Whiz Tips

The park's major focus is on the natural pleasures of sea & sand. Man's mark on this island is clearly of secondary status and then only in relation to how he has tried to cope with the elements with lighthouses and life-saving battalions. In summer, interpretive programs on these subjects are offered at the various visitor centers.

From Apr.-Sept., you can tour the William Floyd Estate. Floyd was a signator of the Declaration of Independence from a Loyalist controlled state - New York.

Kids' Stuff

★ The park is a boon for natives, with beaches and dunes to explore. Kids love to splash in the surf and build sand structures that continually get washed away.

★ During summer, every Wednesday, there's a Jr. Ranger program. Most Sundays, there's a specific ranger-led children's activity.

★ There are two beaches with national park lifeguards in attendance: Sailors Haven & Watch Hill. There's also a special children's guide to the Sunken Forest.

Access: You can drive to the eastern or western ends of the park, but that leaves a very healthy hike to the more popular areas. Ferries to those areas (Sailors Haven and Watch Hill Visitor Centers) leave from Long Island from May-Nov. **Days/Hours:** William Floyd Estate, F-Su 10-4; Smith Point, mid-Apr.-Dec. 8-4; Watch Hill & Sailors Haven Visitor Centers, summer, W-Su 10-4; Fire Island Lighthouse, summer, daily 9:30-5. **Camping:** Park's Watch Hill Campground (20 sites-516/597-6644); Fahnestock State Park (83 sites), Carmel; Harriman State Park (220 sites), Stony Point; Hither Hills State Park (165 sites), Montauk; Wildwood State Park (322 sites), Wading River. **Teacher's Package:** Available. **For info.:** Superintendent, Fire Island National Seashore, 120 Laurel St., Patchogue, NY 11772. 516/289-4810.

Fort Stanwix National Monument

Allow: 2 hrs. *Fee*

For the Bi-Centennial celebrations, the city of Rome, the state of New York and the federal government acted in concert to raze 4 downtown city blocks. Underneath the Sears department store, warehouse and office buildings, lay the original foundations for Fort Stanwix. Today, as you drive into this gateway to the Adirondacks, you're confronted by a recreated wooden fort, literally bristling with sharply pointed staves which held British reinforcements from joining General Burgoyne at Saratoga (see Saratoga NHP, NY).

Highlights

★ The living-history interpreters at the fort are very proud of the preciseness with which their historic site was reconstructed. They will patiently explain why certain "tourist" forts suffer in their authenticity and freely offer information on their daily chores.

Fort StanwixNational Monument

Whiz Tips

In the face of superior numbers and cannon fire, Fort Stanwix held its ground until assistance could be sent. This prevented British Colonel St. Leger's 200 regulars, 500 loyalists and 1,000 Indian allies from linking up with General Burgoyne at Saratoga. And like the proverbial nail, for want of larger cannons the fort was not taken; the armies were not linked. The battle and, ultimately, the war, was lost when Burgoyne, with his 6,000 men, was forced to surrender at Saratoga.

Kids' Stuff

★ Fort Stanwix was a star fort built along the prescribed lines of the day. Each point (bastion) juts out so guns positioned in it could cover almost 360 degrees and protect all the walls. If a force tried to breech the walls, they had to contend with a dry moat or ditch at the base of the fort's walls. In the case of Fort Stanwix, breaching the wall would not have been a good idea as there were almost 800 armed men inside. Kids find this fort appealing because of its appearance. The living-history guides throughout the enclosure are a real bonus.

Access: Downtown Rome. **Days/Hours:** Daily 9-5 Apr.-Dec. (clsd. Thanksgiving & Dec.25). **Camping:** N 6 mi., Delta Lake State Park (101 sites, elec. & shwrs.). **For info.:** Superintendent, Fort Stanwix National Monument, 112 East Park St., Rome, NY 13440. 315/336-2090.

Gateway National Recreation Area

Allow: 2-3 days *FREE*

"Along this coast, each summer, the greatest number of hot-weather holiday rovers in the United States happily congregates."

Carl L. Biemiller
New Jersey

South of Manhattan lie four separate waterfront havens protected and preserved as part of Gateway NRA. Three, Breezy Point, Jamaica Bay and Staten Island, lie in New York State and the fourth, Sandy Hook, reaches up from New Jersey as if trying to join them. At Jamaica Bay, the park service is reclaiming many wildlife sanctuaries. Breezy Point has a wealth of marine and dune creatures and plants. Woods, grasses and dunes are being allowed to return to their pristine states at Staten Island while Sandy Hook preserves significant cultural and natural features. Together Gateway comprises 26,000 acres on which 3 forts, a wildlife refuge, 2 historic airfields and the country's oldest operating lighthouse sit.

Highlights

★ With the country's greatest concentration of humanity, the preservation of easily accessed public ocean front is laudatory. Here there are beaches where the throngs can gather to bake their weary bones and feel a natural beat as the surf pounds the shore.

Whiz Tips

The rangers conduct an amazing array of activities which are designed to educate city-dwellers to the natural and historical pleasures that surround them. Each unit has interpretive programs tailored to the general public, as well as special offerings for schools and seniors. On certain weekends at Breezy Point, you can join a "Photo Safari" and tour the dunes or you can attend an historical tour of Fort Tilden. Bird fanciers make it a point to go to sessions to learn more about the many birds which use the refuge at Jamaica Bay. Staten Island is a favored fall migratory stop for Monarch butterflies and the rangers show visitors why. Sandy Hook's special programs include touring its holly forest and Fort Hancock.

Kids' Stuff

★ While the beaches are the main

attraction for the young, parents who want their children to learn more can have them attend any of the park's programs. In addition, the rangers put on presentations or walks aimed more directly at young people. For example, at Sandy Hook, they have a Jr. Ranger program and puppet shows.

Access: All units can be reached by taking mass transit or auto. Breezy Point, exit 11S on Belt Pkwy. S across the Marine Parkway Bridge to Beach Channel Dr.; Jamaica Bay, exit 17S on Cross Bay Blvd.; Staten Island, take I-278 exit Hylan Blvd. S; Sandy Hook, Garden State Pkwy. to NJ 36 to Highlands. **Days/Hours:** Daily, summer 9-8:30; Sandy Hook winter wknds. 10-5, spring, summer & fall; Jamaica Bay (clsd. Dec.25 & Jan.1). **Camping:** Fahnestock State Park (83 sites), Carmel, NY; Harriman State Park (220 sites), Stony Point, NY; Hither Hills State Park (165 sites), Montauk, NY; Wildwood State Park (322 sites), Wading River, NY; Fire Island National Seashore's Watch Hill Campground (20 sites). **For info.:** Superintendent, Gateway National Recreation Area, Floyd Bennett Field, Bldg. 69, Brooklyn, NY 11234. 718/338-3338.

General Grant National Monument

Allow: 1 hr. *FREE*

"I have carefully searched the military records of both ancient and modern history, and have never found Grant's superior as a general."
General Robert E. Lee

Unfortunately, the same could not be said for his presidency, which is probably why this monument is called "General Grant" and not "President Grant." Grant's Tomb, as it's popularly called, is the largest mausoleum in the country. For 12 years after his death, Grant lay in a temporary vault until money for the building could collected. Visitors are still awed by the architecture as they tour the park's exhibits.

Highlights

★ Renewed interest in the Civil War has made most of us more aware of this momentous domestic

General Grant National Monument Courtesy Jim Miller

squabble and the significant role Grant played in it. The monument provides a comprehensive picture of the storied career of this uncomplicated hero.

Whiz Tips

❢ The rangers give interpretive talks on Grant's life and the memorial. Although many people know Yellowstone was the world's first national park, how many realize it was Grant's administration that created it?

❢ Baptized Hiram Ulysses Grant, the president had his name inadvertently changed when West Point enrolled him as Ulysses Simpson Grant and, for some reason, he adopted the new signature. His early career gave little indication of the fame that awaited him. After West Point, he campaigned in the Mexican War then languished in remote peacetime postings. At 32, he tried civilian life and had a series of failures before the Civil War came along and saved him from ignominy. A number of national battlefields detail his (and the union's) progression during the war (see Fort Donelson NB, TN; Shiloh NMP; TN, Vicksburg NMP, MI; Chickamauga & Chattanooga NMP, GA; Fredericksburg/Spottsylvania NMP, VA; Richmond NBP, VA; Petersburg NB, VA; Appomattox Court House NHP, VA). He became the first full General of the Armies in American history. It was probably inevitable that he would be convinced to run for the nation's top office and it was probably just as inevitable that he would do poorly. In a polling of noted historians in 1983, Grant was placed 35th out of 36 U.S. presidents and was classified as one of only 5 "failures." His two terms in the office were tainted by scandals as his friends used their positions for personal gain. It is fairly clear from his own finances that Grant did not share their acumen as he struggled to leave money for his family before he died.

Kids' Stuff

★ Grant's legacy is that some people need to find the right niche at the right time to achieve greatness. Children should recognize that because a person fails at one thing, it does not make them a failure. Indeed, all of us should be so fortunate as to find one thing we could do as well as Grant could general.

Access: In Riverside Park in Manhattan, at Riverside Dr. & W 122nd St. **Days/ Hours:** W-Su 9-5. **Camping:** Fahnestock State Park (83 sites), Carmel, NY; Harriman State Park (220 sites), Stony Point, NY; Hither Hills State Park (165 sites), Montauk, NY; Wildwood State Park (322 sites), Wading River, NY. In addition, Fire Island National Seashore Watch Hill Campground (20 sites). **For info.:** Superintendent, General Grant National Monument, 26 Wall St., N.Y., NY 10005. 212/666-1640.

Hamilton Grange National Memorial

Allow: 1 hr. *FREE*

"He is enterprising, quick in his perceptions, and his judgment intuitively great."
George Washington

During the formative years of the American governmental system, Alexander Hamilton was the quintessential power-broker. His first step to power was serving as General Washington's aide - de - camp. Throughout Washington's career, Hamilton continued to aid and influence the nation's first leader. After Washington stepped down, Hamilton's philosophies of a strong central government had attracted many followers, making him a force to be reckoned with. The Grange was Hamilton's suburban home, his get-away. He wanted his children raised far from the dirt and grime from the city. Today, it sits in the heart of Manhattan.

Highlights

★ While much is made of presidents, little is heard of their hard-working confidants. The Grange, while still being restored to its former glory, serves as a locale for personifying the performance of one of the country's ablest administrators and a man whose philosophies still influence law-givers.

Whiz Tips

The park services' tour of the mansion provides colorful background which helps humanize this extraordinary historical personage. Alexander Hamilton was the illegitimate son of a Scottish nobleman. He grew up in the West Indies and showed enough promise at a formative stage in his youth that he was financed to continue his studies in America. Like many a bright college student, Hamilton found himself absorbed in the movements of the day. He championed the revolution and soon was embroiled in the fight for freedom. An ideologue, he left a confusing legacy. While he championed freedom for African Americans, stating they would prove as worthy and capable as European descendants, he owned slaves. Yet his final act shows a man willing to risk his life for his beliefs. He accepted Aaron Burr's challenge of a duel to defend his honor and fired in the air. Burr hit what he had aimed at and Hamilton died from his bullet.

Kids' Stuff

★ The site is better suited for children who are familiar with the first years of the country's federal government.

Access: Downtown Manhattan at Convent Ave. & W 141st St. **Days/Hours:** Daily 9-5. **Camping:** Fahnestock State Park (83 sites), Carmel, NY; Harriman State Park (220 sites), Stony Point, NY; Hither Hills State Park (165 sites), Montauk, NY; Wildwood State Park (322 sites), Wading River, NY. In addition, Fire Island National Seashore Watch Hill Campground (20 sites). **For info.:** Superintendent, Hamilton Grange National Memorial, New York Group, 26 Wall St., N.Y., NY 10005. 212/283-5154.

Home of Franklin D. Roosevelt National Historic Site

Allow: 2-3 hrs. *Fee*

"Meeting Franklin Roosevelt was like opening your first bottle of champagne; knowing him was like drinking it."

Winston Churchill

Certainly one of the boldest presidents this country has ever seen, Franklin Delano Roosevelt dominated the political arena like no other. When Arthur Schlesinger, Sr. published a poll of 50 American historians, who ranked him behind Lincoln and Washington, no less a personage than Winston Churchill declared that Roosevelt was unquestionably first in terms of the impact he had on the world and not just in America (it should be noted that Winnie was a seventh cousin once removed). Even today, we liken the nation's leaders to this man who has been dead for almost half a century. For example, Ronald Reagan is said to have been the first president to use the media as effectively as F.D.R. Democrat leaders are likened to him and the party is still criticized for supporting the government spending programs enacted by him to defeat the depression. In a subsequent 1983 poll of 900 historians, FDR had passed Washington and risen to second place among the 36 presidents rated. His grand Hyde Park estate gives no hint of a man who would so clearly be seen as the little man's president.

Highlights

★ For many, the house is a pilgrimage. Here is where FDR read, and this room is where he entertained the Queen. This is his bedroom and his mother's and over here is where Eleanor, his wife, stayed during his illness. At the end of your tour, you are left with the distinct impression that this was Roosevelt's childhood home rather than the home of a president.

★ The museum and library details Roosevelt's life. He was the only president to be re-elected not thrice but four consecutive terms (after his presidency, they made a law that twice-in-a-row was the maximum). His storied illness and courageous comeback is detailed with pictures and his wheelchair. His celebrated first hundred days, during which he launched truly gigantic social programs to confront the depression, are illustrated.

Whiz Tips

FDR, influenced by his admiration of his cousin, President Theodore Roosevelt, ran on the 1911 Republican ticket for State Senator in a Democrat borough. Spending a huge amount of money (his family had holdings in the Bank of New York), he won the seat. This dramatic victory propelled him to national attention and in 1913, he was appointed Assistant Secretary of the Navy, a job he wanted dearly because his cousin had held the position and because he was in love with ships. In 1920, although he ran unsuccessfully as vice-president, his candidacy was quite a leap from his previous positions. In 1921, he had a bout with polio that left him with limited use of his legs. However, with Eleanor's encouragement, he again gained public office as the 1928 Governor of New York. In 1932, in the height of the Great Depression, he became the nation's 32nd president, a position he would hold until his death in 1945.

Historians don't even refer to the year or the man when they use the terms the "New Deal" or the "First Hundred Days." What was the New Deal and what significance was the First Hundred Days that every president since has been measured against?

On March 4th, 1933 Franklin D. Roosevelt was sworn into the presidency of the United States. Just the week before, banks were forced to close, cities defaulted on payrolls and a quarter of a billion dollars in gold had been drawn from the federal re-

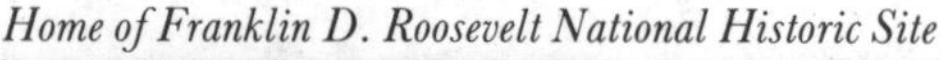
Home of Franklin D. Roosevelt National Historic Site

serve by citizens trying to protect their savings. "First of all, let me assert my firm belief that the only thing we have to fear is fear itself nameless, unreasoning, unjustified terror which paralyzes needed efforts to convert retreat into advance." And so saying, he advanced.

On March 5th, he declared an unprecedented four-day banking holiday and made it illegal for Americans to own gold. On March 9, he convened Congress for a banking act and to grant him control of the nation's currency. On the morning of March 10, he signed the quickly passed banking bill (think it could happen today?). On March 11, he signed the bill giving the president powers to maintain the country's credit. On March 12, he initiated his famous fireside chats, this one clearly explaining banking. March 16th saw the president asking Congress to pass the *Agriculture Adjustment Act* providing crop curtailment and farm mortgage refinancing.

On the 21st, he asked for governmental approval for the Civilian Conservation Corps to reforest, fight forest fires and build dams and roads to relieve unemployment and give young men work experience. Also on the 21st, he enacted the biggest welfare program in the country's history when he asked for federal grants to help the states relieve unemployment. On March 22nd, he got the Beer Bill or *Volstead Act* passed, which once again allowed the sale of beer and light wines with a federal tax attached. March 29th, he asked for laws controlling the sale of new investment securities to protect potential investors. On April 10, he proposed the establishment of the Tennessee Valley Authority to develop power resources and inject new capital into that area's economy. Three days later, he extended mortgage relief to home owners, one of his most popular acts. May 4th, F.D.R. asked for a coordinator of transportation to eliminate duplication of public carriers and to reorganize the finances of the railroads. On May 12th, he got more money for the states through the *Federal Emergency Relief Act*. The next day, he asked for a shorter work week, a minimum wage, unfair practice measures and a huge employment program, which, after being savaged in Congress, came out as the *National Industrial Recovery Act*.

F.D.R.'s family relationship with Churchill also links him to George Washington. Other presidents he could claim as family include: John Adams, James Madison, John Quincy Adams, Martin Van Buren, William Henry Harrison, Zachary Taylor, Ulysses S. Grant, Benjamin Harrison and of course, T.R (1/3 of all presidents who preceded him). Who says there's no such thing as American royalty?

Kids' Stuff

★ Certainly families visiting here with children who have studied F.D.R. will benefit. The museum has a number of his childhood toys and pictures, which children take great interest in. The very scope of his presidency, from the throes of the Depression to the waning days of WW II, provides enough color and drama for a century, let alone the 12 years he toiled.

Access: On Rte. 9 in Hyde Park. **Days /Hours:** Daily, Apr-Oct & Th-M, Nov.-Mar. 9-5 (clsd. Thanksgiving, Dec.25 & Jan.1). **Camping:** Just N of Hyde Park, Margaret Lewis Norrie State Park (45 sites & shwrs.). **For info.:** Superintendent, Home of Franklin D. Roosevelt National Historic Site, Hyde Park, NY 12538. 914/229-9115.

Martin Van Buren National Historic Site

Allow: 1 hr. *Fee*

"He is one of the gentlest and most amiable men I have ever met with."

Washington Irving, author

In the still-rural town of Kinderhook, the 8th president, Martin Van Buren, lived out most of his life. The mansion stands in lonely vigil over the broad green yard. The house interior bespeaks of a man with cultured tastes. His wallpaper was imported from France, his plumbing was indoors and his lighting was oil. Indeed, it was these refined tastes that led to his downfall in his attempt to be re-elected. His opponent, William Henry Harrison, who was of the Virginia gentry, drew attention to Van Buren's redecoration of the White House while the country was in the throes of its first major depression. Van Buren's supporters mistakenly tried to portray Harrison as a country bumpkin who would be most comfortable in a log cabin. Unfortunately for Van Buren, most Americans at that time lived in log cabins.

Highlights

★ The house tour relates the life and times of a country lawyer turned master politician. Although Van Buren continued to live away from the big city action, his tastes were decidedly up scale. Not a rich man, he not only had in-door plumbing but a sophisticated heating system. To his credit, he made the property a working farm which supported his family.

Martin Van Buren National Historic Site

COURTESY NPS

Whiz Tips

The first "American"-born president, Van Buren, became a U.S. Senator by the age of 40. He helped form the Democratic party and supported Andrew Jackson's 1828 presidential campaign. After a very short stint as Governor of N.Y., he returned to Washington as Jackson's Secretary of State. Jackson nominated Van Buren for ambassador to Great Britain (a key career move for many past presidents). Jackson's then vice-president placed a critical tie-breaking vote to defeat Van Buren's nomination, so enraging the president that he replaced him with Van Buren in the 1832 election. As Jackson's choice to succeed, Van Buren waltzed into the presidency just as the country fell into its first major depression. In 1840, he was defeated by the Whig Party. In '44, when he objected to Texas joining the Union as a slave state, he was defeated by Polk in his bid for the Democrat nomination. In '48, he again ran for president as a Free-Soil anti-slavery candidate and again lost, splitting the Democrat vote and ending his political career. While many debate whether the depression greeting Van Buren's reign as president dictated his efforts or whether Van Buren's lack of measures deepened the depression, few would question his abilities as a back room wheeler-dealer. His establishment of an independent treasury, the forerunner to the Federal Reserve system, may have influenced the historian's poll of 1983, which ranked him 20th of 36 presidents; not bad, given his circumstances.

Kids' Stuff

★ President Van Buren is not one whom history celebrates. He is pictured, and perhaps rightly so, as an "organization" man opposed to an ideologue. It's sometimes hard for younger children to appreciate and understand these subtleties.

Access: 25 mi. S of Albany on Rte. 9H. **Days/Hours:** Daily 9-5 late Apr.-Oct & W-Su 9-5 Nov.-Dec.5. **Camping:** Lake Taghkanic State Park (62 sites & shwrs.). **Teacher's Package:** Available. **For info.:** Superintendent, Martin Van Buren National Historic Site, P.O. Box 545, Kinderhook, NY 12106. 518/758-9689.

Sagamore Hill National Historic Site

Allow: 2-3 hrs. *Fee*

"No President has ever enjoyed himself as much as I have enjoyed myself..."
Theodore Roosevelt

The "Summer White House" was but one symbol of the most energetic and enthusiastic president the country had yet to witness. Roosevelt not only had time to run the nation but he had time to run with his large brood of kids. Theodore Roosevelt spent his summers at Sagamore Hill, Long Island, within an easy commute of New York. The president's home is a large estate with a big rambling house reflecting his persona.

Highlights

★ One of the questions asked of our children by a ranger was "Did you have a favorite room?" The true measure of the extent of memorabilia in the house is reflected by the range of responses she received. Nothing about Roosevelt was modest. His furniture is either large or exotic and frequently both. One of his children is to have said the following about him, "When father goes to a wedding, he wants to be the bride; when he goes to a funeral, he wants to be the corpse." He would enjoy the attention visitors pay to his Sagamore Hill home today.

Whiz Tips

The Old Orchard Museum has exhibits and uses Walter Cronkite's "Twentieth Century" TV biography of Roosevelt to introduce you to the park. There are several ranger talks given throughout the summer. These include: T.R.'s role in creating the navy, as a Rough Rider, a family man, a father and a famous American.

Roosevelt lived a full and colorful life. He was a college boxer, a New York police commissioner, a cowboy, a rough rider, an Assistant Secretary of the Navy, a New York Governor, a trust-buster, a wealthy man, a vice-president, the first president to travel abroad while in office, the first to ride in an automobile, a third-party presidential candidate, a big game hunter, a conservationist, an author, a historian and a Nobel Peace Prize winner. In short, an man who enjoyed himself.

Kids' Stuff

★ One of the interpretive programs at Sagamore Hill is the explanation for Theodore Roosevelt's association with the teddy bear. Children can relate to the story that the president refused to shoot a tied-up bear and that an entrepreneur would capitalize on this image to successfully launch a new toy.

Access: 3 mi. E of Oyster Bay on Cove Neck Rd., from the Long Island Expwy. take Exit 41N to Rte.106N. **Days/Hours:** Daily 9:30-5 (clsd. Thanksgiving, Dec.25 & Jan.1). **Camping:** Fahnestock State Park (83 sites), Carmel, NY; Harriman State Park (220 sites), Stony Point, NY; Hither Hills State Park (165 sites), Montauk, NY; Wildwood State Park (322 sites), Wading River, NY; Fire Island National Seashore's Watch Hill Campground (20 sites). **For info.:** Superintendent, Sagamore Hill National Historic Site, Cove Neck Rd., Box 304, Oyster Bay, NY 11771. 516/922-4447.

Saint Paul's Church National Historic Site

Allow: 1 hr. *FREE*

A wooden church was originally constructed on this affiliated national park site in 1665. About a hundred years later the building of the current structure was begun. While the church's sheer longevity makes it a significant historical site, its role in the establishment of freedom of the press makes it of national importance. In 1773, the High Sheriff tried to use a number of loopholes in the voting laws to get his candidate elected. He failed.

However, the people weren't satisfied with this small victory for democracy as they knew it but convinced John Peter Zenger to start the "New York Weekly Journal" newspaper and run an account of the incident. Zenger did so and he continued to print satirical accounts of other governmental misdeeds and officials.

Zenger was brought to trial for libel (see Federal Hall, NY) and subsequently set free as it was determine that his abuses of the governor among others were based on fact.

This was the first legal ruling establishing freedom of the press and was used in discussions regarding the Bill of Rights and the establishment of The First Amendment. The church is representative of American colonial architecture.

Access: Downtown Mount Vernon. **Days/Hours:** Tu-F 9-5 by appt. or Sat. 12-4. **Camping:** Fahnestock State Park (83 sites), Carmel, NY; Harriman State Park (220 sites), Stony Point, NY; Hither Hills State Park (165 sites), Montauk, NY; Wildwood State Park (322 sites), Wading River, NY; Fire Island National Seashore's Watch Hill Campground (20 sites). **For info.:** Superintendent, Saint Paul's National Historic Site, 897 S. Columbus Ave., Mount Vernon, NY 10550. 914/667-4116.

Saratoga National Historical Park

Allow: 2-3 hrs. *Fee*

The turning point in the American Revolution, the second battle at Saratoga resulted in the surrender of General Burgoyne's entire army. After news of the outcome of this battle reached Europe, France decided to join America in its fight for independence and Great Britain decided to abandon northern efforts to enlist the aid of the more loyal southern colonialists and to rely on its might at sea. The battlefield itself rests on the hills between Saratoga Lake and the Hudson River in eastern New York.

Highlights

★ The living-historians make special efforts to explain the battle in its context in the Revolution. Logs and diaries of the combatants on both sides show how the British expectations of great public support of the Crown never transpired. This lack of a general uprising in support of the crown was a major factor in Burgoyne's defeat.

Whiz Tips

! The American victory at Saratoga, described as "one of the fifteen most decisive battles in world history," was the culmination of a poorly executed British initiative. First, General Howe took his New York troops to capture Philadelphia, making them unavailable to provide relief for Burgoyne. Second, Burgoyne completely underestimated the strength and resolve of the rebels and overestimated the remaining loyalist support. Third, Burgoyne counted on St. Leger to succeed in capturing Fort Stanwix (see Fort Stanwix NM, NY) and to provide reinforcements. The upshot? Burgoyne was badly out numbered. The British won the field of battle in the first collision on Sept. 19. However, on Oct. 7, 1777, out-offavour, soon-to-be-traitor, General Benedict Arnold performed heroic feats of valor, pushing the British back. Nine days later, Burgoyne surrendered.

Typically there are at least two full-dress encampments each year. Visiting during one of these sessions enhances your appreciation of the site ten-fold.

Kids' Stuff

★ This is a battlefield to be experienced on bike. Families pedal from marker to marker reading about the ebb and flow of the fight. They pull up at the historic buildings so they can chat with the living-historians. They brake at the overlooks and gaze on the magnificent Hudson River valley. You can hike the grounds if bicycling isn't an option, but plan on a good long hike or make use of loop trails to shorten your journey.

Access: 30 mi. N of Albany on US 4 & NY 32. **Days/Hours:** Daily 9-5 (clsd.Thanksgiving, Dec.25 & Jan.1). **Camping:** Morreau Lake State Park on 17S (144 sites, elec. &shwrs.). **Teacher's Package:** Available. **For info.:** Superintendent, Saratoga National Historical Park, R.D.2, Box 33, Stillwater, NY 12170. 518/664-9821.

Statue of Liberty National Monument

Allow: 1 day *FREE (access by fee ferry)*

"That tall Liberty with its spiky crown that stands in New York Harbor and casts an electric flare upon the world, is, in fact, the liberty of property, and there she stands at the Zenith. "

H.G. Wells
The Future in America

The Statue of Liberty, on Liberty Island, is a constant. It has always stood for freedom. Ellis Island has become a symbol for many Americans of where their ancestors first touched American soil. For the approaching ships full of immigrants, it wasn't seen as a gateway, so much as it was a test they must pass. They called it the "isle of tears." The authorities coded the people by attaching symbols to them. The two feared symbols were "E" for trachoma, an eye disease and the dreaded circle with a "+", the symbol for feeble-mindedness. Although two out of every ten applicants failed the preliminary physical examination, only 2%

Saratoga National Historical Park

were sent back. Family members faced the immediate and difficult decision to return with the rejected relative or to go on. For many, this was a life or death decision. 12 to 16 million made it to the waiting ferries and a whole new world. The park has two sites: Liberty Island and Ellis Island.

Highlights

★ "Once in a lifetime!" These are words you'll hear repeatedly as you shift your weight from foot to foot, waiting to inch into and up the Statue of Liberty for a view of the New York/New Jersey harbor. On hot, humid days the toll is taken, with the weakened and perhaps wiser souls settling for the museum and a slightly lower view. The temperature inside the statue averages about 20 degrees hotter than the air outside. On the day we visited, it reached 120 degrees.

★ At Ellis Island, there are scores of pictures painting vivid images of the mix of peoples who came together to form one nation. Their dress, their language, their customs, their religions and their foods would blend to form a magic elixir keeping the country young and vibrant. Each new flow added something else to the already dynamic nation.

Statue of Liberty National Monument

Whiz Tips

In the Statue of Liberty's museum you can see its history. In 1865, at a French dinner party, Frenchman Frederic Auguste Bartholdi became impassioned with the idea of a gigantic statue recognizing the special relationship between the United States and his country. In 1871, Bartholdi came to America to present his proposal and sight-see (a round-trip train ride to San Francisco). America wanted to see what France was committing to this project. France commissioned Bartholdi to produce a more modest statue for the American Centennial celebrations. The work enabled him to lobby support for the big statue. In 1876, with the help of French donors, Bartholdi displayed the statue's 30-foot-high arm and torch at the Philadelphia Centennial Exhibition. Philadelphia, among others cities, vied for the completed statue. But Bartholdi was emotionally committed to placing it in New York's harbor even if New Yorkers were reacting skeptically toward the gift. France asked America to donate the pedestal upon which to set the lady. The New York sentiment was, "It's their gift. Let them pay for it." In his *New York World* newspaper, Joseph Pulitzer lobbied for the rich to help and cheered on the common folk who contributed. When it became clear the statue was on its way, civic and national pride spurred 100,000 individual donors to come up with the needed $102,000 for the pedestal.

Kids' Stuff

★ The ferry trip to the island is a good prelude to the visit. Children sense the anticipation everyone experiences as they sail here. The Statue of Liberty's very size affirms its importance even to the very young.

School-age children need no introduction to the ideals the statue stands for.

★ Ellis Island provides families the opportunity to explain the advantages of America's tolerance of others. Few nations in the world have been so willing to open their doors to people from such disparate backgrounds. While the country has always had to adjust to its new citizens, it has flourished.

Access: Ferry from Battery Park, NY & Liberty State Park, NJ. **Days/Hours:** Statue of Liberty & Ellis Island daily 9-5 (clsd. Dec.25). **Camping:** Fahnestock State Park (83 sites), Carmel, NY; Harriman State Park (220 sites), Stony Point, NY; Hither Hills State Park (165 sites), Montauk, NY; Wildwood State Park (322 sites), Wading River, NY; Fire Island National Seashore's Watch Hill Campground (20 sites). **For info.:** Superintendent, Statue of Liberty National Monument, Liberty Island, N.Y., NY 10004. 212/363-3204.

Theodore Roosevelt Birthplace National Historic Site

Allow: 2-3 hrs. *Fee*

"To announce that there must be no criticism of the President, or that we are to stand by the President, right or wrong, is not only unpatriotic and servile, but is morally treasonable to the American public."

Theodore Roosevelt

This rebuilt birth home of Theodore Roosevelt has been enveloped by the urban pulse of downtown Manhattan. "Teedie" Roosevelt was a frail child, suffering from severe asthma. His father encouraged him to build his body to be as good as his mind. This legacy never left T.R. as he remained active, espousing physical fitness to his last days. Indeed, it was his adventurous spirit which took him to the Amazon, where he contracted malaria and a leg infection which caused his death at age 60. Visitors are given a tour the home and can linger in the accompanying museum.

Theodore Roosevelt Inaugural National Historic Site

Highlights

★ The home is reflective of a wealthy New York family in the late 1800s. Of special interest is a chair T.R. used as a child because he was allergic to horsehair, the typical filler for seats, and a nursery with a gymnasium.

★ At the museum we were able to trace his career through the exhibits, seeing the full spectrum of his accomplishments.

Whiz Tips

Most of us know T.R. was president. We think he led his Rough Riders on a charge up San Juan Hill (he didn't; he led them up Kettle Hill from where he watched the charge up San Juan Hill). We recognize his long-lasting contribution to preserving the nation's landmarks, and we see his face on Mount Rushmore. However, how many of us know he won a Noble Peace Prize, he "cowboyed" and he was a prolific author and academic. In 1906, Roosevelt was the first American honored with the prestigious Peace Prize for his efforts as a mediator ending the Russo-Japanese War. After his mother and first wife died on the same day, Feb. 14, 1884, Roosevelt left his daughter Alice in the care of relatives and went to the badlands of North Dakota, where he took up cattle ranching. One of the few money-making enterprises Roosevelt had was the publishing of 19 books and a host of articles in magazines like "National Geographic." His first novel, *The Naval War of 1812*, is still used as reference material for scholars. In 1983, when 900 historians were polled on where each of the presidents ranked, T.R. ranked 5th of 36.

The Roosevelt family motto, "He who has planted will preserve" is very fitting for the prime mover in establishing so many national parks.

Kids' Stuff

★ This is a good stop for children who have studied Theodore Roosevelt or 19th century social history. T.R.'s exploits translate well for kids. After all, what child isn't intrigued by a small, weak child building his body and mind to become the nation's leader and a cowboy to boot.

Access: Downtown Manhattan at 28 E 20th St. **Days/Hours:** Wed.-Sun. 9-5. **Camping:** Fahnestock State Park (83 sites), Carmel, NY; Harriman State Park (220 sites), Stony Point, NY; Hither Hills State Park (165 sites), Montauk, NY; Wildwood State Park (322 sites), Wading River, NY; Fire Island National Seashore's Watch Hill Campground (20 sites). **Teacher's Package:** Available. **For info.:** Site Manger, Theodore Roosevelt Birthplace National Historic Site, C/O Manhattan Sites, 26 Wall St., N.Y., NY 10005. 212/260-1616.

Theodore Roosevelt Inaugural National Historic Site

Allow: 1 hr. *Fee*

The Wilcox Mansion, a reminder of early New York architecture, is the site of Theodore Roosevelt's inauguration as the nation's 26th president after the tragic assassination of President McKinley. Initially built as a barracks for troops protecting the northern border against Canadian attack, the building was converted into the mansion as the neighborhood became fashionable. T.R. stayed as a guest of the Wilcox's at the mansion shortly after hearing McKinley was shot. It was here he returned when McKinley succumbed to his wounds, and it was here he accepted the office of president of the United States. Visitors can tour the mansion and learn more about T.R. and the role this building played in his and Buffalo's life.

Highlights

★ The home contains some of the furnishings of the auspicious occasion as well as many period pieces. As you tour the house you are reminded of life at that time. In addition, the events leading up to McKinley's death are detailed.

Whiz Tips

The house, like the city, has seen better days. Buffalo was a key port for the trade that plied the Great Lakes. Its importance to America at the turn of the century was underscored by its hosting of the Pan-American Exposition, where President McKinley was assassinated. The Exposition proved to be Buffalo's. By the 1930s both Buffalo and this building had fallen on hard times. The mansion was eventually converted into a restaurant in the 40s, but again fell into disrepair until the park service recovered it and, with several other organizations, maintain its historical significance.

On President's Day, Sept. 5, 1901, Leon F. Czolgosz, an anarchist, shot President McKinley through a handkerchief which is on exhibit at the site. When it appeared the president was recovering, Roosevelt took an Adirondacks vacation. While there, he was notified the president was failing. T.R. made a harrowing journey from the mountains in order to reach the president in time.

Kids' Stuff

★ Our kids were captivated to hear that teddy bears were named in honor of Theodore (Teddy) Roosevelt. Apparently, when T.R. was out hunting for bear with little success, some friends of his decided to help out and captured a bear which they tied to a tree. T.R. was brought to the bear for his kill. He balked at shooting such a defenseless creature and had the bear set free. This act of sportsmanship so endeared him to the people that a Bronx entrepreneur wrote the president and asked him if it was O.K. to use his name to market a line of toy bears called "teddy bears." T.R. told him if anyone was inclined (foolish enough) to buy a toy bear just because it was called a "teddy bear," that was fine with him. As we all know, this became the generic name for all stuffed toy bears. The entrepreneur built the still-thriving Ideal Toy Co. with his profits. The "Teddy's Treasures" shop

Theodore Roosevelt Inaugural National Historic Site

in the house has a great variety of "teddy bears" on sale.

★ There's a Victorian Touching Museum which features games, toys and artifacts from that era in the viewing room. In addition, as you tour the house, there are some "hands-on" Touching Baskets associated with some of the rooms.

Access: Downtown Buffalo. **Days/Hours:** Daily, M-F 9-5 & S&S 12-5 (clsd. fed. holidays). **Camping:** Allegheny State Park and Darien Lakes State Park (150 sites & shwrs.). **Special Events:** Easter children's program; Teddy Bear Picnic and; Christmas offering. **For info.:** Superintendent, Theodore Roosevelt Inaugural National Historic Site, 641 Delaware Ave., Buffalo, NY 14202. 716/884-0095/0330.

Upper Delaware Scenic and Recreational River

Allow: 2-3 days *FREE*

The Delaware River is the eastern border of Pennsylvania, separating it from New York and New Jersey. It wends its way down to Delaware Bay, where it provides life to the marine creatures. The Upper Delaware is that stretch of clear free-flowing waters Pennsylvania and New York share. The waterway and information centers comprise the park service's domains.

Highlights

★ Most of the 73 miles of river is classified as Class I, "moving water with few riffles," which makes it prime water for most of us novist canoeists. However, hypothermia is an ever-present risk for unwary or careless boaters and class II rapids do exist.

Whiz Tips

! On certain Sundays, rangers lead 5-7 hrs. long canoe tours (you provide your own canoe). On weekends, interpretive talks and walks are scheduled at various locations.

! The park also oversees the Zane Grey Museum and the Roebling Delaware Aqueduct, the forerunner to the Brooklyn Bridge and the nation's oldest wire cable suspension bridge. The museum contains the famous novelist's memorabilia. Grey was an

Vanderbilt Mansion National Historic Site

eastern dentist who took to writing and is considered by some to be the father of the western novel. He was also an renowned outdoors man, who held many fishing records.

Kids' Stuff

★ The river is a good place to try your luck fishing. Kids may catch brown and rainbow trout, walleye, bass and panfish.

Access: Take NY 17 & I-84 to southern access or NT 17 & I-81 to northern access, NY 97 mirrors the river shore. **Days/ Hours:** Visitor center, summer daily, fall W-Su & winter weekends, 9-4:30 until Dec. Information kiosks, summer, hrs. vary. **For info.:** Superintendent, Upper Delaware Scenic and Recreational River, P.O.Box C, Narrowsburg, NY 12764-0159. 717/685-4871.

Vanderbilt Mansion National Historic Site

Allow: 1-2 hrs. *Fee*

"Here [Hyde Park] the misty summit of the distant Catskills begins to form the outline of the landscape; it is hardly possible to imagine anything more beautiful than this place."

Frances Trollope, 1832
Domestic Manners of the Americans

As you drive along Hwy. 9 through Hyde Park, you would be hard put not to notice the palatial grounds of the Vanderbilt Mansion. Stately stone walls don't hide the stream running through the property, the gently rolling hills or the huge monolith which intrudes upon this pastoral scene. The property is an outstanding example of how the pre-income tax rich spent their fortunes. The pieces in the mansion are of exceptional illustrations of this point. The grounds are utilized by many for recreational walks.

Highlights

★ The mansion is chocked full of exotica. You want gilding, they got it. You want a Louis XV bedroom with a rug so plush that it weighs over a ton, it's here. Statues and ornaments abound.

Whiz Tips

💡 Benjamin Franklin was wrong. In 19th century America, there was only one sure thing in life instead of two and taxes wasn't it. There were no income taxes and the rich got richer. How rich? Well, consider that this property was only one (and not the plushest) of seven seasonal homes these Vanderbilts owned. Emulating the nobility of Europe, which their forefathers had rebelled against, the rich in America were spending freely.

💡 The extent of how rich the Vanderbilts were, came out in all its fullness, when the self-made patriarch, the Commodore, passed on at 83 and left a will designed to bring out the worst in his heirs. The hotly contested document entertained America for months. His off-spring, recognizing the enormous wealth their daddy tried to keep from them, fought their battles through the courts and through the media.

Kids' Stuff

★ Visiting the mansion is similar to visiting a museum for most kids. However, there is a self-guiding brochure and nature trail detailing the property's trees. There are also some superb views of the Hudson River.

Access: N entrance to Hyde Park on US 9. **Days/Hours:** Daily, Apr-Oct & Th-M, Nov.-Mar. 9-5 (clsd. Thanksgiving, Dec.25 & Jan.1). **Camping:** Just N of Hyde Park, Margaret Lewis Norrie State Park (45 sites & shwrs.). **For info.:** Superintendent, Vanderbilt Mansion National Historic Site, Hyde Park, NY 12538. 915/229-9115.

Women's Rights National Historical Park

Allow: 2-3 hrs. *FREE*

"Social science affirms that a woman's place in society marks the level of civilization."
Elizabeth Cady Stanton

In the resort town of Seneca Falls, part way between Buffalo and Syracuse, is a park devoted to the majority of American citizens: women. Elizabeth Cady Stanton, a pre-eminent leader in the early women's equal rights movement, lived in this town in the mid-1800s. In 1848, she and other like-minded women, held the first Women's Rights convention here and introduced the Declaration of Sentiments outlining the convention's demands. Stanton's home is but one of a number of buildings representing aspects of the movement.

Highlights

★ The Stanton House at first seems to be curiously empty (the park service could find very few of Stanton's possessions and chose to go with what they had). However, as we find out how little women were entitled to, perhaps the near-empty rooms are very appropriate.

★ The ranger-led town tour presents the social and economic backdrop to the drama. The walk takes you past the picturesque river and a knitting mill where women were free to toil.

Women's Rights National Historic Park

Whiz Tips

In the 1800s, Seneca Falls was a mill town. Its women worked at mills or did piecework at home for drastically lower wages than men. In the 1830s and 40s, women weren't even entitled to their wages if they were married. They couldn't own property, couldn't inherit their husband's estates, couldn't attend college and couldn't vote. On July 9, 1848, at a tea party Elizabeth Cady Stanton voiced opinions about the second class status of women that echoed the other attendee's experiences. From that tea party the idea of a convention was born and Stanton began a long career lobbying for women's rights. The Declaration of Sentiments, a document based on the Declaration of Independence, "outrageously" declared "all men and women were created equally" and went further in its "audacity" suggesting women should be able to vote. It was this latter stand that caused many kindred spirits to decline signing the document because it went too far! Frederick Douglass (see Frederick Douglass NHS, DC) chose to support an equally downtrodden group of Americans when he signed this declaration.

Even important human rights battles have their lighter side. Amelia Bloomer, one of the women's rights advocates, started a fashion trend when she chose to protest the hoop dresses which were deemed appropriate for women. Donning pantaloons under her skirts and dresses, she introduced the famed "bloomers" which set a short-lived fashion trend. Unfortunately, this lady's apparel was to be associated with "radical" women and, like the 1960s bra-burning trend, fell into disrepute.

Kids' Stuff

★ The site serves as an important historical setting for children. Although for many children it will be difficult to understand a time when women were considered inferior, it is instructive to show them how dissent can have positive results.

Access: 7 mi. from NY Thruway off exit 41 on NY 414 & NY 5/20, downtown Seneca Falls. **Days/Hours:** Visitor center daily 9-5, tours June-Aug.; Stanton House limited winter access. **Camping:** 3 mi. E on Lake Rd., Cayuga Lake State Park (286 sites, elec. & shwrs.). **Teacher's Package:** Available. **For info.:** Superintendent, Women's Rights National Historical Park, P.O. Box 70, Seneca Falls, NY 13148. 315/568-2991.

NORTH CAROLINA

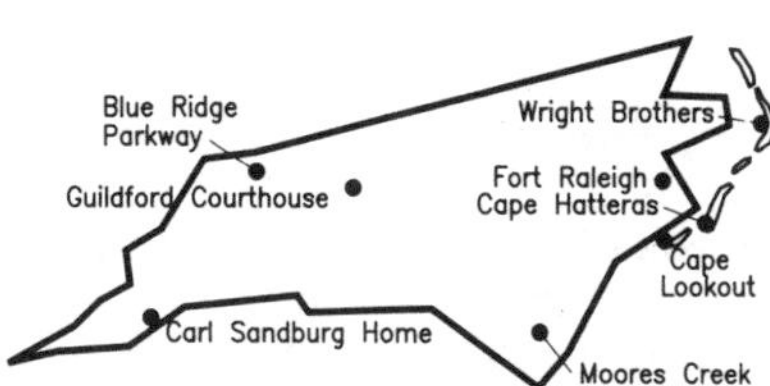

Blue Ridge Parkway

Allow: 2-3 days *FREE*

"Indeed, it would seem as if nature had selected this region for the display of her fantastic power in uplifting the earth, and giving to it strange shapes and startling contrasts imparting curious physiognomies to the mountains and evoking melody from the waterfalls."

F.G. DeFountaine
Picturesque America, 1872

The national park brochure of the parkway is 12 panels long, covering 469 mi. of roadway. Designed to link the two national parks, Great Smoky Mountains and Shenandoah, the roadway provides a cross-sectional view of Virginia's and North Carolina's hill country. Averaging 30 m.p.h. (the speed limit is 45 but the mountains demand their own tempo), visitors who wish to traverse the entire span will find this slow journey visually rewarding. You feel as though you are looking through a one-way mirror at a unique mixture of backwoods, farmyards and backyards.

Highlights

★ The Parkway's north border joins Shenandoah's Skyline Drive near Waynesboro, VA. Between here and the Peaks of Otter Visitor Center (mi.86) is a trail to a reconstructed mountain farm (mi.6), Sherando Lake (mi.16) with camping and swimming, canal locks (mi.64) and innumerable vistas. 5 hrs. south is the parkway's most famous human landmark, Mabry Mill (mi. 176) which, while undergoing renovation, still provides a quaint photo for your memories.

★ Thomas Jefferson's father was one of the surveyors who laid out the Virginia/North Carolina border (mi. 217). Folks come from all over the country to take in North Carolina parkway's three craft centers; the Northwest Trading Post (mi.257), the Parkway Craft Center (mi.293) and the Folk Art Center (mi.382).

Whiz Tips

❢ The parkway has a wealth of interpretive programs at nine visitor centers and nine campgrounds. They cover the wildlife you may encounter (no, not the other drivers). You can find out about the people who took to these hills to make their lives. The need for self-sufficiency caused the hill people to produce their own furniture and equipment, which became an art form. The Folk Art Center endeavors to show you how these gifted artisans evolved their mountain crafts.

Kids' Stuff

★ Nature trails, carriage roads, cycling, old cabins, waterfalls, lookout towers, canals, a mineral museum, wildlife, fishing, picnicking, camping: nah, there's nothing here for kids.

Access: Pkwy. intersects I-64, 77, 40 & 26. **Days/Hours:** Roadway, Daily. Visitor centers June-Oct. **Camping:** Parkway's 9 campgrounds (over 1,000 campsites); mi.170, Clayton Lake State Park near Dublin, VA (132 sites, elec. & shwrs.). **For info.:** Superintendent, Blue Ridge Parkway, 700 Northwestern Plaza, Asheville, NC, 28801. 704/259-0701/0717.

Cape Hatteras National Seashore

Allow: .5 days *FREE*

Three buffers of sand stretching over one hundred miles of North Carolina's northern coast comprise the elements of Cape Hatteras National Seashore, the first national seashore. Today's boon for sun-seekers was the bane of sailors. Cape Hatteras was responsible for so many shipwrecks that 30 lifesaving stations had to be built just to service the poor souls who floundered on the "Graveyard of the Atlantic." The three islands are interconnected by roads and ferries allowing vast numbers of visitors to utilize the beaches.

Highlights

★ As always, it is the ocean meeting the land that attracts visitors. Sure, the park has lighthouses and tours explaining the life-saving techniques employed to save survivors of shipwrecks but sun, sand and sea is the magic elixir. Surfing and surf fishing are popular pastimes.

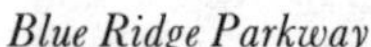

Blue Ridge Parkway

Whiz Tips

❢ At Chicamacomico Station in Rodanthe you can see a demonstration of the old breeches buoy life-saving techniques each summer Thursday. Other programs the Cape runs during the peak season are nature walks, birding hikes, historical talks and special programs requiring lottery selections (you put your name in the "hat" the day before). Some of these specials are canoeing, snorkeling, fishing, boogie boarding, the pony pen or weather station tours. Although the Cape is famous for its life-saving stations and lighthouses, you are unable to tour them.

❢ You pass through Pea Island National Wildlife Refuge as you travel the length of Cape Hatteras National Seashore. The refuge hosts migrating waterfowl and year-round residents, which can be seen from observation platforms and walking trails. On most summer weekdays, they have guided bird walks.

Kids' Stuff

★ Kids 13 and under can earn a Seashore Ranger patch by attending four-six interpretive programs and completing assignments from their worksheet. It takes children two or more days to complete their tasks. The park also has programs tailored for kids, like Pirate Times, Especially for Kids, Ocracritters, Crabs & Things and Bodie Island Beasties.

★ There are three swimming beaches with lifeguards within the park.

Access: N intersection of US 158 & NC 12 & US 64-264 at Nags Head; toll ferries to Ocracoke from S - Cedar Islands & W - Swan Quarter; FREE ferry from N - Hatteras Village to Ocracoke. **Days/Hours:** Daily 9-5 (clsd. Dec.25) **Camping:** Park has 5 campgrounds; Ocracoke (reserve-Ticketron or 900/370-5566). **Special Events:** July 4th Sand Sculpture Contest on Ocracoke Island. **For info.:** Superintendent, Cape Hatteras National Seashore, Rte. 1, Box 675, Manteo, NC 27954. 919/473-2111.

Cape Lookout National Seashore

Allow: 1-2 days *FREE*

At first glance on a map, you wonder why Cape Lookout is separate from Cape Hatteras. They're both part of the so-called Outer Banks. However, man retains a firm grip on Hatteras. Cape Lookout has thus far won the battle against man and with the help of the park service, by and large, has returned to its wild state. Portsmouth Village, ferry landings, a lighthouse and "wild" farm animals remain the last vestiges of civilization's claim on the land.

Highlights

★ Each year, approximately 250,000 visitors come to these barrier islands to enjoy the sun, the sea, the sand and the solace. Many tour the restored "ghost" Portsmouth Village to see the seaside architecture. Many wander the seashore in search of the interesting array of shells the ocean expels on the beach. Binoculared birders come in spring and fall to catch the migratory flocks that use the islands to refuel their energies.

Whiz Tips

❢ Your best bet for an introduction to the pleasures the Seashore offers is to visit either the temporary visitor center at Harkers Island or stop into the Oracoke Visitor Center (part of Cape Hatteras NS). There are also rangers on the islands who can help you out with your visit.

Kids' Stuff

★ While the islands have plenty of great beaches, parents should be aware that they must monitor their own children as there are no lifeguards.

Access: Toll ferry or private boat. **Days/ Hours:** Daily. **Camping:** Primitive camping. N nearby Cape Hatteras National Seashore has 5 campgrounds; Ocracoke (reserve-Ticketron or 900/370-5566); S Fort Macon State Park. **For info.:** Superintendent, Cape Lookout National Seashore, 3601 ridges St, Ste. F, Morelead City, NC. 919/240-1409.

Carl Sandburg Home National Historic Site

Allow: 2-3 hrs. *Fee*

"Always the path of American destiny has been into the unknown. Always there arose enough of reserves of strength, balances of sanity, portions of wisdom to carry the nation through to a fresh start with ever-renewing vitality."

Carl Sandburg, 96th anniversary of Gettysburg

Carl Sandburg, noted poet, author, biographer (Lincoln) and songster, moved here for the warmth in his later (certainly not declining) years. He wanted to devote his energies to writing; his wife, to raising prize-winning goats. Like his thoughts about America at Gettysburg, Sandburg found his necessary reserves of strength, balances of sanity and portions of wisdom to produce some of his finest works here. Ironically, the house he and his wife chose, had been built in 1838 by Christopher Memminger, the first Secretary of the Confederate Treasury. The home is big and rambling, sitting atop a knoll overlooking a picturesque pond. It is precisely the place many of us dream of owning one day.

Highlights

★ The tour of the home demonstrates the earthiness of its occupants. One of Sandburg's quaint habits was to use wooden crates to store things and every room features some variation of this peculiarity. His wife caused a stir in the neighborhood when she showed up with her slew of goats. The park has several of these mobile lawn mowers that you and your family can pet.

Whiz Tips

Sandburg was and remained a social activist. He met his wife at one such meeting. He came by his philosophy honestly as he left grade eight and set forth upon the world. He hoboed, served in the Spanish-American War, did odd jobs and learned

Carl Sandburg Home National Historic Site

about the life of the have-nots. When he was 20, he returned home and went to Lombard College where he began to write. At 26, he had his first poems published and by 36, he had his first big success when his "Chicago" poem was published as one of a set. He wrote for many newspapers to keep his poetry viable and his young family fed. At 48, he established himself as Lincoln's biographer with *Abraham Lincoln: the Prairie Years*. By 54, he was a full-time writer publishing poetry, biographies, histories, children's books, studies of American folk music and a novel. He won a Pulitzer Prize at age 62 for his *Abraham Lincoln: the War Years*. At the end of WW II, he moved to Connemara. Here he continued to write and again won a Pulitzer Prize, this time for poetry, the *Complete Poems*.

Kids' Stuff

★ Besides petting the kids (as in goats), your children can take in the pleasant 1.3 mi. nature trail. Sandburg believed each child has the innate gift to write poetry and many of his works were devoted to them. Some of the notables you might read before your visit are; *The Rootabaga Stories*, *The Rootabaga Pigeons*, *The American Sandbag*, *Early Moon* and *Wind Song*.

Access: 3 mi. S of Hendersonville off US 25 on Little River Rd. **Days/Hours:** Daily 9-5 (clsd. Dec.25) **Camping:** Nearby Pisgah Forest. **Teacher's Package:** Available. **For info.:** Superintendent, Carl Sandburg Home National Historic Site, Box 395, Flat Rock, NC 28731. 704/693-4178.

Fort Raleigh National Historic Site

Allow: 1-2 hrs. *FREE*

Was there ever more strange a story? One hundred and sixteen men, women and children, including the first American-born child of English descent, disappeared after being abandoned on Roanoke Island for three years. All they left of their passing was the word "CROATOAN" (the name of a nearby island) carved on a tree, the ruins of their fort and their governor's rusted armour. By prior arrangement, a special code of a Maltese cross was to indicate trou-

Fort Raleigh National Historic Site

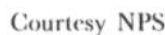
Courtesy NPS

ble. It was not included in the cryptic message. John White, the returning governor and grandfather of the first Anglo-American child, was delayed when the Crown seized his ships to use against Spain. He was to be further frustrated in his search for his family when he was prevented from going on to Croatoan Island by the privateers who brought him. He never saw his progeny again. Although his sponsor, Sir Walter Raleigh, made several attempts to find the colony, it was forever lost.

Highlights

★ The reconstructed fort is based on excavated evidence of its moat. It was constructed the same way the original fort was by digging the moat and throwing the earth inward to form its walls enclosing 50 sq. ft.

★ The evening performance of *The Lost Colony* (fee), flushes out the drama that might have taken place.

Whiz Tips

The park has guided talks and tours daily during the peak summer season. In addition, they regularly put on a living history tour.

This was Sir Walter Raleigh's third attempt at colonization. He was to enjoy but a few more years of success and favor with the British royalty. Seeds of distrust proved to be his undoing and he was executed because it was felt he was plotting to overthrow the Crown.

Kids' Stuff

★ Kids can become a Roanoke Ranger by attending interpretive programs and completing a worksheet. They get a ranger patch for their efforts.

★ Try to catch the living history program so your children can get a better understanding of what transpired here.

Access: 3 mi. N of Manteo on US 64-264 or 67 mi. SE of Elizabeth City. **Days/Hours:** Daily 9-5 (clsd. Dec.25). **Camping:** Nearby Cape Hatteras National Seashore's Oregon Inlet on Bodie Island. **For info.:** Superintendent, Fort Raleigh National Historic Site, Cape Hatteras National Seashore, Rte.1, Box 675, Manteo, NC 27954.

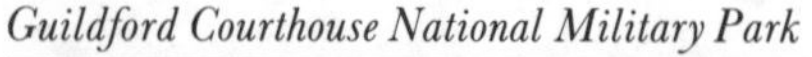

Guildford Courthouse National Military Park

Guilford Courthouse National Military Park

Allow: 2-3 hrs. *FREE*

In central North Carolina, the patriot army lost a battle but, in so doing, helped to win a war. It was encounters like Guilford Courthouse that demonstrated the rebel's resolve and decimated Cornwallis' army. Today, the park commemorates the historic fight with its small wooded area, a paved one-way roadway and walking trails leading to each significant landmark.

Highlights

★ The visitor center relates the interesting characters who fought this battle. General Cornwallis voted against the tools and taxes levied on the American people but felt it his duty to command troops fighting for the crown. General Nathanael Greene was a Quaker from New England who lost more battles than he won but ultimately wore down the British, defeating their attempts to raise loyalist support. In the middle of the battle, an American Goliath, Peter Francisco wielded a 5 ft. long saber, felling a number of enemies.

Whiz Tips

There are interpretive programs offered in the summer, including talks, walks and living history presentations.

At Guilford Courthouse, the Continental Army's untested militia was placed on the front lines in hopes it might slow the British attack. Facing the well-trained red coat troops, they each managed one shot and headed for the hills. "Light-Horse Harry" Lee wrote, "...not a man of the corps had been killed or even wounded.... they rushed like a headlong torrent through the woods." However, the second line made up of Virginians exacted a higher fare for ground gained. Col. William Washington, a cousin of George, led his cavalry among the British. The third line consisting of Maryland regulars was so punishing the British Guards that Cornwallis ordered his cannons to fire even though his own men were mixed in. The result was that he drove off the rebels but at a great loss of men. Cornwallis who had left some of his army in South Carolina, decided not to chase Greene anymore but to go on to Virginia. This allowed Greene to reclaim the Carolinas and left Cornwallis with an outnumbered army at Yorktown (see Colonial NHP, VA).

Kids' Stuff

★ There are a number of seasonal programs appealing to children.

★ The park is a good place for learning about its history while cycling or walking. Children who have studied the Revolutionary War will benefit from touring the battlefield and learning what transpired.

Access: In NW Greensboro near intersection of US 220 & New Garden Rd. **Days/Hours:** Daily 8:30-5 (clsd. Dec.25 & Jan.1). **Camping:** Near Danbury, 36 mi. N, Hanging Rock State Park (74 sites & shwrs.). **Teacher's Package:** Available. **For info.:** Superintendent, Guilford Courthouse National Military Park, P.O.Box 9806, Greensboro, NC 27429-0806. 919/288-1776.

Moores Creek National Battlefield

Allow: 2 hrs. *FREE*

The losses were small, 1 patriot and 30 or so loyalists, but the consequences were critical. In southeastern North Carolina, not far from Wilmington, 1,000 rebels met and defeated a force of 1,600 loyalists. The park marks the spot where the battle occurred, preserves the battle's monuments and relates the history surrounding the encounter.

Highlights

★ The visitor center has a number of exhibits detailing the happenings at Moores Creek. The exhibits show the colorful dress of the loyalists, a sharp contrast to the "lobster-back" uniforms we all envision for troops loyal to the king. Like so many revolutionary encounters, this was a fight between neighbors, not some foreign oppressor and the locals.

★ There are two interpretive trails you can take. The first leads you to the bridge site past reconstructed earthworks and a cannon reproduction. The second trail tells you about the important resources North Carolina held for the British navy.

Whiz Tips

The loyalist troops were offered free land and tax exemption. Nevertheless, they set out with supplies to meet the British who were arriving by sea. Their failure to accomplish this dampened early British attempts to control the South and gave cause for hope among the patriots. Not long after, North Carolina became the first colony to vote for independence.

Kids' Stuff

★ Both trails are relatively short, ideal for children. The park is of interest to those children who have studied the Revolutionary War. It was at small places like this where the patriots turned the tide, winning battles or exacting such a large price that their resolution became certain and their foe's determination questioned.

Access: 20 mi. NW of Wilmington on US 421 & NC 210. **Days/Hours:** Daily 9-5 (clsd. Dec.25 & Jan.1) **Camping:** S of Wilmington, Carolina Beach State Park (83 sites & shwrs.). **Special Events:** Feb.'s last weekend, battle's anniversary with living history encampments and musket firing demos. **Teacher's Package:** Available. **For info.:** Superintendent, Moores Creek National Battlefield, P.O.Box 69, Currie, NC 28435. 919/283-5591.

Wright Brothers National Memorial

Allow: 2 hrs. *Fee*

"The Wright brothers flew right through the smoke screen of impossibility."

C.F. Kettering, VP of Research, GM

Moores CreekNational Battlefield

Courtesy NPS

Among the windswept sand dunes of North Carolina's Outer Banks, rests a stone monument on a high dune. From 1900-1903, two bicycle repairmen without a high school diploma between them, dragged a funny-looking thing made with pieces of wood and sack cloth up and down these hills. Why? What drives the human spirit to toil so? To commit time, money and reputation to a task that to much of the world seemed unnatural, let alone possible. It is because of these two bachelors that the North Carolinians drive around with car license plates bragging "First in Flight."

Highlights

★ Sitting in the great glassed hall watching the ranger render the fascinating saga of the Wright brothers, you can't help but realize the backdrop through the walls is the hallowed ground where man first flew. Remote (they had to take a boat to it), desolate and continually windswept, it must have seemed paradisial to the Wrights.

★ Going outside to pace off the slow progress made on the first day of flight, then climbing the dune is as mandatory as going to the top of the Statue of Liberty.

★ Seeing the full-scale replicas of the 1902 Wright Glider and the succeeding 1903 Flyer is a thrill. We've come such a long way and yet the basic technology is encapsulated within these tenuous structures.

Whiz Tips

As Orville Wright put it in 1903, "Isn't it astonishing that all these secrets have been preserved for so many years just so we could discover them!" This is the place to learn about the secrets of flight. The flight room talk, first flight tour, things that fly presentation and kite flying demonstration are but some of the interpretive programs offered. The exhibits in the visitor center also detail the mechanics of flight, as well as the chronology and the first flight honor roll.

The key reasons for the Wright brothers' success was a home-made wind tunnel. They concluded that the air pressure tables in common use were faulty. They also discovered the way to control balance, elevation

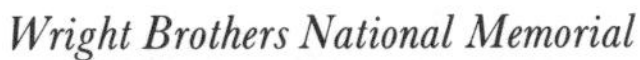
Wright Brothers National Memorial

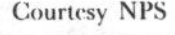
Courtesy NPS

and steering, principles that are still in use today. To provide optimum power they designed and constructed a lightweight motor and efficient propellers.

❢ The Smithsonian did not recognize the Wright brothers' accomplishment as the first to fly because another had falsely claimed the honor. It wasn't until the 1908 that France recognized their accomplishment. The Smithsonian had to agree to recognize the Wright's achievement and it wasn't until after Orville's death in 1948 that they were able get the Wright's first aircraft because of their original slight.

❢ Although Kitty Hawk is regarded as the location of the first manned propelled flight, in fact, the site is almost 7 miles south at Kill Devil Hill. Another interesting fact is that neither Wilbur nor Orville piloted a plane for which they didn't make the engine and propeller.

Kids' Stuff

★ Children under 13 can become Flight Rangers by attending the ranger-led programs and completing activity assignments. If successful, they get a patch with an image of the first airplane saying they are a Wright Brothers Flight Ranger.

★ The visitor center has two full-size planes for children to peruse and ponder. The kite-flying demonstration is a sure-fire winner with children who can grasp the mechanics.

Access: 15 mi. NE of Manteo on US 158. **Days/Hours:** Daily 9-5 (clsd. Dec.25) **Camping:** Nearby Cape Hatteras National Seashore's Oregon Inlet on Bodie Island. **For info.:** Superintendent, Wright Brothers National Memorial, Rte. 1, Box 675, Manteo, NC 27954.

NORTH DAKOTA

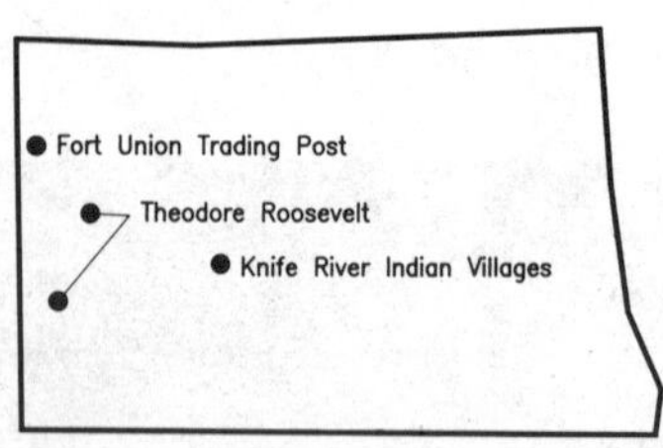

Fort Union Trading Post National Historic Site

Allow: 2 hrs *FREE*

"The country is far from being without character; on the contrary it has a very distinct stamp, but somber, inexorable, it grips the soul much more than it pleases the eye...More than anything else, it is an impression of immensity, of open space, and of an individual left to his own resources in the midst of nature where nothing belongs to anyone and everything belongs to everyone."

Philippe Regis de Trobriand
Military Life in Dakota, 1860

Furs, the gold of the great northwest, were there for any trader who could win the confidence of those who trapped and hunted. One such man was Kenneth McKenzie, who left the British North West Company to join what became John Jacob Astor's American Fur Company, to set up shop here in northwest North Dakota. Although the beaver trade dropped off with a fashion switch to silk hats, McKenzie and his successors continued to haggle with the natives and frontiersmen for buffalo robes and other furs. The park service has uncovered the ruins of the old fort and reconstructed portions so visitors can visualize what it was like in the 1850s.

Highlights

★ The site provides a glimpse of the adventuresome men who left the cities and their own kind to live among the Native Americans. This strange land and its people cast a spell over most who visited. They stayed, married, had children and thought little of the busy places back east or in Europe. Their concerns were to cope with the elements, to compete with other fur traders and to coexist with the others who shared the land.

Whiz Tips

The fort has interpretive programs relating to its history. George Catlin, the great Western artist, was on the first paddle-wheeler that navigated the Missouri to the fort. His art, and that of many others, provides us with images of these times when the Assiniboine, Crow and Blackfeet still controlled the region. Later, the Sioux pushed in and wrested control.

Kids' Stuff

The reconstructed fort fires childrens' imaginations as they prowl about the 18-foot-tall walls and massive stone bastions or explore the Indian tepees. They picture a wild country where brave people performed brave deeds.

Access: 24 mi. SW of Williston, ND or 21 mi. N of Sidney, MT. **Days/Hours:** Daily, summer 8-8 & winter 9-5:30 (clsd. winter fed. holidays). **Camping:** 2 mi. E at Fort Buford State Historic Site; 19 mi. SE of Williston, Lewis & Clark State Park (58 sites, elec. & shwrs.). **Special Events:** Mid-June, Fur Trade Rendezvous. **For info.:** Superintendent, Fort Union Trading Post National Historic Site, Buford Rte., Williston, ND 58801. 701/572-9083.

International Peace Garden

International Peace Garden, Inc., an affiliated organization, administers the 888 acre site commemorating the peaceful relations between Canada and the United States.

For info.: International Peace Garden, P.O.Box 419, Dunseith, ND 58637.

Theodore Roosevelt National Park Courtesy NPS

Knife River Indian Villages National Historic Site

Allow: 2-3 hrs. *FREE*

"The earth is North Dakota's treasure..."
Pearl S. Buck
America

And so it was for the Mandan and Hidatsa people, who relied a great deal on their agricultural produce. 60 miles N.W. of Bismarck where the Knife River joins the Missouri, visitors can see the undulating features marking three villages of these sedentary people. Evidence of almost 12,000 years of occupation has been found here. The park focuses on the agricultural lifestyle and trade network of these tribes who played kind host to the Lewis and Clark Expedition during its first winter (see Fort Clatsop NHS, OR & Jefferson N. Expansion Mem., MO).

Highlights

★ While the park is in the process of building a new visitor center and an earth lodge, there's still plenty of interpretive programs you can take advantage of. You can take two self-guiding or ranger-led hikes to three village sites where you can see evidence of their domiciles and artifacts.

Whiz Tips

The Knife River villages were primary exporters of agricultural foods and flint. These fortified villages served as trade centers for people of the Northern Plains. A little-known facet of Native American life was the high degree of trade that went on. Most portrayals show each tribe subsisting on its own through farming or hunting and gathering. Several park service sites seek to correct this stereo-type (see Salinas NM & Pecos NHP, NM; Pipestone NM, MN; Alibates Flint Quarries NM, TX). Trade goods flowed east and west along the Missouri. Not just foodstuffs, but copper from the Great Lakes (perhaps from Isle Royal NP, MI), obsidian from Wyoming and shells from the Pacific and Gulf of Mexico found their way to the Knife River villages.

Theodore Roosevelt National Park Courtesy NPS

❢ Reservations can be made to canoe the Knife River with a ranger.

Kids' Stuff

★ The park has a "hands-on" display of gardening tools and household items for children to inspect.

Access: 68 mi. NW of Bismark on US 83 to ND 200A to ND 31 and Stanton. **Days/ Hours:** Daily, summer 8-6 & winter 8-4:30 (clsd. Thanksgiving, Dec.25 & Jan.1). **Camping:** 17 mi. N. near Garrison Dam. **Special Events:** July, village Indian trade encampment; Aug., historical drama. **For info.:** Superintendent, Knife River Indian Villages National Historic Site, Stanton, ND 58571. 701/745-3309.

Theodore Roosevelt National Park

Allow: 2-3 days *Fee*

"Lighting up the dull strata of the buttes are the ever-present pinks and reds of scoria-clay burnt into a brick-like shale by the centuries-old fires of burning coal veins."

WPA–North Dakota: Guide to t'he Northern Prairie State

The park consists of two parcels of badlands, the North and South Units and the small, undeveloped Elkhorn Ranch Site. First-time visitors are stunned by the change in landscape from flat unending prairie to land that appears to have been flogged more than weathered. The scars of water and wind look raw and unhealed. Reds, blacks, blues and purples stratify the exposed knolls. The sun beats down relentlessly, casting an ethereal hue over the terrain. Visitors enjoy both the prairie and badlands scenery by getting out in it through hikes, horseback riding, float trips, bird-watching or driving.

Highlights

★ Unusual as it may seem, this desolate-looking region hosts an extensive wealth of wildlife. Pronghorn antelope, bison, deer, longhorn cattle, wild (feral) horses and elk compete for grazing rights in the grasslands. Prairie dogs which once numbered as high as 5 billion, find sanctuary from a largely inhospitable ranching community within the park's boundaries. Golden and occasionally bald eagles dine on the unwary of these chirpy ground squirels. A pair of bi-

Theodore Roosevelt National Park Courtesy NPS

noculars proves invaluable when scouting for wildlife.

★ The land fascinates. It's like watching a fire or waves, each shifting as the light presents a new face, a new image. Scenic drives in North and South Units allow visitors to take in the scenery even if they aren't up to battling the elements.

Whiz Tips

The daily interpretive programs include hikes and campfire talks. They cover the region's geology, prairie pioneers, open-range cattle, Native Americans, T.R. and the park's flora and fauna.

Theodore Roosevelt suffered a calamitous day when, on Valentines Day, Feb. 14, 1884, he lost both his wife and his mother. Some say it was a broken heart; others say it was political problems; whichever, T.R. headed West and took up ranching just 7 miles south of Medora. For two years, T.R. tried to make a profit out of his efforts to turn beef into dough. He credited his time in this wild country with putting him, a wealthy Harvard-trained New Yorker, in tune with middle America. One of T.R.'s many exploits during his tenure here was the capture of some boat thieves.

Kids' Stuff

★ There are some interpretive offerings targeted for kids and the visitor centers have touch tables for children. Families can explore several self-guiding nature trails which make for a fun outing. Good bets are: South Unit Ridgeline Nature Trail & Coal Vein Trail and North Unit Squaw Creek Nature Trail & Caprock Coulee Nature Trail. A concessioner-guided horseback ride in the badlands can be an exciting family experience.

Access: North Unit, 15 mi. S of Watford City or 52 mi. N of Belfield on Hwy. 85; South Unit, in Medora off I-94 17 mi. W of Belfield. **Days/Hours:** Summer, daily, Medora and Painted Canyon Visitor Centers 8-8 & North Unit Visitor Center 9-5:30. **Camping:** South Unit's Cottonwood Campground (77 sites) & North Unit's Squaw Creek Campground (50 sites). **For info.:** Superintendent, Theodore Roosevelt National Park, Medora, ND 58645. 701/623-4466.

OHIO

Cuyahoga Valley National Recreation Area

Allow: 1 wk. *FREE*

22 miles of river valley and uplands plateaus lying between Cleveland and Akron are being returned to their natural state while preserving significant cultural landscapes. In conjunction with public and private owners, the park service restores past glories and preserves nature's wonders for the benefit of all. Hikers, bik-

ers and skiers pass by existing golf courses as well as historic buildings. Cleveland Metroparks, Metro Parks, serving Summit County and the Western Reserve Historical Society work hand-in-hand with national park personnel to provide a profusion of public offerings.

Highlights

★ This is an urban recreation bonanza. Among the wide open spaces are hundreds of miles of trails where joggers meet riders on horseback and kids peddle furiously to their fish pond. In winter, the hills are alive with sleds and toboggans and the ponds become outdoor ice rinks. At Happy Days or Canal Visitor Centers there are introductory AVs and park rangers who can alert you to what to see and do. The Canal Visitor Center, housed in a 150 yr. old lockhouse, features the days when the canals were a vital transportation link.

★ A relatively new feature at the park are the walkways along Brandywine Gorge leading to platform overlooks of the falls. Try to visit after a rainfall if you want to see them at their zenith.

Whiz Tips

❢ The rangers present a wide variety of interpretive programs throughout the year. They explore the history of the valley, its wildlife, the canal, pioneer pastimes, recreation possibilities and a host of other subjects with interested visitors.

Kids' Stuff

★ Families visiting or living in the Cleveland/Akron area can find plenty of entertainment here. The children's interpretive programs include Pre-Schoolers Enjoy Nature, Family Matinee and Saturday Morning Special series. The visitor centers have "hands-on" displays and kids get a kick out of seeing the Canal Visitor Center's working model of a canal lock.

Access: Happy Days Visitor Center, 2 mi. E of Peninsula on OH 303; Canal Visitor Center in Valley View. **Days/Hours:** Visitor centers, daily summer 8-6 & winter 8-5 (clsd. Thanksgiving, Dec.25 & Jan.1). **Camping:** Dover Lake Park, private water sports park within the NRA; Findlay, Portage Lakes, Punderson & West Branch

Cuyahoga Valley National Recreation Area

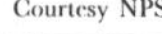
Courtesy NPS

State Parks within 45 min. **Special Events:** Last Oct.Sat., Halloween Celebrations; 1st May Sun., May Day Festival; late summer, Cuyahoga Valley Festival. **For info.:** Superintendent, Cuyahoga Valley National Recreation Area, 15610 Vaughn Rd., Brecksville, OH 44141. Happy Days Visitor Center, 216/650-4636; Canal Visitor Center, 216/524-1497.

James A. Garfield National Historic Site

The Western Reserve Historical Society operates the site which includes Lawfield, home of the nation's 20th president, a carriage house, a pump house and a campaign office. James Garfield died in Office from wounds caused by a .44 British Bulldog handgun fired by Charles Guiteau.

For info.: Superintendent, James A. Garfield National Historic Site, Lawfield, 8095 Mentor Ave., OH 44060.

Mound City Group National Monument

Allow: 1-2 hrs. *Fee*

"...ten thousand in the valley of the Ohio River alone-that they seemed surely to be the work of a vanished race which with incredible persistence had erected them...and then disappeared from our land."

Robert Silverberg
American Heritage

It's hard to believe these man-made knolls sparked academic debates throughout the last century. Many people refused to consider that a Native American culture could have constructed these large geometrically shaped earthworks and created the artifacts buried within. Often the embankments were formed into squares, circles, octagons and long parallel walls, some miles long. Indeed, there intricate designs created a romantic legend about a "lost race." Two Chillicothe residents, Ephraim G. Squier and Edwin H. Davis pursued the notion that the Mississippi Valley natives had connections with prehistoric Mexican

Mound City Group National Monument Courtesy NPS

cultures and researched this area as part of their study. Further research demonstrated the mound builders were indeed the product of local Native Americans. The park contains 23 mounds with a remarkable number of artifacts created "with exquisite skill."

Highlights

★ The visitor center has exhibits showing the mound builders artistry and a short video telling what we know of them. Mound City Group represents the largest grouping of Hopewell burial mounds in the country. One of the mounds has been opened so you can see how it was constructed and the type of items that were placed in it. The mound trail is self-guiding with three audio stations and interpretive signs. Summer visitors should try to catch a ranger-led tour.

Whiz Tips

Several of the park system's sites (Knife River Indian Villages NHS, ND, Salinas NM, Gila Cliff Dwellings NM and Pecos NHP, NM) demonstrate the degree of commerce and interaction that took place between the far-stretched tribes of North America. At Mound City silver from Ontario, copper from northern Michigan, obsidian from Yellowstone, shells from the Gulf of Mexico, mica from the Smokies and shark teeth, probably from Chesapeake Bay, have been found.

Mound City was a burial ground. Experts are unsure where the Hopewells who built these mounds lived in relationship to the site. It's fairly clear from the burial practices that the mound builders had a social stratification in their society much like medieval Europe and Hawaii.

Kids' Stuff

★ Visits to Native American sites help children to recognize the skills of first Americans. When they see the level of trade that existed without the assistance of any easy mode of transportation other than canoe and walking, they can't help but appreciate what was accomplished.

Access: 3 mi. N of Chillicothe on OH 104. **Days/Hours:** Daily 8-5 (clsd. Thanksgiving, Dec.25 & Jan.1). **Camping:** W on US 50 Pine Lake State Park (112 sites, elec. & shwrs.). **For info.:** Superintendent, Mound City Group National Monument, 16062 State Rte. 104, Chillicothe, OH 45601. 614/774-1125.

Perry's Victory & International Peace Memorial

Allow: .5 days *FREE (Fee elevator ride)*

"DEAR GENL: We have met the enemy, and they are ours-two ships, two brigs, one schooner, and one sloop. Yours with great respect and esteem, O.H.PERRY."

On South Bass Island in western Lake Erie stands a large Doric column, a testament to Perry's naval victory and the peace that has coexisted between the United States and Canada since the Treaty of Ghent. The Battle of Lake Erie during the War of 1812 was one of the few American victories. It turned out to be significant in the treaty negotiations at Ghent. With control of the then American Northwest re-established, the British were forced to remove their demands for a neutral Indian buffer state between the two countries.

Highlights

★ Rangers relate the happenings of the battle and the unique relationship Canada and the United States share. The elevator ride to the top of the memorial affords a view of the battle scene and the lake's islands.

Whiz Tips

Most historians have generally concluded that the War of 1812 was started by the U.S. for expansionist reasons. The new nation wanted room to grow. The rationale used by the "war hawks" was that England was infringing on America's rights at sea ("Free Trade and Sailor Rights") and was encouraging the Indians to attack American pioneers. Interestingly, the maritime states were opposed to the war because they felt the government, specifically the southern and western representatives were over-reacting to Britain's infringement on trade (see Salem Maritime NHS, MA). The Treaty of Ghent put everything back the way it was before the war commenced. Historians credit the American negotiating team with great skill at having achieved even this outcome in light of the U.S.'s performance against the British forces.

"More than any other battle of the time, the victory on Lake Erie was won by the courage and obstinacy of a single man." So said noted American historian, Henry Adams of Perry's victory. With the war going badly for the country, Perry's victory was all the more crucial. The British had gained control of Detroit and were pressing the forts along Lake Erie. Perry was feverishly building his ships, which he then had to haul over sandbars to sail. Perry had twice as much firepower but was limited to half the range of the British guns. He managed to get close enough to take advantage of his firepower and was fortunate that the two larger British vessels became entangled. His victory allowed Gen. Harrison to launch a successful ground attack on Lake Erie's northern shore.

Kids' Stuff

★ The ferry ride over to the islands and the story of this freshwater naval battle makes for an enjoyable family outing.

Access: Auto ferry from Catawba Point (3 mi.) or Port Clinton (10 mi.). **Days/Hours:** Mid-Apr.-mid-Dec., daily. **Camping:** South Bass Island State Park (135 sites & shwrs.). **For info.:** Superintendent, Perry's Victory & International Peace Memorial, P.O.Box 549. Put-in-Bay, OH 43456. 419/285-2184.

William Howard Taft NHS

William Howard Taft National Historic Site

Allow: 1 hr. *FREE*

"...my ambition is to become a justice of the Supreme Court...however, there are very few men who could refuse to accept the nomination...for the presidency, and I am not an exception."

William Howard Taft

President Taft's birth home in the Cincinnati suburb of Mount Auburn is an 1840s Greek Revival mansion befitting his family's social position. Having one leg up on the social, economic and political ladder, "Big Bill" put it to good use. He excelled scholastically, placing second in his class at Yale. Trained as a lawyer, he steadily balanced legal and political offices until he ascended the presidency. He was to go on to realize his true ambition of Chief Justice of the Supreme Court almost ten years after he left the nation's top post.

Highlights

★ The guided tour of the home introduces visitors to a truly remarkable man and his beginnings. Set in Taft's pre-puberty years, the furnishings reflect Ohio's post-Civil War era. The president's illustrious career is lovingly detailed.

Whiz Tips

Everyday interpretive talks focus on coming of age in the Victorian era and Big Bill's career. Other less regular programs are neighborhood walking tours, musical recitals and dancing performances.

Twice Theodore Roosevelt offered to bring Taft's goal of Supreme Court Justice, into reach. But each time, Big Bill felt other duties took preference. The first time he was serving as Civil Governor of the Philippines. Taft didn't believe the country should be controlling this former Spanish possession and tried to establish civil rule. On the second occasion, Taft was serving as Secretary of War when there was unrest in the Panama Canal.

"No one candidate was ever elected ex-president by such a large majority." So saying William Howard Taft demonstrated his good nature regarding his fall from popular-

Perry's Victory & International Peace Memorial Courtesy NPS

ity. In the end, although historians don't rate him highly (19th of 36 in '83 poll) Taft's tenure produced more anti-trust actions than T.R.'s, initiated a federal income tax (read his lips), established a postal savings system, started the Interstate Commerce Commission which set railroad rates and brought about direct voting for Senators.

Kids' Stuff

★ Your children can earn a Jr. Ranger designation as they learn about this multi-faceted president. There are several "hands-on" exhibits reflecting the period in which "Big Bill" grew up. Kids are in awe of Taft's size; he weighed in at 300+ lbs; that's bigger than most NFL linemen.

Access: In Cincinnati. **Days/Hours:** Daily 10-4 (clsd. Thanksgiving, Dec.25 & Jan.1). **Camping:** SE on SR 125 East Fork State Park (416 sites, elec. & shwrs.) & NW on SR 732/177 Hueston Woods State Park (502 sites, elec. & shwrs.). **Special Events:** Monthly events; Christmas open house. **For info.:** Superintendent, William Howard Taft National Historic Site, 2038 Auburn Ave., Cincinnati, OH 45219-3025. 513/684-3262.

OKLAHOMA

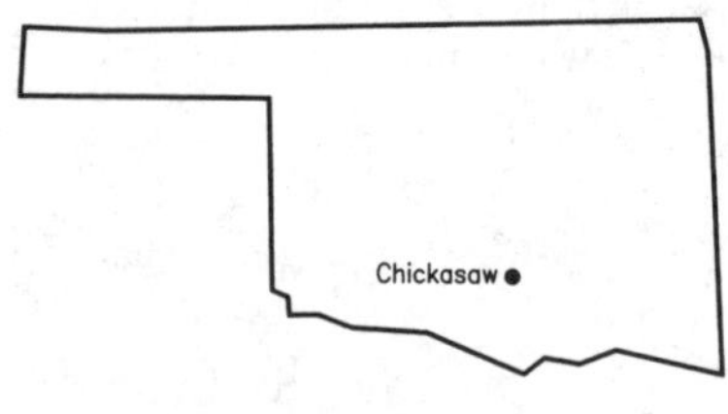

Chickasaw National Recreation Area

Allow: 2 days *FREE*

It's hard to imagine that these hills were once as massive as the Rockies. True, they provide welcome relief from the surrounding prairie land. But for those of us who have driven the Sierras, the Cascades and the Rocky Mountains, it's hard to imagine those walls of granite being transformed into knolls like these. Shaded forests and cool clear waters attract today's visitors to places their grandparents visited for the supposed curative powers of mineral waters.

Highlights

★ People still come to partake of the bromide and sulfur spring waters. Even skeptics have a hard time convincing themselves these odorous waters don't have some medicinal qualities.

Whiz Tips

The park rangers lead interested folks on nature walks and conduct nightly campfire programs.

The more popular springs are found along Travertine and Rock Creeks. Pavilion, Bromide and Medicine Springs contain mineral waters, while Buffalo and Antelope are pure.

Kids' Stuff

★ Swimming, biking, boating, fishing and hiking are the kids' alternatives for outdoors fun. Most of the 8 miles of developed trails in the park are child-sized.

Access: 10 mi. from Davis off I-35. **Days/Hours:** Daily. **Camping:** Park has 5; Rock Creek (106 sites), Cold Springs (64 sites), The Pint (52 sites), Buckhorn (172 sites) and Guy Sandy (39 sites). **For info.:** Superintendent, Chickasaw National Recreation Area, P.O.Box 201, Sulfur, OK 73086. 405/622-3161.

OREGON

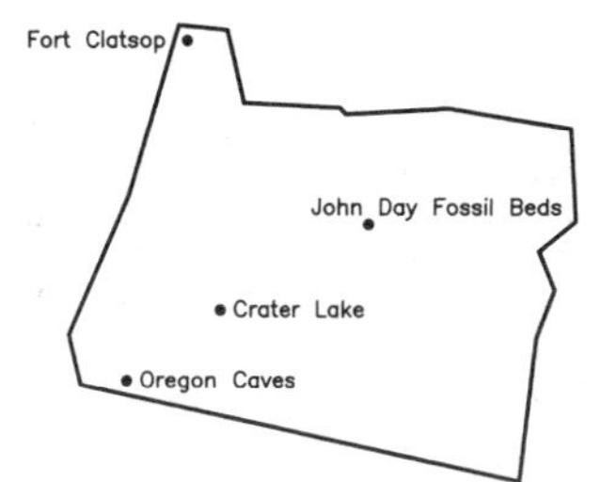

Crater Lake National Park

Allow: 1-2 days *Fee*

"It is unique in all the world. The day is coming when people of all nations will arrive to view its grandeur, then return to their homes to ponder that such things can be."
William Gladstone Steel, 1885

West Coast flyers who glance out their windows and behold a startlingly blue lake set in the middle of a mountain, have perhaps the best appreciation of this remarkable Southern Oregon landmark. Crater Lake sits in the middle of a mountain which literally "lost its head." The road encircling the lake is one of the most beautiful drives in the world. For those who like to see things up close, they can hike down to the water and take a boat ride (fee) with a ranger around the lake.

Highlights

★ Most visitors barely take the time to complete the drive around Crater Lake. Sure, that alone is worth the trip, but there are so many other ways to appreciate the volcano's effort. Short walks or longer hikes introduce you to the country while continually offering different angles from which to view the lake.

Whiz Tips

The park has a nightly campfire program during tourist season as well as hikes, historic tours, geology talks and, of course, the boat tours.

Native Americans recounted the time when Mt. Mazama towered over its neighbors. It was formed by

Crater Lake National Park Courtesy NPS

a stratovolcano which alternately spewed out layers lava or ash. After its central conduit became plugged by cooled lava, fissures in its sides released the internal pressure. Lava flows or cinder cones formed at these holes. Less than 7,000 ago, these pressures became intense and forced the fissures to spread, collapsing the top of the mountain. The remaining bowl-like structure is called a caldera. Wizard Island is the cinder cone of a small volcano which formed after Mt. Mazama's collapse. Because the snowfall and rain have no surface outlet, Crater Lake has created an island of the cinder cone. It should be noted that until man introduced fish, there was very little life in the lake. The steep walls make animal access difficult and the water only contained microscopic plant and animal life.

❢ Crater Lake is the nation's deepest lake (the world's 7th) reaching down almost 2,000 ft. It's a surprising 6 miles across at its widest point with 21 square miles of surface. The reasons for its color are its water purity and remarkable depth.

Kids' Stuff

★ Your kids can become Jr. Rangers, complete with a badge, by attending the prescribed interpretive programs and demonstrating their new-found knowledge. Our children also had to pledge they would conserve the environment. There are a number of self-guided family walks, like Annie Creek Nature Trail.

Access: Off OR 62 or Hwy. 138 (summer only). **Days/Hours:** Park H.Q. Visitor Center, daily 8-5 (winter 8-4:30) (clsd. Dec.25). Rim Visitor Center, daily June & Sept. 9-4 & July-Labor Day 9-7. **Camping:** Park's Mazama Campground (198 sites); National Forest campgrounds nearby. **Special Events:** Aug., Crater Lake Rim Run; Feb., Ski Race. **Teacher's Package:** Available. **For info.:** Superintendent, Crater Lake National Park, P.O. Box 7, Crater Lake, OR 97604. 503/594-2211.

Fort Clatsop National Memorial

Allow: 1-2 hrs. *Fee*

" It continued to rain and blow so violently that there was no movement of the party today."

William Clark, Feb 25, 1806

Near the mouth of the mighty Columbia River, Lewis and Clark and some of their expedition spent probably the most miserable winter of their lives. Of their 106 days in tiny Fort Clatsop, they only experienced 12 days when the sky shed not a tear. Think about it. For two years they travelled the breadth of the continent and when they finally reach their goal, they are besieged by rains of Biblical proportions. However, they used their time well as they updated their records of their historic expedition and prepared for their trip homeward.

Highlights

★ The reconstructed fort, named for the region's Clatsop Indians, is little more than 2 rows of wood huts joined by gates. Although it looks like a determined foe could have easily breached its walls, the tiny outpost was well-guarded.

Whiz Tips

❢ During the spring and fall, there are weekend living history programs showing how these stalwart explorers occupied their days. In summer, these programs swing into full gear supplemented by regular ranger talks. Their demonstrations range from musket loading and firing to tanning and woodworking as they emphasize the expedition's historical importance and the obstacles it overcame.

❢ Meriwether Lewis was a protege of President Thomas Jefferson who had long envisioned this expedition. When the Louisiana Purchase became a reality, Lewis, with the help of William Clark, was sent to enlist a band of sturdy lads to explore the land included in the Purchase. Clark was the brother of Revolutionary War hero, George Rogers Clark (see George Rogers Clark NM, IN). Sailing 1,600 mi. up the Missouri, they endured temperatures as low as -45 degrees F. as they wintered at Fort Mandan, ND. Here they met Sacagawea, who helped the expedition as an interpreter and in the acquiring of horses to cross the Rockies. Sacagawea, kidnapped from her Shoshone tribe as a child, recognized the site of her enslavement, her tribe's summer hunting grounds. The tale has a storybook ending. As good luck would have it, her family was there and, of course, her brother was a sub-chief. "Hey, you want horses? You got them. Anything for my sis." Well not quite. Lewis and Clark did pay a good price for their horses. Lewis and Clark only lost one man (probably to appendicitis) while journeying over 4,000 mi. of unfamiliar territory. The helpful and peaceful role of the Native Americans cannot be minimized.

Kids' Stuff

★ The living history programs and "hands-on" replica items and "try-on" clothing are sure winners for children.

★ The site has short walks taking you to the canoe landing area where the party embarked on hunting forays. Our children had plenty of questions about the construction of the canoes exhibited here.

Access: 5 mi. SE of Astoria off US 101. **Days/Hours:** Daily, summer 8-6 & winter 8-5 (clsd. Dec.25). **Camping:** Nearby Fort Stevens State Park (605 sites, elec. & shwrs.). **Special Events:** End of Dec., holiday fort program. **For info.:** Superintendent, Fort Clatsop National Memorial, Rte. 3, Box 604-FC, Astoria, OR 97103. 503/861-2471.

John Day Fossil Beds National Monument

Allow: 1 day *FREE*

"Here the mountains have cut off most of the moisture coming in from the Pacific, and aridity spells the terms of existence. This is

Fort Clatsop National Memorial

tough, hard uplands terrain of mountains and plateaus."

Neal R. Pierce
The Pacific States of America

It wasn't always this way. 50 million years ago, there were no Cascade Mountains and the region received about 100 in. of rain per year, leaving it verdant. This was the beginning of the Age of Mammals. In mid-eastern Oregon, John Day Fossil Beds contain one of the most comprehensive records of the various stages of mammal development. As the mighty Cascades rose to block the rain (today's 10-12 in./yr.), the flora and fauna changed. Each generation was entombed with volcanic ash. The park has three major sites spread over a couple of hundred miles.

Highlights

★ The best place to see the actual fossils are at the Visitor Center at Sheep Rock. The exhibits clearly delineate the differences in the fossils. You may be fortunate enough to see a museum technician working on a fossil in the lab.

★ The best places to see replica fossils placed where originals were found are on the Island-in-Time Trail at Sheep Rock and The Trail of Fossils at Clarno Palisades.

Whiz Tips

At Clarno Palisades, the oldest fossils were found. The ancient ancestor of the modern horse (Epihippus), a primitive rhinoceros, an early tapir, a Telmatherium (a huge vegetarian) and Hemipsalodon (a meat eater) were found. At Painted Hills, scientists uncovered more recent fossils (40 million yrs.). This era's plant life included the dawn redwood, still found in China, early oaks and myrtles. Sheep Rock has still more recent findings with sabertooth tigers, slightly larger horses, larger rhinoceroses and mouse deer.

These sites played an interesting role in the academic wars among 19th century scientists. Thomas Condon, a minister and amateur pa-

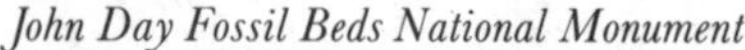
John Day Fossil Beds National Monument

Courtesy NPS

leontologist, tried to interest the nation's first official paleontologist, Othniel Marsh, in the region. Marsh bribed two of Condon's assistants into supplying him with one of Condon's discoveries, a tiny horse, which he then passed off as his own discovery.

Kids' Stuff

★ Many of the trails are ideal in size and grade for even small children. In summer, care should be taken because of the intense heat and aridity. Small children dehydrate very quickly.

★ The park occasionally demonstrates fossil identification for kids.

Access: H.Q. in John Day; Sheep Rock & visitor center 9 mi. N of Dayville; Painted Hills 9 mi. NW of Mitchell; Clarno 20 mi. W of Fossil. **Days/Hours:** Visitor center, daily, summer 8:30-6 & winter 8:30-5 (clsd. winter weekends & fed. holidays). **Camping:** 9 public campgrounds in the region (ask at the park for an area map), Clyde Holliday Wayside near Mount Vernon (shwrs. & elec.). **Teacher's Package:** Available. **For info.:** Superintendent, John Day Fossil Beds National Monument, 420 West Main, John Day, OR 97845. 503/575-0721.

McLoughlin House National Historic Site

Allow: 1 hr. *Fee*

Mcloughlin House is an affiliated park service site encompassing homes of 2 men who played significant roles in white settlement of the northwest. Known as the "Father of Oregon," Dr. John McLoughlin, as chief factor of Fort Vancouver (see Fort Vancouver NHS, WA), was supposed to discourage American immigration into the territory. On the contrary, his assistance to the new arrivals encouraged permanent settlement. For example, his home which can be toured, was known as "the house of many beds" because of his hospitality to immigrants. The other tour home was the residence of Dr. Forbes Barclay, an associate of McLoughlin's. The site emphasizes the importance of fur-trade in opening up the Pacific northwest and the role people like Dr. McLoughlin played in deciding who would claim the region. There are "hands-on" furs and pelts for children to examine

McLoughlin House National Historic Site Courtesy McLoughlin House NHS

and the interpreters will tailor their talks for families.

Access: Downtown Oregon City, 9 blks. from I-205. **Days/Hours:** Tu-Sa 10-4 & Sun. 1-4 (clsd. M, holidays & Jan.). **Camping:** Nearby Washington state parks; Paradise Point State Park (79 sites & shwrs.), Battle Ground Lake (35 sites &shwrs.) & Beacon Rock State Park (35 sites & shwrs.). **Special Events:** 1st Aug. wknd., McLoughlin House Pioneer Festival; 2nd Feb. Sa, Pioneer Days; June, Father's Day Open House; Oct., McLoughlin's Birthday Party; 1st Dec. wknd., Candlelight Tours. **For info.:** McLoughlin House National Historic Site, McLoughlin Memorial Assoc., 713 Center St., Oregon City, OR 97045. 503/656-5146.

Oregon Caves National Monument

Allow: .5 days *Fee (cave tour)*

Close to the California border is the unique marble Oregon Caves National Monument. Carved out of a marble mountain, the cave (there is only one cave) has several unusual formations. Some of the calcite formations you can find here are stalactites, stalagmites, draperies, soda straws and flowstone.

Highlights

★ Although it's a steep climb up (it looks worse than it is), don't miss the optional "Paradise Lost." The flowstone and draperies which are pictured in the monument's brochure don't do justice to the feeling you experience surrounded by these magnificent natural sculptures.

★ The big room has volcanic and fault evidence and its roof is covered in "clay worms." These worms are fashioned much like the calcite formations when mineral-laden water evaporates leaving a clay formation instead of a calcite one. The room once served as a dance hall when an early entrepreneur tried to strike it rich with eccentric toe-tappers.

Whiz Tips

The emphasis of the tour is on cave restoration. Since the cave was discovered in 1874 by Elijah Davidson, man and the elements have done considerable damage to it. When we touch the calcite forma-

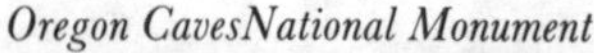

Oregon CavesNational Monument

tions, the oils from our skin remain, preventing further growth, in essence "killing" them. Attempts to make the caves accessible to visitors have opened airways which allowed unfiltered air to discolor the calcite formations. The monument is taking out antiquated and obtrusive lighting systems, metal lint-catching walkways and asphalt paths and replacing them with less offensive materials. In addition, a number of doors now block the air and return the cave's interior environment to its original state.

🌡 To get some idea of how quickly this cave is forming you can see some stalactites that were broken off at the end of the last century. There's about a dime's width of new growth over the past hundred years. The stalactites which "grow" from the ceiling, drip down, forming stalagmites on the floor that "grow" upward until they touch and become columns. The draperies, straws and flowstone create their own patterns for reasons not yet clear to us. Prior to the cave's formation, the mountain experienced a mild volcanic occurrence. Its trail of lava rock can be clearly seen in the caves' largest room. You'll also see some fault action in many parts of the cavern.

🌡 The cave's temperature is 41 degrees F., so dress accordingly.

Kids' Stuff

★ Although the cave tour is limited to children who can safely negotiate the tour route, it's still a good stop for a family that qualifies. Basically, your kids have to be able to climb ladders (up & down). With all the twists and turns over a mile of tunnel ways, kids enjoy a real sense of discovery at each corner.

★ The mandatory lights-out stop is near the beginning of the tour, so stay near your children at the outset to offer a hand before total darkness ensues.

Access: 20 mi. SE of Cave Junction on OR 46. **Days/Hours:** Daily, cave tours run from; spring & fall 9-5, summer 8-7 & winter 10:30, 12:30 2 & 3:30. **Camping:** 2 national forest campgrounds nearby, Cave Creek (primitive) & Grayback. **For info.**: Superintendent, Oregon Caves National Monument, 19000 Caves Hwy., Cave Junction, OR 97523. 503/592-2100.

Oregon National Historic Trail

Thousands of pioneers, gold seekers and missionaries loaded up conestoga wagons and followed the footsteps of the Whitmans (see Whitman Mission NHS, WA) and the fur traders on the 2,000-plus mile Oregon Trail to reach the continent's most western states. Upon their arrival in Portland, OR, many of them were assisted by Dr. John McLoughlin, the chief factor of Fort Vancouver (see McLoughlin House NHS, OR & Fort Vancouver NHS, WA). Their sheer numbers and subsequent settlement resulted in England relinquishing its hold on the Old Oregon Territory. The park service has designated 125 sites (only 28 have been so designated thus far) to commemorate and interpret significant events and landmarks along the route. Other park service sites include Chimney Rock NHS, NE, Scotts Bluff NM, NE and Fort Laramie NHS, WY.

For info.: Oregon National Historic Trail, Pacific Northwest Region, National Park Service, 83 South King St., Ste. 212, Seattle Washington, WA 98104.

PENNSYLVANIA

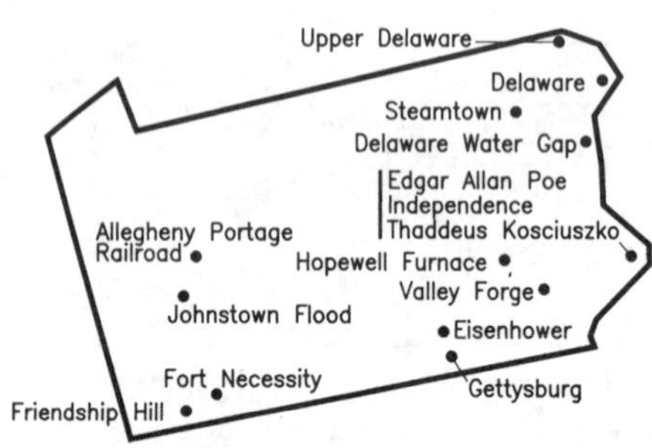

Allegheny Portage Railroad National Historic Site

Allow: 1-2 hrs. *FREE*

"At four o'clock we began to ascend the Allegheny Mountains...The almost incredible variety of plants, and the lavish profusion of their growth, produce an effect perfectly enchanting."

Frances Trollope, 1832
Domestic Manners of the Americans

About 45 min. northeast of Johnstown is one of the most intriguing chapters of American transportation history. Acting as city states, the great eastern seaboard cities coerced their state governments to finance transportation systems so they could compete for the Ohio Valley trade. New York built the Erie Canal, Bal-

Allegheny Portage Railroad National Historic Site Courtesy Holiday Films of Berkeley, CA

timore built the Chesapeake and Ohio Canal and Philadelphia built the Main Line Canal. However, Philadelphia's system had to contend with more mountainous terrain. They designed a multi-mode transportation system incorporating rail and canal. By building railroad tracks over the Cresson Summit, they were able to pull rail cars up over the mountain, linking the Johnstown Main Line Canal to the Hollidaysburg Main Line Canal. In 6 hours, 36 miles were traversed using 33 changes in power source. The system ultimately reduced the trip from Philadelphia to Pittsburgh from 23 days to 4.

Highlights

★ Today's site has examples of these tracks, models of the modes of transportation used and an AV telling the tale. In summer, the rangers interpret the site for visitors through guided walks and occasional living-history demonstrations.

Whiz Tips

In the early mid-1880s, steam engines were not very powerful, so an intricate set of tracks had to be set up to surmount the mountains. Using cars going downhill to help cars being pulled uphill, the company was able to "walk" the cargo over the summit in ten "steps" or incline planes. They replaced the laborious off-loading of passengers and freight from the boats to the rail cars and from rail cars to boats, with the inventive "piggy-backing" of loading the boats directly onto the rail cars. Technology advanced, allowing trains to traverse the Alleghenies year-round, making the canals outmoded because they froze in winter.

Kids' Stuff

★ There are nature trails, a steam engine and a Deputy Historian Program which allows anyone to earn a certificate and a badge upon successful completion of a set of activities. But mostly there remains in your mind's eye, the vivid images of boats with bowler-hatted men with canes and hatted ladies holding parasols being slowly cranked up the hill in boats on the backs of rail cars.

Access: Between Cresson & Duncansville on Old Rte. 22 off new Rte.22. **Days/Hours:** Daily 8:30-5, (summer extended hrs.) (clsd. Thanksgiving, Dec.25 & Jan.1). **Camping:** 20 "hilly" mi. E Blue Knob State Park (75 sites) & N Prince Gallitzin State Park. **Teacher's Package:** Available. **For info.:** Superintendent, Allegheny Portage Railroad National Historic Site, P.O.Box 247, Cresson, PA 16630. 814/886-8176.

Delaware & Lehigh Navigation Canal National Heritage Corridor

Various public and private interests administer this affiliated site containing 2 19th century canals and their associated railroads. These transportation systems were vital in the opening up of the state's rich anthracite coal fields. The Hugh Moore Canal Museum in Easton has many exhibits explaining the importance of the canals and railroads and coal in the industrialization of America.

For info.: Delaware & Lehigh Navigation Canal National Heritage Corridor, c/o Mid-Atlantic Region National Park Service, 143 S Third St., Philadelphia, PA 19106.

Delaware Water Gap National Recreation Area

Allow: 1-2 days *FREE*

Encompassing 37 miles of the Delaware National Scenic River dividing Pennsylvania and New Jersey, the park includes land on both banks. The free-flowing river you see today is not quite what the originators of the park proposal had in mind. Instead of a mature river bed and meandering waters, the original plan was to flood the valley with a 37 mile long dammed lake. However, the high costs attached to the military action in Viet Nam delayed building the dam. By the 70s, the environmental effects of such an enterprise were better understood and the government declared it a National Wild & Scenic River. The dam is still up for review after the turn of the century.

Highlights

★ Millbrook Village is a recreated rural 19th century town that bustles with living historians during summer weekends and provides solitude for weekday wanderers.

★ Canoeing is big here. The park's rangers will help you out on Saturdays if you make reservations. They also have five-hour-long interpretive canoe trips every summer Sunday beginning at 10 a.m. (again reservations and your own canoe 717/828-7802).

Whiz Tips

At Slateford Farm during the summer afternoons (Th-Su), costumed park rangers lead tours through the 1800s farm and explain the slate industry that thrived in the area.

There are several nature walks to chose from and geology talks are for the asking at the Kittatinny Point Visitor Center.

Kids' Stuff

This outdoor natural playground offers swimming, hiking, boating and fishing. The river isn't exactly of the whitewater variety so parents should feel fairly safe around it. However, the park warns all to swim where there are lifeguards.

Access: Kittatinny Point Visitor Center just off I-80 in NJ; Dingmans Falls Visitor Center 1 mi. off US 209 in PA. **Days/Hours:** Visitor centers daily 9-5; Dingmans' Apr.-Nov. **Camping:** Park's boater's primitive campsites; Worthington State (NJ) Forest (75 sites). **For info.:** Superintendent, Delaware Water Gap National Recreation Area, Bushkill, PA 18324. 717/588-2435.

Delaware Water Gap National Recreation Area Courtesy NPS

Edgar Allan Poe National Historic Site

Allow: 1-2 hrs. *FREE*

Ah, dream too bright to last!
Ah, starry Hope! that didst arise
But to be overcast!
A voice from out the Future cries,
On! On!-but o'er the Past
(Dim gulf!) my spirit hovering lies
Mute, motionless, aghast!

Edgar Allan Poe
"To One In Paradise"

Edgar Allan Poe, like many artists, won more acclaim after his passing than while he lived. His house in Philadelphia was and remains in a run-down part of town. Empty rooms remind us that Poe had no material goods worth saving and that no one thought to save what little he owned. To most he was an embittered critic, harsh in his judgment and miserly with his praise. He viciously attacked the most eminent writers of his time. He took particular displeasure with Longfellow (see Longfellow NHS, MA), who had attained a great following. You can tour his hollow home and contemplate its great black raven.

Highlights

★ Poe stands on his own at this site. The park service has chosen not to focus on period furnishings to recreate his era. But rather we are told of the public man.

Whiz Tips

Poe's life has been termed a "long, slow suicide." Orphaned by age 3, Poe spent his life looking for someone to replace his beautiful actress mother. His birth mother, his adoptive mother and his wife were all claimed by consumption (T.B.). A love lost then found, was again lost with his death. Victor Hugo described him as "the prince of American literature." Stephane Mallarme said that he learned English just so he could read Poe in his own tongue. At 18, he published his first volume of poems. Barely keeping the wolf at bay, he wrote stories for magazines. His major ambition was to publish a successful magazine, a dream he would fail to achieve. Although Poe contin-

Edgar Allan Poe National Historic Site

ued to publish widely, there were no copyright laws for literature and he remained poor. "The Raven" was an immensely popular piece, reprinted many times, but all he received for it was $8.00. Poe's reputation as a drunk and drug user has been repudiated. While it is known that he could not hold his "likker" and was a poor drinking companion, there is little evidence of drug use. Poe's literary executor, Rev. Rufus Griswold, detested Poe and smeared his character. European literati firmly established Poe as one of the literary giants of the New World. Recognized today as a world class poet and horror story author, Poe is also credited with creating the murder mystery genre and pioneering science fiction.

Kids' Stuff

★ Although better suited for older children, the park has involved local kids by getting them to write their own poetry. Clearly, Poe's dark images appeal to side of us (and our children) we don't always like to acknowledge. If your kids have to satisfy this bent, better it be with Edgar Allan Poe than Freddie Kruger.

Access: Downtown Philadelphia. **Days/ Hours:** Daily 9-5 (clsd. Dec.25 & Jan.1) **Camping:** 30 mi. W, French Creek State Park (260 sites, elec., shwrs. & reservations). **For info.:** Superintendent, Edgar Allan Poe National Historic Site, 313 Walnut St., Philadelphia, PA 19106. 215/597-8780.

Eisenhower National Historic Site

Allow: 2 hrs. *Fee*

"When I die, I'm going to leave a piece of ground better than I found it."

Dwight David Eisenhower

Where do generals go to die? Old battlefields! However, it does feel strange to drive past the corn fields and country yards littered with Civil War monuments and cannons to visit the home of so recent a presi-

Eisenhower National Historic Site Courtesy NPS

dent. Even after visiting his home, it's less clear why this reluctant president would wish to surround himself by the memories of war. True, he had fond memories of his stay here in 1918 and he was a history buff but as Richard Nixon said of the man he served with as vice-president, "...that no one hates war more than one who has seen a lot of it."

Highlights

★ The tour of Eisenhower's home is ample evidence of how representative he was of middle-America. In fact, the room containing the many gifts he and his wife received while in office and the putting green with the General's five star flag stand out in contrast. Their favorite room wasn't the "gift" room which was rarely used because it was too "stuffy" but rather the covered porch. They ate here, he painted here and they entertained here. The fact of this old warrior's life was that this was the first home he and his wife ever owned, having lived in 37 different governmental houses in 35 years of marriage.

Whiz Tips

Walter Cronkite talks with Ike at his retirement home in a *Twentieth Century* TV program shown at the visitor center. Ike's reason for buying a farm is summed up in the introductory quote, a worthy sentiment for anyone.

Unlike many presidents, Eisenhower's ascendancy owes more to his works than those of his family's wealth. A West Point graduate, Ike demonstrated exceptional administrative abilities paving the way for his rise to Supreme Commander of the Allied Forces invading Europe. After WW II concluded, both political parties hounded Eisenhower to run for president. While he was assembling the newly organized NATO troops, the Republicans finally convinced him to run. In the '83 historians' poll of presidents, Ike ranked 11th of the 36 rated. Today, his presidency is highly regarded, faulted primarily for his lack of initiative in the Civil Rights area. Of his own performance, Ike had this to say; "The United States never lost a soldier or a foot of ground in my administration. We kept the peace. People ask how it happened-by God, it didn't just happen, I'll tell you that." Would that his fellow presidents could all claim the same.

Kids' Stuff

★ As with most historical tours, the benefits are magnified if your children have studied something of the historic figure. Ask a ranger about the President's grandchildren, David, Anne, Susan and Mary who met world leaders, had Secret Service agents protecting them and played at the farm.

Access: Bus from National Park Visitor Center. **Days/Hours:** Apr.-Oct., daily 9-4:15; Nov.-Mar., W-Su 9-4 (clsd. 4 wk. in Jan. & Feb., Thanksgiving, Dec.25 & Jan.1). **Camping:** Caledonia State Park E on US 30 (185 sites, elec. & showers) & Codorous State Park W on SR 216 (198 sites, elec. & showers). **Special Events:** Oct., Ike's art displayed, both mid-July and Aug., Field Days. **For info.:** Superintendent, Eisenhower National Historic Site, P.O.Box 1080, Gettysburg, PA 17325. 717/334-1124.

Fort Necessity National Battlefield

Allow: 1-2 hrs. *Fee*

"...(Washington's) features were indicative of the most ungovernable passions, and had he been born in the forests...he would have been the fiercest man among the savage tribes."

Gilbert Stuart, Presidential portraitist

Just north of West Virginia lies the battlefield where George Washington experienced his first command in battle and his first and only surrender. Ever the expansionist, Washington was determined to control the

Ohio Valley before the French did. He engaged the French in a skirmish, where he had unfortunately embarrassed them. In what proved to be the first major North American action in the French and Indian War, a force of 700 French troops, French Canadians and Indians, met Washington and 400 others in tiny Fort Necessity. Making use of the forest that Washington had left too close to the fort, the constant barrage of French fire reduced Washington's force by 1/4. Washington had no choice but to surrender or face annihilation. He and his men were permitted to leave the fort as a condition of their surrender.

Highlights

★ The reconstructed fort and the grounds provide ample proof of the desperation Washington and his men must have felt. It's not a pretty site picturing 400 men pinned down by a shower of musket shot.

★ The 1820s Mount Washington Tavern has a tenuous relationship to the fort (Washington once owned the land it rests on). Built to service travelers on the nation's first federal highway (Hwy. 40), it reminds us of early westward expansion. As you tour the tavern, the rangers explain the era's lifestyles.

Whiz Tips

Fort Necessity was built as a fortification against the French. Washington and his men were building a road through the hills and chose the Great Meadow, which Washington ironically refers to as a "...charming field for an Encounter" to build the fort. Little did he know.

Kids' Stuff

★ The park has costumed living historians to explain things during the summer and kids enjoy the reconstructed fort.

Access: 11 E of Uniontown on US 40. **Days/Hours:** Daily 10:30-5; (summer extended hrs.). **Camping:** E at Confluence (US 40), Tub Run Recreation Area (101 sites, elec. & showers) & Youghiogheny Lake Recreation Area (75 sites, elec. & showers). **Special Events:** Aug., Family Days. **For info.:** Superintendent, Fort Necessity National Battlefield, Rte. 2, Box 528, Farmington, PA 15437. 412/329-5512.

Fort Necessity National Battlefield Courtesy NPS

Friendship Hill National Historic Site

Allow: 2-3 hrs. *FREE*

"Pennsylvania has produced but two great men: Benjamin Franklin of Massachusetts, and Albert Gallatin, of Switzerland."
Senator J.J. Ingalls, 1885

Friendship Hill preserves the county estate of Albert Gallatin. Gallatin, a Swiss immigrant, served his adopted country for nearly seven decades. Gallatin made significant contributions to the young republic in the fields of finance, politics, diplomacy and scholarship. He is best known as the Treasurer Secretary under Thomas Jefferson and James Madison, during which time he developed the concept of the National Road.

Highlights

★ Gallatin's home is undergoing extensive restoration and is closed to interior tours. Ranger-led tours of the exterior are available during the summer.

★ The park has 5 mi. of hiking trails and 7 small waterfalls.

Whiz Tips

During the summer, there are special programs covering a variety of subjects both natural and historical.

Kids' Stuff

★ Children enjoy exploring the historic area as well as the hiking trails.

Access: 3 mi. N of Point Marion on SR 166 mid-way btwn Uniontown, PA & Morgantown, WV. **Days/Hours:** Summer, daily & winter wknds. 9:30-5. **Camping:** Ohiopyle State Park on Rte.381 (224 sites); Tub Run Recreation Area (101 sites, elec. & shwrs.) and Youghiogheny Lake Recreation Area (75 sites, elec. & shwrs.). **For info.:** Superintendent, Friendship Hill National Historic Site, R.D. 2, Box 528, Farmington, PA 15437. 412/329-5512.

Gettysburg National Military Park Courtesy NPS

Gettysburg National Military Park

Allow: 1 day *FREE*

"Four score and seven years ago our fathers brought forth on this continent, a new nation, conceived in Liberty, and dedicated to the proposition that all men are created equal."

Abraham Lincoln
Gettysburg Address

Cornfields, stone monuments, rolling pastures, cannons, farmhouses, flags, orchards and tombstones: such is Gettysburg, a small town in south /central Pennsylvania. It's enough that this battleground proved the furthest Bobbie Lee's army of North Virginia reached into Federal territory. It's enough that almost as many men were casualties here (51,000) in three short days as were lost in Viet Nam. It's enough that the 16th president of the United States should say in three minutes more about the essence of this nation than his peers would speak in volumes. Gettysburg, a word that summed up all the battles before it and spelled the doom of the Confederacy. The fighting would continue for two more years and the bitterness would claim the great man who sought only to make the house whole. But Gettysburg would continue to reverberate through time as the turning of the tide.

Highlights

★ Because of its name recognition, Gettysburg shares the same over-success other famous national parks experience. There's almost too much to do and sometimes, there are too many people all trying to do it. You can hire a personalized guide who'll ride in your vehicle giving you his/her personal view of the battlefield. Or you can go with a group in a charter bus, or you can go on your own. There's an Electronic Map (fee) showing the ebb and flow of the troops. There's the Cyclorama, a pre-moving-picture form of enter-

Gettysburg National Military Park Courtesy NPS

tainment which features a 360 degree painting of the battle and a spotlight narration. Then, there are the highly recommended park service interpretive programs.

Whiz Tips

❢ Enjoying a long string of successes, Robert E. Lee saw the opportunity to win ground on Federal soil. He felt by so doing he could make northerners question their involvement just as Lincoln's first term was coming due. Secondly, he felt a victory here would legitimize the Confederacy in Europe. However, J.E.B. Stuart, the epitome of Southern derring-do, recklessly led his scouts on a revenge raid. Without his "eyes and ears," Lee stumbled into the northern army on June 30th. At first Lee's army was able to push Union General George Meade back. However, nightfall and replacement troops allowed the Federals to regroup. On July 2nd, Lee split his forces to press both Northern flanks, gaining a modicum of success at a tremendous price, then couldn't hold the ground. On July 3rd, uncharacteristically, Lee sent 12,000 warriors across the mile of open field into the teeth of the opposition in "Pickett's Charge" (although Pickett led the assault, it wasn't his plan nor were his men in the majority). Only 4,000 made it back unscathed. Wave after wave of fearless soldiers dressed in nut brown and gray were shredded by cannon grapeshot and rifle slugs. The day was done and so the battle and so the Confederacy.

❢ Although he won the battle, Meade was replaced by Grant because Lincoln was upset that Meade had not pressed his advantage. A National Cemetery was established to commemorate the Union dead and the ceremonies included the president among the roster of speakers. Lincoln, who worked hard on his speech (no, it wasn't written on the back of a match cover), felt at the time that it hadn't come off. However, the preceding speaker who had taken most of the afternoon to express himself, said the president's few words spoke volumes more than his many. The Gettysburg Address still stands the test of time.

Kids' Stuff

★ A lot of the park is on busy thoroughfares. However, most travelers are park visitors and go slow enough that bicycling is an option. In any event, you and your family can walk many parts of the battlefield. The High Water Mark tour guides you through the fighting that occurred in the area immediately next to the visitor center.

★ Make sure your kids see the downstairs exhibits in the visitor center. The "pirate-like" get-ups the New York regiments wore, as these troops sought to emulate the fashion-conscious French soldiers.

Access: Downtown Gettysburg. **Days/Hours:** Visitor Center, daily, summer 8-6 & winter 9-5. Cyclorama, daily 9-5. **Camping:** Caledonia State Park E on US 30 (185 sites, elec. & showers) & Codorous State Park W on SR 216 (198 sites, elec. & showers). **Special Events:** The park usually has an encampment on the anniversary of the battle, July 1-3, where some of the famous encounters are re-enaeted. **Teacher's Package:** Available. **For info.:** Superintendent, Gettysburg National Military Park, Gettysburg, PA 17325. 717/334-1124.

Gloria Dei (Old Swedes') Church National Historic Site

Founded in 1667, this is the second oldest Swedish church in the country. The structure you'll see was completed around 1700 and is an excellent example of this period's Swedish architecture.

For info.: Gloria Dei (Old Swedes') Church National Historic Site, Delaware Ave. & Christian St., Philadelphia, PA 19106.

Hopewell Furnace National Historic Site

Allow: 1-2 hrs. *Fee (FREE Dec.-Feb.)*

In the picturesque countryside of southeastern Pennsylvania sits Hopewell Furnace, a quaint 19th century hamlet. It's fitting that the state known for its steel mills should have a national historic metal factory, in this case, an iron plantation. Hopewell Furnace was more than an industrial complex; it was a community that sprang up to work at the furnace. Visitors can learn about pre-Industrial Revolution industry.

Highlights

★ In summer costumed park rangers go about the daily rigors of early American life. They'll guide you through the village and demonstrate molding and farming. The park takes great pains to ensure visitors understand the furnace workers lived on the plantation, farming to supplement their lifestyles. The short 10 min. audio-visual program introducing the park is one of the best produced productions we saw.

Whiz Tips

❢ While the furnace initially made stove plates, it began large-scale production of other iron products with the advent of the Revolutionary War. Using iron ore, limestone and hardwood for charcoal, the founder mixed these ingredients together under high heat and a cold air blast to create the molten iron and its residual, slag. The molten iron was appraised by the founder for its purity and then either put directly into molds or sent to a forge as pig iron to be hammered into usable goods. Although the furnace saw its share of ups and downs, it ultimately failed because of the advent of using coal in the process of making iron. The owners built an anthracite furnace, but it failed.

❢ Mark Bird, the original founder of the furnace, suffered a fate many

Hopewell Furnace National Historic Site Courtesy NPS

Revolutionary patriots suffered: financial ruin. British law forbade colonies to produce finished iron products. So it was natural that Bird and other ironmasters would support the revolution (two of Bird's brother-in-laws, who were also ironmasters, signed the Declaration of Independence would you call them "foundry" fathers?). Bird, with little compensation, served as a colonel, raised a militia, sent Washington's troops at Valley Forge 1,000 barrels of flour and supplied armaments. Hopewell lived on after Bird sold out and it reached its peak in the 1830s. An ironic [no pun intended] side note is that Bird used a large number of slaves at the furnace and the last owner of the furnace was an adamant abolitionist who probably employed runaways in addition to free black workers.

Kids' Stuff

★ The furnace is a fascinating place for kids. The "olden days" scene sparks their curiosity. The sprawling community allows them to expend their energies as they explore it (beware the slag piles as some children get cut). Costumed living historians and a farmer add to their pleasure as they show them how things worked as well as tell them. Plus, there are the farm animals that even the tiniest tot enjoys seeing.

Access: From I-76 take Exit 22 to PA 10 to PA 23 to PA 345 or 5 mi. S of Birdsboro on PA 345. **Days/Hours:** Daily 9-5 (clsd. Thanksgiving, Dec.25 & Jan.1). **Camping:** Adjacent French Creek State Park (260 sites, elec., shwrs. & reservations - 215/582-1514). **Special Events:** Late Feb., Black History Program; March, Woman's History Program; April, Sheep Shearing Program; Aug.4, Establishment Day; Sept., Apple Schnitz Day; Dec., Iron Plantation Christmas. **For info.:** Superintendent, Hopewell Furnace National Historic Site, R.D. 1, Box 345, Elverson, PA 19520-9505. 215/582-8773.

Independence National Historical Park

Allow: 1 day *FREE*

"I can say in return, Sir, that all the Political sentiments I entertain have been drawn, so far as I have been able to draw them, from the sentiments which originated in and were given

Independence National Historical Park Courtesy NPS

to the world from this hall (Independence Hall)."

Abraham Lincoln

As Athens and Rome were for their respective civilizations, so was Philadelphia for America. Boston may have led the way for the Revolution, but Philadelphia led the way for the nation that was to be borne from the fire. What era in American history produced such brilliance? In over two hundred years of meetings, when has the House of Representatives and the Senate ever wrought anything as dynamic as the Declaration of Independence or the Constitution. Of all the quotes in American literature, what is more compelling than, "We hold these truths to be self-evident, that all men are created equal, that they are endowed by their Creator with certain unalienable Rights, that among these are Life, Liberty and the pursuit of Happiness." The only other quote that comes close is Lincoln's Gettysburg Address, and it is in reference to this passage.

Highlights

★ Across the Delaware River from New Jersey sits old Philadelphia. For the most part, the city's inhabitants have joined the park service in refurbishing the historic neighborhood. Independence Square is anchored by Independence Hall, Congress Hall, Old City Hall and Philosophical Hall, all of which played key roles in the establishment of our government. It was at this square the Declaration was first read in public on July 8, 1776. This event must have caused some second thoughts as the signators had earlier joked about losing their lives for their seditious actions. Independence Hall is the most historic building in America. It was here the Declaration was voted on and proclaimed. It was here Washington was chosen for and accepted command of the Continental Army. It was here the Constitution was adopted.

★ The visitor center, a striking modern building, has an AV featuring famous American actors portraying even more famous founding fathers. Utilizing touch-computers, you can pick and choose aspects of the constitution which have been challenged or amended and in the process receive abbreviated history lessons.

★ When visiting historic places, it always seems as though the symbols we have associated with events have been invented after the fact. The Liberty Bell, no longer ensconced in the Pennsylvania State House (Independence Hall), apparently wasn't rung to announce the Declaration of Independence. It was immortalized as having done so in 1847 by one George Lippard in his *Legends of the American Revolution*. It came by the name Liberty from a anti-slavery pamphlet in 1839, when it was used to symbolize the freedom of enslaved African Americans. Today, it rates its own pavilion.

Whiz Tips

❢ Philadelphia was to play so many roles in the founding of the country, it's hard to account for them within this one park. The city's leading citizen, Benjamin Franklin, was probably the country's most world renowned personage during his day. When the country began fomenting rebellion, Ben, at 70 years old, had already lived a full and noteworthy life.

By age 24 he owned his own printing business and newspaper. He did so well, he was able to retire at 44 and begin his long career as a statesman. He also had time to devote to his passion, electricity, where his work still ranks him as one of the great American researchers in pure science. One of only six signators of both the Declaration of Independence and the Constitution, it was said the task of drafting the Declaration wasn't given him because the delegates feared he would cleverly weave a joke into the middle of the document.

Franklin Court on Market St., the site of his home, contains an underground museum, an AV about the Franklins, a period printing exhibit and post office and an archaeological exhibit. In the rotunda of the Franklin Institute, the Benjamin Franklin National Memorial, an affiliated site, honors Philadelphia's leading citizen with a colossal statue.

Brigadier General Thaddeus Kosciuszko, a Polish emigre, used his engineering skills to fortify Saratoga, West Point and Ninety-Six. His expertise is credited for the victory at Saratoga, the fact that West Point was never attacked and the near capture of the fort at Ninety-Six. Kosciuszko returned to Poland and attempted to overthrow Russia's domination of his homeland. Today, he is considered a hero in both the United States and Poland. You can tour his Philadelphia home, the Thaddeus Kosciuszko National Memorial.

Kids' Stuff

★ The park is about the very stuff that made this country what it is today. Great men met, discussed, debated and ultimately compromised so the nation could move forward. The park is literally awash with school children in May and June every year. If at all possible, avoid Fridays in those months as big city schools inundate the city. And for good reason.

Access: Downtown Philadelphia. **Days/ Hours:** Daily 9-5 (summer late openings at some buildings) **Camping:** 30 mi. W, French Creek State Park (260 sites, elec., shwrs. & reservations). **Teacher's Package:** Available. **For info.:** Superintendent, 313 Walnut St., Philadelphia, PA 19106. 215/597-8974 (voice or TDD).

Johnstown Flood National Memorial

Allow: 1-2 hrs. *FREE*

It began just 13 miles north of Johnstown, where the visitor center now overlooks. The heavens opened and the rain came. Wealthy Pittsburgh industrialists had rebuilt old South Fork Dam to create a recreational

Johnstown Flood National Memorial

reservoir which stood 450 feet higher than Johnstown. They hadn't used the services of engineers and many in the area worried each spring whether it would be the dam's last. In 1889, their worries were realized in one of the worst "natural" disasters 19th century America witnessed.

Highlights

★ There's a parental warning on the door leading into the theater about the movie *Black Friday*. You think to yourself that the park service is playing it safe. Let us assure you, the park service is NOT playing it safe with either the sign or with this emotional rollercoaster production. This film is without doubt the BEST AV production the national parks have to offer.

★ The exhibit hall has a stunning wall montage and an equally arresting audio program featuring a 92-year-old vividly recounting his experience as a 16-year-old survivor.

Whiz Tips

The statistics are compelling: 12,209 people dead. 27,000 homeless. A wall of water 90 feet high swept down at 40 miles per hour carrying trees as though they were toothpicks. It left the town of Johnstown under a 30 foot lake, while the debris and people jammed against the stone bridge were consumed by a raging two-day fire. One looks for heroes and villains when disaster strikes. And in this case, some of both were to be found but not to be found guilty by the law. The irresponsible scions from Pittsburgh should have done more to ensure their "lake" was secured, but a judge and jury ruled the rains were too fierce to hold mere mortals accountable.

The people and their officials should have heeded the warnings, but there's a story about that too, called "the boy who cried wolf." John Parke, the club engineer, was caught in a moral quandary. He could alleviate the dam by allowing some

Steamtown National Historic Site

Courtesy NPS

flooding (and maybe some deaths) or hope the whole thing would hold. It didn't and a huge disaster occurred. History has recognized his conundrum. The heroes range from neighbor helping neighbor to the folks who flooded the drowned town with tons of goods. Clara Barton, the founder of the American Red Cross, proved her organization's worth by providing care for the traumatized flood victims (see Clara Barton NHS, MD).

Kids' Stuff

★ Speaking of conundrums, do you want your children to experience the tragedy that occurred near here so they can deepen their concern for humanity, or do you want to prevent the possible aftershock? The rangers told us kids don't seem to react as strongly as the adults do (our kids will look unaffected by the *Three Little Pigs* then have nightmares about the wolf).

★ Fortunately for families who chose to avoid the AV, the park has costumed interpretive programs relating the roles of many of the key players in the drama. The South Fork Fishing & Hunting Club members, the Pennsylvania Guardsmen and Clara Barton are some "figures" you might see. Plus there are guided walks of the dam and St. Michael's historic district.

Access: 10 mi. N of Johnstown on US 219 & PA 896. **Days/Hours:** Daily 8:30-5 (clsd. Dec.25 & Jan.1). **Camping:** E Blue Knob State Park (75 sites) & N Prince Gallitzin State Park (75 sites). **For info.:** Superintendent, Johnstown Flood National Memorial, P.O.Box 247, Cresson, PA 16630. 814/495-4643.

Pinelands National Reserve

Exceeding 1,000,000 acres of undeveloped land, the largest on the eastern seaboard, the reserve contains marshes, bogs, ponds and dwarfed pines. This affiliated site is managed by the three levels of government as well as private interests.

For info.: Pinelands National Reserve, c/o Mid-Atlantic Region National Park Service, 143 S Third St., Philadelphia, PA 19106.

Steamtown National Historic Site

Allow: 1-3 hrs. *FREE*

"The train, panting up past lonely farms,
Fed by the fireman's restless arms...
Past cotton grass and moorland boulder,
Shovelling white steam over her shoulder."
W.H.Auden

Downtown Scranton is fast becoming the hub of the national park's tribute to the days of steel and steam. The park site is an operating rail yard that has seen better days and hopes to see more. Loving hands reconstruct the structures which serviced the iron horses and many fine examples of these bygone beasts are on display.

Highlights

★ There are plenty of things to do here, from the film car where there are continual flicks on railroading to the short interpretive ride aboard a train. In addition, there are locomotives, passenger cars, a postal car and cabooses to explore. The park's piece de resistance is its 3-hr.-long, warm-weather excursion train ride.

Whiz Tips

❢ In *The Life I Really Lived*, Jessamyn West said it succinctly: "A big iron needle stitching the country together." The steam railroad was the catalyst for America's tremendous growth. Before the turn of the 1800s half-century, track had duplicated Lewis & Clark and spanned the continent. The parallel lines of steel replaced the famed Oregon and Santa

Fe Trails. Around the clock, goods flowed back and forth as the river of commerce filled the world's demands and America realized its potential. During the Civil War, trains revolutionized fighting as troops and supplies could be transported quickly. The Civil War's aftermath left displaced young men, who stole aboard these smoky power horses and the hobo was born. Like the railroads they ran, railroad magnates steamed full speed ahead with little regard for what was in their way. They brought about the end of the buffalo (the great herds clogged their path so they paid big game hunters, like Buffalo Bill Cody, to accelerate their extinction); they taxed the South and the West; they rough-shodded competing interests. Finally, they gave Teddy Roosevelt a cause, "trust-busting," and the *Sherman Act* was introduced. What really controlled them were the break-neck technological advances that outstripped their ability to compete.

Kids' Stuff

★ This is a great place for kids of all ages. They can pretend they're driving a locomotive, pump a hand-car, make a hobo sign, scramble through all kinds of rail cars and see the inside of a caboose. The old films have a kind of Charlie Chaplin air about them which greatly amuses the kids. Even the short ride on the train is a thrill.

Access: Downtown Scranton off I-81 take Exit 53. **Days/Hours:** Summer, daily 9-6, rides 10-4 & winter, daily 10-4. **Camping:** 10 mi. N, Lackawanna State Park (96 sites & shwrs.). **For info.:** Superintendent, Steamtown National Historic Site, 150 South Washington Ave., Scranton, PA 18503. 717/961-2033.

Valley Forge National Historical Park

Allow: 2-3 hrs. *Fee*

"To see men without clothes to cover their nakedness, without blankets to lay on, without shoes, by which their marches might be traced by the blood from their feet, and almost as often without provisions as with; marching through frost and snow, and at Christmas taking their winter quarters within a day's march of the enemy, without a house or hut to cover them till they could be built,

Valley Forge National Historical Park

Courtesy NPS

and submitting to it without a murmur, is a mark of patience and obedience which in my opinion can scarce be paralleled."

George Washington

Named for the iron forges that had utilized its ready supplies of wood, iron ore, limestone and running water, Valley Forge owes its fame more to the army's lack of preparedness than to the conditions it encountered. Washington would endure a colder, deeper winter at Morristown and lose far fewer men. In the winter of 1777-78, Valley Forge, a pretty Pennsylvania valley, witnessed the death of almost 2,000 soldiers as they fell not from bullets but from dysentery, typhoid, typhus and pneumonia.

Highlights

★ The town of Valley Forge is a pretty place. Quaint stone buildings mark Washington's quarters while the nearby soldiers' wood huts provide a glimpse of life in the ranks.

★ At the visitor center, a modernistic piece of architecture, you can see an introductory AV and a small museum.

Whiz Tips

During summer several interpretive programs are presented daily. At Washington's H.Q., you can take part in a guided walk detailing the encampment's conditions. From the visitor center you can hear why Valley Forge was chosen as a winter encampment.

Many historians count this encampment as the turning point in the American Revolution. By maintaining a standing army throughout the winter, even at so great a loss, Washington was able to establish a modicum of order. He utilized German General Von Steuben to forge his masses into the semblance of a fighting army and he succeeded.

Kids' Stuff

★ The 6 mile long recreational trail makes for a good family cycling place. If you didn't bring your two wheelers, you can rent.

★ During the summer there are costumed living historians at some of the stops.

Access: 20 mi. W from Philadelphia on PA Turnpike at Exit 24. **Days/Hours:** Daily 8:30-5. Self guiding drive, 6 a.m.-10 p.m. **Camping:** 25 mi. W, French Creek State Park (260 sites, elec., shwrs. & reservations). **Special Events:** Wknds., special interpretive programs; Dec.19, anniversary of the army's entry into Valley Forge; mid-Feb., Washington's birthday week; May 6, French Alliance Day; June 19th, encampment's coming out party. **Teacher's Package:** Available. **For info.:** Superintendent, Valley Forge National Historical Park, Box 953, Valley Forge, PA 19481. 215/783-1077.

PUERTO RICO

San Juan National Historic Site

Allow: 2-3 hrs. *Fee*

In 1898 the United States took over control of this island that for four centuries had been ruled by Spain. Shortly after Columbus sailed into the Caribbean claiming all he saw for Spain, the first settlement on Puerto Rico was built by Ponce de Leon. In the intervening years, the island was recognized as an integral part of the defenses needed to protect the shipping lanes for the Spanish galleons carrying riches gleaned from the New World. Generation after generation of fortification was added to Old San Juan. The park encompasses the oldest masonry fortifications in the United States: Castillo San Felipe del Morro, Castillo de San Cristobal, Fort San Juan de La Cruz (El Canuelo), as well as most of the city walls.

Highlights

★ Touring Castillo San Felipe del Morro is humbling. Purportedly the second largest Spanish fort built in the New World, its six levels rise 140 ft. above the sea with a complex system of tunnels running beneath. The bomb-proof buildings are connected by a series of ramps and stairways allowing visitors to tread where soldiers scampered to man the walls in defence of their city against English and Dutch brigands.

Whiz Tips

The rangers conduct guided tours of Castillo San Felipe del El Morro and Fort San Cristobal. There's an introductory AV and a museum featuring Spanish military architecture and history.

Puerto Rico was one of two vestiges of Spanish might at the close of the last century. The Spanish-American War was precipitated by expansionists in America epitomized by Theodore Roosevelt and local Cuban discontent with Spanish rule. The major fighting took place in Cuba with the final rewards being the annexation of Guam and Puerto Rico by the States and the freedom of the Philippines and Cuba from Spanish control.

Kids' Stuff

★ These massive fortifications prove great getaways for families visiting this sunny isle. Here's a great opportunity to expose your children to 16th and 17th century European history. Imperialistic nations were clashing over control of vast new lands. Pirates were legally sanctioned to war on people who spoke another language or attended a different church. A visit here is a great way to introduce your children to these times and to the rich Puerto Rican past.

Access: In Old San Juan. **Days/Hours:** Daily 8-6. **For info.:** Superintendent, San Juan National Historic Site, Fort San Cristobal, Norzagaray St., P.O.Box 712, Old San Juan, Puerto Rico 00902. 809/729-6536.

San Juan National Historic Site Courtesy NPS

RHODE ISLAND

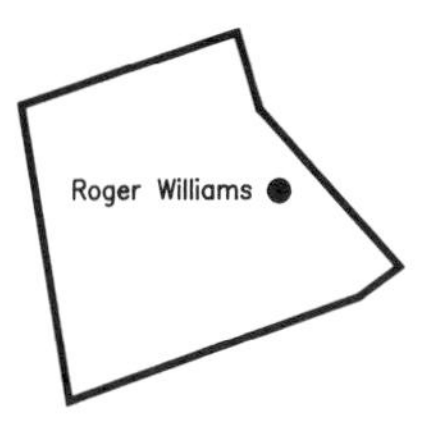

Roger Williams National Memorial

Allow: 1 hr. *FREE*

"The people of Rhode Island have it much in their hearts, if they may be permitted, to hold forth a lively experiment, that a flourishing and civil state may stand...with a full liberty in religious commitments."

John Clark, 1663 petitioning Charles II

It's no coincidence that the Touro Synagogue National Historic Site (affiliated) and Roger Williams National Memorial are within the same state. Roger Williams, the founder of Rhode Island Colony, was expelled from Massachusetts for his religious beliefs. This experience caused him to establish the nation's first pluralistic society. People from all faiths could practice their beliefs without fear. This right attracted those of the Jewish faith, who built the Touro Synagogue in Newport, their first North American place of worship.

Highlights

★ At the visitor center you learn about this little-known yet colorful figure of American history. Roger Williams was a fore-runner to the revolutionary leaders of the War for Independence.

Whiz Tips

Originally an Anglican minister, Williams converted to Puritanism. So strong were his ideals that upon his arrival in New England he quickly fell into conflict. Banished for objecting to the expropriation of Native rights and for insisting that magistrates had no power over an individual's conscience, he moved south of the Massachusetts border and started a community of "Seekers." His first act of ensuring religious freedom was to allow Quakers, whose beliefs he personally found blasphemous, to settle in his colony. Williams sought to establish a social order which regarded men as brothers irrespective of rank, caste or race, words that have never left this land since. Long-lived, he died in obscurity and was buried next to a spring which had an appropriate sign reading, "Liberty is reserved for the inhabitants to fetch water at this spring forever."

Kids' Stuff

★ Like the state itself, this early New World personage, while overlooked, established an early tone for the philosophies this country now prides itself on possessing. The ideals may have been written into the Declaration of Independence and the Constitution in the 18th century, but they were practiced here in the 17th.

Access: Downtown Providence at cnr. of Smith St. btwn. Canal & North Main St. **Days/Hours:** Summer, daily & winter, wknds. 9-5. **Camping:** E at Chepachet on SR 102 at US 44, George Washington State Area (72 sites) or W near Taunton, MA, Massasoit State Park (126 sites, elec. & shwrs.). **For info.:** Superintendent, Roger Williams National Memorial, P.O.Box 367, Annex Stn., Providence, RI 02901. 401/528-5385.

Touro Synagogue National Historic Site

Allow: .5 hrs. *FREE*

"These are the lawes that concerne all men...and otherwise than...what is herein forbidden, all men may walk as their consciences persuade them, everyone in the name of his God."

Rhode Island Code of Laws of 1647

The news of these laws reached the Sephardim, Jews of Spain and Portugal, who had suffered persecution for their beliefs. Around 1660, they came to the colony and established themselves in Newport, a bustling center of trade. Later, Jews from central and eastern Europe known as Ashkenazim came and melded with the original settlers establishing a large enough community to build a synagogue. With help from Jews in New York, Jamaica, Curacao, Surinam and London, they were able to complete their task by 1763. The synagogue has experienced much during its history. The most significant event was an 1790 letter sent to its congregation by George Washington which reaffirmed not only its right to worship but demonstrated Washington's vision of brotherly love and mutual respect. The classically designed small synagogue is an affiliated national park site. Visitors should note that the building sits diagonally on the property so the worshipers can face eastward toward Jerusalem.

Access: In downtown Newport. **Days/ Hours:** Su-F, summer 10-5; spring & fall 1-3 & Sun. only, winter 1-3. **Camping:** Fort Getty Camping & Recreation Area near Jamestown (32 sites, shwrs. & elec.) & Melville Ponds Campground near Portsmouth (123 sites, shwrs. & elec.). **Special Events:** Aug.'s 3rd Sun., Anniversary of George Washington's letter. **For info.:** Touro Synagogue, 85 Touro St., Newport, RI 02840. 401/847-4794.

Touro Synagogue National Historic Site Courtesy Touro Synagogue

SOUTH CAROLINA

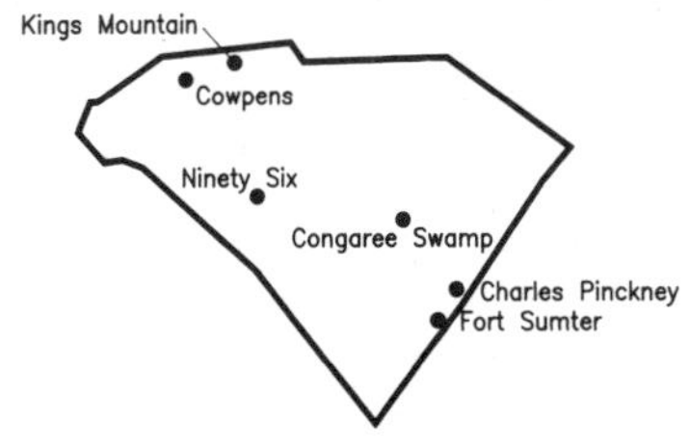

Congaree Swamp National Monument

Allow: 2 hrs. *FREE*

"One by one, the swamp forests fell to the broad axe and cross-cut saw...now, there is only the Congaree Swamp in South Carolina to remind us..."

Gary Soucie
Audubon Magazine, July '75

Man's seemingly insatiable need to convert land, any land, into something he could use led to the leveling and filling in of most of the swamp land in the South. Congaree Swamp was declared a national monument in order to save the last significant stand of bottomland hardwood forest in the southeast. Opossums, raccoons, deer and river otters are among the common mammals that call this place home.

Highlights

★ An eerie yet safe adventure can be had by taking the wheel-chair access boardwalk. What's so adventurous about a boardwalk? You'll see when you're out in the middle of the swamp listening to the sudden rustling noises that come from beneath your feet, then off to the side and more worrisome yet, from behind you. What lives out here?

Whiz Tips

Every Saturday at 1:30, the park puts on a 2 hour guided walk that covers about 1.5 mi. of the swamp. On the trek you'll learn how to identify hardwood trees and distinguish

Congaree Swamp National Monument

them from the loblolly pines, cypress and tupelo trees. When we asked the ranger what we could expect to find here, she said "Big trees!" She was right, but be careful not to miss this forest for the trees. The undergrowth has a charm of its own.

Kids' Stuff

★ There are over 20 miles of hiking trails, two boardwalks, canoeing and fishing. The boardwalk trail is a great family outing.

Access: 20 mi. SE of Columbia off SC 48. **Days/Hours:** Daily 8:30-5 (clsd. Dec.25). **Camping:** Park has primitive camping. **For info.:** Superintendent, Congaree Swamp National Monument, 200 Caroline Sims Rd., Hopkins, SC 29061. 803/776-4396.

Cowpens National Battlefield

Allow: 1-2 hrs. *Fee*

Not the most romantically named battlefield, in 1781 it proved by design or accident to be one of the shinier victories for the Patriots. Daniel Morgan and his country sharpshooters were in full retreat. The British leader, 26 year old Tarleton, had an elite group of dragoons and accompanying infantry in full chase. Unfortunately for Tarleton, his adversary had badger-like tendencies and took a dim view of being cornered. Choosing ground just south of North Carolina and suitable for blunting British fighting strategies, Morgan dug in.

Highlights

★ As you walk, cycle or drive the battlefield, you can see that Morgan designed his defenses to get the most out of his men. He recognized their strengths and more importantly their weaknesses. He put his least dependable forces, the Carolinian and Georgia militia in the second line of defence and asked of them no more than they could give. His vaunted sharpshooters were in the first line to blunt the initial charge, and his crack northern militia were the final line to allow the sharpshooters time to recover and assist. The effects were devastating, as the British infantry were routed before the dreaded dragoons could come into play. The final stats? The Brits lost 110, with

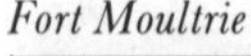
Fort Moultrie

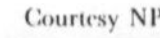
Courtesy NPS

200 wounded and another 500 captured. The Yanks? A mere 12 lost and 60 wounded.

Whiz Tips

- The park's 22 min. AV production and its fibre-optic map are excellent introductions to your 1.3 mi. walking tour or 3.8 mi. driving tour of the battlefield.

- In the fall of 1780 and the spring of 1781, General Cornwallis' troops either suffered morale-shattering losses or pyrrhic victories which depleted their existing ranks and provided little motivation for loyalists to join up. Other national parks recounting Cornwallis' folly are: Colonial NHP, VA; Guilford Courthouse NMP, NC; Moores Creek NB, NC; Kings Mountain NMP, SC & Ninety Six NHS, SC.

Kids' Stuff

★ Cowpens is a good park to explore with children. Unlike many other battlefields, it is self-contained, so cycling or hiking pose little risk.

Access: 11 mi. W of Gaffney & I-85 or 2 mi. E of Chesnee & US 221. **Days/Hours:** Daily 9-5. **Camping:** W, Croft State Park (50 sites, elec. & shwrs.). **Teacher's Package:** Available. **For info.:** Superintendent, Cowpens National Battlefield, P.O.Box 308. Chesnee, SC 29323. 803/461-2828.

Fort Sumter National Monument

Allow: .5 days *FREE (ferry ride fee)*

"In your hands, my dissatisfied fellow countrymen, and not in mine, is the momentous issue of civil war."

Abraham Lincoln, Inaugural Address, 1861

Fort Sumter has become the symbol for this "momentous issue." It was here the South fired its first shots in anger at Federal troops which had remained fortressed on the island after South Carolina had voted to secede from the Union. This lonely island, way out in Charleston harbor, hardly looks like such an important player in this heart-rending American drama. The park also maintains Fort Moultrie.

Fort Sumter National Monument Courtesy NPS

Highlights

★ The main access to Fort Sumter is by tour boat which crosses the Charleston Harbor (private boats can visit FREE). Once on shore, visitors are given a short briefing by the rangers.

★ Fort Moultrie which played a major historical role, has a modern visitor center, a very interesting introductory AV and a really intricate fortification you can explore.

Whiz Tips

Fort Sumter was in use up until the late 1940s. Its most stalwart defence wasn't the two days of shelling Major Anderson, Captain Abner Doubleday (regarded as the father of baseball-a popular misconception) and the Federal troops experienced during the fateful April of 1861. It was the 17 months of shelling the Confederate troops underwent during the war itself. By the end of the siege, the fort, reduced to sand and smashed brick, was better able to withstand the shelling by rifled cannon than when it had the original masonry walls.

At Fort Moultrie you can learn a great deal about American coastal defence systems. First constructed during the Revolutionary War, Moultrie has experienced every phase of fort modification up to and through World War II. Originally the fort was constructed from available materials, palmetto logs, which turned out to be a blessing in disguise. Although the wood in the immediate area wasn't prized as a building material, its soft rubber-like mass proved invaluable for absorbing cannon fire during the British assault of 1776. The present fort, built in 1809, was the third effort.

Kids' Stuff

★ Kids can see some of the largest muzzle-loading cannon in the world and a scale model of the fort.

★ Children find the ferry ride across Charleston Harbor and scouting around the forts exciting. At Fort Sumter, tell your kids to look out toward the Atlantic for dolphins and pelicans.

Access: Fort Sumter by private or tour boats at 17 Lockwood Dr., Charleston or Patriots Point Naval Museum, Mt. Pleasant; Fort Moultrie on 1214 Middle St. on Sullivan's Island. **Days/Hours:** Daily, Fort Sumter varied hrs. & Fort Moultrie summer 9-6 & winter 9-5 (clsd. Dec.25). **Camping:** James Island County Park (795-7275). **For info.:** Superintendent, Fort Sumter National Monument, 1214 Middle St., Sullivan's Island, SC 29482. 803/883-3123.

Historic Camden

In the 1730s a colonial village known as Fredricksburg Township was started here. By 1768 it was renamed Camden in honor of Lord Camden, a champion of Colonial rights. This affiliated site was one of a few places to witness 2 Revolutionary War battles (Aug. 16, 1780 & Apr. 25, 1781).

For info.: Camden District Heritage Foundation, Camden Historical Commission, Box 710, Camden, SC 29020.

Kings Mountain National Military Park

Allow: 1-2 hrs. *Fee*

One of the biggest misconceptions about the American Revolution is that the rebels used guerrilla-like tactics. Hiding behind bushes and trees they would pick off brightly colored puppet-marching British redcoats. Although this was one of the few battles where American warriors would employ these guerrilla techniques, it wasn't against the British redcoats; it was against their fellow Americans who remained loyal to Britain. The loyalist troops fatally adopted their British mentors practices and tried to charge a hidden force through dense underbrush while brandishing bayonets. Sheer folly! Their captors displayed none of the courtesies European armies provided. They continued to fire on a white flag. Several days later, they hung nine of their prisoners for treason. Whether the rebels' harsh tactics or the loss caused the ensuing slide in loyalist support, we'll never know.

Highlights

★ As you walk around the hill (mountain?), you begin to see why the outcome was inevitable. Yes, the Tories had the benefit of the high ground, but the heavily wooded knoll provides ample protection for advancing troops. The rebel forces were made up of men who were more comfortable nestling down against a tree than sitting in a porch rocker. They came from the back hills of the Carolinas and Virginia. They came angry after having their families and farms threatened. Many came from French, Scottish, Irish and Welsh stock which had been pressed under the heel of the English for centuries. Mostly, this loosely organized band of 1,000 strong came for blood.

Whiz Tips

After failing to attract sufficient local support in the northern colonies, the British turned to their loyal southern citizenry to put down the rebellion. The British encountered little difficulty in Georgia and South Carolina. They led their colonial legions into the interior and northward. However, a series of battles like Kings Mountain gradually decimated their Tory support and diminished their own ranks to the point where they were forced to surrender at Yorktown (see Colonial NHP, VA).

Kids' Stuff

★ Touring the site is a pleasant nature outing, but children who have studied the War for Independence will be more appreciative of the historical aspects.

Access: 10 mi. from Kings Mountain, NC on SC 216 or 15 mi. SW of Gastonia, NC & NE of Gaffney, SC. **Days/Hours:** Daily 9-5 (clsd. Thanksgiving, Dec.25 & Jan.1). **Camping:** Adjacent Kings Mountain State Park (118 site, shwrs. & laundry). **For info.:** Superintendent, Kings Mountain National Military Park, P.O.Box 40, Kings Mountain, NC, 28086. 803/936-7921.

Kings Mountain National Military Park

Courtesy NPS

Ninety Six National Historic Site

Allow: 1-2 hrs. *FREE*

By the time the War for Independence had begun, Ninety Six was a thriving village. However, as in much of the South, there were competing loyalties. The first significant infantry battle in the South took place here. 1,800 Tories attacked roughly 500 patriots and were held to a stand-still. By 1781, the loyalists had gained control of the area and constructed a star fort. This time the patriot army had the man advantage which proved no more beneficial than in the first encounter. With news that the British were sending reinforcements to aid the 500 Tories they had penned up in the fort, General Greene saw the merit in living to fight another day. The fact that Greene was able to apply so much pressure to the fort made the British realize holding it was untenable. They abandoned the site to withdraw closer to the coast.

Highlights

★ The remnants of the British fortification can still be seen. You can see how Thaddeus Kosciuszko (see Independence NHP, PA), who engineered many American fortifications, designed the siege lines. There is a reproduced siege tower (1/3 scale) that allowed Patriot sharpshooters to pinion the loyalist troops while trying to tunnel under the Tory walls and blow them up.

Whiz Tips

British minions waltzed back and forth across South Carolina with various patriot forces. Winning most encounters, the British forces slowly recognized the resistance to their presence was substantial. Ninety Six was but one of several encounters which demonstrated that, without a greater commitment from Britain, the end result was inevitable.

The tiny village has two legends of romantic rescue. Twice ladies risked their lives to bring their "man" news that would ultimately save them. The first lady was Cateechee, a Cherokee maid, who rode the 96 miles from Keowee to warn her En-

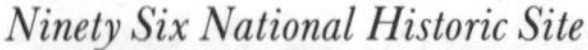

Ninety Six National Historic Site

glish trader lover of her tribe's attack. The town was saved and the lovers married to live happily ever after. The second lady played a role in the siege the park interprets. Kate Fowler got word to the besieged Loyalists that help was on the way, thus fortifying their courage and determination.

Kids' Stuff

★There's a furnished log cabin (circa 1880) which replicates life in the 1700s. Rangers will use the cabin to interpret frontier life for visitors (especially children) and open it upon request.

★ Kids like the short walk through the battle area. Although only the remnants of the structures remain, the nature of the siege can be easily pictured. The fact that much of the war took place between two groups of people who shared the country is an important one for children. It recognizes that strong differences of opinions have often existed between Americans.

Access: 2 mi. S of Ninety Six off US 248. **Days/Hours:** Daily 8-5 (clsd. Dec.25 & Jan.1). **Camping:** Greenwood State Park, 10 mi. away (125 sites elec. & showers). **Special Events:** April, Historical Heritage Festival; October, Autumn Candlelight Tout. **Teacher's Package:** Available. **For info.:** Superintendent, Ninety Six National Historic Site, Hwy.248, Ninety Six, SC 29666. 803/543-4068.

Overmountain Victory National Historic Trail

The trail follows the 272-mile path taken by revolutionary patriots who gathered from the hills of Virginia, Tennessee and North Carolina to Kings Mountain where they defeated a sizable force of British Loyalists (see Kings Mountain NMP, SC).

For info.: Overmountain Victory National Historic Trail, Southeast Region, National Park Service, 75 Spring St., SW, Atlanta, GA 30303.

SOUTH DAKOTA

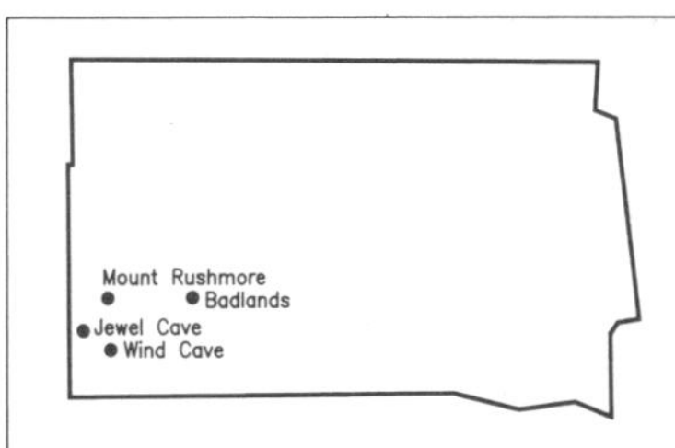

Badlands National Park

Allow: .5 days *Fee*

"I was not prepared for the Badlands. They deserve this name. They are like the work of evil child."

John Steinbeck
Travels with Charley

Southeast of Wall, about one and a half hours east of Rapid City is a national park preserving a section of one of the continent's more unusual geologic formations, a raw display of multi-hued hills. Badlands generally occur in semiarid climates where torrential rain is followed by extended periods of drought. South Dakota's Badlands are layers of alluvial and volcanic ash deposited some 35 million years ago. The great sheets of rain have gradually worn away the plain creating a depression full of spires and mounds of unusually tinted colors. The change from prairie grassland to this depression is so dramatic it can even catch a rider on horseback unprepared. Suddenly the prairie gives way to a hundred foot drop-off into a moon-scape. As you stand on the prairie plateau looking down, you feel no urge to trek across it without ample support.

Highlights

★ Entering the park from the monotonous prairie and discovering the barren but striking display of erosion is at once a shock and a pleasure.

★ Driving through the park at sunset affords colors more beautiful than those seen in the full daylight. An added bonus to dusk or dawn drives is the abundance of pronghorn antelope feeding on the open fields. Not truly an antelope, the pronghorn antelope is unique to North America. Reaching speeds of 60 miles an hour, they rely on their quickness to evade carnivores. Pronghorns can survive long periods of drought by relying solely on the plants' moisture for sustenance. Their adaptability and protection from wanton hunting has allowed them to grow from 15,000, in 1910, to 500,000. You might also to see some of the park's coyotes, deer or recently reintroduced bison and big horn sheep.

Whiz Tips

❢ The park offers a comprehensive interpretive program each summer. There are 3 hour hikes, nature walks, sessions along the Fossil Exhibit Trail and evening presentations daily (if good weather Night Prowl or Night Sky viewing programs).

❢ There's a creative presentation of fossils "au naturale" at the Fossil Exhibit Trail. The Badlands surface is easily eroded and "new" fossils can be found after almost every rainfall. The Badlands was home to ancient ancestors of land turtles, horses, tapirs, camels, deer and rhinoceroses. Other inhabitants like the saber-toothed cats and a giant wolf-like "hyaenodon" preyed on these prehistoric plant eaters.

Kids' Stuff

★ The nature walk and Fossil Exhibit Trail are naturals for families. The walk is relatively short and easily handled by children in this area of extreme temperatures. The visitor center's touch-room caters to children's tactile needs. The park also has a Jr. Ranger program.

Access: 8 mi. S of I-90 & Wall. **Days/Hours:** Cedar Pass Visitor Center, daily, summer 7-8 & winter 8-4:30 (clsd. Thanksgiving, Dec.25 & Jan.1); White River Visitor Center; summer only 9-5. **Camping:** Park's Cedar Pass Campground (110 sites) & FREE primitive sites. **Teacher's Package:** Available. **For info.:** Superintendent, Badlands National Park, P.O.Box 6, Interior, SD 57750. 605/433-5361.

Jewel Cave National Monument

Allow: 2-3 hrs. *Fee*

Southwest of Rapid City is the second largest (over 82 mi.) cave in the country and fourth largest in the world and they are still discovering more passages. Surprisingly, it was not this fact that caused Jewel Cave to be made a National Monument. Indeed, it was almost half a century later that its immense size was discovered. Initially, what was thought to be a small cave was of national interest because of its jewel-like crystal formations.

Highlights

★ The peak season-only guided tours of the cave describe this cave and how it compares with others. You are introduced to the indomitable duo, Herb and Jan Conn, who discovered the extent of this underworld. After 20 years the Conns "retired" from their engrossing pastime of mapping this underground labyrinth. It was only recently that a whole new section has been discovered by someone other than the Conns. Herb Conn's legacy lives on in the cave's lighting system. He recognized lighting was necessary to allow more people to enjoy the cave but he also realized it could be a distraction. His efforts result in a dramatically lit cave formations with little evidence of wires and light bulbs, something you appreciate more when you visit other caves.

Whiz Tips

The crystal glazed walls aren't the only calcite formations at Jewel Cave. Over the millennia, millions of drops of water have deposited minute mineral calcite forming draperies, stalactites, soda straw stalactites, stalagmites and columns. You may be fortunate enough to see some rare finds like hydromagnesite balloons, moonmilk, helictites, popcorn, frostwork, boxwork and scintillites.

Jewel Cave has a very small visitor center. If you want an introduction to caves before beginning your trip, we would strongly suggest you visit Wind Cave National Park (45 minutes SE).

The temperature in the cave is 47 degrees F., so dress accordingly. Plus the cave trail can be slick so rubber-soled shoes are a good idea.

Kids' Stuff

Hey, this is a real cave. Need we say more. Our kids loved every cave tour they went on.

Access: 13 mi. W of Custer on US 16. **Days /Hours:** Daily, summer 8-7:30 & winter 9-4. (clsd. Thanksgiving, Dec.25 & Jan.1). **Camping:** Black Hills National Forest 7 mi. E.; 20 mi. E Custer State Park (295 sites & shwrs.); Wind Cave N.P. 35 mi. SE (100 sites). **For info.:** Jewel Cave National Monument, Rte. 1, Box 60AA, Custer, SD 57730. 604/673-2288.

Mount Rushmore National Memorial

Allow: 2-3 hrs. *FREE*

"Carved upon the mighty mountain,
The heroes' faces, pale
In the misty moonlight."
Emiko Takase Matsumoto,
Kugenuma

Mount Rushmore National Memorial COURTESY NPSc

South of Rapid City is the area's big draw: Mount Rushmore. Carved with dynamite from the mountain face are the visages of four prominent American presidents: George Washington, Thomas Jefferson, Abraham Lincoln and Theodore Roosevelt. It's hard to fathom given our current environmental sensitivities, how somebody could have received public monies to create such sculpture. And yet it beckons. Jefferson isn't the dominant figure he once was and isn't that the wrong Roosevelt up there (to be fair to the sculptor, he began work in 1927, well before F.D.R. became president). Nevertheless, Washington and Lincoln are truly pillars of American history (most would argue the same for the other two).

Highlights

★ Seeing the faces lit by lights in the dark of night is the best way to experience the enormity of Gutzon Borglum's feat.

★ Visiting the sculpture's studio (open May-Sept. 9-5) with a ranger provides more insight into the accomplishment. Borglum was Idaho born and bred. He converted from painting to sculpting while studying in France.

Whiz Tips

This monument acts as a good refresher regarding the four Presidents and their contributions. In 1962, American historians ranked the country's presidents. Lincoln was first, Washington second, Jefferson fifth and T.R. seventh (Franklin was third). Each of these great leaders has one or more national parks dedicated to explaining some component of his lives.

The construction of the monument is a remarkable feat and a tribute to explosive experts and hard-rock miners. Gutzon Borglum realized the sculptures would have to be planned like the excavation of a mine. Each part of the rock to be chipped off had to be measured and the right size hole drilled for the correct amount of explosive. For visitors unfamiliar with the size and scope of the task, one thing certainly becomes clear it was a monumental piece of work.

The faces are only lit for a short time each night (1 hr. in summer & .5 hr. in winter), so plan accordingly. When we visited, a lot of people arrived late, missing the spectacle.

The park suggests the sculpture is best viewed (filmed) in the morning light as the southeastern exposure eliminates shadows then.

If the voice narrating the video introduction seems familiar, it should be. The narrator is Tom Brokaw, N.B.C. television's anchor man for its national news program and a native South Dakotan.

Kids' Stuff

★ The summer sculpture studio programs are oriented to families. Kids, like all of us, are awed by the size and scope of this undertaking.

Access: 3 mi. W of Keystone on SD 244 & 25 mi. S of Rapid City on US 16. **Days/Hours:** Visitor center daily, summer 8-10, winter 8-5. Monument can viewed at any time. **Camping:** Nearby Custer State Park (310 sites & shwrs.); several national forest campgrounds. **For info.:** Superintendent, Mount Rushmore National Memorial, P.O.Box 268, Keystone, SD 57751. 605/574-2523

Wind Cave National Park

Allow: 2-3 hrs. *Fee*

To the south of Rapid City is Wind Cave National Park and its 37 plus miles of tunnels beneath the rolling prairie. Renowned for its unusual formations, it has "boxwork," "popcorn," "frostwork" and "helictite bushes." "Boxwork," the formation the cave is most noted for, is a pattern of thin fins of calcite on ceilings or walls which intersect and bisect each other much like a honey-comb. "Popcorn" is small nodules of white calcite which seem to grow on one another much like coral. "Frost-work" is sheer curtains of white calcite formations which look like spider's webs. "Helictite bushes" are calcite formations which twist and tangle as they defy gravity in their delicate growth.

Highlights

★ The cave tour explains the various formations and the cave's history. In every cave we visited, we were always surprised by the size of caverns. Not that we had a specific idea of how big a cave should be; it's just that when you can't see into corners or know what to expect around the bend, you can't help feeling amazed at how extensive it is.

★ Perhaps because it's a national park and not just a monument, this park has much better exhibits explaining caves. There are fun "hands-on" quizzes introducing notable world caves and other national park caves.

★ The park also features a wide range of wildlife, from roaming bison (buffalo) to bugling elk. Together with its adjacent neighbor, Custer State Park, it forms one of the largest game reserves in North America.

Wind Cave National Park

COURTESY NPS

Whiz Tips

Aside from its tours, the park offers other interpretive programs. For example, fall visitors can learn about elk, including a trip to hear their bugling.

Wind Cave has the most extensive display of "boxwork" in the world. Like most caves with formations, Wind Cave was created by water dissolving the limestone to form halls and chambers. No one seems to know why Wind Cave has the proliferation of "boxwork" it does. Indeed, the surprising thing about Wind Cave is its paucity of more common large calcite deposits like stalagmites and stalactites.

The temperature in the cave is always about 53 degrees, cool in the summer and warm in the winter, so dress accordingly.

The "wind" of Wind Cave comes from the cave's "inhalation" or "exhalation" due to differences between its atmospheric pressure and the surface's. Depending on the changes in the surface's pressure the "wind" will either be blowing in or out of the cave at velocities of up to 50 miles/hour.

Kids' Stuff

★ This is a real cave. Most children enjoy the feeling of being underground and find it exhilarating when the lights go out. Every cave reeks with adventure. Big and little seem full of anticipation as they explore a cave for the first time. Don't wander from the tour! You don't want to end up being a lost and wandering tourist.

★ The freely-ranging wildlife competes with Yellowstone's offerings. Buffalo, deer, and prairie dogs can be seen fairly easily. Coyotes, eagles and elk are more hit and miss.

Access: 11 mi. S from Hot Springs on US 385. **Days/Hours:** Cave tours daily, (winter tours generally limited to the same FREE visits given mobility impaired visitors) (clsd. Thanksgiving, Dec.25 & Jan.1). **Camping:** Park's Elk Mountain Campground (100 sites). Nearby Custer State Park, several campgrounds (295 sites & shwrs.). **For info.:** Superintendent, Wind Cave National Park, Hot Springs, SD 57747. 605/745-4600.

TENNESSEE

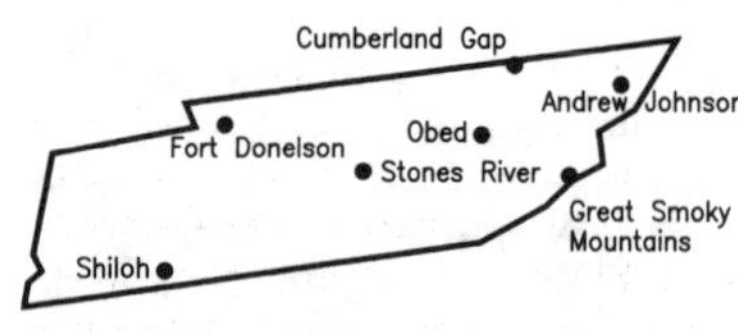

Andrew Johnson National Historic Site

Allow: 2-3 hrs. *Fee*

"I love the Constitution and swear that it and the Union shall be saved as 'Old Hickory' Jackson did in 1832, Senators, my blood, my existence, I would give to save this Union."

Andrew Johnson

In East Tennessee, folks were generally in favor of staying with the Union. Few of them had slaves. So it really shouldn't be too surprising to learn that Johnson was the only Southern Senator to remain loyal to the Union. His loyalty earned him the Military Governorship of Tennessee during the Civil War's early years and Lincoln's choice as his running mate in 1864. Johnson rose to the penultimate post upon Lincoln's assassination. His term was marked by a political divisiveness every bit as fierce as the Civil War.

Highlights

★ The park oversees three of Johnson's properties. Inside the visitor center is the rough-hewn tailor shop he first owned in Greeneville, TN. Across the lane is one of his finished homes and within a couple of blocks is his final well-furnished house.

Whiz Tips

Johnson ran away from home at age 15. Penniless, he chose to become a tailor and through tireless effort accumulated enough wealth that he had 8 slaves, several properties and a number of industrial holdings. For all this material wealth, he was a man who wanted to have a say in government. He is regarded as one of four presidents who truly rose from poverty to the nation's highest office.

"In Egypt, the Lord sent frogs, locusts...He has sent us worse than lice, and has afflicted us with Andrew Johnson." So said Thaddeus Stevens, a leader of the so-called Radical Republicans who attempted the only presidential impeachment in the country's history. Johnson faced what many believe to be the most difficult period in American history, the period of healing the wound along the Mason-Dixon Line. A stubborn man, Johnson was unable to achieve compromise with his governing bodies. The southern states were passing "Black Codes" which were slavery in another form. For example, one code made it an offense for a freedman to leave his employment. To counteract these unfair laws, Congress passed the Freedmen's Bureau. Johnson vetoed the legislation and for the first time in the nation's young history, Congress overruled a presidential veto. This was to happen twice more with the *Tenure of Office Act* and the *Civil Rights Act*. Historians believe his stand in dismissing his Secretary of War was within the purvey of the *Tenure of Office Act* even though his contemporaries tried to impeach him for it. They also believe the failure to impeach Johnson was important in maintaining the differing roles between the legislative bodies and the executive. An interesting side-note is that in 1875 he was once again elected to the Senate. In a 1983 historians' poll, Johnson was ranked 32nd of 36 presidents in terms of effectiveness.

Kids' Stuff

★ The park has a Jr. Ranger program in place. Interested 7-12 year olds must attend both ranger-led orientations, take the self-guiding tour, visit each site within the park, collect a full bag of litter, complete the work booklet and answer the ranger's oral test to qualify for a Jr. Ranger Badge.

Access: Downtown Greeneville. **Days/Hours:** Daily 9-5 (clsd. Dec.25). **Camping:** 9 mi. E, Horse Creek National Forest Campground (10 sites), 12 mi. S, Paint Creek National Forest Campgrounds (21 sites) & Davy Crockett Birthplace State Park 73 sites, elec. & shwrs.) 25 mi. E. **Teacher's Package:** Available. **For info.:** Superintendent, Andrew Johnson National Historic Site, Depot St., Greeneville, TN 37743. 615/638-3551.

Big South Fork National River & Recreation Area

Allow: 2-3 days *FREE*

Truly a park in transition, Big South is co-managed by the park service and the U.S. Army Corps of Engineers. This portion of the Cumberland Plateau bridging East Kentucky and East Tennessee was devastated by misuse. Played-out coal mines and denuded forests had left the land barren and even unsafe for human habitation. The two government agencies were charged with reclaiming it for recreational use which would in turn inject money into the local economy. Today, the streams are prime waters for kayakers and canoeists, and the surrounding hills make for good hiking.

Andrew Johnson National Historic Site

Highlights

★ While experienced boaters check the water levels before embarking here to test their skills, the rivers usually offer some opportunity to wet a paddle. The landscape you float past is slowly recovering to the greenery that greeted Daniel Boone.

★ Yahoo Falls, Devils Jump and East Rim are scenic overlooks easily reached by passenger vehicles.

Whiz Tips

The army engineers are responsible for planning and development of the river basin reclamation. After they complete their task, they will turn the area over to the park service for public use. The Kentucky section of the park is administered by the Daniel Boone National Forest.

Kids' Stuff

★ While much of the region is accessible only by water or four-wheel-drive, families can find access points to swim, fish and even waters safe for boating.

Access: 12 mi. W of Oneida or 12 E of US 154 off TN 297. **Days/Hours:** Daily. **Camping:** Park has 3 campgrounds: Alum Ford-KY, Blue Heron-KY (showers) and Bandy Creek-TN (elec. & showers); nearby Pickett State Rustic Park-TN (32 sites, elec. & showers). **For info.:** Superintendent, Big South Fork National River & Recreation Area, P.O.Drawer 630, Oneida, TN 37841. 615/879-4890.

Fort Donelson National Battlefield

Allow: 2 hrs. *FREE*

"No terms except unconditional and immediate surrender can be accepted. I propose to move immediately on your works."

General Ulysses S. Grant

With these words, Grant set his mark upon the nation. Perhaps it was fate that he led the first major victory for the Union. His reputation as an uncompromising warrior would be earned again and again throughout the remainder of the Civil War. At Fort Donelson visitors can drive, walk or bike through the battlefield, reading the interpretive signs describing the fighting that took place. Here was the fort, over

Great Smoky Mountains National Park

there the Rebel earthworks and here's where the Confederates beat back the mighty gunboats which had battered Fort Henry into submission.

Highlights

★ The Dover Hotel, the only original building in which a surrender of a major battle took place, still stands for viewing.

Whiz Tips

❢ In a surprising maneuver Grant had marshalled 27,000 Federal troops around the fortifications and had been fortunate enough to rebuff a Rebel counter-attack and recover the lost territory. His quick action forced the Confederates to reconsider their position and cut their losses. Although 13,000 men surrendered, another 2,000 escaped during the night. The Northern victories at Forts Henry and Donelson forced the south to abandon Kentucky and most of Tennessee, thus opening the way south to the Mississippi River.

Kids' Stuff

★ Probably the best way to enjoy the park is to do it on foot or by bike. The tour route is relatively short, allowing you to get a better feeling of the lay of the land. This is a great way to introduce your children to the particulars of this battle and its context within the Civil War.

Access: 1 mi. W of Dover. **Days/Hours:** Daily, 8-4:30, summer extended hrs. (clsd. Dec.25). **Camping:** 3 mi. W Land Between the Lakes National Recreation Area's Piney Campground (382 sites, elec. & shwrs.) & Paris Landing State Park (61 sites, elec. & shwrs.). **For info.:** Superintendent, Fort Donelson National Battlefield, P.O.Box 434, Dover, TN 37058. 615/232-5706.

Great Smoky Mountains National Park

Allow: 2 days *Fee*

"There are trees here that stood before our forefathers came to this continent; there are brooks that still run as clear as on the day the first pioneer cupped his hand and drank from them."

Franklin D. Roosevelt, dedicating Great Smoky Mountains National Park

While the park is famous for its natural pleasures, it recognizes its function in preserving history as well. The evidence of the early settlers is featured at the park. Their homes, farms and churches are lovingly kept, allowing visitors to view and capture on film this period of Americana. Great Smoky Mountains National Park is the most visited park in the country, with over 8,000,000 people passing through yearly.

Highlights

★ Rolling wooded mountains are covered with smoky haze like a bride's veil, slightly revealing and full of promise. Any road, path or viewpoint in the park can provide you with a variance of this image. The highest such viewpoint is Clingman's Dome observatory tower. An unencumbered view from there (go early on a good day before the clouds roll in) offers a panoramic perspective on why this place is designated a World Heritage Site.

★ At the western end of the preserve is one of the park's more popular attractions, Cades Cove. Named for its early settlement, you can see some of the pioneer buildings and a wealth of wildlife (deer and bear were our rewards) here. Many visitors take to walking or cycling Cades Cove rather than joining the snail's pace line-up of cars during peak visitor seasons on the one-way back-country road.

★ 900 miles of hiking trails take the hardier back into the new growth eastern forests. Some animals these intrepid trekkers might encounter include black bears, deer, raccoons, weasels, bobcats, coyotes, skunks and the recently introduced river otters and peregrine falcons. The red wolf may soon join this group as efforts are being made to reintroduce it to its native habitat.

Whiz Tips

The park newspaper outlines the wealth of ranger-led programs. A brief glance shows the visitor that the campfire programs, nature walks and orientation meetings are in place. In addition, the park has storytellings, crafts and pioneer food preparation demonstrations, as well as history walks and talks about the mountain folk.

The Great Smoky Mountains were made into a national park to preserve a section of one of the oldest mountain ranges in the world. However, it wasn't environmentalists or outdoors men who spearheaded the drive for a park; rather it was auto club members who wanted access to the beautiful countryside.

Kids' Stuff

★ To become an official Great Smoky Mountains National Park Ranger, kids from 8-12 can pick up a Jr. Ranger booklet and complete the activities described including attending ranger talks or walks, taking a self-guiding nature trail, visiting an historic area, collecting a bag of litter and answering questions on what they've learned. Plus the park has fishing, hiking and cycling opportunities.

Access: 2 mi. S of Gatlinburg, TN or 2 mi. N of Cherokee, NC. on US 441. **Days/ Hours:** Daily (clsd. Dec.25). **Camping:** Park has 10 campgrounds (over 1,000 sites), 3 (Ticketron-reservations); Blue Ridge Parkway's Mt. Pisgah Campground, about 50 miles N (137 sites). **Teacher's Package:** Available. **For info.:** Superintendent, Great Smoky Mountains National Park, Gatlinburg, TN 37738. 615/436-1200.

Great Smoky Mountains National Park

Obed Wild & Scenic River

Allow: 2 Days *FREE*

As befits a wild area, there is little development. Located in central East Tennessee, visitors will find their activities dictated by the water conditions. Portions of four waterways comprise the park: the Obed River, Daddy's Creek, Clear Creek and Emory River.

Highlights

★ Although fishing, swimming, picnicking and hiking can be enjoyed here, floating the streams is the main event. The Obed in particular is classified as a whitewater river and delivers on that promise when the weather complies. Cut into the Cumberland Plateau sandstone, the waters flow through gorges as high as 500 ft. providing spectacular scenery as well as thrills.

Whiz Tips

To demonstrate how fickle these waters can be, canoeists enjoyed outstanding runs in 1989, while there were only a few days after May, '90 when they could wet their paddles.

The Wartburg Visitor Center has an introductory AV showing the region's moods.

Kids' Stuff

★ There are swimming, fishing, hiking and even non-whitewater boating activities for families. Obviously in a park designated as "wild," care should be taken.

Access: In Wartburg, TN via US 27 or TN 62. **Days/Hours:** Visitor center, daily 8-4:30 (clsd. Dec.25). **Camping:** Near Wartburg, Frozenhead State Park (20 sites & shwrs.); near Crossville, Cumberland Mountain State Park (155 sites, elec. & shwrs.). **Special Events:** During May, Annual River Clean-up. **For info.:** Superintendent, Obed Wild & Scenic River, P.O.Box 429, Wartburg, TN 37887. 615/346-6294.

Obed Wild & Scenic River Courtesy NPS

Shiloh National Military Park

Allow: 2-3 hrs. *Fee*

"On Shiloh's dark and bloody ground, the dead and wounded lay; amongst them was a drummer boy, who beat the drum that day."
Traditional Civil War song

The drummer boy was one of over 23,000 lost in two days of fighting near a church called Shiloh. Ostensibly a Union victory, Shiloh resulted in no accolades for the northern generals. Grant and Sherman were held to be responsible for the Union's lack of preparedness. As you tour the battlefield, you can see the ground lost by the surprise Rebel attack and retaken by the precipitous arrival of the Ohio boys under General Buell. 152 monuments, the Shiloh National Cemetery and the over 475 iron tablets serve to remind visitors of the struggle that ensued here.

Highlights

★ Park rangers interpret the ebb and flow of the battle at various sites. The one-way tour route can be hiked, biked or driven. It takes you to many of the critical spots where the final outcome was determined. The park has interesting if gruesome points of interest. The Hornets' Nest demonstrates the value of heroics paying off. The union soldiers withstood 11 charges before succumbing to cannon fire. Their resolute performance allowed their whole army to recover and win the day. Bloody Pond was turned red from the wounds of men and beasts who died in the waters. The peaceful Peach Orchard suffered an early blossom fall as bullets shredded its branches.

Whiz Tips

❢ Regular points interpreted are the Final Stand, the Hornets' Nest, the Peach Orchard and weapon demos. In addition, you may hear about Civil War medicine, the soldier's letters and diaries or why the battle oc-

Shihoh National Military Park Courtesy NPS

curred. This was the first battle where the physicians centralized their work with the wounded and, as a result, saved many lives.

The Union army was flush from the total routing of the Confederates after Fort Donelson (see Fort Donelson NB, TN). While they were surprised at the sudden abandonment of most of Tennessee, they felt it was final. Grant put a priority on drilling his green troops rather than fortifying his position. Sherman discounted reports of a large Rebel force in the vicinity. The South suffered their own problems and were so delayed in their attack that Gen. Beauregard wanted to call off the assault. General A.S. Johnston who was killed during the fighting insisted on pressing forward. With both sides awaiting reinforcement, the North's arrived first and the Confederates fled before overwhelming odds. The way to the Mississippi was clear. The South's fate was all but set.

Kids' Stuff

★ There is a "hands-on" display of reproduced period pieces and dress-up uniforms. You can get great shots of your kids in Civil War get-ups.

★ You may be fortunate to visit when they have their children's "Uniform and Equipment of the Civil War Soldier" program. Rangers provide children with an understanding of how soldiers prepared themselves. For children who have studied the Civil War, Shiloh was a major turning point.

Access: 50 mi. S of I-40 on TN 22 or 150 mi. E of Memphis on Hwy. 57 & 64. **Days/Hours:** Daily, summer 8-6 & winter 8-5 (clsd. Dec.25). **Camping:** Pickwick Landing State Park & TVA Public Use Area, both 15 mi. SE. **For info.:** Superintendent, Shiloh National Military Park, Shiloh, TN 38376. 901/689-5275.

Stones River National Battlefield

Allow: 2-3 hrs. *Fee*

Surrounded by the creeping industrial growth of Murfreesboro is the site of one of the fiercest battles fought in the Civil War. 23,000 men

Shiloh National Military Park

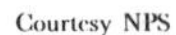
Courtesy NPS

were killed or wounded in two days of fighting. Both sides declared victory. However, General Rosecrans and his Army of the Cumberland would retain control of this vital railway link and the Confederate army from Tennessee would head south to fortify Chattanooga. It was the beginning of a Union offensive which culminated in Sherman's "march to the sea."

Highlights

★ The oldest Civil War monument, the Hazen Brigade Monument, was erected by the Federal combatants to commemorate the Struggle for the Round Forest, the only ground the Federals didn't give up during the course of the battle.

Whiz Tips

During summer weekends, the park has living-history demonstrations featuring artillery firing.

As you travel the South there seems to be battlefield after battlefield, each with horrifying statistics as to the number of men lost or wounded. One narrator on the PBS production *The Civil War* likened the losses at one of the first battles as greater than those suffered at the Battle of Waterloo. He then went on to note that little did the participants know but they would have many more like it. So was Stones River. Here, as at many sites, Confederate Generals and their men would get the best of the Federal forces. But superior numbers and technology would ultimately force the men in butternut and grey to withdraw and entrench further south.

Living History

Kids' Stuff

★ A relatively small site, many visitors walk the battlefield rather than drive. We would recommend such an excursion for your kids. This way you can see the battlefield as it was on New Years of 1863. This mixture of fields and woods is what soldiers on both sides had to contend with.

★ The cannon firing AV intrigues many children. The night before the fighting commenced the Federal and Confederate bands engaged in their own battle. The music program at the visitor center reproduces that particular contest. While the bands initially played competing tunes, both sides joined in the rendition "Home Sweet Home." This proved a fitting sentiment and an unrealized dream for thousands of "fighting boys."

Access: 27 mi. S of Nashville on US 41/70S in NW corner of Murfreesboro. **Days/Hours:** Daily 8-5. **Camping:** 25 mi. N, Cedars of Lebanon State Park (128 sites, elec. & shwrs.); Old Stone Fort State Park, 28 mi. S.E. **Special Events:** 1st July wknd., special battery firing programs. **For info.:** Superintendent, Stones River National Battlefield, 3501 Old Nashville Hwy., Murfreesboro, TN 37129. 615/893-9501.

TEXAS

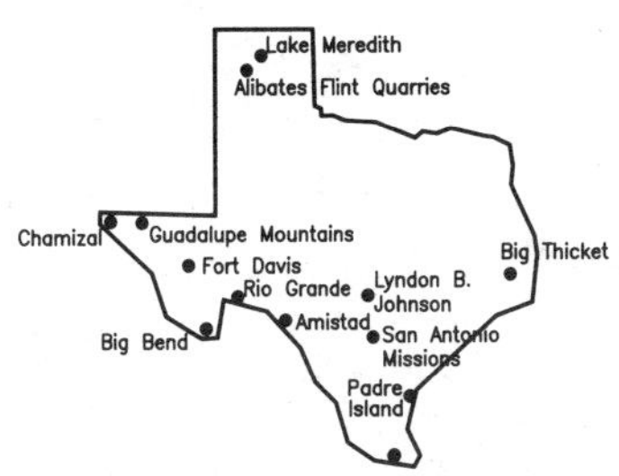

Amistad National Recreation Area

Allow: 2 days *FREE*

The park is as much a tribute to international cooperation as it is a recreational bonanza. Both Mexico and the United States teamed together to build the Amistad Dam. The bronze eagles, each nation's emblems, at the structure's center reminds us of this spirit. The resulting 85 mi. long reservoir, Lake Amistad, is well used by boaters and fishermen.

Highlights

★ The park is utilized by swimmers and water sports lovers nine months a year. Only in the height of winter do temperatures ever reach the low 30s. Scuba diving is a popular pastime for many visitors because of the water's clarity.

Whiz Tips

The park has interpretive nature walks, archaeological talks and evening programs that are presented at the park's H.Q. in winter and at the campgrounds in summer.

Native Americans have inhabited this region for over 12,000 years. The earliest people shared the land with mammoths, camels, bison and horses which no longer exist. More recent inhabitants left behind a wealth of pictographs. There are 400 pictograph sites within the park and in the surrounding area.

Kids' Stuff

Good places to go swimming with children are the protected beaches at the Dam, Governor's Landing and Rough Canyon.

Families can try their luck fishing for over 30 different kinds of fish in the waters including muskie, bass, sunfish, crappie, perch, walleye, pike, gar and perch.

Access: W of San Antonio on Rte. 90 in Del Rio. **Days/Hours:** Visitor Center, daily 8-5. **Camping:** Park has 5 FREE primitive campgrounds; nearby Seminole Canyon State Historical Park (showers). **Special Events:** "Black History Week," "Parade of Lights" (early Dec.), "Spanish Heritage'" "Take Pride in America'" and the "Amistad Parade." **For info.:** Superintendent, Amistad National Recreation Area, P.O.Box 420367, Del Rio, TX 78842-0367. 512/775-7491.

Big Bend National Park

Allow: 2-3 days *Fee*

A gift from Texas to the nation, Big Bend NP was named by the park service for the great U-turn in the Rio Grande. Beginning in the mountains of Colorado the river travels southward until it forms the border between Mexico and Texas as it gradually makes its way to the Gulf of Mexico. Here it veers to the north as it follows a river bed cut through the mountains. In 1978, Rio Grande Wild & Scenic River was added to Big Bend's administration to protect a 191.2 mi. stretch of the river that runs eastward out of the park.

Highlights

★ This is a wild, untamed land. The

Chisos Mountains encircled by the Chihuahuan Desert and arid lands are a natural wildlife oasis. The river breathes its own life into the area and the surprising desert, providing a rich ecosystem for those creatures who adapted.

Whiz Tips

As the region's climate changed the mountains became a land-locked "Galapogos Island." Species found nowhere else, evolved and adapted to their new environment. Some of these are: a mosquito fish found in only one pond and the Carmen Mountains white-tail deer. There are also some species where this is their only toehold north of the border. Two of these are the Chisos Oak and the Colima Warbler. Two animals who have adapted to the desert are: jackrabbits who use their over-sized ears for listening for predators and for expelling excess heat from their bodies and kangaroo rats who satisfy their water requirement by metabolizing the carbohydrates from their food. Other animals you might see here are gray foxes, ringtails, tarantulas, the roadrunner and, of course, his buddy, the coyote. Rarely sighted but present in the area are golden eagles and peregrine falcons.

Kids' Stuff

★ The park is noted for its walking and hiking trails. However, the warning to wait until you get to the park before planning any backcountry trips because of the fickleness of water holes, demonstrates the care hikers must take to carry sufficient H2O. In the unlikely but possible event you see a mountain lion (there have been 800 sightings in the last 40 years, an average of 20/yr.), pick up your small children, make yourself as big as possible and throw stones to make the lion realize you are dangerous.

Access: 69 mi. S of Marathon on US 385 or 103 mi. S of Alpine on TX 118 or 92 mi. E of Presido on TX 170. **Days/Hours:** Daily. **Camping:** Park has 5 campgrounds, Rio Grande Village (elec.). **For info.:** Superintendent, Big Bend National Park, Texas 79834. 915/477-2251.

Guadalupe Mountains National Park

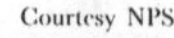

Big Thicket National Preserve

Allow: 1-2 days *FREE*

"Resting hard on the western edge of the southern pine forest, the Big Thicket has been called "the biological crossroads of North America," the intersecting point of eight wholly separate ecological systems, the only spot on the continent where sub-tropical and temperate vegetations overlap."

Al Reinert
Texas Monthly Political Reader

In southeastern Texas is a patch of land that was lightly regarded by settlers but has become highly regarded by scientists. Several ecosystems are found in the eight tracts of land and four riverways encompassing the park. Lifeforms found in the swamps of the Everglades are found here. Appalachian forests preserved in Great Smoky and Southwestern deserts celebrated at Big Bend are evidenced in the Thicket. Trees and plants from Ohio's Cuyahoga Valley and savannah seen at Florida's Timucuan Ecological Reserve appear together.

Highlights

★ The best way to appreciate the wide variety of life, is to get out onto the trails or waterways. Four of the units have developed trails: Turkey Creek, Beech Creek, Hickory Creek and Big Sandy Creek. Each offers its own distinct ecosystem.

Whiz Tips

❢ The park has naturalist-led interpretive walks and talks explaining exactly how this region has been created (reserve well in advance for a tour). Where do foothills becomes mountains or plains? Where does the north become the south? Big Thicket is unique in that it forms not just the apex of two ecosystems but as many as eight. Species forced south from the days of the Ice-Age have been able to hang on and co-exist with species who returned with the retreat of the glaciers. The climate, topography and geology have conspired to protect and nourish the plants which in turn protect and nourish the animals. The density of the growth forestalled civilization long enough so that these surviving areas could be saved.

Kids' Stuff

★ The Thicket's trails are fairly flat and very accessible to families. The preserve's naturalists present several programs designed to delight children if you book well in advance. The Jr. Ranger Program can be completed on your own or by taking part in ranger-guided activities.

Access: Bounded by US 96 on E, US 90 on S, US 59 on W & US 190 on N. **Days/ Hours:** Turkey Creek Unit Information Center, summer, daily & winter Th-M (clsd. Dec.25). **Camping:** Martin Dies Jr. State Park on Hwy. 190 (182 sites, elec. & shwrs.); Alabama-Coushata Indian Reservation btwn. Livingston & Woodville on US 190. **For info.:** Superintendent, Big Thicket National Preserve, 3785 Milam, Beaumont, TX 77701. 409/839-2689.

Chamizal National Memorial

Allow: 1 hr. *FREE*

"I see where America and Mexico had a joint earthquake. That's the only thing I ever heard we split 50-50 with Mexico."

Will Rogers
The Best of Will Rogers

Chamizal National Memorial, in El Paso near the Mexican border, has a visitor center and museum dedicated to preserving the peaceful settlement of a century of dispute between the U.S. and Mexico. The memorial and its park grounds often host mutual festivities celebrating the good relations these two cultures and neighbors now share.

Highlights

★ The documentary film and the museum exhibits detail the boundary dispute and its resolution. They demonstrate the kinds of difficulties international/intercultural negotiations can encounter. The achievement of the Solomon-like settlement also shows how dealing in good faith can work wonders and that even Will Rogers can be wrong.

Whiz Tips

The Rio Grande, which was the settled borderline between the U.S. and Mexico, was known to change course. During the last century, both countries agreed to a method of settling border changes made by the meandering stream. If it was merely a change in the channel, the deepest channel would become the border. However, if the river was naturally diverted from its old path to a new route, the old river bed would remain the national division. Of course, when this was decided almost all of the river's banks were uninhabited. The change in the river at Chamizal took place between El Paso, the largest American city along the border and Juarez, which dwarfs El Paso. Both sides claimed the river's change was caused by that phenomenon most advantageous to them. In 1962, J.F.K. and President Adolfo Lopez Mateos decided enough was enough and a deal was cut. Today, the Chamizal National Memorial stands on that portion Mexico ceded to the U.S. On the other side of the constructed concrete-lined border channel, Mexico has established its own commemorative park.

Kids' Stuff

★ This is an excellent place to show children the difficulties in reaching agreements and the kinds of barriers people can construct.

Access: South/central El Paso adjacent international border. **Days/Hours:** Daily 8-5 (open until 11 during scheduled performances). **Camping:** 35 mi. E on US 62/180, Hueco Tanks State Park (20 sites (shwrs.). **Special Events:** The park is a showcase for intercultural fiestas, celebrations and shows; Oct.'s 1st wknd., Border Folk Festival with Native Americans, Bluegrass, Hispanic and Cajun performers. **For info.:** Superintendent, Chamizal National Memorial, 700 E. San Antonio, D-301, El Paso, TX 79901. 915/534-6277.

Fort Davis National Historic Site Courtesy Fort Davis NHS

Fort Davis National Historic Site

Allow: 1-2 hrs. *Fee*

In the middle of West Texas sits Fort Davis, the most outstanding surviving example of an Indian Wars frontier southwestern fort. Modern-day visitors can see how frontier soldiers survived, by touring over 20 restored buildings. While no fighting occurred at the fort (few western forts were attacked by Indians), the soldiers played a key role in guiding travelers on to their next destination. The fort was named for then Secretary of War, Jefferson Davis, who went on to become the President of the Confederate States of America.

Highlights

★ During summer, visitors touring the fort can interact with living-history soldiers, officers' wives and servants. Many rooms are furnished as they would have been during the fort's occupation. You can hear the sounds of an 18 min. dress retreat parade and occasionally see weapons firing demonstrations.

★ The fort's location in the box canyon offers a surprisingly pleasant setting and provides camera buffs with great shots to show the folks back home.

Whiz Tips

When the fort was occupied in 1854, the Apache and Comanches just avoided the soldiers and continued raiding settlers and travelers. During the Civil War, they even lured some of the fort's Confederate cavalry into an ambush and massacred them. After the war, the U.S. sent black soldiers under white officers to protect the area. Buffalo Soldiers! So the Indians called the black soldiers whose hair reminded them of buffalo fur. "Black-white men", another of the printable names the Indians called these soldiers who proved an effective thorn in their sides. There is cause to believe that the black soldiers were sent to these parts because of the then racist belief that African-Americans could better survive the heat. An interesting footnote of Americana is that these "buffalo soldiers" who served so well for so long were unable to serve with white soldiers until the Second World War. Today the highest ranking military person in the United States if met by these same Indians, would also be called a "buffalo soldier".

Kids' Stuff

★ Children recognize that Fort Davis soldiers had to cope with a life of constant readiness. This fort sitting in a remote frontier fires the children's imaginations.

Access: N edge of Fort Davis. **Days/ Hours:** Daily, summer 8-6 & winter 8-5 (clsd. Dec.25.) **Camping:** Davis Mountain State Park (88 sites, elec. & showers). **Special Events:** July 4, Independence Day and Sat. Labor Day wknd., Restoration Festival. **For info.:** Superintendent, Fort Davis National Historic Site, P.O.Box 1456, Fort Davis, TX 79734. 915/426-3224.

Guadalupe Mountains National Park

Allow: 2-3 days *FREE*

Nestled along the Texas-New Mexico border, Guadalupe Mountain Park is in effect the headland of a prehistoric reef. An ancient marine fossil reef was thrust up from the encircling desert lowlands. Looking like a ship's prow, the spectacular escarpment is called "El Capitan," a fitting name. Primarily a wild park, it is a hiker's paradise.

Highlights

★ McKittrick Canyon, fed by a natural spring, has been called "the most beautiful spot in Texas." Nature flourishes. You can spot jackrabbits, coyotes, porcupines, grey foxes, mule deer, elk and, less likely, mountain lions. There is a 4.6 mile round-trip hike to a "neat" stone cabin.

Whiz Tips

❢ This part of Texas and Big Bend National Park almost due south constitutes Texas' high country. You'll see mountain vegetation and animals you won't find anywhere else in the Lone Star State. The park incorporates the climates and life found in the Chihuahuan Desert, pine-oak woodlands and high plains grasslands. Aspens, maples, oak, walnut, ash and chokecherry trees flourish in the protected sanctity of the canyons. Elk, reintroduced after the native elk were exterminated in the early part of the century, can be found in the higher altitude regions, along with mule deer. The almost ghostly mountain lions and black bears are unlikely to be found by even the most seasoned woodsperson. Unfortunately, while bighorn sheep would probably thrive under the protection of the park service, they were eliminated long before the sanctuary was established.

❢ For the true adventurer, fossil viewing is a major thrill here. Ancient sea creatures, trapped in time by the reef formations, are found in a place hundreds of miles from where their offspring still flourish.

❢ During the summer there are evening interpretive programs guided nature hikes and special programs.

Kids' Stuff

★ During summer, there's a Jr. Ranger Program held once each week. Plus, there are "Adventure Pacs" available as check-out items for all families.

★ Hiking in the park is a challenge for families with small children. For some, the key is the older the child the better. Two good family walks are the 2.3 mi. Smith Spring trail and the 1 mi. McKittrick Canyon Nature Loop. The first leads to a desert oasis and should take less than 2 hrs.

Access: 55 mi. SW of Carlsbad, NM or 110 mi. E of El Paso, TX on US 62-180. **Days/Hours:** Pine Springs Visitor Center & McKittrick Canyon area, daily, 8-4:30 (summer extended hrs.) (clsd. Dec.25 & Jan.1).

Guadalupe Mountains National Park Courtesy NPS

Camping: Park's Pine Springs (39 sites) & Dog Canyon (5 drive-in & 18 walk-in sites). **For info.:** Superintendent, Guadalupe Mountains National Park, HC 60, Box 400, Salt Flat, TX 79847-9400. 915/828-3251.

Lake Meredith Recreation Area

Allow: 1 hr. *FREE*

Lake Meredith in the Texas panhandle was created because the Canadian River is one of the very sources of above-ground water in the region. The surrounding plain, known as the Llano Estacado, has been described as flat as any in the world. On the lake's west side is Alibates Flint Quarries National Monument, the Native American flint quarry sites whose product has been found throughout the Southwest and Great Plains. You can see how distinctive the coloring of its flint is.

Highlights

★ The reservoir has become a boon for outdoor fans. Hunters, anglers, boaters and swimmers make use of its waters. The waters hold bass, catfish, crappie, sunfish, carp and walleye.

Whiz Tips

Twice daily rangers lead a tour of the quarries explaining how the Native Americans dug the rock from the ground and the many uses it was put to. The Indians valued the flint so much that one tribe, the Panhandle Pueblo Culture, set up shop here for 250 years, trading its supply for other goods. Archaeologists believe they were probably a plains tribe that took up farming and mining. As part of their adjustment from a nomadic hunting lifestyle, they also adopted the fixed pueblo-style housing found further to the west and north.

Kids' Stuff

Kids make good use of the lake as they seek relief from the hot summer sun. Our children were always surprised by how much industry the Native Americans demonstrated, contrary to popular myths about them.

Guadalupe Mountains National Park Courtesy NPS

Access: In Fritch on Hwy.136. **Days/ Hours:** Lake Meredith, daily; Alibates Flint Quarries NM, summer only tours, daily 10 & 2. **Camping:** Park has 7 campgrounds with differing avail. **For info.:** Superintendent, Lake Meredith National Recreation Area & Alibates Flint Quarries National Monument, P.O.Box 1438, Fritch, TX 79036. 806/857-3151.

Lyndon B. Johnson National Historical Park

Allow: .5 days *FREE*

"As President, his brilliant leadership on the Civil Rights Act of 1964 and the Voting Rights Act of 1965 has earned him a place in the history of civil rights alongside Abraham Lincoln."

Senator Edward Kennedy

When President Johnson was in the White House, he brought a little bit of Texas, down-home style, to the national scene. With Texas barbecues, a homey approach and a visible family, voters saw LBJ as a "real" American. About an hour from Austin is the town this master-politician's family founded, Johnson City. The park's town site property includes LBJ's boyhood home, his grandaddy's log house and other buildings reminiscent of the settlement's early days. You can tour his ranch lands, childhood schoolhouse and reconstructed birthplace.

Highlights

★ You get a real up close look at the nation's 36th president and the evolution of a small Texas town. The Johnson clan can trace its roots in this region back to the Civil War. Both Johnson's father and grandfather experienced widely shifting fortunes. Sam Sr. first made it big driving wild Texas longhorns north to Kansas rail heads. Sam Jr. made a fortune speculating on cotton which provided for a well-to-do childhood for the future president. But he stayed in the speculating game a little too long and LBJ's teenage years were spent doing odd jobs after school to help out. One constant was the family's sense of public service. Even at his poorest, Sam Jr. served his community in the state legislature.

San Antonio Missions National Monument Courtesy Jim Miller

Whiz Tips

LBJ epitomized what some feel is the essence of the American political system's success, the art of compromising. It was said he was best when he talked to people one-to-one. He was the youngest Senatorial Minority and Majority Leader ever. As president, he instituted Medicare, the aforementioned *Civil Rights* acts, the *Fair Packaging & Labeling Act*, the *Water Quality*, *Clean Water Restoration*, *Clean Air*, *Air Quality* acts, the Space Program and the War On Poverty. However, he continues to be linked to the Vietnam War, which ultimately proved his undoing. In the 1983 historians' poll, LBJ ranked 10th of 36 presidents in effectiveness' fairly high.

Kids' Stuff

★ LBJ could link his family back to pioneer days. His grandaddy ramrodded huge cattle drives employing over 100 cowboys. His grandmother had to hide from Indians. His own life was no bed of roses as he experienced a roller-coaster ride in his family's fortunes. However, he persevered to achieve the nation's highest post, a good lesson for children. Children who are currently studying American history or the presidents will come away from here a great deal more knowledgeable about Lyndon Johnson.

Access: Johnson City Unit in Johnson City; LBJ Ranch Unit bus only from LBJ State Historical Park. **Days/Hours:** Johnson City Unit, daily 9-5; Johnson Settlement, daily 9-4:30; LBJ Ranch Unit, 10-4 (clsd. Dec.25 & Jan.1). **Camping:** 14 mi. E Pedernales Falls State Park (69 sites, elec. & shwrs.) **Special Events:** Crafts Day; Aug.27, LBJ's birthday : Dec., Annual Christmas Tree Lighting. **For info.:** Superintendent, Lyndon B. Johnson National Historical Park, P.O.Box 329, Johnson City, TX 78636. 512/868-7128.

Padre Island National Seashore Courtesy Jim Miller

Padre Island National Seashore

Allow: 2-3 hrs. *Fee*

"Her treasure is the gold of her sun, the silver of her moonlight, and the sapphire of her pearl-crusted waves."

1766 survey report

Protecting the part of Texas stretching down the Gulf of Mexico to the Mexican border is a chain of barrier islands, the largest of which is Padre Island. Although man has attempted to bend and shape these lands, wind and water remain the rulers. The prime pleasures found here are swimming and fishing.

Highlights

★ You can enjoy the water and sun year-round. Surfers and surf-fishermen find waves and fish. Beachcombers pick up a wide variety of treasures washed ashore.

Whiz Tips

The Malaquite Beach Visitor Center has interpretive displays, an introductory AV and ranger-led programs. Some of these include discussions on the water creatures, the birds and the things that get washed ashore.

Kids' Stuff

★ Families enjoy the endless sand, warm waters and exploring opportunities. Kids love the tales of Spanish gold and pirate treasures that are said to be buried beneath the surface. It puts a little extra zest into their sandcastle digging.

Access: From Corpus Christi on Park Rd. 22 or Port Aransas on Park Rd. 53 then left on Park Rd. 22. **Days/Hours:** Daily. **Camping:** Park's Malaquite Beach & primitive beach camping; nearby to the N Mustang Island State Park, Nueces County Park & Padre Balli Park (showers). **For info.:** Superintendent, Padre Island National Seashore, 9405 South Padre Island Dr., Corpus Christi, TX 78418-5597. 512/949-8068.

San Antonio Missions National Historical Park Courtesy NPS

San Antonio Missions National Historical Park

Allow: .5 days *FREE*

"We have never really captured San Antonio, we Texans somehow the Spanish have managed to hold it."

Larry McMurty
In a Narrow Grave

One reason for the above statement has been the invisible cementing of faith and culture which has allowed these four missions in San Antonio to withstand Apaches, Comanches and Texans. The Coahuiltecans, the local native hunter and gatherers, were early and steadfast converts to both Catholicism and mission life. When the French made the Spanish missions untenable in East Texas, the Franciscans and the Coahuiltecans reestablished their missions here in the heart of Apache/Comanche territory. The park service administers four of these missions (Concepcion, San Jose, San Juan and Espada) as well as an aqueduct system.

Highlights

★ Along with the famed Alamo, the 18th century missions provide a rich legacy of San Antonio history and striking architecture. Faded by time and the elements, they remain stalwart structures of the faith. Each presents historians with confirmation of building practices and design elements meant to enhance spiritual and physical existence in the face of external hostile forces.

★ Mission Road is the celebrated pathway the friars and Native Americans travelled. Along the route you can see the historic irrigation system, the Acequia, which has been in use since its inception.

Whiz Tips

❢ Rangers are located in each mission to assist visitors on their tour of the still viable establishments. An interesting facet is the fact that many of today's parishioners can trace their Christian roots back to the first missions.

Kids' Stuff

★ Just off the Mission Parkway are two good family excursions, the Hike and Bike Trail and the Espada Dam. You can also take your kids on the Woodland Nature Trail at Mission San Juan or introduce them to mission life in the 1700s through the audio-interpreted model of Mission San Jose.

★ This is one of the few park sites that shows how early Spain was involved in a very concrete way with Native Americans. While these missions were educating the native children, the English colonies had not yet founded Georgia and were restricted to coastal settlements. Most children are unaware of how much the Spanish accomplished in the west during the country's pre-independence days.

Access: Southern San Antonio on Mission RD. **Days/Hours:** Daily, summer 9-6 & winter 8-5 (clsd. Dec.25 & Jan.1). **Camping:** E at Sattler, the Corps of Engineers has 4 campgrounds; Canyon (287 sites), Comal (30 sites), Cranes Mill (72 sites) & Potters Creek (119 sites, elec. & shwrs.). **Special Events:** May, Mission San Jose participates in the Harlandale School District Annual Festival, with a parade, games, talent & art contests, cultural dances and food. **Teacher's Package:** Available. **For info.:** Superintendent, San Antonio Missions National Historical Park, 2202 Roosevelt Ave., San Antonio, TX 78210. 512/229-5701.

UTAH

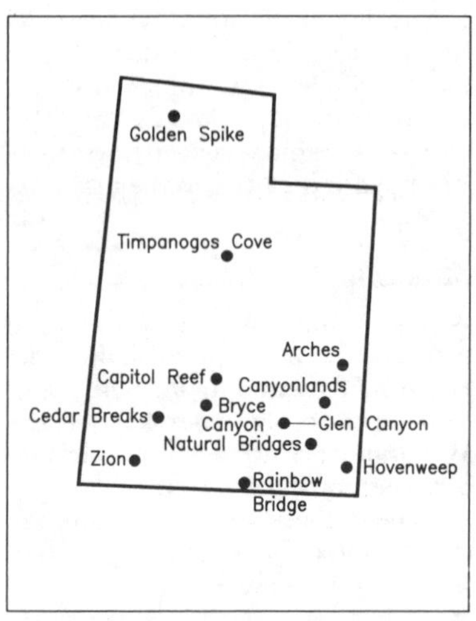

Arches National Park

Allow: 2 days *Fee*

In southeastern Utah is some of the most extraordinary scenery in North America. Advertised as having the greatest density of arches in the world (over 500 in the park), the phrase doesn't begin to describe Arches National Park's beauty. Arches, balanced rocks, eroded fins, towers and spires dot the landscape. You can see the dominant features as you drive through, but to fully experience them, you should take short hikes.

Highlights

★ A visit to the Windows section finds you ringed by arches with such names as Double Arch, Turret Arch and Ribbon Arch. It's a photographer's delight as silhouettes and contrasts evolve from sunrise to sunset. On your way into the Windows area you pass Balanced Rock, a recognized landmark which graces many calendars.

★ The guided Fiery Furnace hike takes in a giant's garden of rocks. Clambering over game trails and through narrow crevices, you can be-

Arches National Park

gin to appreciate the necessities of the early and late starting times and the need for a guide. The mid-afternoon summer heat would quickly take its toll on those who lost their way or tarried too long.

Whiz Tips

❢ A full slate of interpretive walks will accelerate your comprehension of nature's powers. As this is a high desert area, the park makes a special effort to introduce you to the desert flora and fauna that have adapted to this severe climate. For example, prickly pear cacti have tiny needles that provide shade, protect the plant from animals who might want to eat it and help channel water to the plant when it rains.

❢ You learn the difference between an arch and a natural bridge. (An arch is formed by water freezing in cracks and breaking the rock away. A bridge is formed by moving water using sand like a drill to scour a hole through the rock.) Additionally, you'll learn about the different layers of earth and how they were compacted by pressure.

Kids' Stuff

★ A challenging but highly enjoyable jaunt for kids is the (2 hr.) Fiery Furnace interpretive hike. Hikers have to squeeze through rock crevices and balance on ledges but the kids on our hike could cope, with a little help. In return for our efforts, we came upon foraging mule deer.

★ Sand Dune Arch offers a giant sand box amidst the towering rock steeples. The sand is so fine and shaded for most of the day that you don't have to worry about burning bare feet or hands. Our kids played in the sand and used the towering rocks for "hide 'n seek".

★ Because the area looks so mountainous, most visitors don't recognize it is part of a desert. Remember, little children get dehydrated much quicker than adults, so make sure they have lots to drink.

Access: 5 mi. N of Moab on US 191. **Days/Hours:** Visitor center, daily, summer 8-6 and winter 8-4:30 (clsd. Dec. 25). **Camping:** Park's Devil Gardens (52 sites). **For info.:** Superintendent, Arches National Park, P.O.Box 907, Moab, UT 84532. 801/259-8161.

Bryce Canyon National Park

Allow: 1-2 days *Fee*

There are some who say Bryce is more beautiful than the Grand Canyon; there are many who dare to compare; there are few who deny it its place. The land of the HOODOO! Are they castles? Nay! Soldiers at attention? Nay! For each of us, these seemingly impossible Southern Utah rock formations create different but no less striking images. Hoodoos were so named because in the dying light these stone sentinels have the appearance of ghostly hooded creatures.

Bryce Canyon isn't a canyon at all but a 20 mile long escarpment comprised of several amphitheaters. Ebenezer Bryce, a rancher who worked this acreage accessed the area through an individual canyon which was named for him. The name was then applied to the whole area. It is said, he called the region "a helluva place to lose a cow." Who should know better than he?

Highlights

★ For a single one-on-one view, Inspiration Point rivals any. The shadows, the light and the stone combine to create a visual playground for the mind. Imagine what you will, it's there. Sunset and sunrise pictures of this point attract photographers from around the world, as they try to best what the naked eye beholds.

★ Natural Bridge, so close and yet so timeless, appears to be within touching distance. Every viewpoint along the Rim Drive offers scenes most of us only see in National Geographic or Sierra Club publications. Driving or hiking through the park provides any visitor with enough scenery to make the trip and subsequent slide or video shows raving successes.

Whiz Tips

- The best time to photograph the colors is while the sun is going down...don't wait until sunset or you'll be too late as the formations are on the northeastern side. Go at least an hour before official sunset. The many colors making Bryce's formations so awe-inspiring are caused by two minerals in the rock. Manganese accounts for the lavender and green hues, while good old rusted iron oxides are responsible for the pinks and red.
- In winter, if you're so inclined, you can borrow snow shoes for FREE from the visitor center and trudge around the park.
- The 125 mile drive between Bryce and Capitol Reef National Parks (SR 12) is spectacular. It offers a range of geological highlights including stops at Anasazi ruins, pictographs and petrified forests.

Kids' Stuff

★ Bryce has a Junior Ranger program for 5 to 12 year-olds in which they have to complete a booklet.

★ Hiking in Bryce means a steep return trip unless you take the rim walk. Recommended short hikes into the canyons are the Queens Garden Trail and the Navajo Loop Trail.

Access: 7 mi. S on US 89 from Panguitch, then 17 mi. E on UT 12 from Bryce Jct. **Days/Hours:** Visitor center daily, winter 8-4:30 & summer extended hrs (clsd. Dec.25). **Camping:** Park's two campgrounds (206 sites). **For info.:** Superintendent, Bryce Canyon National Park, Bryce Canyon, UT 84717. 801/834-5322.

Bryce Canyon National Park Courtesy NPS

Canyonlands National Park

Allow: 2 days *Fee*

On their way to the Grand Canyon, the Green River and Colorado River meet in Canyonlands National Park in southeastern Utah. Encompassing the high mountain plateau and the river valleys below, Canyonlands is two parks in one: Island in the Sky and the Needles area. The rivers carve large valleys on either side of a mesa leaving Island in the Sky. At their confluence they form a much larger, more destructive river. The geologic remains of this meeting is known as the Needles area.

Highlights

★ At Island in the Sky, you climb to the mesa top and drive until you have no place to go but straight down (fortunately there's a fence to stop those of us too enamored with the view). Along the way you can stop for rewarding views at the end of short walking trails. Mesa Arch is a photographer's delight because the arch acts as a frame to the river valley below.

★ The Needles area, no slouch when it comes to scenery, was more fun for our children to explore. With three different thematic hikes we learned about cowboys in the area, ancient Indians and how life can mystically occur in a puddle.

Whiz Tips

As in most National Parks, Canyonlands has interpretive talks and hikes. During the Mesa Arch walk, the most popular at Island in the Sky, the ranger told us about the cold desert. She identified what the plants were and how they have adjusted to cope with long periods without water. In addition, she told us about the many animals that frequent the area and their special adaptations. As the walk proceeded, she described the geology of the area and how the arch, the mesa and the river valley were created. In a little more than an hour we had a very good introduction to our natural surroundings and reached our goal, magnificent Mesa Arch.

At Needles, the Pothole Point

Canyonlands National Park Courtesy NPS

Trail takes you over a petrified sand dune which, because of its composition, is pitted by holes worn by water, wind and sand. Remarkable as it may seem, these holes can be bone dry for months, then with a rainstorm, spring to life. Snails, tadpoles, worms, shrimp and insects lie in hibernation in eggs which hatch with moisture. While alive, these tiny creatures have to mature, mate and ensure the next generation, all before the desert winds whisk their life-giving moisture away.

We found late afternoon forays into the park rewarded us with solitude, better picture light, many wildlife sightings and cooler temperatures. As an extra bonus, as we left Island in the Sky at dark, we saw some fantastic natural light and sound shows as summer storms brewed in the distance.

Kids' Stuff

★ The hands-down winner was the Cave Spring Trail leading us through caves, up rock faces, down Anasazi ladders to the cave spring itself. Finally, we "discovered" the cowboy line camp cave, complete with corral, stove, cooking utensils and tools of the day. We marveled at what it would be like to live under this overhang with your animal stock within smelling distance.

★ We were fortunate enough to find potholes with some water left in them, brimming with life. Our kids couldn't believe the empty holes we passed were as filled with little critters ready to explode into existence.

Access: Island in the Sky N of Moab off US 191 on UT 313 & Needles S of Moab off US 191 on UT 211. **Days/Hours:** Visitor center in Moab and park info. centers, weekdays 8-4:30. **Camping:** Island in the Sky, Willow Flat Campground (12 sites & no water) & Needles, Squaw Flat Campground (26 sites); On Island in the Sky is Dead Horse Point State Park (21 sites) and on the way into Needles is Newspaper Rock State Historical Monument (8 sites & no water). **For info.:** Superintendent, Canyonlands National Park, 125 West 200 South, Moab, UT 84532. 801/259-7164.

Capitol Reef National Park

Allow: 1-2 days *Fee*

Capitol Reef is a simple, timeless oasis. In the main part of the park are pioneer farm buildings in a peaceful valley. At a nearby picnic areas families bring out their supplies. Moms and Dads root about putting together the final touches of lunch. Kiddies run through the fruit trees to see the deer foraging for orchard droppings. The petroglyphs etched upon the stone walls seem as if they could have been done by the class of '29 from the log-cabin one-room school house. Sure the park has its fair share of natural geologic wonders but the real essence of this place is its grace.

Highlights

★ The petroglyphs and pictographs left by the Fremont Indians provide excellent examples of primitive art. The Fremont, although not the great builders their contemporaries to the south were blessed with artistic inclinations. The Fremont Indian culture relied on hunting and foraging to satisfy its nutrition requirements. Some believe they were the ancestors of the Utes and Paiutes who later occupied this territory and survived similarly.

★ The trail to Hickman Natural Bridge offers a worthwhile reward as you come to a 133 ft. wide natural rock bridge which rises 125 ft. Along the way, you find more evidence of the prehistoric Fremont Indians in the form of "pit house" ruins and a granary.

★ The 25 mi. Scenic Drive along the 1,000 ft. escarpment provides remarkable overlooks of a truly wild area.

Whiz Tips

❢ On summer weekends, at the Fruita Schoolhouse, you can learn about the days when the schoolhouse was teeming with little tykes. Park rangers and audio programs recount school days and blacksmithing.

❢ When is a reef not a reef? When it's Capitol Reef, a 100 mile barrier of sandstone creating ridges of 1000 feet. The earth forced a massive uplift exposing layers of sedimentary rock which had lain beneath the earth's surface for millennia.

Kids' Stuff

★ This summer the park was studying programs for kids, so there were many alternatives. A Junior Geologist program was the official name for programs conducted this year. Whatever the name, our youngsters looked forward to each opportunity to participate.

★ The park has lots of interpretive trails suitable for families; Fremont River and Hickman Bridge are two of the shorter trails. Kids really enjoy the Capitol Gorge Trail where they can play hide 'n seek in the tiny caves eroded in the gorge's walls.

Access: 11 mi. E of Torrey on UT 24. **Days /Hours:** Visitor center daily; winter 8-4:30 & summer extended hrs. (clsd. Dec.25) **Camping:** Park's Fruita Campground (71 sites). **Special Events:** In Sept., Harvest Homecoming. The park has a schedule of different fruit harvesting times in which you may partake (fee). **For info.:** Superintendent, Capitol Reef National Park, Torrey, UT 84775. 801/425-3791.

Cedar Breaks National Monument

Allow: 2 hrs. *Fee*

Located in southern Utah, early Native Americans more properly named this gigantic amphitheater, the "Circle of Painted Cliffs." With the highest layer of eroded earth strata in the region, the cross-sectional view offered at Cedar Breaks allows you to see the initial erosive effects of time on these stones. Bryce, then Zion and finally, the Grand Canyon demonstrate what each successive lower and older layer of rock offers.

Capitol Reef National Park

Highlights

★ Like Grand Canyon and Bryce, the approach and discovery of nature's work from a seemingly flat plateau is impressive. First you drive up out of a lava strewn forest to the great chasm. There it appears as if the colorful pinnacles and valleys ripple as the sunlight strikes. Layers and layers of geologic time have been ripped open for your pleasure.

★ In early July, fields of subalpine wildflowers paint an impressive collage.

Whiz Tips

Like many National Parks, depending on the time of year, there are interpretive lectures and hikes. The talks here cover the geology and nature within the park's borders. We learned how the different layers were added. First a huge lake deposited its mud and then the land mass uplifted creating a fault which allowed volcanic lava to escape forming another layer. The ranger also explained the reason for the many colors in the eroded rocks: rust. Pretty romantic stuff!

There are no cedar trees here. As a matter of fact, true cedars are not native to North America. Europeans arriving in these parts mistook the junipers for cedars and, hence, the park's first name. The second name, "Breaks," is pioneer-talk for escarpment where the land "breaks away."

It is cooler (more refreshing) in this park because of its elevation (10,000 ft.), so plan your attire accordingly. The park notes freezing temperatures are not uncommon even on summer nights.

Kids' Stuff

★ Upon request at the visitor center, you can listen to audio tapes featuring the park's fauna including mountain lion calls.

★ Our gang enjoyed the nature hike to an alpine pond complete with a self-guiding pamphlet.

Access: 23 mi. from Cedar City off I-15 or 27 mi. from Long Valley Jct. off US 89 on UT 14 or 14 mi. from Parowan on UT 143. **Days/Hours:** Visitor center, daily 8-6 from June-mid-Oct. **Camping:** Park's Cedar Breaks Campground (30 sites); Dixie National Forest, 10 campgrounds within 20 mi. **For info.:** Superintendent, Cedar Breaks National Monument, P.O.Box 749, Cedar City, UT 84720. 801/586-9451.

Cedar Breaks National Monument Courtesy NPS

Glen Canyon National Recreation Area

Allow: 1 week *FREE*

Also known as Lake Powell, this region has been transformed into a major recreational area for boaters and backcountry travelers. Unlikely to be undone, the damming of the Colorado River back into Glen Canyon was completed over many objections and is still an issue today. Senator Barry Goldwater, not your most pro-conservationist politician, called his vote for the project his biggest mistake. Yet, the dam, the lake and the area offer many of us benefits that the river and canyon alone would not. For many the fantastically sculpted landscape hasn't been diminished but enhanced.

Highlights

★ Take the half-day boat tour (fee) to Rainbow Bridge National Monument and see the largest natural bridge in the world. The land access is really not a family trip as visitors have to hike or horseback over 13-14 mi. of rough country. The Navajo believe it is a sacred place and call it "Nonnoshoshi," "the rainbow turned to stone." It stands 290 ft. high and spans 278 ft., with a minimum thickness of 42 ft. Natural bridges are created by running water cutting a hole through the rock. Other nearby parks featuring natural bridges or arches are Natural Bridges NM, Arches NP, Canyonlands NP, all north in Utah.

★ Known as the "Jewel of the Colorado," some believe the pre-dam canyon rivaled Grand Canyon in beauty. While some of this scenery has been submerged beneath the lake, Lake Powell does allow visitors the chance to get closer to the heights.

Whiz Tips

The park rangers offer interpretive programs on the region's ecosystem, geology, wildlife, history and Native American culture. In addition, you can tour Glen Canyon Dam on your own or join a guided session.

The prehistoric builders, the Anasazi, made it into the canyon to fashion some of their classic struc-

Glen Canyon National Recreation Area Courtesy Jim Miller

tures. Petroglyphs, pictographs and ruins of their structures can still be found above the water's level.

Kids' Stuff

★ Although there are hiking opportunities, most families stick close to the water. Water-skiing, fishing and boating provide days of pleasure for kids. The lake and waters around the park provide a world class fishery; 10 lb. rainbow trout, 15 lb. brown trout, 10 lb. largemouth bass, 5 lb. walleye, channel catfish, striped bass, crappies and sunfish give even neophytes a thrill when hooked.

Access: H.Q. in Page at 337 North Navajo Dr.; visitor center 2 mi. from Page on US 89. **Days/Hours:** Daily (clsd. Dec. 25 & Jan.1) **Camping:** Park's Wahweap (189 sites), Lees Ferry (54 sites), Bullfrog (87 sites) & Halls Crossing (65 sites & shwrs.). **Special Events:** During Feb., Big Stripper Derby; in May, Page Rodeo; July 4th, Fireworks Display; in Dec., Festival of Lights Cookie-Baking Contest. **For info.:** Superintendent, Glen Canyon National Recreation Area, P.O.Box 1507, Page, AZ 86040-1507. Wahweap Visitor Center, 602/645-2511; Bullfrog & Halls Crossing Visitor Centers, 801/684-2243.

Golden Spike National Historic Site

Allow: 2-3 hrs. *Fee*

Situated in Promontory, Utah, at the north tip of the Great Salt Lake, the park owes it current isolation to two competitive and combative rail companies, both of whom sought to service the Salt Lake Valley. One company started from the east, the other from the west. Their agreement with the government was they were to be paid for each mile of completed track until they met each other. It was a race fit for gods. The western company had to cross two mountain ranges, the eastern one contended with the war-like Plains Indians. At the end, each company, seeking to gain control of the Valley, continued working past each other, completing some 200 miles of parallel grades. Finally, Congress intervened and forced them to meet at Promontory Summit. On May 10th, 1869, Central Pacific's Jupiter and Union Pacific's 119 met head-to-head at this site, symbolizing the completion of

Golden Spike National Historic Site Courtesy NPS

the first transcontinental railroad. Two golden colored (one was silver and the other an alloy of gold, silver and iron) spikes were driven into the rails, ending what some called "the most significant event of the 19th century." The national park exists as a memorial to this crucial period of American development.

Highlights

★ Two steam engines, Central Pacific's Jupiter and Union Pacific's 119, have been meticulously constructed to precise specifications using pictures of the originals. Even the casual visitor can't help but admire these examples of early American locomotion.

★ During the summer, usually by the re-created 1869 tent city of Promontory, there are a wealth of interpretive programs on locomotives, railroading and some from creative perspectives like the buffalo's and train robber's.

★ The film on A.J. Russell, the photographer who chronicled the event, shows the enormous range of history Russell captured on film. Unfortunately, Russell has slipped into obscurity as many of his pictures are being mistakenly attributed to more famous western photographers.

★ Of special note is a sculpture in honor of the Chinese laborers who toiled thanklessly to complete this monumental task. Paid little more than slave wages, the Chinese were vilified and subjected to the whims of whatever white man chose to harm them.

Whiz Tips

The railroads were to play a vital if short-lived role in the settling of the central and western states. Their construction led to the slaughter of the huge buffalo herds for food to feed the workers driving the mighty beast to near-extinction. It should be noted the rail companies shed no tears over the dwindling of the great herds because the immense migrations of the prairie beast crossed the rail tracks causing major disruptions in rail service.

These tracks nailed to the earth symbolized the permanence the white man sought as opposed to the nomadic existence the Plains Indians led. The towns springing up in the wake of these tracks became jump-off points for cattlemen, miners and homesteaders who coveted the Indian's land.

Kids' Stuff

★ The park has a year-round Junior Railroad Engineer program. When the kids complete their activity booklet, they receive a badge and can purchase a really neat railroad cap for a very good price. Please note, the caps are not for sale to the general public, only to successful Junior Engineers.

★ Some of the summer fare includes living-history programs where rangers don 1860's clothing and demonstrate elements of the era. They also put on a "Just for Kids" program whose primary focus is children's understanding of railroading.

Access: 30 mi. W of Brigham City via UT 83. **Days/Hours:** Daily, summer 8-6, winter 8-4:30 (closed Thanksgiving & Dec.25). **Camping:** E nearby Brigham City, National Forest's Box Elder Canyon Campground (26 sites). **Special Events:** May 10th, at precisely 11:30 a.m., the Last Spike Celebration; mid-August, Railroaders Festival featuring the World Spike Driving Contest & buffalo chip throwing; btwn. Christmas & New Year's, Winter Locomotive Demo & Railroad Film Festival. **For info.:** Superintendent, Golden Spike National Historic Site, P.O.Box W, Brigham City, UT 84302. 801/471-2209.

Mormon Pioneer National Historic Trail

Fleeing religious persecution, approximately 70,000 members of the Church of Latterday Saints (Mormons) left from points east to journey to Utah. Many chose to follow Brigham Young on the 1,300-mile overland route from Nauvoo, IL driving ox-carts or pushing hand-carts. They travelled through Iowa, Nebraska (see Chimney Rock NHS & Scotts Bluff NM, NE), Wyoming (see Fort Laramie NHS, WY) into the Great Salt Lake valley. An auto route has been marked indicating the trail.

For info.: Mormon Pioneer National Historic Trail, Rocky Mountain Region, National Park service, P.O.box 25287, Denver, CO 80225.

Natural Bridges National Monument

Allow: .5 days *Fee*

"Discovered" by a prospector in 1883, the monument which features three large natural stone bridges is remotely situated in the southeastern corner of Utah. The steep cliff sides and the commanding bridges are remaining survivors testifying to the potency of water's force. Native Americans lived among these highly unusual geologic structures for at least 1500 years until they abandoned the region about the fourteenth century.

Highlights

★ There are three Natural Bridges within the park: Owachomo, Kachina and Sipapu, all Hopi names bestowed upon them when President Taft expanded the monument. The bridges were formed by flash flood waters through White and Armstrong Canyons. The water and the sediment it propelled, undercut the rock formations moving by pounding into the softer layers until it had successfully cut through and then expanded the opening. Most visitors stop at the various overlooks along the Bridge View Drive. However, each bridge can be visited by descending into the canyon. Owachomo (rock mounds), the oldest and thinnest of the bridges, spans no water and is reached by a moderate hike. Kachina (Hopi spirits) is reached via a steep trail. It is the newest bridge and the only bridge still being "carved" by stream ero-

Natural Bridges National Monument Courtesy NPS

sion. Sipapu, while spanning water, is a mature structure with its "legs" well up from the stream bed. Sipapu (the hole the Hopi emerged from into the world) is at the end of a steep trail.

Whiz Tips

❢ Between visiting Arches National Park and here, you recognize when an arched rock structure with a hole is a bridge or an arch. Bridges are formed by free-flowing water and arches are formed by water freezing and thawing.

❢ You can visit the photovoltaic system which supplied over 90% of the monument's energy requirements. At the time of its construction in 1980, it was the largest solar power generator of its kind.

Kids' Stuff

★ The hikes to the bridges are relatively short but steep. The trails to Sipapu and Kachina require close supervision of children. If you can only take one hike, the easiest is the .5 mi. Owachomo Bridge round trip trek. Also, worth a visit is the Horsecollar Ruin Overlook trail.

Access: 120 mi. S on US 191 & UT 95 from Moab or 45 mi. W on UT 95 from Blanding or 44 mi. N on Rte. 261 from Mexican Hat. **Days/Hours:** Park daily. Visitor center daily 8-4:30 (clsd. fed. winter holidays). **Camping:** The monument has a 13 site primitive campground. **For info.:** Superintendent, Natural Bridges National Monument, Box 1, Lake Powell, UT 84533. 801/259-5174.

Timpanogos Cave National Monument

Allow: .5 days *Fee*

Picture it. The night before, California has just had its worst earthquake in 80 years. You're waiting to tour a cave of who knows what dimensions. You overhear the rangers telling each other how they should change their little electric sign to read that the cave is a FAULT cave. You hope they're joking. You complete the strenuous walk straight up 1.5 miles of mountainside, only to be told by your guide, it is indeed a FAULT cave. She then goes on to tell you that this is actually the safest place to

Timpanogos Cave National Monument Courtesy NPS

be, because in earthquakes the shock waves cause all the damage. As Bill Cosby used to say ... RIIIIGHT!

Between Provo and Salt Lake City are three small, interconnected limestone caves that make up Timpanogos National Monument. These caves are particularly prized because of their rich and varied helictite formations which "grow" oblivious to the law of gravity. In addition, the caves have many other formations, like stalactites, stalagmites and popcorn. All are calcite residues left by liquefied limestone seeping into the caves. Each formation occurs when the water evaporates from the limestone solution, leaving the solid calcite configurations. Stalactites and stalagmites form icicle-like pillars from the roof or floor, respectively. These can grow to quite large dimensions. Helictites, the stars of this particular attraction, are stalactites that form in any direction other than perpendicular. Usually they're shaped in little spheres one upon another much like magnetic ball-bearings. Popcorn is balled calcite spread out like rust or mildew.

Highlights

★ The helictites in these caves are the most spectacular we've seen. They are countless, stretching and twisting in all directions, defying the understanding of scientists.

★ The view as you trek straight up the mountainside is quite spectacular.

Whiz Tips

The tour is very informative regarding the features in the caves, their formation and history. There's a wonderful origin story about the Indian Princess whose heart still beats in the cave.

On holidays and Saturdays, the cave is a hot item and can be sold out, so go early. Also be sure to dress warmly as the temperature in the cave is quite cool (45 degrees F.).

Kids' Stuff

★ The park has a Jr. Ranger program which allows children to learn more about the park while earning a special patch and certificate. In addition, throughout the summer there are special children's activities, mostly scheduled on Saturdays.

★ These caves are filled with things for kids to look at. The rangers make it really interesting with their stories. Like most cave tours, they turn out the lights. Although most kids marvel at the utter darkness, we recommend you hold your child's hand.

Access: 7 mi. E on UT 92 from I-15. **Days/Hours:** Visitor center daily, summer 8-5:30 & winter 8-4:30 (clsd. Thanksgiving, Dec.25 & Jan.1); Cave tours run from mid-May to mid-Oct. **Camping:** Adjacent Uinta National Forest. **Special Events:** Candlelight & flashlight tours, standard special tours; photography exhibitions & history lectures, less common. **Teacher's Package:** Available. **For info.:** Superintendent, Timpanogos Cave National Monument, R.R. 3, Box 200, American Fork, UT 84003. 801/756-5238.

Zion National Park

Allow: 2-3 days *Fee*

As the Aussies say, Southern Utah is chock-a-block with national parks, monuments and recreation areas. If the surrounding parks offer some of the most beautiful views in the world, what of Zion? How about one of the most beautiful drives in the world! Everything is real up close in Zion. The mountains and cliffs seem to tower around you. In the early days of the national parks, a park service representative was doing a slide show of the parks pointing out their beauty. From the back of the room a voice drawled out that the presenter hadn't seen the most beautiful place yet, that being Zion. After heeding that suggestion, Zion was explored and included in the National Park System.

Highlights

★ In a park with so many overwhelming vistas, it's hard to designate highlights. Certainly, the seemingly unending tunnel (1.1 miles) about which there are so many warnings, offers the thrill of discovery when you burst out into another marvelous setting which includes the Great Arch of Zion.

★ Checkerboard Mesa causes all to wonder at its formation and is an absolute must for the camera-happy. The mesa consists of petrified sand dunes, deposited by wind as the oceans receded, then covered by other sediments, "pressured" into hard rock and cemented by calcium carbonate and iron oxide. The multitude of cross-hatched cracks are the effects of freezing and erosion.

★ Make sure you have plenty of film as the scenic drive past Zion Lodge offers a multitude of "photo ops." If you still have film left continue on foot to the Narrows and, if you're up to some adventure, roll your pant legs up and wade up through the Narrows for some more great shots (the river is subject to flash floods so check with rangers on conditions).

Whiz Tips

Ranger-guided nature talks and walks as well as self-guided walks are available. Everyone in this park seems interested in helping you learn. We got a history of an early forestry operation. that used to harvest the mountainsides in the park, from a ranger who just happened by on his way to clean out the trash barrels.

Kids' Stuff

Zion is justifiably proud of its Junior Park Ranger Program, one of the best in the country. With a nature center classroom and field trips, 6 to 12 year-olds have to complete 2.5 hrs. of "class time" and two guided nature hikes or naturalist programs to successfully complete the requirements.

A challenging but "doable" hike is the Emerald Pools Trail where you get to go under waterfalls and climb up to the upper pools to arrive at a beach (a sandy mountain pool). Interpretive hikes include the Canyon

Zion National Park Courtesy NPS

Overlook Trail, Weeping Rock and the Gateway to the Narrows. They each have self-guiding pamphlets and are all child-size.

Access: I-15 or US 89 to UT 9, Kolob Canyons take Exit 40 off I-15. **Days/Hours:** Visitor centers; Zion Canyon summer 8-9, winter 8-5 & Kolob Canyons summer 8-6, winter 8-4:30. **Camping:** Park's 2 campgrounds; South (141 sites) & Watchman (228 sites) and a FREE summer primitive campground. **For info.:** Superintendent, Zion National Park, Springdale, UT 84767. (801) 772-3256.

VIRGINIA

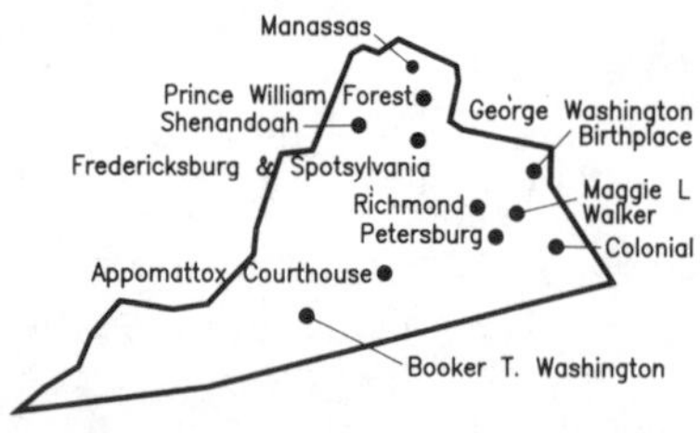

Appomattox Court House National Historical Park

Allow: 2 hrs. *Fee*

"Virginia buried her beloved at Appomattox, as her sons stood by, very ragged. All that she was, all that she hoped, all in which she had taken pride she told herself she had interred there."

Douglas Southall Freeman,
These United States

In Virginia's heartland is a small town whose name was etched in history as the place where the Civil War ended. It wasn't. Lincoln was assassinated after Lee's surrender here and at least three more large confederate forces had to be forced into submission. However, the fact that it was the South's greatest military leader, Robert E. Lee who surrendered, all but sealed the final outcome. In the long run, Appomattox

Appomattox Court House National Historical Park Courtesy Eastern NP&M Assoc.

has retained its significance for historians because of the manner in which the North treated the defeated rebel armies. The park consists of 27 buildings (14 restored & 13 reconstructed) comprising the picturesque village of Appomattox Court House in that fateful year.

Highlights

★ Touring the village, you sense an orderliness that suited the actions taken on that fateful April 9, 1865. The house where Grant accepted Lee's surrender was owned by Wilmer McLean, who had left his previous home on the edge of the Manassas battlefield (see Manassas NBP, VA), appropriately the first major engagement of the war, to escape the war. So the circle is completed by two war-weary generals in his parlor.

Whiz Tips

In summer, the park has living history interpreters who portray characters like a federal provost marshall, an ex-Confederate soldier and the county clerk. Park volunteers staff the Kelly House and Meeks Store while rangers lead tours through the McLean House.

Appomattox is regarded as the "bell cow" for how the defeated South would be treated. Whether General Grant followed his own instincts or the wishes summed up by Lincoln's second address ("With malice toward none; with charity for all;"), it's clear he set a tone for all future arrangements. Grant required little of the Rebel forces other than they lay down their weapons and leave their flags. Lee was finally ground down by Grant's singlemindness. Other Federal generals had their day with Lee. Most regretted the encounter. Lee went on to become the president of a small college after the war, while Grant went on to serve two terms as the nation's 18th president.

Kids' Stuff

The living historians, including some school-age participants, add an entertaining and informative dimension to your tour. For a good family outings, follow some of the five miles of hiking trails to historic Civil War sites.

Access: 3 mi. NE of Appomattox on VA 24. **Days/Hours:** Daily 9-5 (clsd. winter fed. holidays). **Camping:** Holliday Lake State Park (60 sites & shwrs.). **Special Events:** April 7, Anniversary of Battle of Sailor's Creek; April 9, special showings of "Surrender at Appomattox"; April 13, bus tour & week of 13th, living history presentations. **For info.:** Superintendent, Appomattox Court House National Historical Park, P.O.Box 218, Appomattox, VA 24522. 804/352-8987.

Arlington House, The Robert E. Lee Memorial

Allow: 1 hr. *FREE*

"Abandon your animosities and make your sons Americans!"

Robert E. Lee

Towering over the Capital like Mount Olympus (at least in the South's eyes), is the abandoned home of Robert E. Lee, last general-in-chief of the Armies of the Confederate States. The huge columned porch looks more like the entrance to a government building than the front door to a domicile. Perhaps this is fitting, as the finest of Virginia aristocracy are linked by the building. The first owner, George Washington Parke Custis, was the son Martha Washington and the stepson of George. When he died, he left the home to his daughter, Mary and her husband Robert E. Lee. The great mansion now stands sentinel over the most famous American graveyard. At the base of the hill below the home lies the cream of Boston's aristocracy, John Fitzgerald Kennedy and brother Bobby. The Federal forces who occupied the home right after it was abandoned created the cemetery to spite Lee.

Highlights

★ While the family carried away much of its furnishings when Lee made his decision to reject the North and join the South, many pieces have been returned for viewing.

Whiz Tips

Lee's life is a storied one. Leader of the Rebel Southern Army in a bitter war, his reputation remains unscathed in both North and South. Lee seems to have been born for his role. An uncle, Col. "Light-Horse Harry" Lee was a Revolutionary War hero and his ancestry among the cream of Virginia. Lee attended West Point, finishing second in his class. From there he began a solid military career serving in the Mexican War, overseeing the Military Academy and capturing John Brown at Harpers Ferry. Although only a Colonel, his reputation was such that Lincoln offered him command of the entire Federal forces when Virginia seceded. He rejected Lincoln's offer and joined the secessionist Army of North Virginia, eventually taking command of it. During the war he won plaudits for his daring and creative battle plans. He so inspired his men that in one difficult skirmish they ordered him back from the front for they believed if he was lost then so was the South. Robert E. Lee proved he was the best leader of armies in America in the 1860s. This fact says a great deal about him but perhaps more about the president who in 1860, was willing to give him more than the South did, total control of all the armies. Once again, Lincoln, we salute you.

Kids' Stuff

★ The antebellum home and furnishings have trouble competing with the saga of their owner, particularly with children. Those kids who have studied the Civil War are more attune to the historic significance of this place.

Access: Just across the Potomac from Washington, DC in Arlington National Cemetery. **Days/Hours:** Daily, summer 9:30-6 & winter 9:30-4:30. **Camping:** Greenbelt Park (125 sites) & Prince William Park (80 sites). **For info.:** Superintendent, Arlington House, The Robert E. Lee

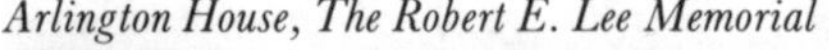
Arlington House, The Robert E. Lee Memorial

Memorial, George Washington Memorial Parkway, Turkey Run Park, McLean, VA 22101. 703/557-0613.

Booker T. Washington National Monument

Allow: 1-2 hrs. *FREE*

"This country demands that every race measures itself by the American standard."
Booker T. Washington,

In the foothills of the Blue Ridge Mountains just north of North Carolina are the decidedly humble beginnings of the founder of Tuskegee College, Booker T. Washington. Born and raised a slave, Booker T. Washington raised himself up to achieve a career in education anyone would envy. His birth home and the farm give you a good idea of how far he came. The log structures seem quaint and picturesque on a sunny day, but when winter strikes, the wind can whistle a cool tune.

Highlights

★ The small farm which Booker called a plantation has a comfortable feel about it. The rough-hewn structures are picturesque. The mid-19th century farm animals are different from those we see today. It is difficult to comprehend how the owners could consider Booker T. and his family as slightly more expensive livestock, to be bought and sold at will, regardless of family ties.

Whiz Tips

Booker was priced at $400 as a slave. He said of his childhood, "There was no period of my life that was devoted to play,... from the time that I can remember anything, almost every day has been occupied in some kind of labor." After having the Emancipation Proclamation read to them, Booker's family journeyed to West Virginia, where at the age of 11, he worked in a salt mine. Later he got a job as a house boy and at 16, he journeyed 400 miles by foot to Hampton Institute because he heard they would teach him in return for work. After graduating, he began his teaching career and returned to the institute as an instructor. In 1881, chosen to start an African American school in Tuskegee, Alabama, he

Booker T. Washington National Monument

Courtesy Booker T. Washington NM, NPS

and his students built the institute brick-by-brick, making it one of the most respected schools in the country (see Tuskegee Institute NHS, AL). Booker T. Washington gained national attention when he introduced the Atlanta Compromise which sought educational advancement for African Americans but condoned segregation. Washington's stand on the Atlanta Compromise came the year Frederick Douglass died, making Washington the preeminent black leader in America. He was often consulted by presidents and, at President Theodore Roosevelt's invitation, was the first African American to attend dinner at the White House.

Kids' Stuff

★ The farm has its own attraction regardless of its historic importance. Kids will enjoy exploring the property and seeing the razorback hogs, horses, cows, turkeys, chickens, ducks and sheep.

★ Booker T. Washington's rise from slavery and his willingness to work for his goals is a testimony to a thirst for knowledge and the rewards of striving for excellence.

Access: 16 mi. NE of Rocky Mount on VA 122N or 20 mi. SE of Roanoke on VA 116S & 122N or 21 mi. S of Bedford on Rte. 122. **Days/Hours:** Daily 8:30-5 (clsd. Thanksgiving, Dec.25 & Jan.1). **Camping:** Blue Ridge Pkwy., Roanoke Mountain Campground (105 sites) & Peaks of Otter Campground, 10 mi. NW of Bedford (148 sites). **Teacher's Package:** Available. **For info.:** Superintendent, Booker T. Washington National Monument, Rte. 1, Box 195, Hardy, VA 24101. 703/721-2094.

Colonial National Historical Park

Allow: .5 days *Fee*

"The Countrie is not mountainous nor yet low, but such pleasant plaine Hils and fertile Valies, one prettily crossing another, and watered so conveniently with their sweete Brookes and Christall Springs, as if Art it selfe had devised them."

Captain John Smith
Purchas his Pilgrimes, 1625

The park encompasses two of the country's most important historic

Colonial National Historical Park

sites: Jamestown, the oldest (1607) continuing English-established settlement in North America and Yorktown, the final important battle scene in the War for Independence. The Colonial Parkway links the legends of John Smith and Pocahontas to British General Cornwallis and George Washington.

Highlights

★ At Jamestown, you take a step back in time to watch the 17th century English immigrant craftsmen ply their hands at glass-making and pottery. Statues of the settlement's prominent people and reconstructed buildings provide you with a glimpse of the past.

★ At Yorktown, you can see many of the buildings that date back to the Revolutionary War era and attend some of the park's interpretive programs.

Whiz Tips

Although the Jamestown settlers felt they could make a good living with a glass-works and by starting a silkworm culture, they hoped to uncover riches of jewels or gold. Imagine their winter dreams when they sent a keg of bright yellow flakes back to England. Oh, what a life they must have banked on! Oh, what misery must have beset them when they learned it was iron pyrite or "fool's gold." The colony achieved a modicum of success with a weed (tobacco) that King James I referred to as "loathsome to the eye, hateful to the nose, harmful to the braine, and dangerous to the lungs," thus predating the Surgeon-General by over 350 years. Pocahontas became America's most famous Native American woman when John Smith claimed she saved his life by begging her father, Chief Powhatan, to let him go. She died at age 22 on her return voyage from England, where she and her husband John Rolfe met with royalty. She wasn't the only casualty as one year, in retaliation for past wrongs, the Native Americans prevented settlers from gathering their food and 9 out every 10 of them died during the winter. Jamestown National Historic Site, administered by the Association for the Preservation of Virginia Antiquities is an affiliated site covering that portion of the first permanent English settlement in North America (1607) not administered by the park service.

Across the peninsula lies Yorktown, the last Southern beachhead for the British forces. Cornwallis lost the war even when he won the battles. Each victory diminished his force; each loss meant more rebels joined the fight. In the end, the assistance of the well-trained French forces enabled the patriots to defeat the redcoats and their loyalist forces. Even in defeat, Cornwallis was unable to respect the colonists as he offered his sword to the French Admiral Count De Grasse. Not only did the French officer refuse his offer but Washington insisted the British surrender to the man the British had defeated at Charleston, General Benjamin Lincoln.

Kids' Stuff

★ The park has a Jr. Ranger program which awards a badge and a certificate to those people who successfully complete the requirements. There is a quiz on the introductory film, questions on the rangers' responsibilities, hands-on programs and work sheets to complete.

★ Kids are quite taken with the large section of a battleship that they can walk through and its top deck where a Pinocchio-like colonial boy, "John Whitney," who describes the battle of Yorktown. In summer, rangers demonstrate 18th century artillery firing.

Access: Jamestown & Yorktown anchor Pkwy. off I-64 or Rte. 17. **Days/Hours:** Daily, summer 8:30-6 & winter 8:30-5:30. **Camping:** 7 mi., Newport News city park has camping. **Teacher's Package:** Available. **For info.:** Superintendent, Colonial

National Historical Park, P.O. Box 210, Yorktown, VA 23690. 804/898-3400.

Fredericksburg & Spotsylvania NMP

Allow: .5 days *FREE*

"It was a great slaughter pen...they might as well have tried to take Hell."

Union soldier at Marye's Height

For over two years a series of battles were fought in the area of Virginia between Washington, DC and Richmond. The park is comprised of the sites of four of the most fiercely fought battles in the Civil War: Fredericksburg, Chancellorsville, Wilderness and Spotsylvania.

Highlights

★ Travelling through each battlefield you get a good sense of what happened from the lay of the land. At Fredericksburg, as you look up Marye's Heights, you understand how even the bravest assault could be broken and you wonder why anyone would attempt such a foolhardy task. The Wilderness seems made for Lee's practiced ploy of creating confusion and evening-up the odds for his outnumbered men. At Spotsylvania's "Bloody Angle," you shudder at how rivals could remain so close to each other through such harrowing fire and death. And at Chancellorsville, you are reminded of the risks of war when you hear of bold Stonewall Jackson's fatal "friendly fire" wound.

Whiz Tips

❢ Park rangers are available at the various locations. Try to time your visit to take in the interpretive programs.

❢ The Fredericksburg Visitor Center is at the base of Marye's Heights where the Rebels under Lee crushed the Federal troops (12,000 men dead or wounded) who tried to take it. This site includes the length of the battlefield and nearby Chatham where Federal officers housed themselves. Fredericksburg was central to most of the fighting in the Eastern Campaign. For example, on July 21, 1861 citizens heard the guns at the Battle of Manassas.

Fredericksburg/Spotsylvania National Military Park

The Chancellorsville Battlefield has its own visitor center and AV explaining the fighting that took place there and at the Wilderness and Spotsylvania. A monument marks the spot where Stonewall Jackson was mistakenly shot by his own men.

After the battle at the Wilderness, Grant tried to sneak past the rebel force and beat them to their capital. Lee won the race and dug in at Spotsylvania Court House. The battle was notable for the "Bloody Angle," a place in the battle lines where 11,800 men were killed or injured during the 24 hours of hand-to-hand combat.

Many rural manor homes and related buildings fall under the care of the Green Springs Historic District, an affiliated park service site.

Kids' Stuff

★ Although the sites are linked by busy highways, each has quieter paved areas where families can walk or cycle as they tour. The fact the park spans three years of the Civil War and four critical battles allows families to learn a great deal about the whole war here.

Access: Visitor centers in downtown Fredericksburg & Chancellorsville. **Days/Hours:** Daily, summer 9-6 & winter 9-5 (clsd. Dec.25 & Jan.1). **Camping:** Prince William Forest Park (80 sites). **Teacher's Package:** Available. **For info.:** Superintendent, Fredericksburg/Spotsylvania National Military Park, Box 679, Fredericksburg, VA 22404. 703/373-6122.

George Washington Birthplace National Monument

Allow: 2 hrs. *FREE*

A peaceful colonial plantation setting, Washington's Birthplace overlooks sprawling Pope's Creek where it joins the mighty Potomac. The park service administers a 1730s mansion and separate workshop and kitchen, to transport you back to George Washington's childhood days.

Highlights

★ The site is actually quite attractive. The creek offers a tranquil set-

George Washington Birthplace National Monument

ting for wintering waterfowl including tundra swans, Canada geese and several varieties of ducks.

Whiz Tips

★ Because the original structures no longer stand, the site uses period-style buildings with interpreters dressed in 18th century-style clothing. In summer, these living historians demonstrate blacksmithing, spinning, ox-driving, candlemaking and open-hearth cooking. For example, on our visit the plantation blacksmith told of his many chores, including the traditional working with iron to the making of shoes and rope. He explained how every part of a cow was put to use including horns to make buttons, spoons, bowls, lantern shades, combs, forks, cups and they were even finely stripped to make translucent book covers.

The visitor center traces the lineage of the Washington clan and displays artifacts recovered from the site. Washington's father, Augustine, died when George was 11. At that time he returned to Pope's Creek to live with his older half-brother and study surveying. At 16, he was "out West" surveying for the King of England. The field across from the family Burial Site was one of his first surveying exercises.

Kids' Stuff

Children get very excited about visiting George Washington's birthplace. They have studied about the nation's first president in detail. The opportunity to see his birthplace is almost overwhelming. Questions come quick and fast. "Where did the cherry tree stand?" "Where did he throw the silver dollar?" "What did he wear?" These questions allow the interpreters to describe Washington's early life to all visitors.

Families find the Dancing Marsh Nature Trail a good place for a hike and a picnic. At a short stretch of the Potomac, kids can search for shells and shark's teeth. The children love to see the 18th century farm animal breeds and learn about the skills the colonials had to practice out of necessity.

Access: 38 mi. E of Fredericksburg on VA 3 & VA 204. **Days/Hours:** Daily 9-5 (clsd. Dec.25 & Jan.1). **Camping:** Prince William Forest Park (80 sites) & Westmoreland State Park (elec. & shwrs.). **Special**

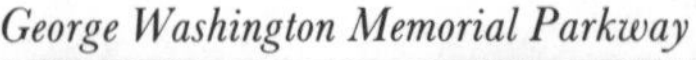

George Washington Memorial Parkway

Events: Children's Day, Wool & Flax Day, Gentry Day, Band Concerts, Native American Heritage Day, Afro-American Heritage Day, Christmas Season and Feb. 22, Washington's Birthday Open House. **For info.:** Superintendent, George Washington Birthplace National Monument, R.R. 1, Box 717, Washington's Birthplace, VA 22443. 804/224-1732.

George Washington Memorial Parkway

Allow: 2-3 hrs. *FREE*

Running alongside the mighty Potomac on the D.C./Virginia border, you travel from the northern stretches of the beltway all the way to the doorstep of George Washington's Mount Vernon estate. Along the way, you pass a plethora of parks, historic sites and bird sanctuaries.

Highlights

★ From north to south, you can take in Turkey Run Park,a wooded park area; Great Falls Park (see Great Falls Park), Claude Moore Colonial Farm, a recreated colonial farm; Glen Echo Park; Clara Barton House NHS, (see Clara Barton House NHS, MD); Fort Marcy, a Civil War era earthen fortification; Theodore Roosevelt Island, a treed island across the Potomac from the Kennedy Center; the United States Marine Corps War Memorial and accompanying Netherlands Carillon (49-belled monument to WW II); Arlington House, the Robert E. Lee Memorial (see Arlington House, the Robert E. Lee Mem., VA); Arlington National Cemetery, the final resting place for so many American notables including J.F.K. & R.F.K.; Lyndon Baines Johnson Memorial Grove, a living memorial to the 36th President of 500 white pines; Roaches Run Waterfowl Sanctuary, a popular fishing spot; Daingerfield Island, a hiking and bird-watching area; Jones Point Lighthouse, an inland lighthouse; Dyke Marsh, a wetlands habitat preserving over 250 species of birds with a boardwalk for cycling or walking; and Fort Hunt, an 1898 gun placement guarding the river approach to the nation's capital.

Whiz Tips

The byway was constructed to save natural greenways around the capital. It was originally planned to complete a loop joining the north and south banks of the river. Today the parkway runs down the Virginia shoreline from I-495 south to Washington's Mount Vernon home and from the American Legion Bridge south along the Maryland shoreline to Cabin John Bridge (this portion is called the Clara Barton Parkway). This parkway is a major commuter route, so beware of Washington's infamous three hour rush "hour."

Kids' Stuff

★ There are plenty of nature trails, picnic sites, fishing holes and interesting sites along the parkway. The colonial farm and forts are good bets. But the best idea is to "drag" the kids to Glen Echo Park and "force" them to take the hand-carved, hand-painted Dentzel Carousel ride (open Wed. 10-2 & Sa & Su noon-6 May-Oct. 301/492-6282).

★ The Netherlands Carillon (open during Bell Tower Concerts Sat. from Apr.-Sept 2-4 & June-Aug. 6:30-8:30) is a great place for kids to climb to the top for a view of the capital city.

★ Theodore Roosevelt Island has a mile-long nature trail leading through a swamp, a marsh and the forest. There's a footbridge where kids can fish from during tidal changes ("small fry for small fry"). Turkey Run Park also has an 8 mi. hiking trail running alongside the Potomac. Spring visitors are treated to a colorful array of wildflowers. Further south near Mount Vernon, there's an 18.5 mi. biking and hiking trail that's great for families.

Access: Off Beltway take Exit 14; from D.C., the 14th St., Memorial or Theodore Roosevelt Bridges. **Days/Hours:** Daily. **Camping:** Prince William Forest Park (80 sites) & Greenbelt Park (175 sites). **Special Events:** Dec. 17-Jan. 6, Christmas at Arlington House. **For info.:** Superintendent, George Washington Memorial Parkway, Turkey Run Park, McLean, VA 22101. 703/285-2598. Claude Moore Colonial Farm-703/442-7557.

Great Falls Park

Allow: 2 hrs. *Fee*

"[the canal will] bind those people to us by a chain which can never be broken."

George Washington

This scenic stretch of the Potomac held a special promise for the country's leading engineer. George Washington hoped to circumvent the falls by building a canal around it. The Patowmack Canal would allow traders access to the eastern seaboard thus opening greater riches from the interior. While Washington's plan couldn't maintain its economic viability, we still benefit from the remains of his efforts because the park preserves the canal ruins.

Highlights

★ The Virginia side of the river is the best place to see the falls. Craggy rocks jut out of the plunging water, sending it tumbling around.

Whiz Tips

Washington's Patowmack Company built five canals, two with lift locks and dredged the river, enabling the company to operate for 26 years. Great Falls, which has a drop of 80 ft. in less than a mile, required a lift lock so the canal boats could be lowered as the river descends. The enormous cost of carving a canal out of the hard rock bordering the falls proved a key factor in the financial ruin of the company. During the company's life it formed a vital link between the Allegheny mountains and the coast. Washington's good friend and fellow Revolutionary War hero, "Lighthorse Harry" Lee, backed the town of Matildaville, named for Lee's first wife, whose fortune closely followed the canal's. It

Great Falls Park

was abandoned shortly after the canal proved unprofitable.

Kids' Stuff

★ The rangers offer interpretive walks and talks about the geology and history of the park. Plus, the park is a favorite picnic site for the locals with the falls as a scenic backdrop. There are also fishing and hiking available. One note of caution: several people have lost their lives due to the treacherous power of the river. As a result, swimming and wading are prohibited.

Access: 15 mi. N of Washington, DC off Beltway Exit 13 in Great Falls. **Days/ Hours:** Park, daily 9-dark. **Camping:** Greenbelt Park (175 sites) & Prince William Forest Park (80 sites). **For info.:** Site Manager, Great Falls Park, P.O.Box 66, Great Falls, VA 22066. 703/285-2966.

Maggie L. Walker NHS

COURTESY NPS

Maggie L. Walker National Historic Site

Allow: 1 hr. *FREE*

"To be a success in business, be daring, be first, be different."

Marchant

In downtown Richmond is a house commemorating a woman who was all these things. Before women had the right to vote and before married women could own property, a woman of African descent, rose up to become leader of a social service organization, editor of a newspaper and founder and president of the first African American bank in the country. It is no small tribute to her that this same bank survived the Great Depression and scores of Savings & Loans failures to exist today. Maggie L. Walker also put her considerable skills to help organize the National Association for the Advancement of Colored People (NAACP) and served as its vice-president.

Highlights

★ You can tour the Walker home and see evidence of Maggie's strong family life. Most of the furnishings are hers or her sons; whose families shared the house with Maggie.

Whiz Tips

Maggie's story is truly an All-American saga. Her mother, a former slave, was widowed while Maggie and her brother were still young. Although Maggie had to do laundry to help the family out, she was able to complete school and become a school teacher. At age 14, Maggie had joined the Independent Order of St. Luke, an order promoting humanitarian causes and encouraging self-help. Maggie took this philosophy to heart and advanced in the organization. Before she became the leader, St. Luke's was floundering. In short order, she increased membership and exacted sound financial plans. In 1901, she established the *St. Luke Herald*, a newspaper servicing the black community. The St. Luke Penny Savings Bank was established in 1903 so Richmond's black community could put their money to work for them, as opposed to putting it into white-controlled banks.

Kids' Stuff

★ Maggie's story and accomplishments are worthwhile examples for any child. She showed how anyone can succeed if they have the will and the ability. She also demonstrates that championing a cause is possible while achieving one's career aspirations.

Access: Downtown Richmond. **Days/Hours:** W-Su 9-5 (clsd. Dec.25 & Jan.1). **Camping:** SW near Burkeville, Twin Lakes State Park (33 sites & shwrs.). **Teacher's Package:** Available. **For info.:** Superintendent, Maggie L. Walker National Historic Site, 3215 East Broad St., Richmond, VA 23223. 804/780-1380.

Manassas National Battlefield Park

Allow: 1-2 hrs. *Fee*

"Night has closed upon a hard-fought field, our forces have won a glorious victory."
Confederate President Jefferson Davis

As Fort Sumter came to epitomize the start of the Civil War, then Manassas or Bull Run (as the Federals called it) epitomized the first significant blood-letting. Just across the Virginia border is the Bull Run ("run" is Virginian for stream), the place of the first major encounter between North and South. The place where all the dreams of early victory and romantic battles would turn to dust as did the bones of the fallen. Manassas had the misfortune to witness two engagements and more death than it cared for.

Highlights

★ There's a plus to visiting a location which has played host to two battles; you get to see so many more skirmish sites. The downside is it's

Manassas National Battlefield Park

easy to get confused as to what happened when.

Whiz Tips

❢ The first battle fought on July 21, 1861, resulted in a union loss and the establishment of Confederate "Stonewall" Jackson's name. Union General McDowell tried to rally the courage of his men by pointing out Jackson's demeanor, likening it to a stonewall, a most curious way to motivate your troops. Although the losses would seem insignificant at the war's end, the 900 men lost in this encounter acted like a cold shower on the men from both sides. Each had convinced themselves that they could "whop" the other in short order. Neither was prepared for the blood and death the actuality of fighting would bring. This battle demonstrated that trains would revolutionize war as large masses of men and material could be transported quickly to needed areas.

❢ At the second battle the Federals were surprised by the strength of the Confederate forces and only valiant efforts at Chinn Ridge and Henry Hill saved them from annihilation.

❢ Wilmer McLean and his family, Southern sympathizers, were residents of the area when the first battle occurred. McLean's house which was struck by a Union artillery shell, served as an office for the Confederates during the fighting. In order to escape the war, he moved his family to Appomattox Court House and into the history books (see Appomattox Court House NHS, VA).

Kids' Stuff

★ The battlefield is cross-hatched by paved country roads. However, there are bridal and hiking trails which make it a nice safe place for a family outing. As is usual with this kind of park, the more familiar your children already are with the events that transpired here, the more fruitful your visit will be.

Access: 26 mi. SW of Washington off I-66 on VA 234. **Days/Hours:** Daily (clsd. Dec. 25) **Camping:** Bull Run Regional Park, Centerville exit off I-66 (150 sites, elec. & showers) & Prince William Forest Park off I-94 (80 sites). **Teacher's Package:** Available. **For info.:** Superintendent, Manassas National Battlefield Park, 6511 Sudley Rd., Manassas, VA 22110. 703/754-7107.

Petersburg National Battlefield

Allow: 1-2 hrs. *Fee*

"The key to taking Richmond is Petersburg."
General U.S. Grant

Why Petersburg? Why not just capture Richmond? Petersburg was Richmond's supply center. By laying siege to Petersburg and cutting off its supplies, the Federals were essentially starving Richmond. The siege lasted 10 months as Grant slowly managed to capture rail line after rail line. Lee tried to slip the tightening noose with a counter-attack, but it failed. The scene was set and the war was soon to be over for the Confederate States of America.

Highlights

★ One of the most unusual actions taken in the entire war occurred at Petersburg. Pennsylvania troops, many of whom were miners, began tunnelling under the city's earthen Confederate fortifications. Their plan was to plant a large explosive under the mound and blow it to smithereens. Whether the Union troops who were poised to attack were overly excited at this accomplishment or their attack was poorly planned, the final result was chaos. Line after line of Federal troops pushed forward into the pit unable to climb out the other side or to retreat the way they came. If the Union men had the presence of mind to go around the hole instead of down through it, the war probably would have ended a great deal sooner.

★ At the City Point Unit, you can see the cabin where Grant spent the siege. Also part of the park is the Appomattox Manor, the home of one Dr. Epps who owned 150 slaves and joined the Confederate Army as a private.

Whiz Tips

❢ During summer, visitors are treated to living-history presentations.

❢ Petersburg was the culmination of Grant's strategy to wear down the Army of North Virginia. With no more resources to call on, the Confederates were in a battle of attrition. Old men and boys were called into action and still they were vastly outnumbered. The siege at Petersburg resulted in 6 major battles, 11 engagements, 44 skirmishes, 6 assaults, 9 actions and 3 expeditions resulting in a total of 70,000 casualties.

Kids' Stuff

★ The 4-mile-long battlefield can be bicycled and there are walking trails explaining the actions that took place. During the peak of summer, there's a union camp and artillery firings. On wknds. you can occasionally see musket drills and firings.

Access: 2.5 mi. E of downtown Petersburg. **Days/Hours:** Visitor center, daily, summer 8-7 & winter 8-5. **Camping:** SW near Burkeville, Twin Lakes State Park (33 sites & shwrs.). **Special Events:** Early Dec., Christmas program at City Point. **For info.:** Superintendent, Petersburg National Battlefield, P.O.Box 549, Petersburg, VA 23804. 804/732-3531.

Prince William Forest Park

Allow: 2 hrs. *FREE*

Like many of the forested parks encircling the nation's capital, Prince William appears to have been established as a federally run state park protecting greenways for camping and picnicking. The plant growth is all new and reflects how this area would have looked before Europeans brought their axes and their plows.

Highlights

★ There is an infrastructure of nature trails and plenty of picnic spots. Lying within an easy 1 hour drive of Washington, DC, the campground is a quiet godsend to visiting campers.

Whiz Tips

❢ The park has a Nature Center where naturalists design day walks and evening programs to teach visitors about the ecosystem.

Kids' Stuff

★ The park personnel make special efforts to make this a family spot with its programs. The rangers put on afternoon sing-a-longs and games days, in addition to the usual walks and talks. While cycling is not allowed on the nature trails, the roads within the park are fairly safe with little traffic and there is a network of fire roads your family can use. There is also fishing in the park's small lakes.

Access: 32 mi. S of Washington, DC off I-95. **Days/Hours:** Daily (clsd. Dec.25 & Jan.1). **Camping:** Park's campground (80 sites). **For info.:** Superintendent, Prince William Forest Park, P.O. Box 209, Triangle, VA 22172. 703/221-7181.

Red Hill Patrick Henry National Memorial

Deep in the wooded hills of Virginia is the small plantation of one of the nation's finest orators. Visitors can see a museum (fee), and a reconstruction of his home.

For info.: Red Hill Patrick Henry National Memorial, Patrick Henry Memorial Foundation, Brookneal, VA 24528.

Richmond National Battlefield Park

Allow: 1-4 hrs. *FREE*

"On to Richmond!"

Union battle cry

Twice along Richmond's eastern flank the Rebel forces had to marshall their defenses to preserve the Confederate capital. As these battles occurred over a vast area, the park consists of ten units: Chimborazo Visitor Center, Cold Harbor, Chickahominy Bluff, Beaver Dam Creek, Watt House (Gaines' Mill Battlefield), Malvern Hill, Garthright House, Drewry's Bluff, Parker's Battery and Fort Harrison.

Highlights

★ Lee's last major victory came during the second assault on Richmond at Cold Harbor. Grant uncharacteristically delayed his attack, allowing Lee's men to dig in. 7,000 Union soldiers were killed or wounded in 20 min as they were pinned in a giant horseshoe of fire. Grant said "I regret this assault more than any one I have ordered." He should have regretted his behavior after the attack even more. It took Lee and Grant three days to agree to a truce allowing the Union troops to remove their wounded. When the truce was settled, only two of the wounded were left alive; the others had succumbed to their wounds, starvation, thirst and exposure. The reason for the delay? To ask for a truce to clear the field was admitting you had lost.

Whiz Tips

★ At Fort Harrison, where today's living historians stand "guard," Grant assembled 15,000 Federal troops under the cover of darkness to capture and defend the well-fortified position. The North's African American troops won 14 Medals of Honor here.

❢ The Union's first attempt to capture Richmond was led by the tentative George McClellan. McClellan didn't want to win as badly as he didn't want to lose. He brought his troops up the peninsula and sat and waited for over two months until Robert E. Lee defeated him at the

Richmond National Battlefield Park Courtesy Richmond NBP

Seven Days' Battles, forcing him back north.

Kids' Stuff

★ Children 7-12 can spend 3-4 hrs. in the park's Jr. Ranger program and earn a certificate and colorful patch. Ask at the Chimborazo Visitor Center about the Gallery Game which is designed to help children get involved in their visit here. The park also has special children-oriented interpretive programs in the summer. There is also the extremely comprehensive EARTH program which incorporates environmental and historical lessons. It's offered weekdays through the summer but does require reservations.

★ There are about a half dozen living-history events where history buffs dress up in full regalia to recreate Civil War encampments. The past schedule has included about one weekend per month starting in May and ending in Oct. If you can catch one of these, you'll find these volunteers more than willing to explain everything and anything about the times, the battles, their equipment and their uniforms.

Access: Chimborazo Visitor Center, 3215 E. Broad St. in Richmond. **Days/Hours:** Chimborazo Visitor Center, daily 9-5 (clsd. Thanksgiving, Dec.25 & Jan.1); Fort Harrison Visitor Center, summer, daily 9-5. **Camping:** Pocahontas State Park, 45 min. from Richmond. **Special Events:** Mid-May, Drewry's Bluff Encampment; late June, Gaines' Mill Encampment; late July & late Aug., Cold Harbor Encampment; end of Sept., Fort Harrison Encampment & Candlelight Walking Tour. **Teacher's Package:** Available plus EARTH materials. **For info.:** Superintendent, Richmond National Battlefield Park, 3215 East Broad St., Richmond, VA 23223. 804/226-1981.

Shenandoah National Park

Allow: .5 days *Fee*

"I ain't so crazy about leavin' these hills...I allus said these hills would be the heart of the world."

Hezekiah Lam, Shenandoah resident

Encompassing the northern crest of the Blue Ridge, Shenandoah maintains a fragile wildlife area. Unlike the Blue Ridge Parkway, its southern

Shenandoah National Park Courtesy NPS

link to Great Smoky Mountain National Park, Shenandoah has wide swaths of land alongside its Skyline Drive which the park rangers encourage visitors to get out of their cars to enjoy. Its 105 miles of roadway passes a myriad of hiking trails leading to overlooks, waterfalls and wildlife.

Highlights

★ Never in all our travels on this continent have we seen so many deer. When you bed down at Big Meadow campground, your nearest companion might be one of these irresistible creatures, who settles in next to your tent. They are as plentiful as squirrels in a city park and wander about the campsite reminding us that we are the visitors, not they. With that thought in mind, please remember feeding them (or any wild animal) is a bad practice.

Whiz Tips

The emphasis at Shenandoah is nature. Almost all of its interpretive programs are focussed on walks or talks that explain the animals, the birds, the forests or the geologic formation. If you want to see some of the wildlife yourself, an early morning or late evening trip is guaranteed to produce results.

Shenandoah and the Appalachians are home to the greatest variety of salamanders in the world. The most common of these amphibians, the red-backed salamander, is also the most common park animal but one of the hardest to spot.

Kids' Stuff

Shenandoah offers a Jr. Ranger program and special summer weekend children's interpretive programs called Just For Kids. The park newspaper codes those programs where adults have to accompany children under 12. Otherwise, there are several programs which cater to all ages. Most of the hikes are accessible for children. The wild flowers in the early part of the year and the proliferation of deer make this park particularly appealing to families.

The park is rift with great short hikes for families. In the North District, good hikes you can take are Fox Hollow Nature Trail (1.2 mi.) which has an interpretive guidebook; Compton Peak (2 mi.) leading to scenic overlook; Fort Windham Rocks (.8 mi.) with lava formations; Traces Nature Trail (1.7 mi.) which has a trail guide. In the Central District, these are good family hikes; Story of the Forest Trail (1.8 mi.) which is a self-guiding nature trail; Lewis Spring Falls (1.8 mi.) with a steep hike to an 80 foot falls; Mill Prong (1 mi.) to a pretty stream. The South District walks include Ivy Creek Spring (1 mi.) leads to a cold spring; Deadening Nature Trail (1.3 mi.).

Access: N entrance - 340 S of Front Royal (I-66 to Front Royal); S entrance - Rte. 250 & I-64; Thornton Gap - Rte.211; Swift Run - Rte.33. **Days/Hours:** Byrd Visitor Center, daily 9-5 (clsd. winter); Dickey Ridge Visitor Center, daily 9-5 (clsd. winter). **Camping:** Park has 4 campgrounds; Big Meadows (peak season -reservations-Ticketron). **Special Events:** May's 3rd wknd., Wildflower Weekend; wknd. closest Aug. 10, Hoover Days. **For info.:** Superintendent, Shenandoah National Park, Luray, VA 22835. 703/999-2229.

Wolf Trap Farm Park for the Performing Arts

Allow: 2-3 hrs. *FREE (except performances)*

Like other Washington area parks, Wolf Trap Farm's role is a little mystifying to tourists. Because of the unique nature of Washington, DC, i.e. it doesn't belong to any state, the parks around it would normally be state parks or city parks. However, here they fall under the control of the park service. Wolf Trap Farm in any other location would be a state or municipal theater. The property includes a large stage where a variety of performances are displayed throughout the summer and a park land for picnicking. Because it is a national facility, it has interpretive programs to help you understand its mandate.

Highlights

★ During the summer, the FREE interpretive performances (reservations required) include opera, ballet, symphony, children's performers, puppetry and musical theater. The performers explain their craft as well as demonstrate their talent.

Whiz Tips

The very nature of the park is to allow visitors access to the arts. Its location, prices and content are designed to facilitate attendance for a cross-section of the public.

Kids' Stuff

★ The interpretive programs are primarily targeted at children although anyone can attend. Several performers do their best to involve kids in their presentations making it a fun learning experience. The park's picnic area make this a pleasant and economical outing.

Access: S from Washington, DC take Exit 11-S off I-495 on Rte.123 to US 7 to Towlson Rd. **Days/Hours:** Daily 830-5. **Camping:** Greenbelt Park (175 sites) & Prince William Forest Park (80 sites). **For info.:** Supervisory Park Ranger, Wolf Trap Farm Park, 1551 Trap Farm Rd., Vienna, VA 22182. 703/255-1820/1800.

VIRGIN ISLANDS

Buck Island Reef National Monument

Allow: .5 days *FREE*

Just north of St. Croix Island is tiny Buck Island and its wondrous reef. The Marine Garden is a swimming and snorkeling paradise, with little to harm you save the sun's intense rays and stings from things you shouldn't be touching in the first place. Caribbean coral reefs are complex, delicate ecosystems. They reward visitors with a multi-hued, multi-varied, multi-shaped world of fishes, corals and plants.

Highlights

★ Buck Reef offers pristine conditions for discovering the addictive pastime of snorkeling. It offers the unique feature of an underwater nature trail complete with signs. Many snorkelers explore reefs without a clue of what they are looking at. This trail provides a great opportunity to learn more about this underwater world.

★ Buck Island has hiking trails leading to an overlook of St. Croix. The park also has picnic tables, grills, a change room, a shelter and restrooms.

Whiz Tips

The coral reef is one of the few ecosystems where animal life exceeds plant life. Although many think of the reef as a geological formation, it is a living thing. Millions of tiny corals attach themselves to the hard skeletons of their predecessors and feed. At the end of their short lives, they have produced a skeleton which becomes a part of the reef. Coral reefs only occur within very limited geographic locations. The water temperature, salinity and flow are the major dictates of their growth. They are only found within 22 degrees latitude of the Equator and on the eastern shores of the continental plates. Coral can be shaped like huge brains, spires, trees, staghorns or shrubs. It can encourage growth of other near relatives which are shaped like sea whips, sea fans and gorgonians. The reefs ultimately host plants which attract small fishes, who in turn attract larger fishes.

Newcomers to snorkeling often make the painful mistake of not protecting their backs from the sun. A form-fitting T-shirt is a must and plenty of waterproof sun screen for backs of necks and legs is advisable.

Kids' Stuff

★ Snorkeling is a great sport for children who can swim. The surprising part of snorkeling is that with the aid of flippers and the diversion of the scenes below you any half-decent swimmer (we barely qualify) can stay afloat for hours.

Access: Private boats carry visitors from Christiansted for a fee. **Days/Hours:** Daily. **For info.:** c/o Superintendent, Buck Island Reef National Monument, Christiansted NHS, P.O.Box 160, Christiansted, St. Croix, V.I. 00820. 809/773-1460.

Christiansted National Historic Site

Allow: .5 days *Fee*

A Danish town on a Caribbean island is the setting for this national park. The Danish West India and Guinea Co. bought St. Croix from the French, the last of three countries (England and Spain) to lay claim to it. From 1733 until 1820, the purchase proved a gold-mine. Sugar cane and slave-labor fueled its success. However, sugar beet competition lowered the prices and black emancipation raised the costs, putting an end to the "Fabulous Sugar Island." The U.S. made tentative stabs at buying the islands but it wasn't until the threat of a German naval base during WW I that they made a firm offer.

Highlights

★ Quaint, exotic, intriguing are adjectives faintly describing a tour of downtown Christiansted and the park's historical sites. The mid-18th century fort is the best preserved of the Virgin Island fortifications. Of the same era are the warehouse and steeple building. The newer 19th century structures you'll see include the customs house, scalehouse and government house.

Whiz Tips

The park's H.Q. can brief you on the walking tour and alert you on what is of significance. Make it your first stop.

Kids' Stuff

★ Your children, like all visitors, will marvel at the different architecture. Truly Old World buildings demonstrate how Europeans carried their familiar surroundings with them as they attempted to adapt to new life styles. A good way to enhance your little ones' learning is to ask them how appropriate or inappropriate features of these buildings are for the climate.

Access: Downtown Christiansted, St. Croix Island. **Days/Hours:** M-Sa 8-4:30. **For info.:** Superintendent, Christiansted National Historic Site, P.O.Box 160, Christiansted, St. Croix, V.I. 00820. 809/773-1460.

Virgin Island National Park

Allow: 1 week *FREE*

"Ocean o'er its reefs and bars
Hid its elemental scars;
Groves of coconut and guava
Grew above its fields of lava
So the gem of the Antilles,-
'Isles of Eden,' where no ill is,-
Like a great green turtle slumbered
On the sea that is encumbered."

Bret Harte
'St. Thomas', A Geographical Survey

And so it is with St. John. In the 1930s, one government official described it thusly: "Three miles westward from St. Thomas, across the flashing blue waters of Pillsbury Sound, lies St. John, most romantic of the Virgin Isles...It is as wild, detached and primitive as if it were lost somewhere on the rim of an unknown sea." Today, the park service manages a good portion of the 9 mile by 5 mile island and much of its surrounding waters.

Highlights

★ The variety of land and ocean life is really amazing for so small a place. There are over 800 species of plants and 100-plus kinds of birds. Feral cats compete with the introduced mongoose, while donkeys and goats wander freely. The seashore is lined with coral reefs which host a multitude of crabs, turtles, fish and plants. You can see these natural wonders by donning walking shoes or flippers and taking to the park's land or underwater nature trails.

★ Some experts rank Trunk Bay as one of the top ten most beautiful beaches in the world. Its downside is that it is a mecca for the tour ships who stop by between 10-2 most days during the peak tourist season. Snorkelers should try Waterlemon Cay for its reefs and Francis Bay for turtles.

Whiz Tips

Occasionally, the rangers don traditional dress to explain the cultural history of the island. There are interpretive walks, boat rides and snorkeling lessons.

The Virgin Islands were Danish possessions until the U.S. purchased them during WW I to prevent German occupation. The park contains many ruins of the sugar plantations which were really only viable when manned by slave labor. As with most West Indian isles, its major attractions are its beaches and warm Caribbean waters.

Kids' Stuff

★ Hawksnest Bay is a great place to teach your children the joys of snorkeling. The bay is shallow enough for taller children to stand and peer down at the small, colorful fish flitting in and out of the elkhorn coral.

★ At the Annaberg sugar refinery children can learn the many uses for sugar cane. Cultural craft demonstrations help interpret traditional basket-making, cooking and gardening.

★ Many families are pleasantly surprised by the wealth of hiking trails they can take. Most are less than 2 miles long. The Cinnamon Bay Trail takes you to a sugar factory, while the Francis Bay Trail leads you past an estate house and a mangrove forest. To see some of the island's older history, try Reef Bay and the Petroglyph Trails and study fascinating rock carvings.

Access: Ferry from St. Thomas. **Days/ Hours:** Park H.Q. at Red Hook, daily 8-5; Cruz Bay Visitor Center, daily 8-4:30. **Camping:** Park's Cinnamon Bay Campground (can bring own tent but also fixed tents & cottages & shwrs.). **For info.:** Superintendent, Virgin Islands National Par, #10 Estate Nazareth, Charlotte Amalie, St. Thomas, VI 00801. 809/776-6201.

WASHINGTON

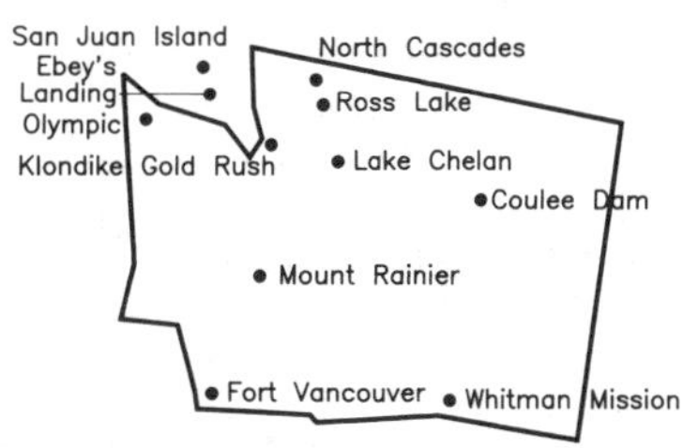

Coulee Dam National Recreation Area

Allow: 2 days *FREE*

The Coulee Dam is the first in a chain of eleven U.S. dams which capture the natural power of the Columbia River and convert it into energy. By doing so, it created 151 mi. long Franklin D. Roosevelt Lake, better known as Lake Roosevelt and backed up the Spokane River, boons for summer visitors. The dam also regulates the water flow for irrigation and flood control. When conditions are favorable, vibrant sails dot the blue expanse, motor boats skirt past coasting canoes and water skiers smear the smooth lake, as children ruffle its borders. At the park's two visitor centers you can find out about the best places for your particular recreational pursuits.

Highlights

★ Western rivers, once dammed, resemble enormous thick snakes as they follow glacial troughs. Whether by boat or car, people touring the lake find themselves compelled to go around the next corner.

★ For most visitors (we're talking Pacific coastal residents), the weather is the main attraction. It offers a respite from rain, a surety of sun and warmth.

Whiz Tips

There are a variety of interpretive programs. Some of these are recrea-

Coulee Dam National Recreation Area Courtesy Jim Miller

tional activities in the region, the lake's ecosystem and the history of Fort Spokane and the native people.

❢ You can tour the Grand Coulee Dam, where you learn about its purpose, its workings and the role hydroelectric generators serve in the total energy generating plan. If you time your visit right, you can take in the spectacular evening laser light show when the dam's waterfall is splashed by zaps of light as you listen to a narration of the Columbia River story.

Kids' Stuff

★ Family interpretive programs include environmental education, snorkeling and canoeing instruction, guided hikes and evening family canoe trips during the summer months.

★ With 16 FREE boat ramps, lifeguard beaches, several ideal water skiing areas and a multitude of fishing spots, there's plenty of opportunity to introduce your children to the pleasures of the lake.

★ Hot spots for catching fish are the Confluences, High Cliffs, Spokane River, Kettle River, Sanpoil river and Sherman Creek. Walleye, rainbow trout, kokanee, whitefish, perch and sturgeon patrol these waters.

Access: Visitor centers at Fort Spokane & Kettle Falls. **Days/Hours:** Fort Spokane and Kettle Falls Visitor Centers, summer, daily & winter, intermittently; park H.Q., weekdays year-round 8-4:30. **Camping:** 32 campgrounds, 24 drive-in. **For info.:** Superintendent, Coulee Dam National Recreation Area, P.O.Box 37, Coulee Dam, WA 99116. 509/633-9441.

Ebey's Landing National Historical Reserve

Allow: 2 hrs. FREE

Located on Whidbey Island just northwest of Seattle in the Puget Sound, is a collection of historic buildings and lands which are currently being developed by the park service to become an affiliated local historical site. The site will detail the native people and early settler's history. While its story is specifically the area encompassing Ebey's Landing, Coupeville and Monroe's Landing, it also serves as an example of other

Fort Vancouver National Historic Site

similar early American pioneering efforts.

Access: From Seattle by I-5, ferry and WA 525 or from Burlington/Mount Vernon on WA 20. **Camping:** Within the reserve, Fort Casey State Park (35 sites & shwrs.) & Fort Ebey State Park (53 sites & shwrs.). **For info.:** Project Manager, Ebey's Landing National Historical Reserve, P.O.Box 774, Coupeville, WA 98239.

Fort Vancouver National Historic Site

Allow: 2 hrs *Fee*

The British flag still waves over this last bastion of the Hudson's Bay Fur Trading Company south of the 49th parallel.

The reconstructed fort standing on the banks of the Columbia staring balefully across at Portland, OR, is not some clever ruse to wrest Canadian tourist dollars. Rather, the stockade and buildings recreate an era when the British tried to assert their claim to the region. Their interests were represented by the Hudson's Bay Company, the oldest incorporated trading company in the world, which virtually ruled all of Canada and what is now Washington, Oregon and Idaho. Fort Vancouver, its main base in the Pacific Northwest, supplied its outposts with trade goods and sea biscuits baked at the fort.

Highlights

★ The reconstructed fort is ever adding buildings as funding becomes available. Presently, you can enter the walls, climb the bastion, watch blacksmiths practice their trade, visit with the trader clerk, stop in at the doctor's home and company hospital, tour the chief factor's home and watch the baker work.

Whiz Tips

After checking out the visitor center and seeing the AV, you should be able to grill the "British" living-history guides or park volunteers on life at the fort. Some of the things you'll learn are the roles of the various people who worked here. The chief factor was usually an educated man who was very similar in stature to

Fort Vancouver National Historic Site

the captain of a ship. The workers for the company received no pay but kept a running tally of currency and expenditures at the fort. The fort attracted adventurers of many nationalities. One account names an Iroquois, a Creek/Frenchman, some Hawaiians and Canadians as well as Britons.

Kids' Stuff

★ Although the fort wasn't built to defend against attack but rather to protect the supplies, children still get a kick out of exploring it. The bastion was of particular fascination to our children as they imagined holding a fictitious enemy at bay by firing through the slots. They also enjoyed learning about the bakery and seeing what kinds of things people bought from the store.

Access: Just N of Portland, OR, E of I-5 (Exit 1C) in Vancouver, WA. **Days/ Hours:** Daily, summer 9-5 & winter 9-4 (clsd. Thanksgiving & Dec.25). **Camping:** Paradise Point State Park (79 sites & shwrs.), Battle Ground Lake (35 sites &shwrs.) & Beacon Rock State Park (35 sites & shwrs.), all within 30 mi. **Special Events:** May 19, Queen Victoria's Birthday; Surprisingly (for a British fort), a 4th of July Celebration; late July, an encampment; mid-Oct., a candlelight tour; early Dec., Christmas at Fort Vancouver. **Teacher's Package:** Available. **For info.:** Superintendent, Fort Vancouver National Historic Site, 612 East Reserve St., Vancouver, WA 98661-3897. 206/696-7655.

Klondike Gold Rush National Historical Park

Allow: 1-2 hrs. *FREE*

"Alaska and the Klondike are big and gold has no legs."

Dawson City News, Dec. 15, 1899

The California Gold Rush of 1849 left an indelible stamp on the generations that followed. However, the California fields were panned out and civilization had crept into every corner of the lower 48. All that remained for the adventuresome was the Great North: Alaska and northern Canada. In 1896, an American named Carmack made the Klondike gold strike in Canada's Yukon Territory. News trickled out that people

Klondike Gold Rush National Historical Park (Seattle, WA)

were picking up gold right off the ground! The only problem was, "How to get there?" The answer came from the newspapers: Seattle to Alaska then on to the Yukon's Klondike region. It must have seemed that every yahoo in the world used Seattle as a jumping-off point to the gold fields. The Canadian authorities added to the city's boon when they began enforcing a law stating the miners had to have enough food supplies to last them one year before they could cross the border. This provision prevented a disaster of major proportions if ill-prepared gold-seekers had been allowed to proceed. Two parks with the same name commemorate this last great gold rush; Seattle's Pioneer Square Historic District and the second one in Skagway, AK.

Highlights

★ The visitor center in Seattle's Pioneer Square has a veritable feast of films about the gold rush and its effect on Seattle. Fortunately, this last frontier was to be uncovered during a frenzy of photography. Hundreds of graphic depictions of the gold rush remain and are incorporated in the park's programs.

Whiz Tips

Of the 100,000 or so who started the journey to the gold fields, only 300 succeeded in getting rich ($10,000 or more) from their gold finds and only 50 of them had anything to show from their bonanza two years later. By the time most gold seekers reached the newly constructed Dawson City, most of the gold-producing claims had been staked. The lucky found "placer" gold, a gold found on the surface in streams or on stream banks, as opposed to "lode" gold, which has to be dug out. Prospectors pan the stream and if there is a sufficient quantity of gold to warrant it, they will build rocker or sluice boxes so they can extract more gold in a shorter time. Because gold is heavy, the water's swirling motion acts to sift out all the other minerals leaving the bright shiny gold.

What's a year's worth of food supplies? 100-200 lbs. of bacon, 400 lbs. of flour, 75 lbs. of dried fruit, 50 lbs. of cornmeal, 20-40 lbs. of rice, 10-25 lbs. coffee, 5-10 lbs. of tea, 25-100 lbs. of sugar, 100 lbs. of beans, 1 case of condensed milk, 10-15 lbs. of salt, 1 lb. of pepper, 25-50 lbs. of rolled oats, 25-100 lbs of potatoes, 25 cans of butter and evaporated vegetables and meat. Prospectors also had to buy equipment and clothing, bringing their load to about one ton. Poorer prospectors had to carry this load up through the Chilkoot Mountain pass on their backs. It took them 20-30 trips to get their stuff to the top; then they had to take it down the Canadian side once they passed through customs.

Kids' Stuff

★ A children's activity guide to the Klondike Gold Rush with a "deed" to a Klondike claim is available from the information desk.

★ Kids of all ages enjoy the old time movies. On the first Sunday of every month, Charlie Chaplin's silent classic "The Gold Rush" is shown at 3. The park's summer offerings include gold-panning demonstrations and costumed interpreters who try to "sell" you a ticket to Skagway and a year's worth of gear. Every summer Saturday, you can join a 1:30 walking tour of the Historic District.

Access: Downtown Seattle. **Days/Hours:** Daily, 9-5 (clsd. Thanksgiving, Dec.25 & Jan.1). **Camping:** Fay Bainbridge State Park, 30 min. by ferry from downtown Seattle (36 sites & shwrs.). **Special Events:** Around June 6, Seattle Fire Festival. **Teacher's Package:** Available. **For info.:** Klondike Gold Rush National Historical Park, 117 S. Main St., Seattle, WA 98104. 206/553-7220.

Mount Rainier National Park

Allow: 2-3 days *Fee*

"After mounting the steps, I rang the doorbell, then idly turned around and froze. For there, staring me in the face, was the most enormous mountain I had ever seen...so big it seemed to fill the sky. Its base was obscured by a thin white haze, so that the entire mass appeared to hover above the horizon like an alabaster apparition immense, awesome, serene."

Patrick Douglas
Saturday Review, Aug.21, 1976

And so it seems from Seattle on a clear day. About 70 mi. as the crow flies, it looms so large that its glacial cap must be magnified by the atmosphere. Mount Rainier is one of a chain of formidable Cascade volcanic giants which remain covered in winter's blanket.

Highlights

★ Rainier is a year-round recreational dream. Skiing, snow-shoeing, climbing and hiking are the predominant choices of outdoor enthusiasts. Sightseeing the mountain vistas from the highway and short walks are the choices of most casual visitors. A special treat for those who leave their cars are the wildflower patches.

Whiz Tips

❢ You can learn a great deal about the park at the visitor center's introductory AV and by asking the rangers. In summer, there are interpretive walks and talks covering the park's geology, wildlife, plantlife and Native American history. Rainier was created about the same geologic time as Mounts Hood, Baker, Adams and Glacier Peak, approximately 11 million years after the Cascade Range was formed. Rainier is part of the American portion of the Pacific Ring of Fire which extends from Lassen Volcano (see Lassen Volcano National Park, CA) to the Alaskan Range. Although the park has black bears, elk and mountain goats, the mammals you're most likely to spot are chipmunks, pikas, marmots and squirrels. The mountain attracts climbing aficionados from around the world. Rainier Mountaineering Inc., a guide service, will assess your level of fitness, prescribe programs, put on seminars and guide you to the top.

Kids' Stuff

★ Ideal family hiking trails include Nisqually Vista Trail, Bench & Snow Lakes, Silver Falls, Grove of the Patriarchs, Natches Peak Loop, Shadow Lake, and Lake George. All are less than 2 hrs. in duration, about all our children can take without complaining.

Access: 74 mi. SE of Tacoma on Rte. 7 & Rte. 706 or 87 mi. W of Yakima. **Days/ Hours:** Longmire Museum, daily 9-4:30; other visitor centers & Sunrise Rd., summer only. **Camping:** Park has 5 campgrounds (675 sites). **Teacher's Package:** Available. **For info.:** Superintendent, Mount Rainier National Park, Ashford, WA 98304. 206/569-2221.

North Cascades National Park Complex

Allow: 2 days *FREE*

"The mountains of the Pacific Northwest are tangled, remote and high. They have the roar of torrents and avalanches in their throats."

William O. Douglas
Of Men and Mountains

Straddling the Cascade Mountains, North Cascades, a wild mountain park, is somewhat unusual because it is adjacent to 2 National Recreation Areas. Ross Lake National Recreation Area contains the major thoroughfare, Hwy. 20 while Lake Chelan National Recreation Area attracts the Stehekin Ferry boat riders.

Highlights

★ The "Cascades Loop" drive on Hwy. 20 through the park and Hwy. 2 to the south ranks with the most spectacular in the world. The mountain vistas are comparable with the Swiss Alps. Aquamarine lakes nestle in wooded mountain valleys like rare gems thrown upon a dark green lawn.

★ By taking the Lake Chelan Ferry to Stehekin you can leave civilization in a most civilized way.

★ Access to Ross Lake is via 40 miles of gravel road from Canada. The reward for this sojourn is a huge clear lake, enclosed by snow-capped mountain peaks fed by picture-postcard waterfalls and filled with 20-inch rainbow trout.

Whiz Tips

The park offers interpretive programs during the summer season. They focus primarily on the geology and wildlife of the Cascades. The Stehekin shuttle bus and Golden West Visitor center provide interpretive information as well.

Kids' Stuff

There are separate children's interpretive programs, even though most of the park's offerings are tailored to include rather than exclude youngsters. The park also has an information sheet detailing its many family hikes.

Access: E from Burlington or W from Winthrop on WA 20. **Days/hours:** Hwy. 20 summer only; ranger station 8-9. **Camping:** Park has 3 developed campgrounds (over 300 sites); W on Hwy. 20 Rockport State Park (50 sites, elec. & showers) & E Pearrygin Lake State Park (83 sites, elec. & showers). **For info.:** Superintendent, North Cascades National Park, 2105 Hwy. 20, Sedro Woolley, WA 98284. 206/856-5700.

Olympic National Park

Allow: 3-5 days *Fee*

"Virgin evergreen rainforests are so thick that sunshine rarely reaches the ground and dark ferns grow to the height of small trees."

Neal R. Pierce
The Pacific States of America

Olympic National Park, isolated in the northwest corner of the lower 48,

North Cascades National Park Complex

is a wild coastline, a rainforest and glacier-laden mountains. It is classified by most experts as the best hiking park in the country.

Highlights

★ On clear days (no certainty here) Hurricane Ridge offers glacial mountain vistas usually only high country hikers ever see. The 17-mile drive up to the ridge provides panoramic views of the San Juan Islands and British Columbia.

★ The park has clear lakes and rivers offering fishing, plus there are miles and miles of wild coast and mountains to explore. Sol Duc Hot Springs is an accessible, popular natural hot spring within the park.

Whiz Tips

Although visitors come for the recreation, many expand their knowledge by participating in the rich offering of interpretive programs. During summer, there are regularly scheduled tidepool, rainforest, beach and sub-alpine meadow walks. The Pioneer Visitor Center in Port Angeles recounts the park's natural history.

The Olympic Mountains rise right out of the ocean. The Pacific winds bring water-laden clouds smashing against this formidable wall of rock causing what some visitors feel is perpetual rain or snow. The 60 glaciers found on the mountain tops are one result of this H2O onslaught. Another is a luxurious canopy of rich green growth so thick that some snow never reaches the soil. While there are four types of forests on the peninsula, it is the rare rainforest which has resulted in the park achieving World Heritage Site status. An Alaska cedar, a Douglas fir, a subalpine fir and a western hemlock are some of the park's record-holding trees.

The park was largely created to protect the Roosevelt elk, the largest wild herd in the world. A larger species than their Rocky Mountain cousins, the Roosevelt are more social, living in herds throughout the year.

Kids' Stuff

Tidal pool visits with children are always a hit. Our kids enjoy nothing more than investigating these ocean

Olympic National Park Courtesy Northwest Interpretive Assoc.

puddles to see what has been left. In the visitor center is a touch room for kids where they can closely inspect some of the remains of park creatures.

★ The park has a summer-only Jr. Ranger program with instructions on how to participate carried in its newspaper.

★ If you want to give your kids a thrill of a lifetime, give them an opportunity to hook into a salmon or better yet a steelhead (an ocean-going rainbow trout). These fish are large and very strong (and hard to catch).

Access: US 101 encircles the park. **Days/Hours:** Visitor centers, daily, 9-4:30. **Camping:** Park has 18 campgrounds (close to 1,000 sites); W Bogachiel State Park (41 sites), NE Sequim Bay State Park (86 sites) and SE Lake Cushman State Park (80 sites) & Dosewallips State Park (140 sites). **Teacher's Package:** Available. **For info.:** Superintendent, Olympia National Park, 600 Park Ave., Port Angeles, WA 98362-6978. 206/452-0330.

San Juan Island National Historical Park

Allow: 2 days *FREE*

Dark green emeralds placed on blue velvet and frequently cloaked in dew; these are the San Juan Islands. With the number of beautiful natural retreats diminishing daily, we don't wonder that Great Britain and the United States squared-off over these gems. In 1859, an British pig was shot for rooting around in a American garden. American soldiers were rushed to the island to protect American interests. British warships and Royal Marines were sent to drive them off. The British captain refused to take any action until the commander of the British Pacific fleet arrived (he received a knighthood for his judicious inactivity). For once the bureaucrats in London and Washington displayed common sense. They agreed on a Solomon-like solution of placing balancing forces on the island until its ownership could be decided. It took 12 years before Kaiser Wilhelm I was asked to arbitrate the dispute and he decided in the U.S.'s favor. The park relates this interesting chapter in U.S./Canadian relations.

Highlights

★ When you visit the British and American Camps, you wonder what it must have been like to spend part of the 12 years here as each side protected its purported "(possession) 9/10ths of the law." Did soldiers believe they might have to take up arms against their neighbors? The weekend re-enactment is a special pleasure as you get a better flavor of how these soldiers felt.

Whiz Tips

Oregon and Washington had been disputed territory for some time. This was the West, a land for the taking. Even the settlement of 1846 left questions about this archipelago called the San Juan Islands. The British claimed the agreed-upon channel was the most easterly, the Americans the western channel.

Kids' Stuff

★ The trip to the island by ferry is a winner with children. The "Pig War" story is a great one for the kids to learn about. Forget Aesop's Fables; think about the moral of this event.

★ Children really enjoy the re-enactment, the soldier's uniforms, the historic aura.

Access: By WA State ferry from Anacortes, 83 mi. N of Seattle or from Sidney, B.C. on Vancouver Island, 15 mi. from Victoria, B.C. **Days/Hours:** Daily 8-4:30 (clsd. winter fed. holidays). **Camping:** County campground on island. **Special Events:** July 4th celebrations; San Juan County Fair; Annual Pig Roast BBQ Jamboree. **For info.:** Superintendent, San Juan Island National

Historical Park, P.O.Box 429, Friday Harbor, WA 98250. 206/378-2902.

Whitman Mission National Historic Site

Allow: 1 hr. *Fee*

The mission was located on the famed Oregon Trail near today's Walla Walla. The Whitmans' fate was but a scene of a much larger play called "Homesteading the West." Repeatedly, two very different cultures were to clash, one insensitive to the values of the other, the other unwilling to keep pace with the dramatic changes. The Whitmans came with what seemed to them the best of intentions; they would heal souls and bodies. The Whitmans were true pioneers, one of the first white couples to cross the continent, travelling a path that would become the Oregon Trail. They not only guided others, but allowed their mission to serve as a way station for the rapidly growing immigration. Their demise serves as a testimony to the failure of early European intervention in Native American culture.

Highlights

★ Little more than wagon ruts remain from the time of the Whitmans. The grassy knoll and empty field vibrate with the spirits of the tragic participants in the drama that ended so badly for all. At the park museum you can see some of the Whitman and Cayuse artifacts.

Whiz Tips

💡 During the summer weekends there are pioneer demonstrations. You can listen to audio explanations of the mission as you wander the field.

💡 The Whitmans were highly educated people from New York state. The Cayuse were nomadic people who were well regarded for their horse-back riding prowess. They were a proud tribe who had steadily expanded their territory and influence throughout the region. The Whitmans came to improve them by teaching Christianity and "civilized" ways. The Cayuse weren't aware they needed to change. Marcus

Whitman Mission National Historic Site Courtesy NPS

Whitman, a well-trained doctor was unable to stem the number of Cayuse deaths from European diseases. The Cayuse blamed Whitman because he couldn't cure their diseases. They felt killing him would end the illness. It didn't.

Kids' Stuff

★ Children who have studied about the westward expansion can see its effects in the scars formed by the many wagons who travelled through here to still more western home sites. They also learn how this transition had its negative as well as positive effects.

Access: 7 mi. W of Walla Walla on US 12. **Days/Hours:** Daily, summer 8-6 & winter 8-4:30 (clsd. Dec.25 & Jan.1). **Camping:** Fort Walla Walla Park Campground, city park (showers). **Special Events:** July's third Sat., Pow Wow. **Teacher's Package:** Available. **For info.:** Superintendent, Whitman Mission National Historic Site, Rte.2, Box 247, Walla Walla, WA 99362-9699. 509/522-6360.

WEST VIRGINIA

Appalachian National Scenic Trail

Beginning in the wilds of Maine, the trail follows the meanderings of the Appalachian Mountains for some 2,000 miles through New Hampshire, Vermont, Massachusetts, Connecticut, New York, New Jersey, Pennsylvania, Maryland, West

Harper's Ferry National Historical Park

Virginia, Virginia, Tennessee and North Carolina to Georgia.

For Info.: Appalachian National Scenic Trail, P.O.Box 807, Harpers Ferry, WV 25425.

Harpers Ferry National Historical Park

Allow: .5 days *Fee*

"The trial was fair,
Painfully fair by every rule of the law,
And that it was, made not the slightest difference.
The law's our yardstick, and it measures well
Or well enough when there are yards to measure,
Measure a wave with it, measure a fire,
Cut sorrow up in inches, weigh content.
You can weigh John Brown's body well enough,
But how and in what balance weigh John Brown?"

John Brown's Body,
Stephen Vincent Benet

There are those who claimed John Brown's martyrdom was a falsity. They said he was a madman. They said he was a murderer. They said he was a fool. Many of these same people said the Civil War was fought for states' rights. They said slavery was never the issue. Yet over 100,000 soldiers dressed in blue would face shot and cannon ball singing the praises of John Brown. And yet, Harpers Ferry is more. It is a story of American industry, a story of Civil War clashes and a story of a people who forged an educational institute for those denied access elsewhere. But, it always comes back to John Brown. As Henry David Thoreau put it on July 4, 1860, "Editors persevered for a good while in saying that Brown was crazy; but at last they said only that it was "a crazy scheme," and the only evidence brought to prove it was that it cost him his life...They seem to have known nothing about living or dying for a principle."

Highlights

★ John Brown's Museum has an AV on Harper's Ferry and a film and exhibits on John Brown.

★ Historic Harpers Ferry rests at the juncture of the Potomac and Shenandoah Rivers. Thomas Jefferson was so enamored by its natural beauty that he wrote, "The passage of the Potomac through the Blue Ridge is perhaps one of the most stupendous scenes in nature....This scene is worth a voyage across the Atlantic." You judge.

★ With the Baltimore & Ohio Railroad and the Chesapeake & Ohio Canal servicing the town, it became a merchant's dream. The town's munitions factory established the concept of producing interchangeable parts into an industrial reality, introducing the age of the production line. Living historians relate the town's daily business activities during this era.

Whiz Tips

The role of Harpers Ferry as a key link in the region's transportation system made it a prime military target. Federal and Rebel armies took turns trying to defend what seems to have been an indefensible location. Stonewall Jackson so easily captured 12,500 federal troops here that he was able to leave them under a very light guard and race across Maryland to bale Lee out at Antietam (see Antietam NB, MD).

Kids' Stuff

★ The historic town with its 19th century architecture is a neat place to wander around. Each building has its own surprises, from costumed early 19th century characters and the ammunition storage building Brown holed up in, to overlooks of the picturesque river confluence. Children are well occupied even if they haven't been briefed on the subject matter beforehand.

Access: Downtown Harpers Ferry, visitor center on hill off US 340. **Days/Hours:**

Daily, summer 8:30-6 & winter 8:30-5 (clsd. Dec.25). **Camping:** W in MD, Antietam Creek (20 FREE sites) & N in WV, Sleepy Creek Public Hunting & Fishing (125 sites). **Special Events:** 2nd Oct. Sat., Election Day-1860; 1st Dec. wknd., A Civil War Christmas..The Shattered Piece. **Teacher's Package:** Available & special education programs. **For info.:** Superintendent, Harpers Ferry National Historical Park, Box 65, Harpers Ferry, WV 25425. 304/535-6223.

New River Gorge National River

Allow: 1-2 days *FREE*

"This is the best poor man's country on the globe...You can 'coon hunt all winter and fish all summer."

1894 resident

Fifty three miles of the New River and 40 miles of its tributaries are included in the New River Gorge National River, Gauley River National Recreation Area and Bluestone National Scenic River units. These waters form a recreation haven for whitewater floaters and anglers.

Highlights

★ New River falls 750 feet in 50 miles from the Bluestone Dam to Gauley Bridge, creating some of the best whitewater rafting opportunities in the eastern U.S. Inexperienced boaters use the southern, more placid waters.

Whiz Tips

Each visitor center has interpretive programs covering the river canyon's geology, cultural history (emphasis on coal mining & railroading), rock climbing potential, fishing opportunities, whitewater floating and wildlife. Rangers provide this information through talks, evening programs, hikes and bus tours.

The US 19 bridge, which can be seen from Canyon Rim Visitor Center, is the world's longest single steel arch bridge.

Kids' Stuff

★ Children's programs are available at each visitor center. Each center also has a "Discovery Table" where kids can touch articles associ-

New River Gorge National River Courtesy NPS

ated with the park. At Hinton, kids can use puzzles to study the region's diverse ecology.

★ The lower part of the park, with its calmer waters and good fishing, is really more suitable for families. Prime waters for smallmouth bass, the river also hosts muskellunge, walleye, catfish and carp. The incoming streams are stocked with trout.

Access: Canyon Rim Visitor Center near Fayetteville & Hinton Visitor Center at WV 3 By-Pass in Hinton. **Days/Hours:** Canyon Rim daily; Hinton, daily, summer 9-5. **Camping:** Babcock State Park, Little Beaver State Park, Pipestem State Park, Bluestone State Park and Summersville Lake; Park's riverside permit primitive camping. **Special Events:** On 3rd Oct. Sat., US 19 bridge & 1/4 million pedestrians celebrate. **For info.:** Superintendent, New River Gorge National River, Box 246, 104 Main St., Glen Jean, WV 25846. Canyon Rim 304/574-2115; Hinton 304/466-0417.

WISCONSIN

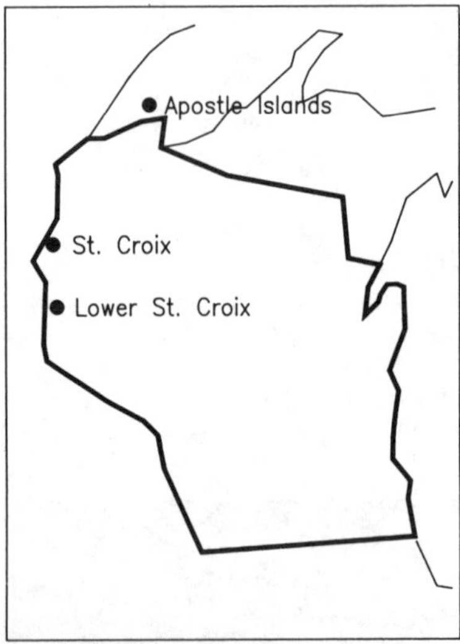

Apostle Islands National Lakeshore

Allow: 2-3 days *FREE*

At Apostle Islands, the Wisconsin Ice Age (see Ice Age NSR, WI) put the force of its one-mile-deep glaciers to work digging trenches around the 22 islands. Recognizing the recreational potential of this freshwater archipelago, the park service acquired 21 of the islands and 12 mi. of mainland shore with the goal of rejuvenating the lands to their previous pristine state.

Highlights

★ The park has a mainland visitor center at Bayfield with introductory AVs, a lighthouse display and natural history exhibits. Little Sand Bay (mainland) and Stockton Island have ranger stations.

★ Scenery stalkers find plenty of picturesque spots like the six historic lighthouses and the sculpted sea caves. By exploring the park, you can still see the efforts of human industry to harvest the region's material riches. Hidden among the trees of the reforested islands, you can still find evidence of the woodsman's axe, the sandstone rock quarries and the camps of commercial fishermen.

Whiz Tips

The park rangers have several guided programs. They provide tours of a fish camp (Manitou Island) and a lighthouse (Raspberry Island). At Raspberry and Stockton Islands, rangers lead birding expeditions, island hikes, beach strolls and bog walks.

Winter usage of this park is growing as cross-country skiers, snowshoers, snowmobilers and ice fishing fanatics discover it.

❢ Boaters should be aware of the immense size and latent power of Lake Superior. With the furthest points between the national park sites at 28 mi., you should be fully aware of the weather forecast. One of our worst memories was a slow motor and a full boat as a Great Lake storm was brewing.

Kids' Stuff

★ The park has special "children's hour" interpretive programs where they tailor their approach and material to families. Families can boat, hike (over 50 mi. of trails) and fish (steelhead & salmon). However, Lake Superior, the only water body within the park, remains about 50 degrees F. throughout the summer, so swimming is limited to very shallow bays.

Access: E from Duluth on US 2 to WI 13 N to Bayfield. Islands accessed by own boat or excursion from Bayfield. **Days/Hours:** Bayfield visitor center summer, daily 8-6, fall, daily 8-4:30 & winter, M-F 8-4:30 (clsd. Thanksgiving, Dec.25 & Jan.1). Ranger contact stations, summer, daily 8-4:30. **Camping:** Permit-only backcountry camping on several of the islands; tribal (Red Cliff Campground); city (30 sites Dalrymple Campground & 45 sites Madeline Island Campground); county, Big Bay State Park (Madeline Island-55 sites). **For info.:** Superintendent, Apostle Islands National Lakeshore, Rte.1, Box 4, Bayfield, WI 54814. 715/779-3397.

Ice Age National Scenic Trail

The trail joins 6 of the 9 units comprising Ice Age National Scientific Reserve with a 1,000 mile hiking path. Almost 1/2 of the trail is open to the public leading them past significant glacial features.

For info.: Ice Age National Scenic Trail, National Park service, 7818 Big Sky Dr., Madison, WI 53719.

Ice Age National Scientific Reserve

Allow: 2-3 days *Fee*

"scientists...have chosen a good name for the last ice age. They call it by the name of the place it found as a waterless plain and altered into magnificence. The last ice age is known the world over as Wisconsin."

Charles Kuralt,
Dateline America

The reserve is the result of a unique relationship between state and federal governments. Wisconsin Dept. of Natural Resources oversees nine units preserving the resulting geologic features left as a result of the Wisconsin Glaciation. The nine sites are spread throughout the state (see **Access:** below).

Highlights

★ Many of the sites are within state parks that offer outstanding recreational opportunities. For example, at Kettle Moraine, you can see interlobate moraines (mounds of earth deposited between lobes of ice), kames (like sand at the bottom of an hourglass, earth plunged through a hole in the ice), eskers (stream tunnels that filled with rocky debris) and kettles (the remains of huge ice boulders that melted leaving the earth on their surface behind). You can also enjoy swimming, boating, hiking and in winter, cross-country skiing. Devil's Lake, Interstate and Mill Bluff are other sites offering recreation and glacial features.

Whiz Tips

❢ Wisconsin offers comprehensive interpretive programs at Kettle Moraine, Interstate, Devil's Lake and Horicon Marsh.

❢ As recently as a hundred years ago, the concept of continental glaciation (ice ages) wasn't accepted. Louis Agassiz, the famous Swiss naturalist, put forward the theory of continental glaciation. Today, we estimate that over 1.5 million years at least four different ice ages occurred covering most of Canada and the northern reaches of the U.S. The ice age named for Wisconsin, resulted in an ice mass about a mile deep, which sheared hills and filled valleys, planing the land. The lakes, rivers and hills we now see are products of this huge glacial event. When it receded in the face of a general warming, the earth "rebounded" 160 ft.

Kids' Stuff

★ Visiting these sites is an excellent way to help school age children understand the effects glaciers played in the development of the country. The geography they carved has provided very different opportunities for man's use than the land masses it didn't reach.

★ There are Jr. Ranger and Wisconsin Explorer programs at Devils Lake, Kettle Moraine, Mill Bluff and Interstate. They are targeted at kids in grades K-6 and require them to complete a workbook for which they receive a certificate and iron-on patch.

Access: Two Creeks 12 mi. N of Two Rivers on WI 42; Kettle Moraine 20 mi. W of Sheyboygan on US 45/WI 67; Campbellsport Drumlins 3 mi. W of Campbellsport on Hwy. Y or V; Horicon Marsh 1 mi. N of Horicon on WI 33; Cross Plains 3 mi. E of Cross plains on US 14; Devil's Lake 3 mi. S of Baraboo on WI 159/123/113; Mill Bluff US 12 or 16; Chippewa Moraine 6 mi. N of Bloomer on WI 40; Interstate adjacent St. Croix on US 8/WI 35. **Days/Hours:** Daily. **Camping:** Devil's Lake, Mill Bluff, Interstate and Kettle Moraine. **For info.:** Superintendent, Ice Age National Scientific Reserve, DNR Box 7921, Madison, WI 53707. 608/266-2181.

St. Croix National Scenic Riverway

Allow: 2-3 days *FREE*

"Here it is possible to be grateful to a glacier. When the last ice age ended and the massive mantle of ice retreated to the north, it left a gift behind the landscape of Wisconsin [St. Croix Valley]."

Charles-Kuralt
Dateline America

Over 250 miles of riverway begin in

St. Croix National Scenic Riverway Courtesy NPS

the wilds of northwestern Wisconsin and terminate in the Mississippi, just south of the Twin Cities, Minneapolis/St. Paul. The escaping waters of Lake Namekagon and the St. Croix Flowage meld to become the St. Croix River which in turn becomes Lake St. Croix and, finally, part of the brown sludge known as the mighty Mississippi. Fortunately for park visitors, its waters are bright and clear until its terminus. The southern stretch of the waterway is known as the Lower Saint Croix National Scenic Riverway.

Highlights

★ Because of the length of the protected waterway, there is a wide variety of pursuits. The Dalles area near Taylor Falls is a noted scenic strip. To get the best view of any portion of the waterway, you have to get out on the water. Canoeing is the preferred method when the water level cooperates.

Whiz Tips

! The visitor centers put on interpretive programs explaining components of the riverway. The bordering state parks also have their own programs.

! Originally the Chippewas and Dakotas (Sioux) shared this land. When the French arrived trading guns for pelts, the Chippewas recognized the value of these new weapons and secured enough weapons to drive the Sioux westward. By the mid-1880s, the Chippewas had lost their dominance and lumber was king. By 1914, the prime forests had been felled and the last log float made its way down the St. Croix.

Kids' Stuff

★ At the visitor centers there are "hands-on" exhibits for children. In addition, there are family-oriented interpretive programs including puppet shows.

★ While the park service doesn't offer a Jr. Ranger program some of the adjacent state parks do.

★ Fishing is a favorite pastime. The Namekagon stretch is noted for its brown trout, while the St. Croix offers a wide variety of northern species like pike, muskellunge, bass, wall-eye and sturgeon.

Access: Park H.Q., downtown St. Croix

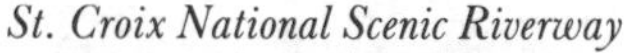
St. Croix National Scenic Riverway

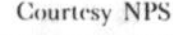
Courtesy NPS

Falls. **Days/Hours:** Visitor centers, daily, summer 8:30-5. **Camping:** Riverway has canoe camping sites; 7 state campgrounds. **For Info.:** Superintendent, St. Croix National Scenic Riverway, P.O.Box 708, St. Croix Falls, WI 54024. 715/483-3284.

WYOMING

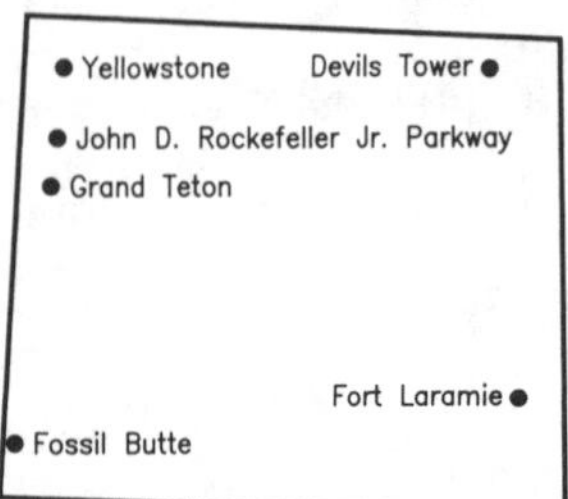

Devils Tower National Monument

Allow: .5 days *Fee*

The startling remains of a volcano's neck rises 865 feet out of a river basin in the Black Hills of north-eastern Wyoming. The Indians' explanation for this phenomenon was that a boy was changed into a bear and began chasing his sisters. His sisters climbed a tree and pleaded with the gods to save them from the bear. The gods changed the tree to a rock and caused it to grow skyward. The bear clung tenaciously to the side, its claws leaving great grooves in the rock. The sisters? They rose to the heavens to become the Big Dipper. Today, the rock has become a favorite of the "do or die" rock climbers. Over 1,000 ascents are made each year with the adventurous bent on establishing "firsts:" first to climb this route, first to free-climb, first to climb in December, first all-women climb, first, first, first. We just wanted our visit to last.

Highlights

★ You can marvel at this geologic wonder, the nation's first national monument, by two trails circumnavigating the tower. Both furnish absorbing views of each side of the tower and the surrounding territory. The 14-foot in diameter rock columns which have crashed to earth from the Tower's top provide a fascinating perspective of its dimensions. Climbers dangling precariously from the still-clinging columns add to your recognition of how big this volcanic stub really is.

Whiz Tips

❢ The rangers put on "how to climb" programs at the kiosk in front of the visitor center. Inside you can examine the pictorial record of progress the scalers have made as they have continued to explore newer and more challenging ascents. The information desk keeps an annual running tally of the successful attempts much like other parks monitor their daily temperatures.

❢ During the summer daily ranger talks, you can learn about the geologic occurrence causing such a curiosity. When you walk around the Tower, you can see the difference between the southern rock which is relentlessly exposed to the sun and the northern "smooth side", which is spared dramatic temperature changes.

❢ Prairie dogs, like the buffalo, once dominated the plains. It's hard to picture 25 billion of these creatures in millions of prairie dog towns. Today, because of widespread eradication, the best places to see a prairie dog town are at parks. The black-tailed species live here and on the prairies while their less numerous white-tailed cousins are found in the mountain plains to the west.

Kids' Stuff

★ The park offers a Junior Ranger Program with a naturalist checklist for your children to complete. If they take a hike around the monument they should be able to fulfill the requirements handily and collect a memento of their visit to boot.

Access: 28 mi. NW of Sundance or 14 mi. N of US 14 on WY 24. **Days/Hours:** Monument year-round; visitor center daily May-mid-Oct., summer 8-7:45 & May & Sept-Oct. 8-4:45. **Camping:** Park's Belle Fourche River Campground (50 sites). **For info.:** Superintendent, Devils Tower National Monument, Devils Tower, WY 82714. 307/467-5370.

Fort Laramie National Historic Site

Allow: 2-3 hrs. *Fee*

Cheyenne and Denver are far to the south. The fort seems small. The Laramie River is more a stream than a river. And yet, Fort Laramie was THE focal point of teems of traders, immigrants and Native Americans who travelled the Wild West. After months of trudging across endless miles of flat, featureless prairie, pioneers stumbled out of Nebraska into Wyoming. Here, they caught their collective breath to prepare for the remaining mountainous leg.

Highlights

★ Several buildings remain intact. Each has been restored with period pieces decorating the rooms. As you peek through the glass doors, you imagine how their residents passed their time. The park rangers who perform living-history demonstrations each summer add flesh to the fort's bones.

Whiz Tips

❢ The Fort takes you back in time, making you realize some of what life must have been like. The Industrial Revolution, while in full progress elsewhere, had little effect on these brave souls. "Hand-made" was not a marketing term but a fact of life. Soldiers had to wash, darn, and iron

Fort Laramie National Historic Site Courtesy NPS

their clothes. They had to care for their horses and their equipment. Near "Fort John," the original fort site, are some pioneer "freezers." In the winter, the soldiers would cut huge blocks of ice from the river and store them in the holes. Summer visitors will find it hard to believe this supply of ice lasted until September.

Each season brought different visitors. Spring brought Indians and mountain men to trade for supplies. Summer saw the arrival of immigrants streaming west. Fall brought supply wagons with goods to feed the fort's occupants. During the winter, stragglers who weren't prepared for its onslaught would come seeking help. It was a good place to find somebody or something you couldn't find elsewhere.

Kids' Stuff

★ In summer, the Fort is a bustle of activity with pioneers, soldiers and Indians, all with stories to tell. Smaller children become so entranced with the show, they have a hard time figuring out what's real and what's make-believe.

Access: 3 mi. SW off US 26 at Laramie. **Days/Hours:** Daily, summer 8-6, winter 8-4:30 (clsd. Thanksgiving, Dec.25 & Jan.1). **Camping:** Nearby (13 mi.) Guernsey Lake State Park (145 sites). **Special Events:** "Moonlight tour" in May and Aug. & an "Old Fashioned 4th of July" celebration. **For info.:** Superintendent, Fort Laramie National Historic Site, P.O Box 86, Fort Laramie, WY 82212. 307/837-2221.

Fossil Butte National Monument

Allow: 1-4 hrs. *FREE*

Around 50,000,000 years ago, 3 lakes covered southwestern Wyoming: Lake Gosiute, Lake Unita and Fossil Lake. What makes the site important is the level of detail preserved in the butte containing the fossilized remains of Fossil Lake. In most fossils, you're lucky to find a clear imprint of the outline of the creature that was encased. Many of these fossils show not just the bones and shape of the species but on fish, their tiny scales and on turtles the crinkles on their shells. Evidence of over 20 kind of fish, 100 varieties of insects, untold

Fossil Butte National Monument

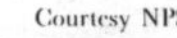
Courtesy NPS

numbers of plants, crocodiles, turtles, bats, snakes, early primates and dog-sized horses have been unearthed.

Highlights

★ In the visitor center you can see exhibits of the paleontologists' efforts. To assist you in picturing what today's high desert once looked like, there's a re-creation of the region when it was well-watered.

★ Make sure you explore one of the two interpretive trails so you can see how the scientists searched for fossils and gain a better idea of the differences between those long-ago days and the current environment.

Whiz Tips

On weekends (at 10 & 1), the park rangers give guided walks explaining facets of the monument and on Thurs., the folks from Kemmerer Fossil Country Museum put on campfire chats.

These fossils were made when the calcium carbonate precipitated out of the water like rain and settled to the bottom of the lake, covering the dead fish and plants lying there. Over hundreds of thousands of years this process continued. At some points, large numbers of creatures were all killed at once, to be entombed. Scientists are still unsure why this occurred.

Kids' Stuff

★ Children really appreciate the fine details these fossils reveal. Two exhibits which get extra close scrutiny are the 13-ft.-long crocodile and the single fossil that has entombed 356 fish.

★ Children can become Jr. Rangers by spending time examining the visitor center offerings, taking a short hike, getting involved in preparing a fossil and picturing how the site looked when these fish were there for the catching.

Access: 11 W of Kemmerer, N of US 30W. **Days/Hours:** Daily, summer 8-7 & winter 8-4:30 (clsd. winter fed. holidays). **Camping:** Bridger-Teton National Forest and Fontenelle Lake (50 mi.); Bureau of Land Management (BLM) lands (primitive). **For info.:** Superintendent, Fossil Butte National Monument, P.O.Box 592, Kemmerer, WY 83101. 307/877-4455.

Grand Teton National Park

Allow: 2-3 days *Fee*

"...few such stand among so broad, deep valleys as to give so great relative elevations and to be seen so prominently...this must become a favorite for tourists."

1872 Hayden survey

Epitomizing the world's view of the Rocky Mountains, Grand Teton National Park in northwestern Wyoming is truly a national treasure. Soaring mountain peaks and crystal-clear lakes provide the backdrops for picture postcard scenes. Grand Teton, the mountain, is the highest peak in the park at 13,770 feet. The mountain and park take their name from French Canadian fur-trappers who named three of the peaks, the Trois Tetons or "three breasts."

Highlights

★ The best way to experience the park is to go to its extremes, the top or the bottom of its perpendicular peaks. You can hike along the Teton crest trail or at Jackson Hole, you can take the Aerial Tram up to 10,000 feet for a panoramic view of the Tetons. To contemplate the vast difference in the landscape, float a boat out on the lakes at the mountains' feet or raft down the Snake River.

Whiz Tips

Grand Teton offers several guided programs from canoe and boat trips to museum tours and tepee building. The Colter Bay Indian Arts Museum has ranger-led tours describing the culture of local 19th century Native Americans.

❢ Only 10 million years old, the Tetons are a relatively new range formed by the earth's thrusts. The reason for the lack of foothills and the resulting dramatic difference in height between the mountains and the land at their base is two-fold. Firstly, the western side of the Teton fault rose while at the same geological time its eastern flank dropped. Secondly, the great glaciers of the ice ages gradually scoured and leveled the Teton's base. The lakes were molded by the tremendous rock residue left by the receding glaciers.

❢ Together with Yellowstone, Grand Teton forms the Greater Yellowstone Ecosystem, the biggest wildlife sanctuary in the lower 48. The park's brochure has a "where to watch wildlife" key. Animals you might spot are moose, mule deer, black bear, bighorn sheep, buffalo, pronghorn antelope and coyotes. Birders may glimpse bald eagles, trumpeter swans, ospreys, great blue herons and Canada geese. The ecosystem is home to the largest elk herd on the continent. Elk or Wapiti (Indian name meaning "light colored deer") can reach 1,000 lbs. and stand over 5 ft. tall. The best season to see them is in the fall when you may be fortunate enough to hear the haunting bugle of the male elk.

Kids' Stuff

★ For a small fee, your kids can participate in a Young Naturalist program by completing specified activities where they learn more about the park.

★ One day a week the park offers a "Little Moccasins" program for 7-12 year olds. This is a fun two-hour introduction to Native American culture.

★ Good hikes for kids are Lunch Tree Hill Trail, Cunningham Cabin Trail, Menor's Ferry Trail and Colter Bay Nature Trail.

Access: 13 mi. N of Jackson on US 26, 89 & 191. **Days/Hours:** Moose Visitor Center daily, summer 8-7, early summer-early fall 8-5, winter 8-4:30 (clsd. Dec.25). Colter Bay Visitor Center summer 8-7, early summer & early fall 8-5 (clsd. winter). **Camping:** Park's 5 campgrounds (907 sites); adjacent Yellowstone NP. **For info.:** Superintendent, Grand Teton National Park, P.O.Drawer 170, Moose, WY 83012. 307/733-2880.

Grand Teton National Park Courtesy Jim Miller

Yellowstone National Park

Allow: 2 days minimum *Fee*

"...the Gorge of the Yellowstone. All I can say is that, without warning or preparation, I looked into that gulf seventeen hundred feet deep, with eagles and fish-hawks circling far below. And the sides of that gulf were one wild welter of colour crimson, emerald, cobalt, ochre, amber, honey splashed and port-wine, snow-white, vermilion, lemon, and silver-grey, in wide washes."

Rudyard Kipling
From Sea to Sea

Located in the Rocky Mountains in northwestern Wyoming, Yellowstone is unlike other mountainous national parks. Its main attribute is its wealth of geothermic phenomena with over 10,000 thermal features, of which there are about 250 active geysers. These features caused the area to gain such prominence that in 1872, Yellowstone became not just the nation's first national park but the world's. To grasp how early in American history this was, early park visitors chanced a run-in with the warring Sioux, Cheyenne and Arapaho who had decimated Custer and the 7th Cavalry at Little Big Horn (see Custer Battlefield NM, MT) and the fleeing Nez Perce (see Big Hole NB, MT & Nez Perce NHP, ID). The park is named for America's longest "wild" river, the Yellowstone River. Although there is a continuing demand for the corralling of this 671 mile long river with dams, it still retains its reputation as the premier trout fishing river in the country. Yellowstone Lake from which it flows is the largest high altitude (7,733 ft. above sea level) lake in all of North America. Yellowstone is linked to Grand Teton National Park by the scenic 82-mile long John D. Rockefeller, Jr., Memorial Parkway.

Highlights

★ The main highlight of the park continues to be its volcanic geothermic phenomena. Old Faithful didn't fail us and we all "oohed" and "aahed" until it had dissipated. However, it has suffered over time as it used to whoosh approx. every 65 min.; today, it's once every 69-76 min.

Yellowstone National Park

★ Yellowstone has two of the most spectacular waterfalls on the continent, Lower & Upper Falls. The view of Lower Falls from Artist Point lives up to its billing and Kodak stock soars with every bright and sunny day as countless of rolls film are exposed.

★ Although, Yellowstone is still the natural sanctuary in the country, no longer do you see roadways strewn with begging bears. At first you are full of anticipation. Then the miles of wooded road seem all too familiar. Where are the famed Yellowstone animals? Firstly, Yellowstone is an enormous park. It takes two solid days to just drive its main roads. Secondly, bears are moved from highways and civilization as soon as they are reported. Bears + humans = Big Problem! The situation has reduced the park's grizzly population to a minimum of 200. Have patience. The further into the park you travel, the more likely you'll see wildlife. Buffalo become old hat. Elk...well, once you've seen fifty or so, you've seen them all. And deer...become commonplace. Moose and bear, now there's excitement. If you see either of these, your trip's a success.

★ At the Boiling River, a natural hot spring flowing into the Gardner River, between Mammoth Village and the North exit, we had a sunset dip. What a marvelous feeling it was to lie in a mountain stream and drift from cold sparkling water back into the hot spring run-off. The outlet is reached from a small parking lot on the east side of the road. It's a five- to ten-minute walk up stream from there. Change at your car because the site is primitive.

★ The mammoth hot spring formation is not to be missed. It epitomizes the unusualness of the park. Abruptly the mountain vegetation gives way to this bubbling cauldron which spills downward forming layer upon layer of thermal sediment not just scarring the hill but building a monument to its passing. The formation constitutes the world's largest hydrothermally-formed terraces still active. In addition, the formation itself is a favorite stop for elk who sidled next to us as they took in the waters.

Whiz Tips

❢ You can learn all you want about geysers, mud pots, mud volcanoes and hot springs. Ditto on fires, a natural aftermath from the big burn of '88. The park has devoted considerable energies in exhibits, videos and literature to explain the fire and its long-term effects.

❢ Yellowstone's buffalo or, more accurately, bison are mountain bison as distinguished from plains bison you may find elsewhere. Once numbering 60,000,000, before the advent of the Europeans, by the turn-of-the-century, all bison were reduced to about 600. They ranged from Oregon to New York State and from Canada to Mexico. Today there are estimated to be 25,000 found in the Great Plains and the Rockies. Adult males can stand up to 6 feet tall, weigh up to a 1 ton and can reach speeds of 30 m.p.h. Armed with sharp hoofs and horns, buffalo are not to be trifled with at any time. Yet, each year people are injured by these great beasts because summer, their rut period, coincides with peak tourist season. Like most animals, buffalo are very irritable during rut season.

❢ Yellowstone and Grand Teton NP are about as far south as moose range in the country. Standing up to 6.5 ft. tall and weighing up to 1,800 lbs., they can be found throughout Alaska and Canada and Montana's Rockies. Moose are notoriously timid. Until researching this book, we had seen moose in the wild only once. Having lived in the backwoods of New Brunswick and spent many years driving backroads in the Northwest, we certainly expected to experience more sightings. However, on our travels this past year, we had three sightings, all in the Rocky Mountains of Montana and Wyoming.

❢ Each of the visitor centers has museums and audiovisual programs. Mammoth Springs had a particularly interesting exhibit area.

Kids' Stuff

★ Our crew was kept occupied by looking at the buffalo, elk and deer and the constant anticipation of sighting a bear.

★ Yellowstone offers many children's programs and is reintroducing a Jr. Ranger program. Hiking is another easily accomplished activity which your children will enjoy. There's also fishing throughout the park for the famed Yellowstone Trout.

★ The Gardner River hot springs was the hit of our visit. The cold mountain stream wasn't too fast when we visited as even our 3 year old could make his way safely up and down to the hot spring flowing in. (We were careful to ensure none of the little guys got too close or stayed in the hot area too long as prolonged exposure to heat can result in damage to their internal organs.)

Access: N entrance, Hwy. 89 from Gardiner, MT; W entrance, Hwy. 89 from West Yellowstone; S entrance, Hwy. 89 from Flagg Ranch, WY; E entrance, Hwy. 16 from Cody, WY; NE entrance, Hwy. 212 from Cooke City, MT. **Days/Hours:** Road between Gardiner & Cooke City, running across the northeast corner of the park, open year-round; other roads closed (usually Oct.-May) until clear of snow. **Camping:** Park's 11 campgrounds (over 1800 sites); 3 campgrounds (shwrs.); Bridge Bay Campground (rsrvtn.-Ticketron); also state or national forest campgrounds at park borders. **Teacher's Package:** Available. **For info.:** Superintendent, Yellowstone National Park, P.O.Box 168, WY 82190. 307/344-7381.

Kids at National Park COURTESTY HOT SPRINGS NP

Index